❖

A LIBRARY OF PROTESTANT THOUGHT

❖

A LIBRARY OF PROTESTANT THOUGHT

✦ ✦ ✦

EDITORIAL BOARD

✦ ✦ ✦

✦ ✦ ✦

The
Mercersburg Theology

Edited by

JAMES HASTINGS NICHOLS

New York

OXFORD UNIVERSITY PRESS

1966

COPYRIGHT © 1966 BY OXFORD UNIVERSITY PRESS, INC.

LIBRARY OF CONGRESS CATALOGUE CARD NUMBER 66-24435

PRINTED IN THE UNITED STATES OF AMERICA

A Library of Protestant Thought

A LIBRARY OF PROTESTANT THOUGHT is a collection of writings intended to illumine and interpret the history of the Christian faith in its Protestant expression. It is as variegated in its literary forms and theological positions as is the movement it mirrors. Tracts, letters, sermons, monographs, and other types of literature comprising the heritage of Protestant thought find a place in this series. Works that were originally composed in English, whether in Great Britain or in the New World, and works that were originally written in other languages, many of them not previously translated into English, are included. But it is neither necessary nor desirable that every segment of Protestant theology, piety, and ethics receive equal space. The trite theology, the conventional piety, and the platitudinous ethics always bulk larger in any tradition, also in the Protestantism of the past four centuries, than does the creative output of the religious spirit. The latter is our primary interest in this Library. While we have not felt obligated to grant them equal attention, we have included works that are typical of the more commonplace literature of the Protestant tradition. On the other hand, some works which logically belong in this series have not been included because they are readily available elsewhere.

In keeping with the fundamental purpose of this Library, the voices of Protestantism are allowed to speak for themselves, with only as much introduction, commentary, and exposition as will in fact allow them to do so. Wherever feasible, documents are reproduced in their entirety. A few representative selections have been preferred to more numerous but shorter passages, for the Library tries to depict the structure of thought rather than the genetic development of a man or a movement. Nevertheless, the variety of Protestant forms precludes a uniform treatment throughout. Our aim has been to be representative rather than exhaustive and to employ the best available tools of critical historical scholarship. Despite its ambitious scope, A Library of Protestant Thought is not an encyclopedia of Protestantism. It is a series of volumes from which not only clergymen and theologians, but students of philosophy, history, literature, political science and other disciplines can gain a more balanced view of

v

how the Protestant mind has thought and spoken since the Reformation.

The Board is grateful to the Hazen Foundation for an initial grant enabling it to begin its work; to the Sealantic Fund, Inc., for a grant making possible Board meetings, consultations, and editorial assistance in the preparation of specific volumes; and to the Oxford University Press for undertaking the publication of the Library.

THE EDITORIAL BOARD

Table of Contents

Part Four

Heteronomous Authority and the Autonomous Individual 283

Part Five

The Ministry 343

✤

THE MERCERSBURG THEOLOGY

✤

Introduction

I

The Mercersburg theology took its name from a remote village in the Appalachian foothills near Mason and Dixon's line, where the college and seminary of the German Reformed Church were located. In the middle of the nineteenth century these institutions acquired theological and philosophical distinction under the leadership of two men in particular, the historian and liturgist Philip Schaff (1819–93), and the theologian John Williamson Nevin (1803–86).

The German Reformed Church had previously made no perceptible contribution to the intellectual life of American Christianity. It was one of the minor Reformed bodies, with a small, mainly rural constituency, isolated by the use of the German language and geographically confined, for the most part, to eastern Pennsylvania, Maryland, and Ohio. It is indeed possible that neither Nevin nor Schaff had ever heard of Mercersburg before they were first approached about joining the faculty there. At the time, Nevin was an established theologian, a product of the Old School Presbyterians, and Schaff, a member of the United Evangelical Church of Prussia, was fresh from his studies at three German universities. They soon discovered that they had come quite independently to share a distinctive theological orientation, and their collaboration in its development produced the Mercersburg theology.

The flood of new ideas and strange categories that erupted at Mercersburg did not receive universal approval in the German Reformed Church. Within a year after the two professors began their collaboration in 1844–45, they were already the defendants in a trial for heresy. This they survived, but it was a portent of the challenge the Mercersburg theology was felt to present to American thought. Nevertheless, in part because of the previous weakness of intellectual life in the German Reformed Church, Nevin and Schaff exercised an overwhelming, if by no means unquestioned, ascendancy in its church courts, educational institutions, and press.

From this base in the German Reformed Church they carried on a series of debates with theologians in other denominations. None of their

German Reformed opponents could meet them on equal terms, nor, for that matter, could the Reformed Dutch or American Lutheran theologians who fought them so bitterly. Nevin and Schaff gave themselves devotedly to the needs of the German Reformed Church, but they conceived of it as called to a distinctive ecumenical task, so that their theological horizons far transcended denominational tradition. Their position was worked out in a series of theological debates. As they saw it, the collective opponent was "Puritanism," by which they meant the individualistic anti-traditionalist evangelicalism then dominant in American religion. With Charles Hodge (1797-1878), the oracle of the Presbyterian Old School and editor of the *Princeton Review*, they debated the Reformed doctrine of the Lord's Supper and the nature of the Church, among other matters. On the Roman Catholic side the American ultramontane, Orestes Brownson (1803-76) was much easier to cope with than the imposing Johann Adam Möhler (1796-1838), whose ideas can be detected in many Mercersburg discussions, even when his name is not mentioned. Nevin and Schaff followed the Anglo-Catholic movement closely, finding in R. I. Wilberforce[1] (1802-57) the greatest theological substance and the closest affinity to their own position. In two or three interchanges with Horace Bushnell[2] (1802-76) there was much mutual respect, though the two parties seem to have talked past each other to a considerable degree. Most important of all were the exchanges with contemporary Germans, chiefly of the so-called "mediating" group which attempted to relate to theological tradition and Scripture the methods and conceptions especially of Hegel and Schleiermacher. In different ways, relations were especially close with Karl Ullmann (1796-1865) and Richard Rothe (1799-1867), and with the speculative Christology of K. T. A. Liebner (1806-71) and of the Danish high-churchman Hans L. Martensen (1808-84). Of all these the most formal *Auseinandersetzung* occurred in Nevin's debate with Isaak A. Dorner[3] (1809-84), Schaff's one-time professor at Tübingen. For all its isolation, Mercersburg may well have had wider horizons than any other center of American theology in its time.

Provinciality was a conspicuous feature not only of that theology, but to some degree of British theology as well. The leading American schools, Andover, Princeton, Yale and Union, all represented the old covenant

1. Cf. E. R. Fairweather, *The Oxford Movement*, (New York, 1964).
2. Cf. H. Shelton Smith, *Horace Bushnell* (New York, 1965).
3. Cf. Claude Welch, *God and Incarnation in Mid-Nineteenth Century German Theology: Thomasius, Dorner, Biedermann* (New York, 1965).

theology associated with the Westminster Confession and with certain of its New England variants. Even in New England, the most productive region, the problems at issue were largely posed by the epigones of Jonathan Edwards. The Presbyterians and the Dutch and German Reformed of the Middle Atlantic States contented themselves with textbook divinity from Dutch, German, or Swiss scholastics—Franciscus Turretinus (1623–87), Joannes Wollebius (1586–1629), Hermannus Witsius (1636–1708), and Joannes Marckius (1656–1731).[4] Some of these schools repeated the same texts and lectures notes for decades. In biblical and historical studies eighteenth-century German texts held a virtual monopoly. Andover was especially active in domesticating the outworn biblical interpretation and exegesis of such "rational supernaturalists" as J. A. Ernesti (1707–81), and church history meant Chancellor Mosheim (1694?–1755). But despite the inclusive range of these Continental manuals, theological interest was largely confined to the issues typical of the English-speaking world since the Puritan Revolution. This Congregational and Presbyterian main stream was paralleled, of course, by Methodist, Episcopal, Baptist, and Lutheran traditions. But these, while varying in emphasis, were even less creative intellectually, and even more practical in orientation. With the resources of the churches largely exhausted by overwhelming practical tasks, American theology generally was traditionalist, sectarian, and provincial.

It was not yet generally appreciated in either America or England that Germany in the late eighteenth century had taken the lead in theological studies and now teemed with an unequalled wealth of scholarship and thought. There were, indeed, rumors that rationalistic error, "transcendentalism," and pantheism were rampant in Germany, and those, such as Hodge or Pusey, who ventured into the maelstrom, were much on guard — while prayers were said at home that they might not lose their faith.

In this situation the bilingual churches in America, especially the German Lutheran and Reformed, were naturally best equipped to mediate between American Christianity and the new developments abroad. The Lutherans, however, led by men like Benjamin Kurtz (1795–1865) of the *Lutheran Observer*, or Professor Samuel S. Schmucker (1799–1873) of Gettysburg, were cut off from the newer developments on the Continent, and were content to take their cue from such centers as Princeton and

4. For some representative texts see J. W. Beardslee, III, *Reformed Dogmatics* (New York, 1965).

Andover. It was rather the German Reformed Church which first established effective communication with nineteenth-century German theology,
both Lutheran and Reformed. The German language and ties which were
in some ways a handicap in American life could thus be a positive re-
source in theology.

Philip Schaff was called by the church fathers to fulfill precisely this
function. He was to replace Friedrich Rauch (1806–41), a disciple of
the conservative Hegelian of Heidelberg, Karl Daub (1765–1836), and
an effective teacher at Mercersburg for two or three years before his pre-
mature death at thirty-five. This had been enough to whet the appetite
for German scholarship, and emissaries were sent to Germany to secure a
replacement. Philip Schaff, then a young docent at the University of Berlin, was recommended, and he was called by the Synod in 1843.

Schaff was a product of that Awakening which had begun on the Continent during the Napoleonic Wars. Swiss by birth, he owed his religious
formation and his education to Swabian pietism. The pietist settlement at
Kornthal prepared him for the university, and for two years at Tübingen
(1837–39) he associated with the leaders of Württemberg pietism. Then
at Halle, F. A. G. Tholuck (1799–1877), the leader of North German
pietism, made Schaff his secretary, and introduced the youngster, when
he transferred to Berlin in 1840, to Baron von Kottwitz (1757–1843), the
pietist patriarch of the Prussian capital. Schleiermacher and Hegel were
both gone, of course, but Schaff heard Schelling's famous lectures of
1841, and became devoted to the great church historian August Neander
(1789–1850). At Tübingen he had also heard F. C. Baur (1792–1860),
dean of the "Tübingen school," and been impressed by his conception of
historical development, even while deploring his radical tendency. Isaak
Dorner, a more conservative idealist, was theologically the most congenial
of his Tübingen teachers. In Berlin Schaff became a protégé of E. W.
Hengstenberg (1802–69), the rigid Biblicist who was also the most powerful ecclesiastical politician in Prussia, and of Ludwig von Gerlach
(1795–1877), the leading spokesman for the theocratic high-church
views of the royal court. Here Schaff's individualist pietism developed
into "evangelical catholicity" not long before he sailed for New York at
the age of twenty-five.

At Mercersburg Schaff was to teach in the German language, while his
older colleague, John Nevin, was to continue instruction in English. But
it happened that Nevin, Scots-Irish, Princeton-trained Presbyterian
though he was, had developed an enthusiasm of his own for contempo-

rary German theology and philosophy. It was partly for this reason that he had been called to Mercersburg in 1839 from the Western Theological Seminary in Pittsburgh, where he had already taught for a decade. He did not share the Scottish empiricism of Charles Hodge, whose Princeton classes he had taught during Hodge's years in Germany. Rather, the influence of Coleridge had brought him, like so many others, to an idealist perspective and a new, less mechanical view of biblical inspiration. The church historian Neander had wakened him, he said, out of his dogmatic slumber to a sense of historical movement even in doctrine, and to a belief, with Schleiermacher, that religion was in itself distinct from either doctrine or ethics. German biblical commentators, especially Hermann Olshausen (1796–1839), proved suggestive to him theologically as well as in exegesis. He was thus, for an American, unusually familiar with current German theology even before he moved to Mercersburg and had the guidance first of Rauch and then of Schaff concerning the German academic scene. By the time of the Civil War there were few, if any, native Americans more familiar with contemporary German theology than Nevin was.

Charles Hodge made of all this a reproach, accusing Nevin of decking himself out with the castoff clothes of Hegel and Schleiermacher. Nevin, admitting that he had read some of Schleiermacher and hoped to read more, answered that the debt to him was chiefly indirect, through such authors as Neander, Tholuck, Mueller, Nitzsch, Ullmann, Dorner, and Rothe. In one sense the significance of Mercersburg is that it introduced this body of German literature into American theology. In so doing it contributed to a revolution which was completed more than a generation later when, as Schaff and Nevin had predicted, the collapse of New England theology finally opened the way to the tendencies of German thinking. By that time, of course, the speculative method had largely been crowded aside by Ritschlianism and the historical approach to the Bible.

Nevin, like Schaff, had been in early years shaped by the individualist piety of the nineteenth-century Awakening. He experienced a conversion as an undergraduate at Union College, and there and at Princeton he pursued "heart religion" in conservative churchly forms. His affiliations were still with the Presbyterian Old School, although he deplored the doctrinal rancor of the 1830's. He was a typical private-judgment Biblicist and evangelical in those years, calling energetically for home and foreign missions, Sunday schools, temperance, and finally, after a colonizationist phase, abolitionism. The last issue seemed to him more profoundly divisive than the doctrinal one in the Presbyterian Church, and he remained unconvinced of the constitutionality of the Acts by which that body was split in 1837.

The German church to which Nevin transferred in 1839 was just beginning to feel the impact of revivalism and of the machinery that had been characteristic of Presbyterianism and Congregationalism for two decades — the agencies for home and foreign missions, moral reform, and the distribution of Bibles and tracts; colleges and theological seminaries; and the religious press. The German congregations, on the other hand, had become accustomed to the chronic shortage of ministers, and often seemed content with monthly church services. There was sometimes bitter resistance to fund-raising for purposes which were suspected by some of tending to re-impose the burden of the state church they had left behind. Even so, Nevin had substantial success in a vigorous campaign to finance an impoverished college and its associated school of theology. By the time Schaff arrived, Nevin was at once president of Marshall College and head of its board of directors, as well as — since the death of Rauch — sole professor in its theological seminary.

But alongside the routine formalism and niggardliness, Nevin found the German Reformed Church threatened from the opposite extreme of wildfire revivalism. In the 1840's the German churches, the Lutheran even more than the Reformed, seemed to be repeating the experience of the Presbyterians and Congregationalists with Charles Finney's revivals twenty years before. Nevin's *The Anxious Bench*, published in 1843 to warn the German churches against "new measures" revivalism, restated the familiar Old School arguments. To him, apart from the unseemly disorder and "quackery," the chief danger of revivalism was doctrinal. Finneyism implied the Pelagian self-salvation of Nathaniel Taylor's theology; and to an Old-School Presbyterian "Taylorism" was the most formidable of current heresies. For Nevin, another danger in "new measures" revivalism was that it often led to censoriousness and divisiveness. Philip Otterbein (1726–1813) had led off one revivalist split from the German Reformed Church, the "United Brethren in Christ," and John Winebrenner (1797–1860) had seceded to form the "Church of God" in the 1820's. Against such dangers Nevin urged the "system of the catechism," careful teaching, preaching, and visitation. In preparing a second edition of *The Anxious Bench* at the beginning of 1844, he added a new chapter, which signalized a new catholicizing phase startlingly parallel to Schaff's new-found evangelical catholicity.

For a decade after their meeting in the summer of 1844, the two Mercersburg professors collaborated in vigorous literary propaganda as well as in their teaching. A stream of books and tracts, and of articles in *The Weekly Messenger*, *The Mercersburg Review*, and the *Kirchenfreund*, elaborated a position which is sampled in the selections that follow.

Americans sensible of the manifold debt of scholarship to Philip Schaff will find several familiar works missing from this volume. But the Mercersburg chapter of Schaff's life comprehended only his late twenties and his thirties; his best-known scholarly achievements were the products of his second career, after the Civil War, in the Presbyterian context of Union Theological Seminary in New York. It was there that he wrote his *Creeds of Christendom*, the seven-volume *History of the Christian Church*, and *Church and State in the United States;* that he edited the twenty-odd volumes of the Lange biblical commentary, as well as the Schaff-Herzog Encyclopedia of Religious Knowledge; that he supervised much of the series of Nicene and Post-Nicene Fathers, planned the thirteen volumes of American denominational church histories, founded the American Society of Church History, and chaired the American committee of the group which prepared the Revised Standard Version of the Bible. No other American theological scholar of the century rivalled this production. But although some of these and other later writings convey echoes of Mercersburg themes, they can scarcely be claimed for the Mercersburg movement and its special perspective.

There was a loss of momentum at Mercersburg, indeed, as early as 1853, when the removal of Marshall College to Lancaster and the retirement of Nevin to private life broke up the inner circle of leaders. Schaff had to resign from the editing of the *Kirchenfreund*, and was left in the lonely isolation of Mercersburg village with a handful of seminary students. His trip to Germany in 1853–54, however, was something of a milestone for him personally. The lectures he delivered in Germany, later published as *America, a Sketch of its Political, Social and Religious Character* (1855), constituted an important corrective to the *Principle of Protestantism*, and showed Schaff as for the first time independent of his German teachers. At the same time he was released from the somewhat overpowering influence of Nevin's personality. At the age of thirty-five he was now ready to stand on his own feet as a theologian and scholar. He reworked his early church history in the following years, publishing the first of the two volumes while he was still in Mercersburg. But his participation in the movement was now confined chiefly to trips to Lancaster for sessions of the liturgical commission. Schaff had inherited the leadership of this enterprise from a despairing Nevin, and the "Provisional Liturgy" of 1857 became his greatest contribution to the movement.

In both Europe and America, the world in which the Mercersburg theology had been formulated was transformed by the events of the 1860's. The Civil War in America, the Seven Weeks' War and the Franco-Prussian War in Europe ushered in a brutal new "realism" in political and economic thinking, beside which the theocratic visions and moral utopianism of the preceding generation seemed naive. Natural science, positivism, and technology elbowed aside metaphysical speculation in the intellectual world. And the triumph of ultramontanism in the Syllabus of Errors and the decree of papal infallibility in 1870 shattered such ecumenical hopes as Schelling and the Mercersburg men had entertained.

In this new environment the scope of the Mercersburg movement was narrowed. It was no longer an aggressive force in the intellectual world. Both Nevin and Schaff significantly modified their own positions, and the old program survived as a mere tradition in the hands of their disciples at the college and seminary. Schaff had gone elsewhere, and Nevin in his old age turned in another speculative direction. The line of Appel, Higbee, Harbaugh, and Gerhart maintained the legacy into the 1890's, but without creative force. The spirit of the movement survived mainly in the liturgy it had molded. The *Order of Worship* embodied a sense of continuity at once with the Reformation and with ancient Catholicism, along with the characteristic views of its compilers concerning Church, ministry, and sacraments. In some congregations it remains to this day the vehicle of a living tradition.

II

It is true that Mercersburg constituted a chapter in the history of philosophical idealism in America which has not been adequately evaluated as compared with the New England transcendentalists and the Coleridgeans. But the most distinctive aspects of the thought of Nevin and Schaff were neither their philosophical views *per se*, nor their ties with the mediating theologians, nor their new sense of history — although the last in particular deserves further consideration. What chiefly identified both Nevin and Schaff, in their own view and in that of their contemporaries, was their interpretation of the Church. When Schaff first met Nevin he noted in his journal, "I feared I might not find any sympathy in him for my views of the Church; but I discover that he occupies essentially the same ground that I do, and confirms me in my position." [5] It is the high-church or catholicizing tendency within the framework of German idealism and historical thought which is the characteristic note of Mercersburg theology.

It has been observed that in the first half of the nineteenth century the Church itself, her nature, calling, and structure, became a central theme of theology as never before among Protestants.[6] Among the various approaches to this theme, the Mercersburg theology is to be grouped with that series of high-church movements which sprang up across the several countries and ecclesiastical traditions in the middle third of the century. The two movements to which Mercersburg was most akin were the neo-Lutheran confessionalism represented, e.g., by Wilhelm Löhe (1808–72), Theodor Kliefoth (1810–95), and August Vilmar (1800–68), on the one hand, and the Anglo-Catholicism of J. H. Newman, E. B. Pusey, and R. I. Wilberforce on the other. The parallels between these two, including their common and ambivalent indebtedness to pietism and evangelicalism, are pointed out by Y. Brilioth, who characterizes the passage from evangelicalism to the catholicizing phase as follows:

> The Oxford Movement was a rediscovery of the historical mediation of salvation, just as the evangelical movement had been the discovery of the immediate relation of the individual soul to its Saviour. The salvation of the soul was no less serious a matter to the Tractarians, but as it involved the questions of the historical church, of episcopacy, and of sacraments, these things, too, gained a tremendous importance. The question of the historical Church became part of the question of the salvation of the soul.[7]

Only a year or two before leaving Berlin, Schaff had become an adherent of the *"Evangelische Katholizität"* of Ludwig von Gerlach, the jurist and counsellor of King Frederick William IV. This movement later turned largely to exclusive Lutheran confessionalism, but in its early phase at the beginning of the 1840's it gloried rather in the unity of Lutheran and Reformed in the Prussian Evangelical Church.

Gerlach himself later contrasted the religious style of the 1820's with that of the 1850's. In the earlier decade the emphasis was on the personal experience of sin and grace, while ministry, worship, sacraments, and the

5. D. S. Schaff, *Life of Philip Schaff*, (New York, 1897), 103.
6. E. Hirsch, *Geschichte der neuern evangelischen Theologie* (Gütersloh, 1949–54), V, 145.
7. *Three Lectures on Evangelicalism and the Oxford Movement* (London, 1934), 57.

form and order of the Church were secondary and instrumental. In the 1850's, however, the focus had moved from subjective experience to the God-given "Objektivitäten" of Church, confession, ministry, worship, sacrament, and discipline. As against all subjectivist arbitrariness the weight now fell on the institutional Church, with its orders and ministry and confession, as the Body of Christ.[8]

Whatever mysterious forces may be supposed to effect such changes between generations, theologically the best key to the catholic movement may be its intoxication with vitalistic categories for the religious community. Since the days of Herder and the early romantics, the ideas of organism and mechanism had been contrasted in the consideration of political and religious forms. Goethe added to the force of such thinking. There was scriptural basis, of course, in the "Body of Christ," but organicist theologians in various communions often pushed the metaphor far beyond what any responsible exegesis would justify. Earlier centuries had thought about the Church on juridical and on mechanical models; now biology supplied the categories. The concepts of potency and actuality so favored by organicist thinkers — concepts which in fact go back to Aristotle — were biologically derived. They were useful in that they underlined certain kinds of change most familiar in living beings. In contrast to inorganic or mechanical processes, the growth of an organic structure is self-impelled and internally governed. Schelling, of course, was ruled by this analogy even in considering what is usually called "inorganic nature."

Concerning Nevin's "churchly" conversion, at least, one suspects that the idea of organism was the intellectual catalyst. He had for some years been philosophically "Platonist," with an intuitionist theory of religious knowledge. Along with Schleiermacher's distinction between piety and theology, he had accepted a measure of historical evolution in the realm of doctrine. His devotional bent seems not to have focussed on concern for justification and conversion. It was mystical in its stress on growth in holiness, on the life of God in the soul. But even with his high-Presbyterian views of ministerial succession and of a Calvinist Real Presence, all this could still be combined with the categories of visible and invisible Church. To judge from his references it was the application of organicist thought to the idea of the second Adam, the new creation, as by Ernst Sartorius (1797–1859) and Olshausen, that became the governing motif in a general reorganization of his theology.

8. E. Hirsch, *op. cit.*, 172f.

A second major tendency was a reverence for tradition as expressing the continuity of the Church. That tradition of course included institutional structure and patterns of worship, but most crucial to it were the classical formulations of doctrine, the ancient Creeds. At Mercersburg the catholic Creeds were exalted as a banner, in a way quite exceptional among American churches. The stimulus here may have come from the debates at the Prussian General Synod of 1846. There, when Nitzsch and Dorner proposed a new formula for ordination, Gerlach campaigned against the "Nitzscheanum" in the name of the Apostle's Creed and the "Niceanum." The ancient Creeds established the common ground of all Christianity — Roman Catholicism and Orthodoxy included — and were not subject to revision by any merely local body. Mercersburg held the same position as against the consensus creed proposed by Samuel Schmucker for his federal union of churches, or the doctrinal articles drawn up by the Evangelical Alliance. What could such private inventions signify as against the universally acknowledged declarations of the Catholic faith?

In its practical effect, on the other hand, the Mercersburg movement was primarily a Eucharistic revival. It did not arise, like the Tractarian development, as a campaign for clerical prerogatives and authority, although in the course of time a comparable doctrine of the ministry did emerge. The first and central concern, and that on which the opposition first fastened, was with the Lord's Supper. "To my own mind," wrote Nevin, "all that is great and precious in the gospel may be said to center in this doctrine. . . . Both for my understanding and my heart, theology finds here all its interest and attraction." [9]

The recovery at Mercersburg of the sacramental emphasis, as at Oxford and among the high-church Lutherans, seemed to be associated with a re-conception of the ministry. Many of the leaders of this movement, including Löhe, Newman, and Nevin, were powerful preachers, but many of them were strangely silent on the Christological significance of the Word preached. With them the constituting function of the ministry became the dispensation of sacramental grace, together with the exercise of ecclesiastical government, and little was said about the ministry of the Word. There was also often a new preoccupation with the legal succession of ordinations as the necessary validation of the sacraments. Hirsch identifies what he calls the "Osiander-Löhe" doctrine of the minis-

9. *The Weekly Messenger*, October 8, 1845.

try as the most distinctive note of the high-church Lutherans as a group.[10]

Gerlach and Stahl insisted on an institutionally defined succession of ministers. They were favorably disposed to diocesan episcopacy, but did not single out this one order as indispensable for the continuity of either ministry or Church. The Mercersburg men maintained this position also, and in this they resembled the Lutherans more than the Anglo-Catholics. They asserted a high doctrine of Church, ministry, and tradition, but without absolutizing the confessions, as the Lutherans did, or bishops, as did the Anglo-Catholics. In America these aspects of ecclesiastical tradition did not function, as in Europe, as defenses against aggression by the civil power. There was little pressure from the state of the sort experienced in either England or Prussia. In England the authority of a legal episcopal succession, if divinely sanctioned, could be appealed to against civil supremacy. In Prussia there was no such ground for the assertion of clerical independence, but the authorized confessions had a juridical status and ecclesiastical authority which provided a comparable bastion for the integrity of religious life. In America, on the other hand, the threat was from revivalistic chaos and sectarian anarchy, against which nothing could be asserted but the catholic nature of the Church itself.

Of various approaches to the Mercersburg theology, as useful as any is one drafted by Nevin himself in the course of the liturgical controversy after the Civil War. In assessing it, one should remember the overwhelming concentration in American Protestant theology at that time on the soteriological topics related to conversion — such as atonement and justification — and, on the other hand, the stress on biblical inspiration and "evidences." The Mercersburg liturgy, said Nevin, expressed a definite theology:

> In the first place, it is Christological, or more properly perhaps, Christocentric; in the second place, it moves in the bosom of the Apostles' Creed; in the third place, it is objective and historical, involving thus the idea of the Church as a perennial article of faith. These three conceptions are closely intertwined; but they admit and deserve separate consideration. . . .
>
> No theology in the country certainly has made more of Christ as the center of its thinking and teaching. No theology has insisted more earnestly on the great cardinal truths of the Trinity, the Eternal Generation, the divinity of the Son, the Incarnation, the mediatorial work and reign of Christ; and no theology, it may be safely

10. Hirsch, *op. cit.,* V, 194.

asserted, has done more, within the same time, to awaken and enforce attention to the practical significance of these truths in the American religious world. . . .

The Creed . . . is no summary of Christian doctrine primarily for the understanding, but the necessary form of the gospel, as this is first apprehended by faith; a direct transcript, we may say, of what the gospel is to the contemplation of the believer, turned wholly upon the Person of Christ. Such faith is necessarily ruled by its object; the Creed, in other words, must be Christological, must unfold itself, first of all, in the order of what are to be regarded as the fundamental facts of Christianity, growing forth from the mystery of the Incarnation.

Starting in Christ, it [the Mercersburg Theology] follows the order in which the facts of religion unfold themselves with necessary connection from his Person. This order is for it not optional simply, but is felt to be inwardly bound to its own principle. . . . It makes all the difference in the world, in this view, whether a system of theological thought be cast in the type of doctrine that is set forth in the Creed, or constructed in some other way. . . . Every doctrine, in this way, becomes Christological, and serves to express a truth which is true only within the orbit of the Creed, and not at all on the outside of it. It would be interesting to verify this in particular cases, by showing how the doctrine of the atonement, for example, the article of justification by faith, the idea of regeneration, the conception of sacramental grace, are found to be always something materially different in the theology of the Creed from what they are made to be in any other theology; but it would carry us too far. . . .

The theology we are defending may be said to be specially identified with the honor of the Apostles' Creed in the religious history of this country. In our Reformed Zion, twenty-five years ago, the Creed had become almost a dead letter. . . . Now, however, all is changed. . . . Can there be any doubt of the source from which this great change has sprung? Do we not owe it entirely to the Christological tendency that has been at work among us for the last twenty years? . . . And no one, who has observed attentively the the course of things, can doubt but that the power of this testimony has been felt also far beyond the narrow limit of our Reformed Church. . . . No other theology in the country, certainly, has labored more to reanimate the symbol with its pristine life. No other has so borne it on high as the chosen banner of its faith.

Starting in the great fact of the Incarnation, and following its movement, our theology has finally the third general character of being objective and historical . . . This objective act [the Incarnation] is itself the gospel, in the profoundest sense of the term. In the very nature of the case, it must underlie and condition all that the gospel can ever become for men in the way of inner experience. True, it cannot save men without their being brought to experience its power; on which account it is that we need to be placed in communication with it by faith; but the power that saves is not, for this reason, in our experience or faith; it is wholly in the object with which our faith is concerned. . . . The objective reality from which Christianity springs, the new order of existence which was constituted for the world by the great fact of the Incarnation, must be allowed also to be historical . . . But this conception of a supernatural economy having place among men under an objective, historical form, an order of grace flowing from Christ, and altogether different from the order of nature, is nothing more nor less than the idea of the holy catholic Church as we have it in the Creed.

The theology we are speaking of, then, is churchly . . . It believes in an economy of grace, a sphere of supernatural powers and forces flowing from the historical fact of Christ's birth, death, and glorification, which are themselves present in the world historically (not magically) in broad distinction from the economy of nature; and in the bosom of which only, not on the outside of it, the gospel can be expected to work as the wisdom of God and the power of God unto salvation.

Such a churchly theology, we feel at once, can never be otherwise than sacramental. Where the idea of the Church has come to make itself felt in the way now described, as involving the conjunction of the supernatural and the natural continuously in one and the same abiding economy of grace, its sacraments cannot possibly be regarded as outward signs only of what they represent. They become, for faith, seals also of the actual realities themselves which they exhibit. . . . In the end, also, unquestionably, the sacramental feeling here cannot fail to show itself a liturgical feeling.

A theology which is truly Christocentric must follow the Creed, must be objective, must be historical; with this, must be churchly; and, with this again, must be sacramental and liturgical. [11]

The Mercersburg theology, then, may be triangulated from high-church Lutheranism and Anglo-Catholicism. In its historical dimensions and enduring influence, of course, it was much less extensive than either of the two. But it is sufficiently individual theologically to warrant attention. It is more akin to the Lutherans in its serious concern for the Reformation and in the range of theological and philosophical interests it maintained. But in America, where the Lutheran movements were little known, the Mercersburg theology was usually associated with "Puseyism." Its ecumenical passion, and the seriousness with which it wrestled

11. "The Theology of the New Liturgy," *The Mercersburg Review*, XIV (1867), 28–44.

with the historical evolution of Church and doctrine, enable it to stand comparison with either of the parallel movements.

III

The dynamics and motivations of the Mercersburg theology are not to be grasped simply by noting its most characteristic themes and positions. The movement is intelligible only if one takes seriously its deeply felt ecumenism. And this yearning for the Church Catholic may perhaps be best understood in relation to its foil, the spirit of sect understood as the Protestant manifestation of Antichrist.

Schaff had spoken out on the curse of American sectarianism in his ordination sermon at Elberfeld and again in *The Principle of Protestantism*. He was then merely repeating the clichés of European state-churchmen, with little grasp of the realities of the American situation. But Nevin — at first scandalized by the Pelagian tendencies of "new measures" revivalism but later more distressed over sectarian anarchy — agreed with him in great part. The American evangelical stress on religious immediacy tended to confine the sense of community to those actually present in meeting, with a minimum of concern for the larger Church, to say nothing of any felt community with generations past. The one sufficient point of reference was the Bible, to which it was generally agreed that all had equal access on the principle of private judgment. The consequence was what seemed to be an incurably progressive disease of subdivision and disintegration. And "Puritanism," as the Mercersburg men labelled the dominant evangelical tendency, seemed to provide no theological anchorage for halting the drift. Although Puritanism was not to be simply equated with sectarianism, it was peculiarly liable to the disease.

The sectarian mentality flourished in part because of the lack in America of historical consciousness. In Britain as well, Christians of the first half of the nineteenth century had, as a rule, not yet acknowledged the historical evolution of Christian doctrine and institutions. Ecclesiastical controversy regularly took the form of an effort to demonstrate that some existing system of thought or polity or worship was in fact the faith once delivered to the saints, and that all proposed alternatives were simply human corruptions. Whether it was Brownson's papalism, Pusey's episcopacy, New England congregationalism or Princeton presbyterianism, each represented a static orthodoxy supposed to have been divinely established from the first or in one of the early centuries, and now represented faithfully by one favored tradition. All of them, consequently, had to rule much or most of Christian history as out of the bounds of the true Church. The development of modern ecumenism waited in part on the development of modern historical consciousness. Both had already made their appearance in Germany, and from Mercersburg they were introduced into the English-speaking world.

In his autobiography Nevin described how the new historical perspective represented by Neander had worked a revolution in his own theological thinking. By distinguishing piety from doctrine Neander could interpret sympathetically figures and movements in Christian history with which he was not wholly in agreement theologically. Thus Nevin had learned for the first time to appreciate and make sense of the Fathers of the early Church, men whom his Princeton mentors had treated as simply wrong and unintelligible. Schaff had received a more sophisticated introduction to the development of doctrine from F. C. Baur and Isaak Dorner, although he too was a grateful student of Neander. In Neander's method a degree of anti-intellectual pietism made doctrine secondary to devotion. But Baur and Dorner endeavored to find, in the changes of doctrine itself, an inner logic whereby conflicting views might be justified in relation to their historical bearings and in this way to all others as well. Responsible theology in a historically self-conscious age must thus be ecumenical theology. What could a purely Methodist or Baptist or Puritan theology be worth henceforth? "Theology can be no science," Nevin now contended, "except as it has to do with the whole of Christianity, and is thus at once both churchly and historical." [12]

In that total sweep of Christian thought since the New Testament there were three great crucial moments that defined the task of the ecumenical theologian. Starting as a Protestant, one must first of all come to terms with the Reformation, from which a perspective on the varieties of Protestantism might be opened. But the meaning of the Reformation itself could be fully grasped only in relation to the preceding Catholicism, and especially to the ancient Church of the Fathers. From this inquiry, finally, there might be expected some guidance as to the lines of future development. The Mercersburg men had something to say on all three questions.

One contribution of Mercersburg to American evangelical theology was in the revival of Reformation studies. In early nineteenth-century England and America the Reformation was generally approached through later Puritanism and scholasticism, and was little studied in itself. Even

12. "The Sect System II," *The Mercersburg Review*, I (1849), 525. See below, 105.

before Schaff's arrival at Mercersburg, Nevin had worked toward an expansion and reorientation of the historical guidelines. When Nevin, an Old-School Presbyterian raised on the Westminster standards, Puritan divinity, and such Reformed scholastics as Turretinus, transferred to the German Reformed Church he obligated himself to the use of the Heidelberg Catechism and to learning the history of the Palatinate Reformation. He made his education a public process, bringing out a series of articles on the history of the German Reformed in the sixteenth century while he preached his way, in Reformation fashion, through the questions of the catechism. He brought both to considerably higher honor and use within the German Reformed Church.

Nevin also retained from his Presbyterian days a high respect for Calvin, even though the German church was accustomed rather to trace its theological lineage to Zwingli. Having been shaken loose from the narrower formulations of later scholasticism and British Puritanism, he cultivated now the freer and more biblical thought of the sixteenth-century Reformers and confessions. The Mystical Presence and "The Doctrine of the Reformed Church on the Lord's Supper" were substantial scholarly investigations which powerfully challenged the conventional understanding of the Calvinist Reformation in Presbyterianism and Anglicanism as well as in the German Reformed Church.

At Princeton and the Reformed Dutch seminary at New Brunswick, Calvin had been customarily interpreted as a systematic predestinarian. Nevin demonstrated that there was a strong sacramental strain in Calvin, whatever the difficulty of reconciling it with his predestinarianism, and that the Calvinist doctrine of the Eucharist had in fact been embodied in the actual constitution of the German Reformed Church while the better known doctrine of the decrees had not. So he wrote of the Reformed Dutch, "We will bear with their Calvinism on the decrees if they will bear with our Calvinism on the sacraments." [13] Nevin himself, perhaps under the influence of Schaff, came to abandon his earlier predestinarianism, and in this sense Mercersburg theology belongs to the nineteenth century revolt against "Calvinism." The Mercersburg men also adopted from Heinrich Heppe [14] the theory of the Melanchthonian character of the Palatinate Reformation, and from about 1850 onward they tended to

13. "The Dutch and German Churches," The Weekly Messenger, September 30, 1846.
14. "Der Charakter der deutsch-reformirten Kirche und das Verhältnis derselben zum Lutherthum und zum Calvinismus," Theologischen Studien und Kritiken, XXIII (1850), 669–706.

hand over Calvin to Hodge as they transferred their historical attention to Melanchthon. Melanchthon and Calvin, Nevin argued, held the same ground on Eucharistic doctrine, but Melanchthon had avoided Calvinist rigor on predestination.

More surprising, and more significant ecumenically, was the Mercersburg contribution to the revival of the historic Lutheran testimony as an indispensable factor in the equation. This was natural enough, of course, for Schaff, who owed much or most of his theological education to Lutherans and who found it painful in America to limit his ecclesiastical affiliation to but one of the two traditions united in his own Prussian church. He paid generous tribute to Luther in his *Principle of Protestantism* and was personally more devoted to Luther and Melanchthon than to Calvin or Zwingli. He was always, like Nevin, Reformed on the doctrines of the Lord's Supper and of ubiquity, but he preferred Lutheran liturgy and devotional forms and loved the Lutheran hymnody. His *Kirchenfreund* served both constituencies in America, and even *The Mercersburg Review* presented numerous German Lutheran theologians to the American public. Lutheran and Reformed congregations were closely related by culture and language, often sharing the same church buildings and hymnals, and intermarrying freely. The Mercersburg movement was almost as much a force in Lutheranism as in the German Reformed Church. Although its full significance in this respect has not been adequately assessed, one may suspect that it played an important role in the shaping of that revolution which occurred in American Lutheranism in the 1850's.

Like Schaff, Nevin deplored what he considered the theological bankruptcy of the "American Lutherans" led by Benjamin Kurtz and Samuel Schmucker, and welcomed with joy the inauguration in 1849 of the *Evangelical Review* as the theological voice, at last, of historically responsible Lutheranism in America. To him it was a great weakness that American theology made no account whatever of the whole Lutheran side of Protestant thought, but assumed in its self-sufficiency that a generically Reformed theology covered the whole ground. American thought was still dominated by New England, where it was taken for granted that "the history of theology in this country, since the days of Jonathan Edwards downwards, may be taken as the comprehension, in substance, of all that is important in its history since the Reformation, or before it. . . . A good theological education is not supposed generally to need any reference whatever to this old Lutheran divinity, except in the way of outward polemic notice, here and there, as in the case of other false systems." [15]

One consequence of this imbalance was that the self-consciousness of the Reformed community had itself evaporated in the absence of its historic counterpart, and Americans had a sharper sense of such superficial divisions among the Reformed churches as were constituted by Methodism, New School Presbyterianism, and Secederism. But the Reformed Church could never fulfill its mission either in theology or practical piety, Nevin and Schaff believed, without the *felt* presence of the Lutheran antithesis.

> We look upon Lutheranism, in the present stadium of Christianity, as a necessary part of the constitution of Protestantism. Our idea of Protestantism is that the two great confessions into which it was sundered from the start, the Lutheran and the Reformed, grew with inner necessity out of the movement itself, carrying in themselves thus a relative reason and right of the same general nature with what must be allowed in favor of the Reformation itself . . . which is destined, accordingly, in due time, to pass away in their inner amalgamation; a result which will involve also, no doubt, a full conciliation of the Protestant principle as a whole, not with Romanism as it now stands . . . but still with the deep truth of Catholicism, from which, by abuse, the Roman error springs." [16]

The theological issues between Lutherans and Reformed churchmen in the sixteenth century arose, of course, precisely from those topics of Eucharistic theology and Christology which to the Mercersburg theologians in the mid-nineteenth century seemed so central, and to most of their contemporaries so marginal.

The references to Catholicism in the passage just quoted bring into view the second great task for the Reformed ecumenical theologian. The greatest scandal of Mercersburg theology was that it attempted to relate itself to Catholicism, both practically and historically, in a positive way. The movement arose at the peak of the violent "nativist" anti-popery agitation of the 1840's. The Charlestown convent had been burned by rioters. In 1844 there was open warfare in the streets of Philadelphia between Irish immigrants and the older Protestant community. There was controversy over the place of biblical material in the schools of New York and Philadelphia. In *Mirari vos* and *Singulari nos*, Pope Gregory XVI con-

---

15. "The Lutheran Confession," *The Mercersburg Review*, I (1849), 473f.
16. *Ibid.*, 470f.

demned the civil and political liberties specified in the American constitution, and increased the fear of Americans that their religious and political heritage was threatened. Philip Schaff arrived from Germany in what was perhaps the time of greatest interconfessional hostility since the colonial period. In his inaugural address, nevertheless, he announced that there was within Roman Catholicism much of the true Church, with which Protestantism should hope to be reconciled.

On this score, among others, Schaff took exception to the program of the Evangelical Alliance. The Alliance purported to be ecumenical, but in the minds of many of its supporters it was quite evidently meant to be a pan-Protestant agency against the encroachments of popery and Puseyism. The implication that Eastern Orthodoxy and Roman Catholicism were wholly outside the true Church and not to be considered as Christian was indefensible to the Mercersburg men, who believed that there was a Christian truth and vitality in Roman Catholicism without which no ultimate Christian unity could be conceived.

The historical basis for this argument was stated in *The Principle of Protestantism*. The Synod which welcomed Schaff from Germany heard a sermon from the retiring moderator, Dr. Joseph Berg, tracing the lineage of the Reformed Church completely outside the Roman apostasy, from the early days through the faithful remnant in the Waldensian valleys during the Middle Ages, and down to Zwingli. When Schaff then stated the contention of Gerlach that the Reformation was the direct offspring and finest flower of medieval Catholicism, a controversy was inevitable. Schaff, of course, could command the overwhelming weight of historical evidence, but Berg had almost as great a preponderance of American opinion on his side.

It is difficult today, with Schaff's position generally taken for granted, to realize how shocking that position was in America a century or so ago. Then it was strange indeed to look upon the Reformers, according to their own intentions, as Reformed *Catholics*, and to take seriously the notion of significant religious and theological continuity from the early Church through medieval Catholicism and the Reformation. Schaff laid out, to be sure, the "formal" and "material" principles of the Reformation as taught by Twesten; but he followed Ullmann's *Reformers before the Reformation* in tracing them back to medieval Catholicism. And he stressed the adherence of the Reformers to the creedal tradition of the Trinity and Incarnation since the ancient Church.

In practice this assertion of a Catholic heritage by the Mercersburg

theologians was an appeal to the patristic tradition. Schaff did share Gerlach's enthusiasm for the theocratic culture of the Middle Ages, and had a
romantic interest of his own in Gothic cathedrals and in Dante's poetry.
Nevin admired the struggles of Hildebrand and Innocent III for the independence of the spiritual power. But apart from casual references to Anselm and Bernard they showed little *theological* interest in the Middle
Ages. Scholasticism did not interest them. Both men, however, wrote extensively and primarily on the early Church in their Mercersburg period,
and the chief theological reference was to the structure of Trinitarian and
Christological thought, with its implications for the Church and sacraments. For this reason their ecumenical tendency related Protestantism to
Orthodoxy as much as to Rome, although there was, of course, no actual
contact with representatives of Orthodoxy. Dorner even said Nevin's
thought had an Orthodox character.[17]

For Schaff this was a relatively unproblematical stance. He adopted
Kliefoth's thesis [18] that the Reformers had built on the Christological and
Trinitarian dogmas of the ancient Church, bringing further clarification
on soteriological doctrine. Ecclesiology would then, as he saw it, be the
task of the nineteenth century. For him this cumulative doctrinal development brought with it no major internal strains. Nevin, however, since
he had discovered the Fathers late in life, and was obliged to wrestle with
theological explication, found matters less simple. He quoted an interesting autobiographical statement from Heinrich Thiersch (1817-85), the
Marburg church historian and spokesman for the Catholic Apostolic
Church, which evidently described his own experience.

> It is a strange impression that the Church Fathers make on one
> who first enters on the study of them under the full force of a
> merely Protestant consciousness. So fared it with the writer himself.
> Nurtured on the best that the old Protestant books of devotion con-
> tain, and trained theologically in the doctrines and interpretations
> of the orthodox period of Protestantism, he turned finally to the
> Fathers. Well does he remember how strange it appeared to him in
> the beginning, to find here nothing of those truths which formed the
> spring of his whole religious life, nothing of the way the sinner must
> tread to arrive at peace and an assurance of the divine favor, nothing
> of Christ's merit as the only ground of forgiveness, nothing of con-
> tinual repentance and ever new recourse to the fountain of free
> grace, nothing of the high confidence of the justified believer. In-
> stead of this, he found that all weight was laid on the Incarnation of

17. See below, 182.   18. See below, 125.

the divine Logos, on the right knowledge of the great object of worship, on the objective mystery of the Trinity and of Christ's Person, on the connection between creation, redemption, and the future restoration of the creature along with the glorification also of man's body, on the freedom of man and on the reality of the operations of divine grace in the sacraments. But he was enabled gradually to live himself into this old mode of thought, and without giving up what is true and inalienable in the Lutheran Protestant consciousness, to correct its one-sidedness by a living appropriation of the theology of the Fathers. He soon saw that over against the errors of the present time, its pantheism and fatalism, its spiritualism and misapprehension of the significance of the corporeal, the Church needs a decided taking up again of what is true in the patristic scheme of thought, and an assimilation of her whole life to the ancient model — in spirit and idea first, as outward relations are not at once under human control. This old primitive Church stood out to his view more and more in its full splendor, in its sublime beauty, of which only fragmentary lineaments are to be recognized in the churches, confessions, and sects of the present day.[19]

This polarity between the theologies of Protestantism and of the early Fathers is typical of Mercersburg. In this respect Nevin had more kinship with such high-church Lutherans as Löhe than with the Tractarians. The Oxford men represented a program of repristination simply, without any concern for, or probably even any understanding of, the Reformation. There was consequently little work to do save to weed out the distinctively Roman elements from the ancient Catholic heritage, and that was not really theological work. But for Nevin there was the task of clarifying the continuities on the one hand, and on the other, of interpreting the discontinuities, between the ancient Catholic Church and the Reformation, in relation to modern philosophy.

Nevin, in working at various aspects of this polarity, was perhaps most effective concerning the Eucharist and the doctrine of the Church itself. He was confident that there was a legitimate development of the patristic Eucharist in the Reformed doctrine. He was less confident that there had been a legitimate development of the doctrine of the Church, although he thought he discerned something different from, but not wholly unlike, the Church of Cyprian and Augustine even within the apparent anarchy of Protestantism. Again and again, however, he was driven to the verge of despair by the propensity within Protestantism to declare itself on princi-

19. H. W. J. Thiersch, *Versuch zur Herstellung des historischen Standpuncts für die Kritik der neutestamentlichen Schriften* (Erlangen, 1845), 280f. Nevin's translation, quoted in "Early Christianity I," *The Mercersburg Review*, III (1851), 555.

ple unchurchly and unsacramental and to cut itself off altogether from its Catholic heritage.

The wavering of Nevin's faith in the viability of "evangelical catholicism" provoked the most dramatic internal crisis of the Mercersburg movement, as Newman's defection had done in the Tractarian movement a decade earlier. Like Newman, Nevin came to wonder whether he served only a "paper church," and he lived for some time with the same "ghost," the thought that Rome might after all be right.

Even though the theological stimulus at Mercersburg came more from Germany than from England, Nevin in particular reacted with intense concern to the dramatic events in British church life about 1850. The notorious Gorham case,[20] on the one hand, and the panic over the re-establishment of a Roman Catholic hierarchy in England on the other, seemed to him to constitute a crisis unequalled since the sixteenth century. The controversy they had unleashed concerning the direction and meaning of Protestantism had repercussions throughout the Protestant world.

The question was not really that of the precise views of baptismal regeneration entertained by Mr. Gorham or Bishop Phillpotts. On this problem the Mercersburg men themselves were not very decided. The more serious question, as revealed in the debates in the religious press generally, was whether English-speaking Protestantism was about to disavow every kind of baptismal grace. Was it possible that these Lutheran, Reformed, Presbyterian, Methodist, and Episcopal writers were struck with no feeling of anxiety and dread at the thought of making Protestantism by its own voice and vote constitutionally baptistic and unsacramental, and of breaking communion on this matter with the Reformers as well as the medieval and patristic Church? [21]

The issue of baptismal grace really involved also the view of the Church, "for the sacraments are the standing sign and seal of whatever power is comprised in the Church; and as we think of this, so invariably also will we think of them." Nevin granted, to be sure, that "the right Church sense is something more general and deep than the right sacramental feeling. The notion of grace-bearing sacraments, sundered from the sense of the Church as still carrying in it the force of its first super-

20. In 1847 Bishop Phillpotts of Exeter had refused to install George C. Gorham as a rector on the ground that his doctrine of baptism was not orthodox. Mr. Gorham had appealed the bishop's ruling, and the court of last resort, the Judicial Commission of the Privy Council, had sustained the appeal, thus by implication defining the Anglican doctrine of baptism. The case led a number of high Anglicans to transfer to Rome.
21. Nevin, *op. cit.*, 372.

natural constitution, would be indeed magical, and must prove quite as pedantical in the end as a supreme regard for bishops in the same dead way. We must believe in a divine Church in order to believe in divine sacraments, or in a divine ministry under any form." [22]

Nevin's pessimism over Anglicanism was the worse because there was no other sect or fragment of Protestantism in which one could put more hope. He had a particular sympathy for Anglicanism, since along with his own denomination it fell at the churchly end of the Reformed spectrum, as opposed to Puritanism at the unchurchly limit. And the Tractarian leaders, whom he admired personally, had made an attempt which Mercersburg emulated to reassert the catholic continuity of the tradition. But was there a real ground to build on in either case, or was Newman right in turning to Rome, which at least desired and claimed to be catholic in the old sense? If it could not be done in Anglicanism, why suppose that it could be done with the little company of German Reformed in Pennsylvania?

The Gorham case had exposed mercilessly the disgrace and misery of the Anglican establishment, its constitutional deficiency and inability "to assert and carry out in full the proper functions of a church." [23] Despite all the Tractarian attempt to reassert old catholic principles against civil supremacy in the Church, "a theological question, not of secondary but of primary consequence — going . . . to the very root of Protestantism — is settled in the last instance by purely civil authority; and the English hierarchy, with his Grace of Canterbury at its head, in the presence of the whole world dutifully succumbs to the insolent and profane dictation." [24] And just at this moment the Roman Catholic establishment of an independent hierarchy revealed that church as taking "with natural ease the very ground which the Tractarian tendency has been reaching after as necessary and right, but reaching after so far in vain." The hysterical reaction against this "papal aggression" only showed that "with all its superiority of patronage and wealth . . . Anglicanism very plainly is afraid to meet Romanism on fair terms, before the tribunal even of the Anglican mind itself." [25]

Nevin anticipated a major secession, either to Rome following Newman and Manning, or into a new body. "It is no more than the beginning probably of a great church-slide, which is destined soon to shake the whole world with its thundering sound. Nearly two thousand ministers at

22. *Ibid.*, 379.   23. *Ibid.*, 388.
24. *Ibid.*, 380f.   25. *Ibid.*, 390.

least are reported as holding ground with regard to the Queen's supremacy, and the late governmental settlement of the questions of baptismal
regeneration, which will hardly allow them to stay much longer with a
good conscience in the government church." [26] The likely outcome
would be "the breaking up of the Establishment altogether." [27]

On what was to Nevin the most crucial issue, the Eucharist, he despaired
of Anglicanism. R. I. Wilberforce had urged the restoration of a daily
service of patristic type. But in Nevin's judgment this construction was
"not in reality the doctrine or practice of the Episcopal Church either in
England or in this country. It will not be accepted on either side of the
Atlantic." These Eucharistic conceptions were "too alien from the reigning
make and genius of the Church altogether to allow the supposition that
they can be practically engrafted into its life." [28] If Wilberforce wished
continuity with the patristic Eucharist in form as well as substance he
might find it in Rome; he certainly would not in Anglicanism.

Nevin assessed the German Reformed Church at this time in similar
fashion. He declined Schaff's invitation to draft a communion service for
the liturgical commission. Such a service demanded "a sort of faith in the
'Real Presence,' which I am afraid goes beyond all that is possible to
engraft on Protestantism, even in our G. R. version of it." [29]

With regard to church order and the ministry, again, Nevin believed
that the German Reformed Church faced the same embarrassments as the
Anglican. In the ancient view of the ministry, its unity, as signalized by
communion with Rome, was more essential than its differentiation into
various orders. By its own and the patristic definition of the Church,
Anglo-Catholicism could never be anything but a schism, as Wiseman had
proved to Newman. The arguments which the Tractarians employed to
insist on the legitimacy of their episcopal succession also proved the necessity of their being re-admitted to communion with the bishop of
Rome. With regard to the German Reformed Church Nevin was not
greatly distressed that its ministry was not differentiated into "orders,"
but he questioned the validity of the functions of any fragment out of
communion with the whole of the Christian ministry.

What should be done in this embarrassment? Nevin saw four options.
He frankly preferred Roman Catholicism to the sectarian denial of

---

26. *Ibid.*, 389.   27. *Ibid.*, 388.

28. "Wilberforce on the Eucharist," *The Mercersburg Review*, VI (1854), 186.

29. Letter to Schaff, December 3, 1855. (Library of the Historical Society of the
Evangelical and Reformed Church, Lancaster, Pa.)

Church and sacraments. There was a third alternative. Some who despaired of the existing churches believed in a new Pentecost in which the Church should be born afresh in spiritual grandeur. Thus the followers of the Catholic Apostolic Church, known as the Irvingites, won surprising support among some highly sophisticated theologians, such as Thiersch, whom Mercersburg found stimulating if not convincing. Mormonism was a kind of caricature of the same judgment of the churches and the same hope for renewal. But for Nevin the implication of the failure of the Church was a suggestion he could never admit. This was the error of Puritanism. For him an unbroken tangible continuity was indispensable.

The single remaining alternative was one not considered by the Tractarians — the possibility of the further evolution of the existing churches into something better. In that event, one's loyalty to a specific denomination or to Protestantism as a whole would have been a provisional matter only. The Church which claimed the full devotion of the Mercersburg men was in this sense an eschatological one. Faith in such a future enabled them to put up with imperfections in the present which would otherwise have been unendurable.

Here, finally, emerged the third dimension of the ecumenical thought of Mercersburg. To admit an evolution of doctrine in the past was also to imply the possibility of further development. Indeed, if some Hegelian anatomy of the Church's movement could be discerned in the past it could be extrapolated into definite predictions for the future. This Schaff attempted with startling boldness, and Nevin followed him, though without his exuberant assurance.

But could Mercersburg really sustain this eschatological assurance? Schaff, with his sanguine temperament and his background of Kornthal adventism, never seemed to waver. But for Nevin it was otherwise. As he wrote Orestes Brownson at the crisis of his doubts, he was unable to relate Protestantism in any fully satisfactory way with the Cyprianic doctrine of the Church. If Protestantism was to be upheld, it could only be as some Providential development of ancient Catholicism, and in the hope of its contributions to a better state to come. "You will observe," he wrote in the summer of 1852, "that I do not venture of late to commit my own mind to it with any absolute assertion. It is presented only hypothetically. *If* our cause may stand, *then* it must be in this general way and no other." [30]

30. Cited in J. H. Nichols, *Romanticism in American Theology* (Chicago, 1961), 212.

Nevin went on in this same letter to Brownson to point out that "all this negative difficulty with Protestantism is no positive conversion to [Roman] Catholicism. I wish at times it were so." Had not Rome, too, undergone some development of doctrine beyond the ancient Church, as in declaring papal infallibility and the immaculate conception of Mary? But the assessment of the problem was complicated by Nevin's physical condition. He broke down, as he had once before, and in his psychically depressed state he could no longer engage in theological work. His emotional disposition was then to lean on authority at a time when the evaluation of Roman claims to authority was precisely the task before him.

Various Roman Catholic intellectuals and bishops interested themselves in Nevin's struggles of conscience, and Roman Catholic newspapers organized campaigns of prayer for his conversion. On the Protestant side, meanwhile, the Reformed Dutch decided in 1853 to send no more fraternal delegates to the German Reformed Synod, since the "continuation of correspondence would seem to sanction sentiments favorable to Rome." The South Carolina classis similarly withdrew from the Synod until it should purge itself of the "Romanizing heresies," the "Germanized Puseyism," of Mercersburg. Individual pastors, such as Berg and Helfenstein, withdrew from the denomination in protest. Editors of the church press of many denominations — Baptist, Presbyterian, Lutheran, and Reformed Dutch — joined in a chorus of censure. But the Mercersburg men rode out the siege, and withstood all attempts to oust them from their positions of influence. By 1854 it appeared that a convalescent Nevin was going to stay with the Mercersburg platform. He himself declared that evangelical catholicism was a reaffirmation of "the original principles and maxims of the Reformation," and that if he were to submit to Rome he could only do so by abandoning the Mercersburg position.[31] He learned to live with his *Kirchenschmerz*, having seen the promises afar off.

Both Mercersburg men entertained an eschatological hope for a fulfillment within the historical process, parallel to the secular eschatology of Progress. The substance of this fulfillment would be the realization of the ecumenical impulse of the institutional and historical Church. Thus Nevin defined his conception of the process of church history, by which

without prejudice to Catholicism first in its own order or sphere, or to Protestantism next as a real advance on this in modern times, though with the full acknowledgement of the faults and [flaws?]

31. "The Dutch Crusade," *The Mercersburg Review*, VI (1854), 227.

of both systems, it is assumed that the whole present state of the
church is transitional only and interimistic; and that it is destined
accordingly through the very crisis which is now coming on . . . to
surmount in due season the painful contradictions . . . of the
Protestant controversy as this now stands, and so to carry it triumphantly forward to its own last sense (the type neither of St. Peter
nor of St. Paul but of both rather as brought together by St. John)
in some form that shall be found at the same time to etherealize and
and save, in the same way, the last sense also and rich wealth of the
old Catholic faith.[32]

ACKNOWLEDGMENTS

Grateful mention should be made here of at least some of the many
from whom help has been received. Professors Bard Thompson of Drew
University and Sydney Ahlstrom of Yale University, the consultants appointed by the editorial board for A Library of Protestant Thought, read
the whole draft and contributed numerous suggestions toward its improvement. Professor Thompson and Professor George Bricker of Lancaster Theological Seminary, as editors of the projected Lancaster Series
on the Mercersburg Theology, generously offered the use of unpublished
editorial matter. Among the many librarians who contributed beyond the
call of duty, mention must be made at least of the custodians of the several Lancaster collections — George Bricker and his predecessor Paul
Stonesifer at Lancaster Theological Seminary, Herbert Anstaett of Franklin and Marshall College, and Elizabeth Kieffer of the library of the Historical Society of the Evangelical and Reformed Church. Research, in
these collections especially, was originally made possible by a grant from
the John Simon Guggenheim Foundation. Miss Amy Clampitt helped to
clarify the editor's exposition and to standardize the styling of the texts.

32. "Anglican Crisis," *The Mercersburg Review*, III (1851), 396.

PART ONE

❖

Christ and the Church

JOHN WILLIAMSON NEVIN

Catholic Unity

Editor's introduction.

   Almighty and everlasting God, who by thine only begotten Son hast made us to be a new creation for thyself, and has bathed us in the new light of thine Incarnate Word; preserve in us, we beseech thee, the works of thy mercy, and cleanse us from all our ancient stains; that by the assistance of thy grace we may be found in his form, in whom our substance dwells with thee; through Jesus Christ our Lord. Amen.[1]

The first significant statement of what came to be called the Mercersburg theology was Nevin's keynote sermon before the joint Convention of the Reformed Dutch and the German Reformed Churches, delivered at Harrisburg on August 8, 1844. The two denominations, intimately related in their sixteenth-century origins, had been also on close terms in America, where the Classis of Amsterdam had supported the struggling German Reformed Church in the colonial period. This very close historical relation and similarity, the small size of each, and their geographical concentration (the Dutch in New York and New Jersey, the Germans in Pennsylvania and Maryland), seemed to constitute a strong argument for closer relations, at least in the common task of home missions in the West, and perhaps for ultimate ecclesiastical union. The joint convention of 1844 was to consider these matters, and accordingly the leading theologian of the German Reformed Church was invited to preach. He took up the ecumenical theme with conviction, affirming catholic unity to be "the most important interest in the world," involving "the conception of the Christian salvation itself."

   1. Collect for the Second Sunday after Christmas, *Order of Worship for the Reformed Church* (Philadelphia, 1866), 54.

The central theological theme of the sermon is a portrayal of the Church in terms of the metaphor of organic life. Developing the theme of the first and second Adam, Nevin traced the growth of that generic life whose "root" or "seed" is in the incarnate Person of Christ, and which is mystically imparted to believers, typically through the Holy Communion, and finally consummated in the glorified life of the resurrection.

Nevin had already outlined this concept in the last chapter of his tract, *The Anxious Bench*,[2] where he acknowledged his debt to Hermann Olshausen and to Ernst Sartorius (1797–1859) for the suggestion. In "Catholic Unity" the theme was sufficiently developed to exhibit many of the characteristic Mercersburg motifs. Among them are the stress on the Apostles' Creed and on the sacraments, especially the Lord's Supper, as genuine means of grace; the analysis of the Church as "idea" and "actuality"; and the "grounding" of forensic imputation within the mystical union. The reference to the "Real Presence" was to be the offense which a year later first occasioned the charge of heresy by Dr. Joseph Berg in *The Protestant Banner*.

The outlines of a specific ecumenical position are clear. Church unity was not to be pursued by administrative stratagem or by any attack on sects which itself concealed a sectarian bias. The unity of the Church could not be a human achievement at all, but rather a gift and the manifestation of the true inner life of the Church. The first duty of churchmen was repentance, "the conviction of deep and radical defect." Nevin believed that the Church, growing toward the actualization of its unity, existed "in every evangelical communion." He made no explicit reference to modern Roman Catholicism or Orthodoxy. The spirit of sect was contrary to Christ and therefore a sin — although here Nevin (for the last time) still reserved the term Antichrist for the papacy. He did not even mention Lutheranism in his appeal for unity, but specified only the churches represented at the memorable Synod of Dort — the Anglicans, the Scots, the Swiss, and the German and Dutch Reformed.

Nevin received gratifying commendation for his sermon from the leading brethren of the Dutch church, and although some were said to have grumbled at his "Hegelianism," there was a vote to have the sermon printed both by the Dutch in *The Christian Intelligencer* and by the Germans in their *Weekly Messenger*. One of the most interested listeners had been Philip Schaff, arrived in America only twelve days before. From this introduction to his future colleague, he was enormously relieved to find

2. Second revised edition (Chambersburg, Pa., 1844).

that he and Nevin occupied essentially the same ground. Schaff's own inaugural followed in the autumn, and when an English translation of his address, *The Principle of Protestantism,* was published in June 1845, at his request "Catholic Unity," now buttressed with references,[3] was printed with it. Thus Nevin's sermon first appeared in book form as part of a joint manifesto. A new and less friendly interest was now taken in "Catholic Unity," and suspicion about the tendency of the Mercersburg professors developed in the Dutch church as well as the German. The hostility to Mercersburg among the Reformed Dutch became so great, indeed, that all hope of closer ties between the two denominations was clearly precluded by the theological views of the very men who had advocated them.

❖ ❖ ❖ ❖

Ephesians 4: 4–6. There is one body and one Spirit, even as ye are called in one hope of your calling; one Lord, one faith, one baptism; one God and Father of all, who is above all, and through all, and in you all.

This is the image of the Church, as delineated by the hand of an inspired Apostle. In the whole world, we find nothing so resplendently beautiful and glorious, under any other form. The picture is intended to enforce the great duty of charity and peace among those who bear the Christian name. In the preceding part of the epistle, Christ is exhibited as the end of all separation and strife to them that believe, and the author of a new spiritual creation, in which all former distinctions were to be regarded as swallowed up and abolished forever. Reference is had in this representation primarily to the old division of Jew and Gentile, but, in its true spirit and sense, it is plainly as comprehensive as humanity itself, and looks, therefore, directly to every other distinction of the same sort that ever has been or ever shall be known in the world. Christianity is the universal solvent in which all opposites are required to give up their previous affinities, no matter how old and stubborn, and flow together in a new combination, pervaded with harmony only and light at every point. "In Christ Jesus, neither circumcision availeth anything, nor uncircumcision, but a new creature" [Gal. 6:15]. "Those who were far off, are made nigh by his blood" [Eph. 2:13, loosely quoted]. "He is our peace, who hath

3. Five footnotes which appeared in the published text of Nevin's sermon have been omitted here. Consisting almost entirely of quotations from Calvin, chiefly from the commentaries on Ephesians and 1 Corinthians, the *Institutes,* and the "Second Defense against Westphal," they documented Nevin's view of the mystical union and of the Eucharistic participation of the humanity of Christ.

made both one, and hath broken down the middle wall of partition between us"; making "in himself of twain one new man" [Eph. 2:14, 15].
In him all spiritual antagonism among men is subverted. The human
world is reconciled first with God, and then with itself, by entering with
living consciousness into the ground of its own life as revealed in his person. Such is the idea of the Church, which is "the body of Christ, the
fullness of him that filleth all in all" [Eph. 1:23, loosely quoted]. And now
at length, passing from doctrine to practice, the Apostle calls upon those
to whom he wrote to surrender themselves fully to the claims of this exalted constitution. "I therefore, the prisoner of the Lord, beseech you
that ye walk worthy of the vocation wherewith ye are called, with all
lowliness and meekness, with longsuffering, forbearing one another in
love; endeavoring to keep the unity of the Spirit in the bond of peace"
[Eph. 4:1-3]. Such a temper, and such a life, are necessarily included in
the very conception of the Church, as here described. "There is one body
and one Spirit, even as ye are called in one hope of your calling; one
Lord, one faith, one baptism; one God and Father of all, who is above all,
and through all, and in you all" [Eph. 4:4-6]. He does not say, *Let* there
be one body and one Spirit, as simply urging Christians to seek such
agreement among themselves as might justify this view of their state; but
the fact is assumed as already in existence, and is made the ground, accordingly, of the exhortation that goes before. There is one body and
Spirit, and *therefore* are ye bound to keep the unity of the Spirit in the
bond of peace. The unity of the Church is not something which results
first from the thought and purpose of the vast membership of which it is
composed, but, on the contrary, it is the ground out of which this membership itself springs, and in which perpetually it stands, and from which
it must derive evermore all its harmony, and stability, and activity, and
strength.

From the beginning this great truth has dwelt deep in the consciousness
of the Christian world. Through all ages, and in all lands, that consciousness has been uttering itself as with one mouth, in the article of the Creed,
I believe in the holy catholic Church. The Church is one and universal.
Her unity is essential to her existence. Particular Christians, and particular
congregations, and particular religious denominations, can be true to
themselves only as they stand in the full, free sense of this thought, and
make it the object of their calling to fulfill its requisitions. The manifold
is required to feel itself one. All particularism here must be false that
seeks to maintain itself as such, in proportion exactly as it is found in con-

flict with the general and universal, as embraced in the true idea of the body of Christ.

I propose to consider, in the further prosecution of the subject at this time, *first,* the nature and constitution of the holy catholic Church, in the view now stated; and *secondly,* the duty of Christians as it regards the unity by which it is declared to be thus catholic, and holy, and true.

I. *We are to consider the nature of Catholic Unity, as comprehended constitutionally in the idea of the Christian Church.*

Unity does not exclude the idea of difference and multiplicity. Indeed it is only by means of these that it can ever appear under an actual, concrete form. Where the one does not carry in itself the possibility of separation and distinction, it can never be more than a sheer abstraction, an absolute nullity. The idea of oneness, however, does require that the different and the manifold, as comprehended in it, should be in principle the same, and that all should be held together by the force of this principle actively felt at every point. Such is the unity of the Christian Church. It is composed of a vast number of individual members, but these are all actuated by the power of a common life, and the whole of this life gathers itself up ultimately or fundamentally in the person of Jesus Christ. He is the principle or root of the Church, and the Church, through all ages, is one, simply because it stands in the presence and power of this root, universally and forever.

Every Christian, as such, is the subject of a new spiritual life that did not belong to him in his natural state. This is in no sense from himself, for that which is born of the flesh, is flesh, and cannot be cultivated into any higher character. Only that which is born of the Spirit, is spirit. The Christian has his life from Christ. He is not only placed in a new relation to the law by the imputation of the Saviour's righteousness to him in an outward forensic way, but a new nature is imparted to him also, by an actual communication of the Saviour's life over into his person. In his regeneration, he is inwardly united to Christ, by the power of the Holy Ghost, and thus brought within the sphere of that "law of the spirit of life," by which in the end the "law of sin and death" [Rom. 8:2] is overpowered and destroyed in all them that believe. A divine seed is im-

planted in him, the germ of a new existence, which is destined gradually
to grow and gather strength, till the whole man shall be at last fully transformed into its image. The new nature thus introduced is the nature of
Christ, and it continues to be his nature through the whole course of its
development, onward to the last day. The believer has indeed a separate
individual existence, but this existence has its ground in the life of Christ,
just as in any other case the individual begins at first and stands always
afterwards, in the force of the generic nature to which it belongs. His
sanctification does not consist in his being engaged simply to copy the excellencies of Christ, as a man might admire and copy the character of a
Moses or a Paul, but it consists in this, that the very life of the Lord Jesus
is found reaching over into his person, and gradually transfusing it with
its own heavenly force. The old nature is not at once destroyed, but the
new nature of Christ is inclosed in it, as the papilio in the folds of the
chrysalis, and in due time this last must triumph over the first entirely,
leaving it behind as an empty sepulcher in the final resurrection. Thus,
emphatically, Christ and the believer are one. Because I live, we hear him
say, ye shall live also [Jn. 14:19]. He that is joined to the Lord is one
spirit [1 Cor. 6:17].

This mystical union, as it is sometimes termed, is much more strict,
there is reason to believe, than is commonly imagined. There is none on
earth more intimate and inward. It is real and close as the union which
binds the branches to the trunk of the vine. It forms such a bond as holds
between the members and the head of the same natural body. "Except ye
eat the flesh of the Son of Man," Christ himself has said, "and drink his
blood, ye have no life in you. Whoso eateth my flesh and drinketh my
blood, hath eternal life, and I will raise him up at the last day. For my
flesh is meat indeed, and my blood is drink indeed. He that eateth my
flesh and drinketh my blood, dwelleth in me, and I in him. As the living
Father hath sent me, and I live by the Father: so he that eateth me, even
he shall live by me" [Jn. 6:53-57]. This is indeed figurative language, but
if it have any meaning at all, it teaches that the union of the believer with
Christ is not simply moral, the harmony of purpose, thought, and feeling,
but substantial and real, involving oneness of nature. "We are members of
his body, of his flesh, and of his bones" [Eph. 5:30].

This may sound mystical; but, after all, it is no more difficult to comprehend than the fact of our union to the same extent with the person of
the first Adam. As descended from him by natural generation, we are not
only like him in outward form and inward spirit, but we participate truly

and properly in his very nature. We are members of his body, of his flesh, and of his bones. His humanity, soul and body, has passed over into our persons. And so it is in the case of the second Adam, as it regards the truly regenerate. They are inserted into his life, through faith, by the power of the Holy Ghost, and become thus incorporated with it, as fully as they were before with that corrupt life they had by their natural birth. The whole humanity of Christ, soul and body, is carried over by the process of the Christian salvation into the person of the believer, so that in the end his glorified body, no less than his glorified soul, will appear as the natural and necessary product of the life in which he is thus made to participate. His Resurrection is only his regeneration, fully revealed at last and complete. Our life now is hid with Christ in God; but when he appeareth, then shall we also appear with him in glory. The Christian is spoken of at times, accordingly, as already the subject of all that has been reached in the personal life of the Saviour. He is not only dead with him, but risen also, and exalted along with him at the right hand of God [Col. 3:1, 3, 4]. This representation rests throughout upon the fact that his life is grounded in the life of Christ, and so includes potentially all that belongs to this from the beginning.

The idea of this inward union on the part of the believer with the entire humanity of Christ has in all ages entered deeply into the consciousness of the Church. Hence, no doubt, much of the favor which has been shown towards popish and semi-popish errors in the case of the Lord's Supper. Hence, too, the earnestness with which the Reformers generally maintained the doctrine of the Real Presence in this sacrament. They saw and felt, more clearly than many of their followers seem to see and feel now, that the life of the believer involves a communion with the body of Christ, as well as with his spirit. Calvin is particularly strong with regard to this point; and some have found it hard to find any sense whatever in his language on the subject. But after all there is no greater darkness in it than is presented by Paul, when he says, "We are members of his body, of his flesh, and of his bones." Thus also we are taught in the Heidelberg Catechism, that to eat the crucified body and drink the shed blood of Christ, is "not only to embrace with a believing heart all the sufferings and death of Christ, and thereby to obtain the pardon of sin and life eternal; but also, besides that, to become more and more united to his sacred body, by the Holy Ghost, who dwells both in Christ and in us; so that we, though Christ is in heaven and we on earth, are notwithstanding, flesh of his flesh, and bone of his bone; and that we live and are governed forever by one Spirit, as members of the same body are by one soul" [Ans. 77].

Partaking in this way of one and the same life, Christians of course are vitally related and joined together as one great spiritual whole, and this whole is the Church. The Church is his body, the fullness of him that filleth all in all. The union by which it is held together through all ages is strictly *organic*. The Church is not a mere aggregation or collection of different individuals, drawn together by similarity of interests and wants, and not an abstraction simply, by which the common in the midst of such multifarious distinction is separated and put together under a single general term. It is not merely the *all* that covers the actual extent of its membership, but the *whole*, rather; in which this membership is comprehended and determined from the beginning. The Church does not rest upon its members, but the members rest upon the Church. Individual Christianity is not something older than general Christianity, but the general in this case goes before the particular, and rules and conditions all its manifestations. So it is with every organic nature. The whole is older and deeper than the parts, and these last spring forth perpetually from the active presence of the first. The parts, in the end, are only the revelation of what was previously included in the whole. The oak of a hundred years, and the acorn from which it has sprung, are the same life. All that we behold in the oak lay hid in the acorn from the start. So, too, the human world all slept originally in the common root of the race. Adam was not simply *a* man, like others since born, but he was *the* man, who comprehended in himself all that has since appeared in other men. Humanity as a whole resided in his person. He was strictly and truly the world. Through all ages, man is organically one and the same. And parallel with this precisely is the constitution of the Church. The second Adam corresponds in all respects with the first. He is not a man merely, an individual belonging to the race, but he is *the* man, emphatically the *Son of Man*, comprising in his person the new creation, or humanity recovered and redeemed as a whole. Whatever the Church becomes in the way of development, it can never be more in fact than it was in him from the beginning. Its life is not multiplied nor extended in quantity by its growth. Christ is the root of the Church, and to the end of time it can include no more in its proper life, however widely distributed, than what is included in the root itself.

The unity of the Church, then, is a cardinal truth in the Christian system. It is involved in the conception of the Christian salvation itself. To renounce it, or lose sight of it, is to make shipwreck of the gospel to the same extent. There is no room here for individualism or particularism as such. An individual dissociated entirely from his race would cease to be a man. And just so the conception of individual or particular Christianity, as something independent of the organic whole which we denominate the Church, is a moral solecism that necessarily destroys itself. Christ cannot be divided. The members of the natural body are united to the head only by belonging to the body itself. Separated from this, they cease to have any proper existence. And so it is here. We are not Christians, each one by himself and for himself, but we become such through the Church. Christ lives in his people, by the life which fills his Body, the Church, and they are thus all necessarily one before they can be many.

The life of Christ in the Church is in the first place inward and invisible. But to be real it must also become outward. The salvation of the individual believer is not complete till the body is transfigured and made glorious, as well as the soul, and as it has respect to the whole nature of man from the commencement, it can never go forward at all except by a union of the outward and inward at every point of its progress. Thus, too, the Church must be visible as well as invisible. In no other way can the idea become real. Soul and body, inward power and outward form, are required here to go together. Outward forms without inward life can have no saving force. But neither can inward life be maintained, on the other hand, without outward forms. The body is not the man, and yet there can be no man where there is no body. Humanity is neither a corpse, on the one hand, nor a phantom on the other. The Church, then, must appear externally, in the world. And the case requires that this manifestation should correspond with the inward constitution of the idea itself. It belongs to the proper conception of it that the unity of the holy catholic Church should appear in an outward and visible way, and it can never be regarded as complete where such development of its inward power is still wanting. "There is one *body*," the Apostle tells us, "and one Spirit, even as ye are called in one hope of your calling." Such is the true normal character of the Church, and so far as it may fall short of this it labors under serious defect.

The Apostle does not mean to affirm, however, that the want of such outward and visible unity necessarily and at once overthrows the existence of the Church. It is seldom that the actual, in the sphere of Christianity, fully corresponds with the ideal. And as a general thing, this correspondence, so far as it may be secured in any case, is reached only in a gradual way. The inward requires time to impress its image fully upon the outward. Religion is a process in the individual soul, and also in the life of the Church. Objectively considered, it is complete, and harmonious, and true to itself at every point, from the beginning; but in becoming subjective, all this may seem for a season to fail. The life of Christ in the Church includes in itself potentially, from the first, all that it can ever become in the end. But it may happen that for a long time this hidden force shall be embarrassed and repressed by untoward influences, so as not to find its adequate form and action in the actual order of the Church. Thus we behold at this time the Christian world, in fact broken into various denominations, with separate confessions and creeds, among which too often polemic zeal appears far more prominent than catholic charity. Such distraction and division can never be vindicated, as suitable to the true conception of the Church. They disfigure and obscure its proper glory, and give a false, distorted image of its inward life. Still the Church is not on this account subverted, or shut up to the precincts of some single sect, arrogantly claiming to be the whole body. The life with which it is animated does indeed seek an outward revelation in all respects answerable to its own nature, and it can never be fully satisfied till this be happily secured; but as a process, struggling constantly towards such end, it may be vigorously active at the same time, under forms that bear no right proportion whatever to its wants. We may not doubt, therefore, but that in the midst of all the denominational distinctions which have come to prevail particularly since the time of the Reformation, the life of the Church, with all its proper attributes, is still actively at work in every evangelical communion. The "one body," most unfortunately, is wanting for the present, but the "one Spirit" reigns substantially notwithstanding through all communions, and binds them together as a great spiritual whole. Joined together in the common life of Christ, in the possession of one faith, one hope, and one baptism, the various divisions of the Christian world are still organically the same Church. In this form, we hold fast to the idea of catholic unity as the only ground on which any true Christianity, individual or particular, can possibly stand.

II. *Having in this general way considered the nature of that oneness which belongs to the constitution of the Catholic Church, we are prepared to contemplate, in the second place, the duty of Christians with regard to it.*

This is comprehended generally in the obligation of all earnestly and actively to seek the unity of the Church in its most complete form. We have seen that, in the actual circumstances of the Church, idea and fact do not for the most part fully correspond. It is only in the way of development and process, most generally, that we find the first revealing itself in the form of the second. Thus the unity of the Church is something which is not at once realized, as a matter of course, by the appearance of the Church in the world. The actual, in fact, stands far behind the ideal. But still this relation cannot be rested in as ultimate and right. It can hold with truth, only as an intermediate stage, through which the life of the Church is constantly struggling towards a revelation that shall be in all respects adequate to its nature. This development is not blind, of course, and necessary, as in the sphere of mere nature, but moral, involving intelligence and will. The Church is required to seek and maintain her own unity, and this obligation falls back necessarily in the end upon Christians as such. They are bound to maintain "the unity of the Spirit in the bond of peace" [Eph. 4:3], and cannot be true to their vocation except as they consciously endeavor, so far as in them lies, to have this unity made in the largest sense complete, so that all Christ's people may be "one body" as well as "one spirit," even as they are called in one hope of their calling.

This might seem to be in some sense the great necessity of the Church. "Neither pray I for these alone," is the Saviour's solemn language, "but for them also which shall believe on me through their word; that they all may be one; as thou, Father, art in me, and I in thee, that they also may be one in us; that the world may believe that thou hast sent me" [Jn. 17:20, 21]. Wonderful words, to be understood only by living communion with the heart of Jesus himself. If such was the spirit of Christ, the spirit of the Church must necessarily be the same. The whole Church then must be regarded as inwardly groaning over her own divisions, and striving to actualize the full import of this prayer, as though Christ were made to feel himself divided, and could not rest till such unnatural violence should come to an end. And so if any man be in Christ, he cannot fail, so far as this union may reach, to pray and work for the same object, the catholic unity of the Church, as the most important interest in the world.

It is the duty of all, then, to consider and lay to heart the evil that is comprehended in the actual disunion and division which now prevail in the Catholic Church. I say in the *Catholic* Church, because the one Spirit of Christ is supposed to pervade the whole body, notwithstanding this vast defect, binding it together through all parts of the world with the force of a common life. But this cannot change the nature of the evil itself. It only renders it, indeed, the more glaring and painful. The Church ought to be visibly one and catholic, as she is one and catholic in her inward life; and the want of such unity, as it appears in the present state of the Protestant world, with its rampant sectarianism and individualism, "is a lamentation, and shall be for a lamentation" [Ezek. 19:14], until of God's mercy the sore reproach be rolled away.

We frequently hear apologies made for the existence of sects in the Church. They are said to be necessary. The freedom and purity of the Church, we are told, can be maintained only in this way. They provoke each other to zeal and good works. Without them the Church would stagnate and grow corrupt. They are but different divisions of the same grand army, furnished for battle variously according to their several tastes, but all moving in the same direction against the common foe, and forming together in this order a more powerful array than if no such divisions had place.

This sounds well, and no doubt many so far impose upon themselves as to think it all correct. But it is false notwithstanding, and injurious to Christ. Our various sects, as they actually exist, are an immense evil in the Church. Whatever may be said of the possibility of their standing in friendly correspondence, and only stimulating the whole body to a more vigorous life, it is certain that they mar the unity of this body in fact, and deprive it of its proper beauty and strength. The evil may indeed in a certain sense be *necessary*, but the necessity is like that which exists for the rise of heresies, itself the presence of a deep-seated evil, in which the Church has no right quietly to acquiesce. Our sects, as they actually stand at this time, are a vast reproach to the Christian cause. By no possibility could they be countenanced and approved as good by the Lord Jesus Christ, if he should appear again in the world as the visible head of his people. This all must feel.

We do not suppose, indeed, that the visible unity of the Church demands a single visible head, like the pope of Rome, who is justly styled Antichrist for this very pretension. We do not suppose that it can hold only under a given organization, stretching its arms from one end of the earth to the other, according to the dream of the high-church Episcopalians. But this much most certainly it does require, that the middle walls of partition as they now divide sect from sect should be broken down, and the whole Christian world brought not only to acknowledge and feel, but also to show itself evidently one. How far it is from this at the present time it is not necessary to say. Now what is wanted, first of all, is a clear perception on the part of the Church, that is, on the part of Christians generally, that the want of such visible unity is wrong, and such a wrong as calls aloud continually for redress. Without this, most assuredly, the captivity of Zion will never come to an end. The heart of the Church must be filled with an earnest sense of her own calamity, as thus torn and rent with such vast division, before she can be engaged successfully to follow after union and peace. It needs to be deeply pondered upon that the spirit of sect and party, as such, is contrary to Christ. The present state of the Church involves the sin of schism to a most serious extent. Denominations are not indeed necessarily sects, and every separate ecclesiastical position is not to be denounced at once as schismatic. But to whatever extent particular denominations may stand justified before God in occupying such positions, it is certain that in some quarter a schismatic spirit must be at work to create and maintain the necessity by which this is supposed to be right. Take it altogether, there is schism in our divisions. The unity of Christ's Body is not maintained. This it is that challenges our attention. This we are called upon to consider and lay to heart.

Nor should it relieve the case at all to our feelings, that we may not be able to see how it is possible to bring this state of things to an end. An evil does not cease to be such, simply because it may seem to exclude all hope of correction. Those who seek to reconcile us to the system of sects in the Church, by insisting on the impossibility of reducing them to the same communion, presume greatly either upon our ignorance or our apathy as it regards the claims of the whole subject. If we know that the Church is called by her very constitution to be visibly, as well as invisibly, one, we are not likely to believe that any difficulties which stand in the way of this are absolutely insuperable in their own nature. And if we have come to feel the weight of the interest itself, as exhibited in the last prayer of the Saviour, we are not likely to be soothed and quieted over the general surrendry of it by a view which cuts off all hope of its ever

being recovered. Let it be admitted that there is no way open by which
we have any prospect of seeing these walls of partition broken down, still
it is none the less the duty of all who love Christ to take to heart the presence of the evil itself, and to be humbled before God on account of it,
and to desire earnestly that it might come to an end. What is most deplorable in the case, is that so many should be willing to acquiesce in it as
something necessary and never to be changed. And what is most needed
in these circumstances, therefore, is that anxiety and concern should take
the place of such indifference, and that men should be brought to acknowledge openly the reigning wrong of these divisions in the Church,
and to inquire earnestly after some way of escape.

To such earnest interest the subject is well entitled, for it includes, as
already said, one of the very deepest necessities of the Church. Can any
one suppose that the order of things which now prevails in the Christian
world, in the view before us, is destined to be perpetual and final? Does it
not lie in the very conception of the Church that these divisions should
pass away, and make room for the reign at last of catholic unity and love?
If sects as they now appear have been the necessary fruit of the Reformation, then must we say that the Reformation, being, as we hold it to be,
from God, has not yet been conducted forward to its last legitimate result
in this respect. What it has divided, it must have power again in due time
to bring together and unite. Our Protestant Christianity cannot continue
to stand in its present form. A Church without unity can neither conquer
the world, nor sustain itself. We are bound therefore to expect that this
unity will not always be wanting. The hour is coming, though it be not
now, when the prayer of Christ that his Church may be one will appear
gloriously fulfilled in its actual character and state throughout the whole
world. But before this great change shall be effected, it will be the object
first of much earnest desire and expectation. Not while Christians continue to rest contentedly in the present system, as either sufficiently good
in itself or at least fatally incapable of remedy, can any such new order
come forward to occupy its place. The result will be reached only after it
shall have come to be generally felt that the present construction of the
Church is false and wrong, and when, with such conviction, the hearts of
men shall have been prepared earnestly to seek, and cordially to welcome,
a more excellent way.

It is not by might and by power, we know, not by outward urging and
driving in the common radical style, but only by the Spirit of the Lord,
that any such revolution as this can ever be accomplished. A crusade
against sects, or a society to put down sects, movements and efforts of

every kind that address themselves to the overthrow of sects simply in a negative way, can answer no good purpose here in the end. If the evil is ever to be effectually surmounted, it must be by the growth of Christian charity in the bosom of the Church itself. No union can be of any account at last, that is not produced by inward sympathy and agreement between the parties it brings together. But this preparation of the heart is itself something to be sought and cultivated; and we may say that the very first step towards it consists in just that consideration and concern which is now represented to be due in the case of Christians to the whole subject. In vain may we look for any such deep inward action in the Church as is needed to make room for a closer external union, if it begin not at least in this form.

Christians, then, are bound to consider and lay to heart the evil state of the Church in the view now contemplated. This might seem to be, indeed, the most they have it in their power immediately to do in the circumstances. It is that, therefore, which is mainly and primarily required. Nor may it be regarded as of only small account. An immense object would be gained, if simply the conviction of deep and radical defect here were made to fasten itself upon the general consciousness of the Church. Without this it is in vain to hope for deliverance from any other quarter. But this is not the entire duty created by the case. There is a call not merely for reflection and concern, but also for action.

It has already been admitted that the interest in question is not to be secured by any attempts towards a simply outward reform. A no-sect party in the Church, bent only on pulling down and having no power to reconstruct, must ever be found itself one of the worst forms of separatism, aggravating the mischief it proposes to heal. It is not by renouncing their allegiance to particular denominations, and affecting to hold themselves independent of all, that men may expect to promote the cause of Christian unity. The union of the Church, in any case, is not to be established by stratagem or force. To be valid, it must be free, the spontaneous product of Christian knowledge and Christian love. It can never hold externally till it is made necessary by the pressure of inward want, refusing to be satisfied on any other terms. But all this does not involve the consequence that there is nothing to be done on the part of Christians to hasten this consummation in its time. It is by inward and spiritual action precisely that the way of the Lord is to be prepared for any such deliverance, and to such action all who love the prosperity of Zion are solemnly bound. Every Christian in his place is required to "keep the unity of the Spirit in the bond of peace" [Eph. 4:3]. All are under obligation to culti-

vate the spirit of Christian charity in their own hearts and to exemplify
the power of it in their own lives. All are bound to pray for the peace of
Jerusalem, and to "bow their knees unto the Father of our Lord Jesus
Christ, of whom the whole family in heaven and earth is named," that he
would grant us all, even his whole Church Catholic, "according to the
riches of his glory, to be strengthened with might by his Spirit in the
inner man; that Christ may dwell in our hearts by faith; that we, being
rooted and grounded in love, may be able to comprehend with all saints
what is the breadth and length and depth and height; and to know the
love of Christ which passeth knowledge, that we might be filled with all
the fullness of God" [Eph. 3:14-19, adapted]. Unto this glorious object
all are required to labor, "striving according to his working, which
worketh in his people mightily" [Col. 1:29, adapted]. It is demanded of all
that they should at least endeavor, more and more, to descend into the
heart of Jesus, and take the measure of this great interest, as unfolded
there, in what might seem to be the main burden of his last priestly
prayer. It is the duty of all to follow after the things that make for holiness and peace, and to seek in every way the coming of God's kingdom,
with new power and glory, in the hearts of his people, that they may be
brought to understand and feel, continually more and more, the force of
that common life by which they are all one in Christ Jesus.

All this would be, in the most important sense, to "prepare the way of
the Lord, and to make straight in the desert a highway for our God"; and
the result of it would soon be that the glory of the Lord should be revealed, and all flesh made to see it together [Is. 40:3, 5, adapted]. When it
shall have come to this, that by such inward and spiritual action the
Church shall be fully ripe for union, the difficulties that now stand in the
way will be soon found crumbling and dissolving into thin air. "Every
valley shall be exalted, and every mountain and hill shall be made low; and
the crooked shall be made straight, and the rough places plain" [Is. 40:4].
It may be utterly impossible for us to anticipate beforehand the way in
which this shall take place, or the form under which it shall appear. But in
the circumstances supposed, the want will provide for itself. The life that
is at work will find room and scope, in some way, for its own free action.
With reference to every such case, it is written: "Behold I will do a new
thing; now it shall spring forth; shall ye not know it? I will even make a
way in the wilderness, and rivers in the desert. The beast of the field shall
honor me, the dragons and the owls; because I give waters in the wilderness, and rivers in the desert, to give drink to my people, my chosen" [Is.

43: 19, 20]. That which is impossible with men is easily accomplished by God.

Then it is the duty of the Church, in the third place, to observe and improve all opportunities by which it is made possible in any measure, from time to time, to advance in a visible way the interest of catholic unity. The reformation that is needed must indeed spring spontaneously from within, but the process can go forward, notwithstanding, only in the exercise of intelligence and will, and by the help of counsel, forethought, and wise calculation at every point. We are not at liberty in the case to run before the Lord, presumptuously taking the whole work into our own hands, but we are bound, at the same time, to follow promptly where he leads. Just so soon, and so far, as the way may be open in any direction for advancing the outward and visible oneness of the Church, without prejudice to its true inward integrity, it is our solemn duty to turn the occasion to this high account. It is not to be imagined, of course, that the general reconciliation of the divisions that now prevail in the Christian world, in whatever form it may at last appear, will be effected suddenly and at once. It must come, if it come at all, as a process, gradually ripening into this glorious result. Every instance, then, in which the open correspondence and communion of particular sections of the Church is made to assume in a free way a more intimate character than it had before, deserves to be hailed, as being to some extent, at least, an approximation towards the unity which the whole body is destined finally to reach. No movement of this sort can be regarded as indifferent. The interest just named is the highest that can occupy the heart of the Church. Whatever can serve in any way to bring together the moral dispersions of the house of Israel must be counted worthy of the most earnest regard. All Christians, then, in their various denominational capacities, are required, as they love the Church and seek the salvation of the world, to encourage with all their might a closer visible connection between the different parts of Christ's body, in every case in which the way is found to be open for the purpose. It is terrible to be concerned, however remotely, in dividing the Church, but a high and glorious privilege to take part, even to the smallest extent, in the work of restoring these divisions where they already exist. I would not for the world be the founder of a new sect, though assured that millions would at last range themselves beneath its shadow, but if I might be instrumental with the humblest agency in helping only to pull down a single one of all those walls of partition that now mock the idea of catholic unity in the visible

Church, I should feel that I had not lived in vain, nor labored without the most ample and enduring reward.

In view of all that has thus far been said, we may now be prepared, respected and beloved brethren in the ministry and eldership of the Reformed Church, to estimate aright the weight of the occasion by which we are brought together this day. The very object of this Convention is to bring into closer visible union the two denominations we have been appointed to represent. Apart altogether from the counsels and action of the Convention itself, the simple fact that these bodies have been engaged to enter into the friendly arrangement by which it is called to meet, deserves to be regarded with special interest. In the midst of the religious divisions and dissensions that are abroad in the land, it is cheering to find in any quarter an active movement in favor of the opposite interest. May we not trust that the measure will be owned and blessed of God, and that through his blessing it may be followed in time to come with consequences of good, far more vast than we have power now to imagine?

It is true, indeed, that the Reformed Dutch and German Reformed churches in this country can hardly be regarded as different denominations, and certainly not as different sects, in any right sense of the term. They have been from the beginning substantially the same church, different national branches only of the one great communion of the Reformed, as gloriously represented in the ever-memorable Synod of Dort. The faith of Switzerland, the faith of the Palatinate and the faith of Holland, in the sixteenth century, were emphatically one faith. Transplanted to this country, too, the same churches have been closely related from the first, in a certain sense borne upon the knees, and nourished from the breast, of the same compassionate mother. For the fostering care of the Synod of Holland was never more active in favor of the scion taken from its own trunk, than it showed itself to be in planting and rearing the kindred vine brought over from Germany. Nor has the sense of this relationship been lost since. Still the two bodies have stood separate and apart as distinct religious organizations, with comparatively little knowledge of each other's circumstances, and nearly as much apparent estrangement as is seen to characterize the relations of sects generally. It is well, therefore, that now in the end we should be permitted to rejoice in the prospect of a communion, from this time forward, more intimate and full. It is well that the claims of our kindred life have come to make themselves so felt on both sides, that we are brought thus openly to recognize their force, and give visible expression to the one spirit by which we are consciously bound together. The Church at large has reason to rejoice in this union. It is something won for the cause of catholic unity, in the broadest sense, that these two divisions of the Reformed Church should thus embrace each other in the presence of the whole world, and proclaim themselves outwardly as well as inwardly the same: "one body, and one Spirit, even as we are called in one hope of our calling."

Nor should it be allowed to impair the force of this declaration, that no such union has been contemplated in this case as might involve a formal ecclesiastical amalgamation of the two churches concerned. All are agreed that nothing of this sort is for the present, at least, to be attempted or desired. Both churches would only be embarrassed by the measure, if it could possibly be carried into effect. But happily no such amalgamation is needed in our circumstances to realize the fullest unity the Church is called to seek. A merely territorial separation, where different religious bodies not only hold the same faith, but are openly identified as one interest, cannot be said in any fair sense to involve ecclesiastical disunion. The Presbyterian Church of this country, for instance, resolved according to the recommendation of some into separate independent synods, would be one church still, if only there might be the presence of one Spirit always, sufficiently active to proclaim this unity and cause it to be felt in a public way. And in the same manner the Reformed Dutch and German churches may be as closely bound together as the honor of religion requires, forming in fact but one communion, while yet they continue denominationally distinct, as before. No closer connection than this, in fact, has yet come to hold between the two synods of the German Reformed Church itself, as here represented at this time. The only visible bond by which they are held together is the present Convention.

In these circumstances it is plain enough that no great amount of action, in the common sense, can reasonably be expected from this body. We must not allow ourselves, however, to estimate the importance of the arrangement by this measure. The simple fact of the Convention itself, as an open public demonstration of the mutual confidence and good will of the churches to which we belong, carries in it a moral value in all respects worthy of the occasion. But the correspondence thus established can hardly fail, besides, to open the way directly for a more friendly state of feeling between the two churches, by bringing them to know each other better, and to feel more extensively the force of that spiritual relationship by which they are united. If this triennial meeting should serve no other purpose than to maintain and strengthen such right feeling, it would well deserve to be perpetuated on this account only. But it may be expected in the end to do more than this. It is the want of mutual familiar knowledge of each other's circumstances, and mutual familiar confidence in each other's feelings, on the part of the two churches, which now more than anything else is likely to circumscribe the range of the Convention's action at this time, by creating delicacy, and caution, and restraint, when under different circumstances no call for any such feeling might be supposed to exist. In the course of time, it may be trusted, the connection which is now established will itself serve to bring each church more clearly before the eye, and thus more near to the heart, of the other. Points of common interest will be multiplied and room for common action extended. The relation of the two bodies may be expected to become more free, as it becomes more familiar. In this way, it is quite possible at least that a much wider field for counsel and action may ultimately be opened for the Triennial Convention than any have yet been led to anticipate.

It would seem to lie in the very nature of the case that churches so related, historically, ecclesiastically, and geographically, as the Reformed Dutch and German Reformed churches in this country, should find occasion for common counsel and common action in many respects. By wise co-operation they may surely expect to make themselves felt with more effect in the land at large than they are likely to be by standing wholly separate and apart. The interests represented in the two churches are in all material respects the same, and this itself would seem to require that they should regard them as a common cause, and combine their strength in carrying them forward. In the great work particularly of home missions in the broad valley of the West, it should be seriously considered at least whether such conjunction of counsels and efforts be not called for at their hands. I shall not pretend, however, to say in what several directions or in what several forms occasion may be found for the two bodies thus to join in carrying forward the same general work. That is a question which as yet none of us can be rightly prepared to answer. Only we may take it for granted that opportunities for such co-operation will not fail to exist, while we trust to the hallowed influences that shall spring from this union itself to bring them in due time to light.

I may be permitted in conclusion to say that the time has come when the churches of the Reformation generally have need to seek among themselves a closer correspondence and alliance than has hitherto prevailed. The work of the Reformation is not yet complete. In every great movement of this kind, the direction taken by the general mind is liable in the end to become more or less extreme, and the consequence is then a reaction towards the abandoned error which is often more dangerous to the cause of truth than all the opposition it had to surmount in the beginning. To such extreme the tendencies taken by the Christian world in the religious revolution of the sixteenth century have been unfortunately carried; not, of course, through the force of the principles which constituted the soul of that revolution at the first, but by reason of the gradual paralysis of these principles, where they previously prevailed. The most distressing phase of this bastard Protestantism, the liberty of the Reformation run mad, has been presented in the modern rationalism of Germany, and the Continent of Europe generally. A different form of it we have in the religious radicalism, with its infidel and semi-infidel affinities, into which the dissenting interest of Great Britain has been to some extent too plainly betrayed. And finally it is the same evil substantially which stares us in the face in the unbridled licentiousness of private judgment, as it appears in the endless multiplication of sects on our own side of the Atlantic. All this may be considered the action of a general force which has been at work for three centuries, but has only come to reveal itself fully in these startling consequences within a comparatively recent period. And now, by a necessity which holds in the inmost constitution of our nature, a widespread reaction has begun to show itself, which may well cause the friends of truth to tremble. This, it seems to me, is the true secret of the mysterious charm which popery is found of late to be exercising again over men's minds, where its power appeared once to be effectually destroyed, and the true secret at the same time of the remarkable success which has attended thus far the progress of the Oxford doctrines in the Episcopal Church, both in England and in this country. In this view the movement must be regarded as specially serious. For it is in no sense the result of accident or caprice. It springs from the deepest and most general ground in the character of the age. It belongs to the inmost history of the Church. It is the grand rebounding movement of the Reformation itself, by which more fully than ever before is to be tried the truth and stability of the principles from which the Reformation sprang, and by which it triumphed in the beginning.

The contest of the sixteenth century then is again challenging the strength of the whole Christian world. The work of the Reformation is still to be made complete. It is not enough now simply to cry out against popery and Puseyism, as a return to exploded errors. The truth, as it wrought mightily in the souls of the Reformers, must be understood as well as felt. There is an opposition to the errors of Rome and Oxford sometimes displayed in our own country, which may be said to wrong the cause it affects to defend almost as seriously as this is done by these errors themselves. In its blind zeal and shallow knowledge, it sinks the Church to the level of a temperance society, strips the ministry of its divine commission and so of its divine authority, reduces the sacraments to mere signs, turns all that is mystical into the most trivial worldly sense, and so exalts what is individual above what is general and catholic, as in fact to throw open the door to the most rampant sectarian license, in the name of the gospel, that any may choose to demand. Opposition to Oxford and Rome, in this form, can never prevail. If the cause of the Reformation is to be successfully maintained in the present crisis, I repeat it, it must be not simply by holding fast stubbornly to the forms in which the faith of the Reformation was originally expressed, but by entering with free and profound insight into that faith itself. What is wanted is a republication of the principles of the Reformation, not in the letter merely that killeth, but in the living spirit of the men who wielded them with such vast effect in the sixteenth century. Never was there a more solemn call upon the Reformed churches to clothe themselves fully with the power of the life that is enshrined in their ancient symbols. And surely, in these circumstances, when the very foundations of their common faith are threatened, not by a casual and transient danger but by a force that is lodged deep in the very constitution of the age, and may be said to carry in itself the gathered strength of centuries; when questions of vital import, which were supposed to have been settled long ago, are again to be encountered and resolved, on an issue that involves the very existence of these churches themselves; when in one word the vast struggle of the Reformation is to be taken up in its original spirit and carried forward, through a crisis that may be considered final and decisive, to its proper consummation; surely, I say, in circumstances like these, the churches in question should feel themselves engaged to narrow as much as possible the measure of their separation, and strengthen the consciousness of their unity. The interests by which they are divided are few and small, as compared with those that should bind them together. The glory of God and the honor of his truth, as well as their own common safety, require that they should stand out to the view of the world, not as many but as one, *the Church* (not churches) of the Reformation, the Body of Christ, "the pillar and ground of the truth" [1 Tim. 3:15], one body and one Spirit, even as they are called in one hope of their calling. May the great Head of the Church himself interpose, in ways that to his own wisdom shall seem best, to conduct the hearts and counsels of his people to this result; and in the meantime bestow richly upon us who are here present the glorious power of his grace, that we may be enabled to be faithful to this high interest, especially in the exercise of the trust now committed to our hands, maintaining the unity of the Spirit in the bonds of peace.

II

JOHN WILLIAMSON NEVIN

The Church

Editor's introduction.

Two years after the Harrisburg Convention Nevin again preached on the Church from a text of Ephesians, this time at the opening of the Eastern Synod of the German Reformed Church at Carlisle on October 15, 1846. Six months earlier, in the preface to *The Mystical Presence*, Nevin had sketched some of the themes he developed in the sermon, which was issued as a pamphlet at Chambersburg in 1847.

The sermon contained a polemic against the categories of a "visible" and an "invisible" Church then prevalent in American Protestantism. Nevin also refused to deal in such static collectivities as those of Christian "professors," or of true believers, or of the elect. Instead, he again developed the image of the Church as a biological entelechy, an Idea in the process of actualization. The notion was applied not only to the Church as a whole but also to each of its attributes in the third article of the Creed, its holiness, catholicity, and unity. In this way Nevin was able to contend that the historical and visible church is always the true Church, although not yet the pure or perfect Church. Although still involved in heresy and schism, error and sin, it was to be regarded as the one, holy and catholic Church *in via*. To consider the Church thus, he believed, gave added significance to the confession, "I believe in the holy, catholic Church" — to which Nevin added, "Lord, help mine unbelief!"

That since the publication of "Catholic Unity" there had been a shift in the ecclesiastical orientations of the Mercersburg group is clear from the preface to *The Church*. The arrival of Schaff with his Lutheran sympathies, on the one hand, and the growing difficulties with the Reformed Dutch on the other, had both had an influence. Nevin was no longer inviting his hearers to exalt the Reformed fellowship signalized at Dort. Now he commended his sermon to the German churches, Lutheran as well as Reformed, and argued that it was the vocation of the German Reformed Church to maintain her sixteenth-century emphasis on "the *catholic* side of the Reformation." Whatever might be said of the Dutch, the German Reformed Church and the Lutheran Church were not and ought not to be "Puritan."

The London meeting of the "Evangelical Alliance," in the summer before the Synod, was the subject of a footnote which has been omitted here. The Alliance, Nevin observed, could never be a church, or more than a voluntary association. Its utter silence with regard to the Apostles' Creed betrayed its unchurchly spirit. And the most active promoters of the enterprise, as Nevin remarked in a footnote to *Antichrist* (see 113f., below), were representatives of "the most violently unhistorical and sectarian" denominations.

Schaff also, in *What Is Church History?*, had entered his "decided dissent" from the movement. For many, he believed, the Alliance was intended as a league against Rome, as if a whole Church might be actualized out of purely Protestant elements. Later Schaff did indeed become a prime mover in convening at New York, where the Alliance met in 1873, the most imposing assemblage of world Christianity that had ever met in America.

❖ ❖ ❖ ❖

Ephesians 1:23. Which is his body, the fullness of him that filleth all in all.

I propose, in connection with this passage, to consider, without further introduction, the nature of the *Christian Church*, for the purpose of ascertaining and determining, in a more general way, by the light of God's most holy revelation, the privileges on the one hand and the duties on the other, which are comprehended in our common Christian profession.

1. *What is the Church?*

To answer this question intelligently, we must make a distinction. The Church exhibits itself to us under two aspects, which are in many respects very different, and yet both alike necessary to complete its proper conception. In one view it is the *Ideal Church*, in another it is the *Actual Church*.

I. IDEA OF THE CHURCH

We do not mean by this, of course, the simple sketch of a certain organization, in the way of thought or plan, to which men may be pleased to attach this name, and which is to be taken then as the model to which the Church should be conformed in fact; as a Fourierist philosopher, for instance, has a certain scheme of social order in his own mind, which he endeavors to reduce to a real character in some associated phalanx, as a sovereign remedy for the evil that is in the world. We take *Idea* here in its true sense, by which it expresses the very inmost substance of that which exists, as distinguished from its simply phenomenal character in time and space. As such it is not opposed to what is actual, but constitutes rather its truth and soul. All life is Ideal, that is, exists truly in the form of possibility, before it can become actual; and it is only in the presence and power of this potential life, this invisible, mysterious living nature which lies behind and beyond all outward manifestations, that these last can ever be said to carry with them any reality whatever. In this sense only do we speak of an Ideal Church. As such, the Church is no fantastic figment of any man's brain, no utopian dream of the closet, no creature of human councils or human popes, no device of the state, and no contrivance of the schools. But it is the most real of all realities that God has established in this world, "the pillar and ground of the truth" [1 Tim. 3:15]; the basis, in one word, of the "new heavens and new earth, wherein dwelleth righteousness" [2 Pet. 3:13].

The Ideal Church is the power of a new supernatural creation, which has been introduced into the actual history of the world by the Incarnation of Jesus Christ; and which is destined to go on, causing "old things to pass away and all things to become new" [Rev. 21:4, 5, adapted], till it shall triumph fully in the end over all sin and death, and the whole world shall appear transformed into its image and resplendent with its light. As such a power, it is actually at work in the world already, and has been so since the time of Christ. Very much is still wanting to the complete triumph of the gospel. But the force by which this full triumph is to be accomplished is not to be expected now, as by the Jews under the old dispensation, in the form of some new order of life supernaturally descending from the heavens to the earth. The new creation is already at hand, not developed, indeed, to its last necessary results, but as an active force, all sufficient for its own ends, and really comprehended in the order of the world's history as it now stands. It is exhibited to us in the Church.

The principle of this new creation is the Lord Jesus Christ. In him the Word became flesh, the divine nature was associated with the human as never before, and life and immortality were brought to light in our fallen world. The fact thus accomplished in his person was at the same time a fact for all time. It included in itself all the resources of life and salvation that were needed for the full redemption of humanity, onward to the grand millennial triumph in which it is destined to have its end. The Church, through all ages, is the depository of these resources. The life with which she is filled, the powers that are lodged in her constitution, were all comprehended originally in the person of Jesus Christ, and are all still the revelation only of the grace and truth which came by him in the beginning. He is the alpha and omega, the beginning and the end, of the Church, which is denominated on this account his body, the fullness of him that filleth all in all.

The general attributes of the Ideal Church, as thus described, are not difficult to determine. It is a living system, organically bound together in all its parts, springing from a common ground, and pervaded throughout with the force of a common nature. In its very conception, therefore, it is catholic, that is, one and universal. The kingdom of God, or the new creation in Christ Jesus, must be regarded in the nature of the case as the highest possible form of humanity itself; and in this view it cannot be less single or less comprehensive than the Idea of the human race as a whole. As a single life, moreover, flowing perpetually from the same fountain, it must ever remain in union with itself, always one and everywhere the same, in the midst of all possible extension and multiplication. There may be many states in the world, but there can be only one Church. Such is the doctrine of the New Testament throughout. Such has been the deep feeling of all Christendom from the beginning, as expressed in that ancient article of the Creed: "I believe in the holy, catholic Church." The Church is one, in all ages and through all lands.

In her Ideal character again, as the article of the Creed implies, the Church is absolutely holy and infallible, free from error and free from sin. Her constitution is derived wholly from Christ, who is the truth itself, and in whom the whole righteousness of the law is completely and forever fulfilled. Hence the Church is represented to be the organ and medium by which the world is reclaimed from the power of error, and transformed into a holy life. Her members are called to be saints [1 Cor. 1:2]. She is the pillar and ground of the truth [1 Tim. 3:15]. The gates of hell shall not prevail against her [Mt. 16:18]. In the end, she will be found holy and without blemish, a glorious Church, not having spot or wrinkle, or any such thing [Eph. 5:27].

The Church, moreover, is the necessary and only form in which Christianity can have a real existence in the world. It is not something added to humanity, as it were from abroad, to assist it in taking upon itself the Christian life as its own highest perfection, but it is this life itself exalting humanity into its own sphere. As the human nature in its own constitution is social, and no individual man can be complete apart from his race, so Christianity, which is only the human nature made absolutely complete, includes pre-eminently the same character. In its very conception, it is the power of a common or general life, which can never appear, therefore, as something isolated and single simply, but always includes the idea of society and communion, under all its manifestations. But this social character of Christianity resolves itself into the conception of the Church. Out of the Church, then, or as separated from the general life of Christ in his people, there can be no true Christian character and no Christian salvation. Christianity and the Church are identical, and it lies in the very Idea of this last, that as it is catholic and universal, so it must be also uncompromisingly exclusive.

Lastly, the Church under its Ideal character includes in itself the necessity of a visible externalization in the world. Without this necessity, it could not be real in any of the respects that have been already mentioned. For it is a fixed law in life, that every spiritual force which it comprehends must take some outward form in order to become complete. Pent up within itself as mere spirit, it must remain always an abstraction only, with no power whatever. The outward must ever be joined to the inward, to give it either reality or strength. And the more intensely spiritual any force may be, the more urgent and irresistible will be found the operation of this law, requiring it to put on a body suitable to its own nature, and to appear thus under a visible form. The Church, then, as comprehending in itself the inmost, deepest life of humanity, cannot possibly exist in the character of a simply inward and invisible constitution. Of all forms of existence known among men, this is the very last of which any such imagination might reasonably be entertained. An invisible state, or invisible family, or invisible man, is not so great an absurdity and contradiction as an absolutely invisible Church. Christianity starts, indeed, as something spiritual and inward, as it is said, "The kingdom of God is within you" [Lk. 17:21]; but it is only that it may reveal itself immediately in the way of external life, both in the single Christian and in the Church as a whole. The Idea of the Church includes visibility, just as the Idea of man supposes a body. And this visibility is demanded for all the attributes, too, under which the Church is properly known. It is not the visibility of single Christians, simply as such, that is required, but the visibility of the Church as an organic body, in whose presence alone all individual Christianity becomes real. The Church is required to be visible as a Church — that is, in the whole character which is comprehended in this idea. Its catholicity, unity, sanctity, all call for externalization. The article, *I believe in one, holy, catholic Church*, contemplates in this view no mere intellectual abstraction. It expresses faith in the Church as one, holy, and catholic, under an outward visible form, and those who give it a different sense, put violence upon the Creed in doing so, and wrong the idea of the Church at the same time. For an invisible unity, catholicity, and holiness can never satisfy the requisitions of the case. The Church, in its very nature, seeks visibility, and to be complete at all, this visibility must extend to all its qualities and attributes.

This brings us, however, to a consideration of the other aspect, in which the Church is presented to our view.

2. THE ACTUAL CHURCH

This is exhibited to us in history, as it reaches from the Incarnation of Christ to the present time, and is destined to run forward still to the end of the world as it now stands. It is the kingdom of heaven, as it is found revealing itself in the way of actual life among men. It may be contemplated without reference to the past or future, under the form simply that belongs to it at a given time. Thus we have the Church of the present age, comprehending in itself the whole extent of the Christian life as it now exists in the world. And in the same way we may speak of the Church of the first century, the Church of the fourth century, the Church of the sixteenth century, or the Church of any other age, as something separate and complete within itself. But the true and proper conception of the actual Church is not reached in this way. This includes always the past along with the present, as well as a reference also to the future. Through all periods the Church remains the same, and from beginning to end, her history is but the power of a single fact. The actual Church is a process, not only covering a large field in space, but reaching over a long tract in time; and to be understood at all, it must be apprehended and viewed in this way. Those who might affect to take the Christianity of America for the whole Church, without regard to the Christianity of Great Britain or of Europe generally, would not commit a greater solecism in the case, than is involved in the judgment by which the Christianity of the nineteenth century is made to stand for the Church in the like separate view. In its very nature, the actual Church is a process which has never yet become complete, but is always pressing forward to its completion, as this will appear in the millennium. So it is always described in the New Testament. It is something that *grows*, in the individual and in humanity as a whole. It works like *leaven* in the mass of the world's life, till in the end the whole *shall be leavened*, that is, transfused with the same divine character and made glorious with the attributes of a new creation. In the view of prophecy, accordingly, the entire period in which this process is comprehended is often represented as a single revelation, all complete at once. The second coming of Christ is made to flow together, as it were, with his first coming, and the whole constitutes one grand spiritual scene, in which old things have passed away and all things have become new. No other conception can do justice to the case. The Church as it now stands is the result of what the same Church has been since the time of Christ; the past is gathered up and comprehended in the present; and the whole is reaching forward to still new developments in the future, that will cease only when the Ideal Church and the actual Church shall have become fully and forever one.

The actual Church, as now described, must be expected, of course, to fall short, in every stage of its historical development, of the perfection which it is destined to reach in the end. This lies in its very conception. The Church is a new creation for the world, complete from the first in Christ, but requiring a process of historical evolution, according to the law of all life, to actualize itself with final, universal triumph in the world as a whole. This process supposes imperfection and defect at every point of its progress, on to the last; for when all defect shall have been surmounted, it will itself, of course, have come to an end. It implies opposition, contradiction, and conflict, disturbing forces, foreign elements, corruptions, distortions, aberrations. The historical Church is always the true Church, but never a pure or perfect Church. It is by no means free either from error or sin. The Church of Rome, in claiming to be infallible, claims to be in fact the Ideal Church itself, as though this had already actualized itself in full in her communion. But this claim is contradicted by palpable and acknowledged signs of imperfection under other forms. It belongs to the Idea of the Church to be holy as well as infallible. To be consistent, then, the Church of Rome should lay claim to sinless perfection, or absolute impeccability, along with her pretension to infallibility. But this she does not venture to do. She acknowledges that she is not free from sin. We will not allow, therefore, that she is free from error. There is no reason to say the actual Church may not err, any more than there is to say that she may not fall into sin. On the contrary, the very nature of the process in which she is involved, and in which her character at present consists, might lead us to presume confidently that she would be liable to error and sin both, more or less, in all ages.

In the same way, we cannot allow that a visible unity of organization and worship is indispensable to the truth of the Church, in the view now under consideration. That all this is required by the Idea of the Church, and that the Church can never become complete without it, has been already admitted. It belongs to the nature of the Church to be one and universal, catholic as well as holy, in an outward visible way no less than in its unseen constitution. Our whole sect system (this testimony we may never cease to reiterate) is something wrong, an abomination in the temple of God that must pass away before it can be clean and fit for the coming of the Lord. But still it does not follow at once from all this that the actual Church can exist only in the form of such visible unity as is contended for by Romanists and high-church Episcopalians. Allow our divisions to be a great and sore defect, they are still not necessarily such a defect as is inconsistent with the conception of the actual Church, whose very nature it is to be involved in a perpetual communication, more or less intimate, with what is wrong, and which always includes in its constitution much that is to be expelled from it in the end. The unchurching dogma of the high-toned Episcopalian falls here into the same difficulty with the doctrine of infallibility as asserted by the Church of Rome. It transfers at once to the state of the actual Church what is true only of the Ideal Church, and identifies this last at the same time with its own particular communion. But to be consistent here, again, the claim should extend to *all* the attributes of the Ideal Church. If division be contrary to the Idea of the Church, the same thing is true also of all error and sin. If separation from a particular communion, the Episcopal Church for instance, be supposed to work a forfeiture of all interest in God's covenant, because visible unity is required by the Idea of the Church, it is hard to see why the want of any other attribute of a perfect Church should not do the same thing. Let us beware of this confusion of things which we are bound to keep separate and distinct. The actual Church is still very far from being a perfect Church. It is not, therefore, necessarily free from either heresy or schism. Its visible unity may be greatly marred by its distribution, more or less, into denominations and sects. This we are bound to lament, but we have no right to resort to the violence of unchurching all beyond some favorite communion in order to remedy the evil. As it now stands, especially, the Church with its divine life powers is not confined to any one organization exclusively, as Romanists and Tractarians believe, but extends its presence, with different measures of power, over different and divided communions. It has no sympathy, indeed, with the spirit of division and sect; but still it allows the evil to be comprehended for a time in the evolution of its own life (just as the abuses of the papacy were comprehended in it before the Reformation), in order that all may be the more gloriously surmounted in the end.

With all their difference, however, the actual Church and the Ideal Church, it must always be borne in mind, are in the end the same. The Ideal Church, as before said, is no abstraction but a living divine constitution, which includes in itself from the beginning all that it is destined to become by development in the end, and whose very nature requires it to show itself real in this way. The history of the actual Church, then, is but the presence and life of the Ideal Church itself, struggling through a process of centuries to come to its last, full manifestation. In the end the process will be complete, and then, though not sooner, the actual will be found commensurate in all respects with the Ideal. Meanwhile, however, they are bound, in the process itself, inseparably together. The Ideal Church can have no reality save under the form of the historical, and the actual or historical Church can have no truth except through the presence of the Ideal. The historical Church may be involved in error or sunk in corruption, filled with heterogeneous elements, overloaded with all forms of perversion and abuse. But still it is always the bearer of the Ideal Church, and the form under which it has its manifestation in the world. However defective and abnormal, in the midst of all excrescences and disproportions it represents always notwithstanding the life and power of the Ideal Church, in the stage of development it has reached at the time. We may not look for this last in any other connection; we may not think of it as something independent wholly of the outward organization and action which constitute the presence of the other. The two can never fall asunder, nor is their conjunction accidental simply and external. The relation that joins them is inward and vital, like that which holds between soul and body. The invisible Church, as it is sometimes called, dwells in the visible, as its only possible home among men; and although it includes in itself much more than is actually revealed in this last at any given period, it is still here and nowhere else that all such hidden power is deposited, always ripening for actual life, and ready to show itself in its own time. The actual is the body of the Ideal in *growth*, the process, constantly changing and flowing, by which it is externalized and so made complete, as the great world-fact of redemption.

II. *Having now explained the general nature of the Christian Church, we are prepared to consider, in a like general way, its prerogatives and claims in the work of salvation. What have we as Christians in the Church, and what do we owe to it?*

What, in other words, is that *faith* in the Church, which is made to stand as a separate article in the Apostles' Creed, close on its declaration of allegiance to the three persons of the ever blessed and glorious Trinity: *I believe in the holy catholic Church?* What is the meaning of this faith? What does it comprehend?

If the view already taken of the Church be at all correct, it is plain that the whole truth of the gospel is comprehended in its presence; and that the entire Christian Creed must stand or fall with the faith of the article just quoted. The Church is the historical continuation of the life of Jesus Christ in the world. By the Incarnation of the Son of God, a divine supernatural order of existence was introduced into the world, which was not in it as part of its own constitution before. This was done, moreover, not in the way of transient phenomenon, but in the character of a grand world-fact, which should become from that time forward the central force of history, the bearer of a new divine creation in the bosom of the old, on to the consummation of all things. Jesus returned to heaven after his resurrection, but it was not in such a way as to abstract again from the world the life which had been incorporated with it in our fallen nature, when the Word became flesh. "Lo, I am with you always," he said, "even unto the end of the world" [Mt. 28:20]. He abides with his people, by the Spirit, in the Church. The new creation which revealed itself originally in his person is here made constant among men, with all its resources, as a real historical process, reaching forward to the end of time. No relation, then, can be more intimate or necessary than that between Christ and his Church. "It is his body, the fullness of him that filleth all in all." The grace and truth that came by him at the beginning, the whole fullness of the Christian salvation of which he is the everlasting fountain, continues to reveal itself here, through all ages, as the power of a permanent life in the world's history. In a deep sense, thus, Christ himself is made perfect in the Church, as the head in our natural organization requires the body in order to its completion. There can be no Church without Christ, but we may reverse the proposition also and say, no Church, no Christ. The Incarnation would be shorn of its meaning, if the fact were not carried out to its proper world development, in the Church. Such is the sound feeling of the ancient Christian Creed. It begins with God, but soon shuts us up to the Church, as the only medium of his saving presence among men. "I believe in God, the Father Almighty, Maker of heaven and earth: and in Jesus Christ his only Son, our Lord" — who by his life and death accomplished our salvation. "I believe in the Holy Ghost" — by whose glorious agency, as the Spirit of Christ, he is still made present in the world; and so next, in the "holy, catholic Church," as the one necessary and exclusive divine constitution, by which this whole revelation is made to include either reality or force. For the Creed evidently — that is, according to the sense of the whole Christian world as it stood in the beginning — faith in the Church is the indispensable condition of all right faith in the only true God, and in Jesus Christ whom he has sent.

There is no opposition, then, between Christ and the Church in the economy of salvation. Let us only have a true conception of the last as she stands related to her glorious head, and we need not fear that we shall think more highly of her than we ought. In honoring the Church, we honor Christ; to believe in the Church, according to the Creed, is to believe in Christ; to lean upon the Church is to lean upon Christ. How should we fear to wrong his grace, by confiding in it as real, under the only form in which it is brought within our reach? Rather, we can never honor him truly without a corresponding regard for the Church. We deceive ourselves if we imagine that we have faith in his salvation, while we refuse to recognize the actual historical presence of it in his own institutions. Without faith in the Church, there can be no proper faith in Christ. If there be no such supernatural constitution in the world as the Idea of the Church implies, the whole fact of the Incarnation is turned into an unreal theophany, and the gospel is subverted to its very foundations. This much, and nothing less, is comprised in the article: *I believe in the holy catholic Church.*

The Church is found to be thus, without any qualification, the "pillar and ground of the truth" [1 Tim. 3:15]. She is not simply a witness to the truth as something lying beyond and out of herself, but she comprehends and upholds the truth, in her own constitution, as being in the fullest sense the depository of the life of Christ himself. The everlasting gospel of the Son of God, the living power that shall in the end regenerate the earth and heavens, the fullness of him that filleth all in all, belong to her, in virtue of the union that binds her continually to her exalted Head. The gates of hell therefore cannot prevail against her. She may fall, within certain limits, into error and sin. But only within certain limits. Sin can never have dominion over her absolutely. Error can never come to a full triumph in her communion, so as to require help from abroad. Her proper life may be turned out of the way or borne down for a season, by the power of falsehood; but it is only that it may recover itself again, by omnipotent reaction, to assert with new determination its original heavenward course. If the Church should fail, all truth and holiness among men must fail irrecoverably at the same time.

It is neither the Ideal Church, of course, nor the actual Church, separately taken, that forms the proper object of our faith, as expressed in the Creed, but the first as comprehended always in the second, and constituting with it the presence of a single life. In this view, it is apprehended as a *real* Church, not a logical figment simply, nor yet the mere creature of human will, but a divine constitution actively present in the world, and steadily unfolding itself to its necessary end. As such, it is a *visible, catholic, historical,* and *life-bearing* Church, and is to be embraced in the way of faith accordingly. It is our privilege and duty to believe and confide in the Church, under this character, and if we fail to do so, we wrong the grace of God, and the true sense of the Apostolic Symbol, to the same extent. It is not as a moral conception merely that the Church is proposed to us as the object of our faith, but as a real abiding constitution in the world, including in itself the resources which are needed for its own ends, and always struggling to actualize in full the divine life of which it is the supernatural bearer among men.

1. The Church of the Creed, the proper object of our Christian faith, we say, is *visible*.

Her nature is indeed spiritual, and must exist in the form of inward invisible power before it can come to an outward revelation. But to become real, the inward is urged from the very start to represent itself in an outward form. This externalization is by no means adequate at first, as we have seen, to the demands of the life which it includes; a process of centuries is needed to make it in this respect complete. Still, as far as it goes, it is always the true outward form of the Church in the world, without which it could not exist at all, so as to be the object either of knowledge or faith. An absolutely invisible Church can never be apprehended as a real Church. The abstraction of the Quaker reduces the Idea to a mere phantom. Nor will it answer to connect the invisible with the visible here, in a merely outward way, as when the first is thought of as an association complete within itself, under cover merely of the second, which is to be considered in fact of a totally different nature. With as much reason might we suppose the fluid which holds some substance in solution to be its proper visible form. A Bible society, a temperance union, a benevolent association of any kind having Christians in its membership, is no Church; just as little as a political party, in the same circumstances, is entitled to any such name. As the Church is an organic body in its own nature, so to appear in the world at all it must appear, not in solution, but in an organized way, and its organization must be at the same time its own, the product of its own life, a true revelation as far as it goes of its own inward constitution. The outward in the case must bear the inward, as the body bears the soul that dwells in it, and makes itself to be known and felt by its presence, so that when we look upon it we may say, not simply "The Church is here," but "This is the Church." Most inadequate though it be to express in full its own divine contents (even as the body of an infant, sickly, perhaps, and out of rule, is most disproportionate to the full life of the future man, which is, notwithstanding, comprehended in it at the time), it is still the very life-process in which the fullness of these divine contents is involved, and by which alone it is possible for them to have any real existence in the world. In the way of actual presence and force upon the earth, the invisible Church, as it is called, can have no being whatever apart from the visible. Such was the universal faith of the early Christian world; and we cannot say truly, "I believe in the holy catholic Church," if we take not the article in this sense.

2. The Church of the Creed is *catholic*.

Unity and universality belong not more essentially to the idea of humanity itself than they do to the conception of the Church; for this last is the form simply, in which the first is advanced to its ultimate significance, and thus made eternally complete. The Church must ever be one, even as Christ is one, and the whole world must be taken up organically, in the end, into her constitution. All this is involved in her very nature; and all this, consequently, according to what has been said already, is actually at hand also in the visible representation of her presence in the world. True, she is exhibited to us as in many respects a divided Church, and her catholicity is sorely marred, on every side, by forms of existence that contradict entirely all such character. Whole spheres of life are either willfully excluded from her communion, or else overwhelmed by it in a merely outward way. But still she is the power by which in the end the entire world shall become new, outwardly as well as inwardly, in the harmonious unity of the Spirit. And she is this power *now*, actually revealing itself, in spite of all divisions and obstructions, in the outward organization by which she is represented among men. We may not locate her unity and catholicity in the region of mere abstract thought, as something purely spiritual, or as a result to be expected at best from some other quarter only in her heavenly state. They belong to her inmost constitution as a real Church upon the earth, at the present time, and to believe in such a Church at all, we must believe in it as one and catholic under this form. That is, we must believe that our sects, so far as they belong to the Church at all, belong to it organically, not as loose transports in its service simply, by which some of God's elect may happen to be conveyed to the heavenly Jerusalem, but as component portions of the one universal body of Jesus Christ in the world, representing collectively for the time, not separately, its life as a whole.[1] We must believe that un-

---

1. The sects then are either not of the Church at all, or they must be of it as so many outward totalities belonging to the body as a whole. How far the Church life may reach in this way, we cannot say. There are sects, of course, that have no part in it whatever; and then there are others again, whose connection with it is sickly and imperfect, though still real. In all cases, however, the relation in question holds of the sect as an organization, and not merely of some individuals that may happen to be living in it, as grains of metal in a heap of sand. To be satisfied with my sect, it is not enough to be sure that it includes some true Christians; I need to be sure that the life of the Church is objectively present in its constitution *as a sect*, giving to its spiritual ministrations the force which belongs to the life of the true Church, and to this life only. If I make no account of this point, I show my want of faith in the Church, and have good reason to tremble for my position.

der all this division is working continually a deeper force, by which even
now the apparently sundered sections of the Church are bound together
as a single visible reality in the world, and that will not rest till its own
unity shall be fully and forever impressed upon the whole. We must believe that our sects, therefore, however necessary, are something wrong, a
most defective, abnormal condition of the Body of Christ, an interimistic
abomination, in the Church but not of it, that is destined in due time to
pass away, and which, while it lasts, all good men are bound to deplore.
To justify the sect system as an order of things right in itself, or to cher-
ish the spirit of sect in any way, is in direct opposition to all true faith in
the holy, catholic Church.

3. The Church of the Creed is *historical*.

It must be so to be real, in the character already described. Once in the
world by Jesus Christ, it must continue to be in the world always to the
end of time. To suppose a chasm in its continuance at any point is in fact
to overthrow its existence altogether. Nor will it do to talk of its being
present at times in a merely invisible way. This is to reduce it at last to an
abstraction, a thing of simple thought or name. But the Church is no
abstraction, and it is far more than a name. It is the depository of a supernatural life, which under all diversities of outward manifestation must always remain one and the same, which is strictly organic in its nature, and
which therefore, to have any force at all, must unfold itself organically in
a standing concrete form. This form may change, in the way of transition
from one stage of development to another; but it can never disappear
from the outward, visible process of the world's history; for it is in truth
itself the central force in this whole process, that may be said to bear and
rule its world-embracing movement, onward to the close of time. To be
real, in this case, and to be historical, are the same thing; and when we
say, *I believe in the holy catholic Church*, we do in fact profess our faith
(except as we may choose to play falsely with words) in the Church as a
visible, outward constitution, that has never failed under this character
since it was first established among men, and that never will fail while the
world shall last. As thus historical, of course, the truth and reality of the
body in any given age must depend necessarily on its connection with its
own life in all previous ages. To suppose that it might take an entirely
new start, under such visible organic character, in the fourth century, or
the sixteenth, or at any other time, springing directly from the Bible or

from heaven — its old life having either failed altogether or run out into universal apostasy — is most assuredly to belie its existence as a real Church entirely; as much so as to imagine any similar void or break in our common human life between its embryo formation in the womb and the full maturity of manhood would be plainly to convert the whole process into a mere Gnostic phantom. We may allow the Church to have become in certain periods very corrupt and false to her proper character, but let us beware of annihilating in thought her outward, visible, organic perpetuity. That were heresy of a very serious and grievous order. No man doing so, can say honestly, in the sense of the Christian Creed: *I believe in the holy catholic Church.*

4. THE CHURCH OF THE CREED, ONCE MORE, IS *life-bearing.*

This is a point of vast consequence, comprehended necessarily in what has been said of the subject already. Christianity, strictly speaking, is not a system of doctrines, nor a code of ethical rules, nor a record of events long since past or passing at the present time, but it is a perpetual fact, that starts in the Incarnation of the Son of God, and reaches forward as a continuous supernatural reality to the end of time. As such a *fact,* it includes life-powers which were not in the world before, but cannot be sundered from its history since. These life-powers belong to its very constitution, and as such are lodged in the Church, which is the "body of Christ, the fullness of him that filleth all in all." They are not to be found elsewhere, but here they are really and truly, always to the end of the world. The Church, too, in which they are comprehended, is the outward, visible, historical Church, which we have now been attempting to describe; for however far short this may come of being a full and sufficient representation of the life it bears, it is still, as we have seen, the actual body of Christ, and the only form under which his life appears in the world, or can be said to be in it at all. The living powers in question are not indeed the product properly of the Church outwardly considered; they spring perpetually from Christ himself, as the vitality of the body descends into it from the head. They are present, too, always and only by the presence of the Holy Ghost. But still they are in the Church without a figure at the same time, as truly as the vitality of the body, though springing from the head, is yet in the fullest sense its own, and not simply represented by it in the way of dumb mechanical show. We do not derogate from the glory of Christ by believing and asserting a real historical revelation of his life in the Church. On the contrary, we show by so doing the fullness of our faith in his Incarnation, as a permanent fact for our salvation. The grace and truth comprehended in this fact are not left to evaporate with us into thin abstraction. They are felt to be with us still, in the form of a real abiding constitution, with the same kind of actualness that belonged to the visible presence of the incarnate Word himself, in the days of his flesh.

This is what we are to understand by the *objective* character of the Church. The Church is not the aggregation merely of all the individual actings of piety that are found in its compass; for, in that sense, we might call a Christian association of any sort by this name; but it is the power of a divine constitution, which lies at the ground of all individual piety, and whose existence is absolutely at hand for the purposes it contemplates, independently of such piety altogether, though never, of course, without its presence. There are resources and provisions in the Church, real supernatural life-powers, which belong to no other constitution, and which our human society, no matter how organized, must ever fail of reaching under any different form. To doubt this is to doubt in fact the reality of the entire new creation in Christ Jesus, and to resolve the historical human Christ himself at last into a Gnostic theophany. So felt the early Christian world when it proclaimed, next to its faith in the Incarnation, that most significant article: "I believe in the holy, catholic Church." To deny the objective character of the Church is to overthrow the Creed.

But now the objective life-bearing character of the Church, to be of any force, must express itself through its actual visible organization, the ordinances and institutions by which its presence is revealed and upheld in the world. This is a wide field, which we cannot be expected now, of course, to enter upon in detail. We may say in a word, however, that all the regular and proper organs and functions by which the life of the Church is carried forward among men for its own ends are divine organs and divine functions. They belong not to the sphere of mere nature, but to the sphere of supernatural grace. They include in themselves a value which transcends absolutely all powers that are lodged in our common human nature, under any other view. The ministry, for instance, is far more than any merely human institution could ever be possibly under the same form. The office is a necessary organ of the Body of Christ, and as such it is the bearer of a divine supernatural power that may never be measured safely by any common standard. Ordination does convey, in this sense, objective virtue or force, such as no man in the ordinary course of things can be allowed to possess without it. So all ministerial functions are as such of more force than any common human transactions bearing a similar form. Not without meaning did our Saviour say: "Whatsoever ye shall bind on earth, shall be bound in heaven, and whatsoever ye shall loose on earth shall be loosed in heaven" [Mt. 18:18]. The Church *has* power to bind and loose upon the earth. The regular functions of the ministry are divine functions. Church censures and church absolutions, too, take hold upon the invisible world. Church services involve the force of a true liturgical sacrifice, which serves of itself to bring men near to God. The sacraments in particular have living power in themselves. They are not signs and shadows only, like the symbols of Freemasonry or Odd-Fellowship, but a divine life is actually comprehended in them for the high supernatural ends they are designed to serve.

On all these things it is not necessary now to insist. After the view we have already taken of the nature of the Church, no disposition will be felt among us, it is trusted, to make them the subject of dispute. If there be no supernatural force in the ministry and sacraments for their own ends, it is plain that the entire objective character of the Church, and with this its true historical character, and at last its character also as a real divine constitution, the "Body of Christ," in the world, must virtually fall to the ground at the same time. And then the great fact of the Incarnation will be found, as before said, to be reduced also to a Gnostic abstraction, a thing of mere memory and notion. Without faith in the holy catholic Church there can be no full, abiding faith in the Word made flesh.

It will appear from all that has now been said, that the *Church Question,* as it is termed, which has come to engage so much attention in our own time, is one of the very highest practical consequence. It would not deserve to be so considered, indeed, if it involved nothing more than many who wish to bring it into discredit are accustomed to represent. They tell us, with vast assumption of evangelical superiority to all who differ from themselves, that the grand controversy in the case is between a religion of forms and a religion of the spirit. They oppose Christ and the Church to one another as rival powers, and will have it that the whole danger of running into a false and ruinous extreme lies on the one side only, and not at all on the other. Strange, however, that no misgiving should be created at times in the minds of such persons by the very unnaturalness itself of what they are pleased to assume as the true state of the case in this form. If the church spirit, as opposed to their bald individualism, were in fact what they continually endeavor to make it, a superstitious zeal for rites and ceremonies only at the cost of all heart-godliness, we must be utterly at a loss to account for the madness and folly with which it has been cherished in all ages by so large a part of the Christian world. But the question is not of this poor, superficial order. Let the Church be apprehended in the character in which it has now been represented, as the actual organic presence of the new creation in Christ Jesus among men, comprising in itself all the supernatural life-powers which were introduced into the world by the Incarnation, and it must at once be felt that the issue which is presented to us in this case is one of the most momentous that could well be made to challenge our considera-tion. If there be such a supernatural constitution among us in truth, not in the character simply of an invisible and impalpable abstraction, but under an outward, real, historical form, it is plain that it must be of the utmost consequence for us all to be fully assured of the fact and to have full faith in it, at the same time, as sufficient in all respects for the ends it is de-signed to secure. Faith in the Church is necessary, according to the Creed, to complete our faith in the Holy Trinity and in the great fact of the Incarnation. Where it is wanting to any considerable extent, the whole theory and practice of religion must suffer. Take in illustration the single case of the religious training of children. In what light are they to be viewed, after baptism? Is their relation to the covenant at last anything more than nominal simply, or does it carry in itself a divine power, that properly improved will issue in eternal life? Shall we treat them as God's children, or as the children of Satan? Shall we lean upon the resources of the Church, faithful parental and pastoral education, to form them to a holy life, or shall we distrust and neglect this whole method, teach them practically to despise their own spiritual birthright, and thrust them out from us as aliens, who are to be recovered to the Church, if recovered at all, by an extraordinary process of conversion in some different way alto-gether? All will depend on our view of the Church, and the faith we may have in its visible institutions. But what a weight of practical interest is suspended on the difference here brought into view! These two theories of education run heaven-wide apart. If one be right, the other must be radically wrong. Allow the churchly system to be that which God has in fact ordained for the use of the world, and who does not see that an incal-culable loss must be sustained, wherever the opposite system is substituted in its place? One of the greatest calamities, clearly, that can fall upon a religious community, is to have its confidence in the objective resources of the Church, for the ends of Christian education, destroyed or seriously shaken. And this, as before said, is one example only of the vast practical consequence of this whole question concerning the Church and its institutions.

We have reason, then, to stand upon our guard against the inroads of an unchurchly spirit. For as it is full of danger, so is it extremely plausible and insidious also in its approach. It comes to men like an angel of light, professing to lead them the only sure way to righteousness and heaven. It magnifies the inward and spiritual, and affects to call the soul away from a religion of forms and outward show. "God is a spirit," it tells us, "and they that worship him must worship him in spirit and in truth" [Jn. 4:24]. He looks upon the heart, and not on empty rites, however solemn and imposing. Religion is a personal thing, a transaction between every individual separately and his Maker, and all reliance on church privileges and church ordinances is to be deprecated as full of peril to the immortal soul. In such style, fair and captivating, does this unchurchly spirit erect itself into notice and power, pretending to exalt Christ and magnify repentance and faith, at the cost of all that is comprehended in the idea of the Church, "which is his body, the fullness of him that filleth all in all." But let us beware of its smooth pretenses. It is a spirit that will conduct us in the end to poverty and starvation. It will leave us without a liturgy, without sacraments, without history. It will reduce the "Body of Christ" to a phantom, a thing of no substance or reality. It is the spirit of the ancient Gnostic and of the modern Anabaptist and Quaker, in close affinity, I may add, with the last form of Hegelian pantheism, as applied to the explanation of Christianity by such men as Strauss and Bruno Bauer. We may say of it, with the apostle John: "Beloved, believe not every spirit, but try the spirits whether they are of God; because many false prophets are gone out into the world. Hereby know ye the spirit of God. Every spirit that confesseth that Jesus Christ is come in the flesh, is of God: and every spirit that confesseth not that Jesus Christ is come in the flesh, is not of God: and this is that spirit of Antichrist, whereof ye have heard that it should come; and even now already is it in the world" [1 Jn. 4:1–3]. There is a spiritualism that turns all religion into a mere idea. It will know nothing of a real revelation of Christ in the flesh. This is emphatically Antichrist, for while it professes to honor the Saviour, and arrogates to itself the highest credit in the name of Christianity, it exalts in fact an unreal phantom into Christ's place, and turns the gospel into a mirror simply of its own dreams. The criterion of all such false spiritualism is found in the apostle's simple rule. It will not confess that Jesus

Christ has *come in the flesh;* that is, it refuses to acknowledge practically a real, historical Christ, in whom the divine nature has come to a full, abiding union with the human, and who has become thus the origin and constant principle of a new supernatural creation in the Church that can never fail till the whole world shall be reclaimed from corruption and vanity by its power. Let us beware of this spirit. Even good men, in our own time, are sadly exposed to its influence, not in the form, indeed, of an open opposition to a real, historical Christ. The old Gnosticism has been long since shorn of its glory. But what is it but a more subtle phase of the same error to deny the existence of a real, historical *Church* in the world? Without a real Church we can have no real Christ. Let us beware of the Gnostic, unchurchly, Nestorian spirit. Let us cleave to Christ in the flesh, in the abiding revelation of his presence in the Church. Let us have no fellowship here with Antichrist.

JOHN WILLIAMSON NEVIN

The Incarnation

Editor's introduction.

According to the view we have of Christ, in the end, will be and must be our view also of the Church. We come to the true conception of the Church through a true and sound Christology (as in the Creed), and in no other way.[1]

In *The Mystical Presence*, published in 1846, Nevin had set forth systematically his conception of a true Christology, with its implications for the Church and particularly for the Eucharist. Selections from this work appear in Part Three, below.

Nevin was stimulated to another comprehensive discussion of Christology by the work of R. I. Wilberforce on the Incarnation, which he probably read in the American edition of 1849. Nevin's essay was not really a review of Wilberforce's book, but a statement of his own kindred conceptions "without any particular respect to the author's plan." The organization and style of the English work, in fact, seemed to him an unfortunate and unnecessary obstacle to its influence. Nevin approached the subject in a different way, but then gave generous excerpts from Wilberforce in support of his own discussion. These quotations, which make up about a third of the original essay, have been almost entirely omitted from the text reprinted below, so that unlike the original, it contains little direct reference to "Wilberforce on the Incarnation."

Nevin and Wilberforce were in general agreement, as was natural enough since both had drawn much from the same German springs. A. M. Fairbairn was to a degree justified, if not entirely accurate or fair, in describing Wilberforce's work as "an expansion of a section in Möhl-

1. "Wilberforce on the Incarnation," *The Mercersburg Review*, II (1850), 196.

er's *Symbolik*, which, in its turn, is an application of the Hegelian idea to the Catholic Church." [2] Nevin, for all his admiration, was also somewhat amused at the Anglican claim that this was the great theological production of the age. It perhaps did mark an epoch in the history of English theology, he granted; but, he went on, "All who are acquainted with the later German theology know that the age abounds with great productions in this form. It would be easy to name many theologians not only of equal but of superior learning, and many works also of far more thorough and complete execution." [3] Nevin had been given harder nuts on which to cut his theological teeth by Liebner, Thomasius, Müller, and Dorner in the Christological debate. Wilberforce rather provoked him to a summary review.

For Nevin any consideration of Christology necessarily led to the Church, and vice versa. Whereas he had begun with a consideration of the Church in his two sermons on that theme, now he began with the Incarnation. He laid his emphasis on the Person rather than the work of Christ, the Incarnation rather than the atoning death, and thus ran counter to the prevailing evangelical theology. His references to the election of grace and to the functions of Scripture and Creed were also calculated to provoke Princeton and New Brunswick.

Nevin later read Wilberforce's two volumes on baptism and the Eucharist, and published an article on the latter in 1854. He had in the meantime received at least two personal letters from Wilberforce, the second "more full and confidential." Both men were then seriously considering the claims of Rome, as against which, in Nevin's judgment, the Anglo-Catholic position was not tenable. Wilberforce evidently came to the same conclusion before the end of that year. Schaff was also in England in 1854, and the two English theologians with whom he spent the most time, Wilberforce and F. D. Maurice, were probably those closest to Mercersburg in philosophical theology. Less than three years later Nevin was writing Schaff [4] of how solemnly he had been affected by the news of Wilberforce's death.

❖   ❖   ❖   ❖

1. The *Mediation* of Christ holds primarily and fundamentally in the constitution of his person. With our current theology this is not admitted.

2. *Catholicism, Roman and Anglican* (New York, 1899), 324.
3. *Loc. cit.*, 166.
4. Letter of March 28, 1857. (Library of the Historical Society of the Evangelical and Reformed Church, Franklin and Marshall College, Lancaster, Pa.)

The mediatorial office is taken to be a sort of outward investiture, for which it was necessary, indeed, that Christ should have certain previous qualifications, but which is to be regarded still in this view as holding out of his person and beyond it, like the work assigned to Moses, for instance, when he was selected and appointed to lead the Israelites out of Egypt, and to give them the Law at Mount Sinai. Two parties, God and man, are thought of as in a state of variance, and as needing reconciliation; a certain service is required for this purpose, it may be in the way of negotiation and persuasion simply, or it may be in the way of work, obedience, sacrifice, atonement; and to meet this requirement, under such purely outward view, Christ is regarded as assuming the character of a day's man or arbitrator, and as coming *between* the parties thus in order to bring them together. He may be considered a mere prophet, in the Unitarian sense, who saves by his excellent doctrine and holy example; or he may be allowed to be far more than this, a Saviour possessed of truly divine powers, according to the orthodox faith, by the mystery of the Incarnation, who takes away sin by suffering the penalty of it in his own person; but still, in either case, the thing done has its proper seat and substance in the relation of the parties concerned by itself considered, while Christ as the doer of it stands always, as it were, on the outside of the transaction, in the character comparatively of an instrument or servant to his own glorious work. Now every such view of redemption we hold to be more or less inadequate and false; and it is of the utmost consequence, we think, that attention should be fully fastened on the point, for the purpose of promoting a more just apprehension of this great mystery in its true nature and power. The mediation of Christ, we say, holds primarily and fundamentally in the constitution of his person. His Incarnation is not to be regarded as a device *in order* to his mediation, the needful preliminary and condition of this merely as an independent and separate work; it is itself the Mediatorial Fact, in all its height and depth, and length and breadth. . . .

It makes all the difference in the world for our theology, whether the Christian salvation be apprehended as a living fact thus starting in the person of Christ, or as an arrangement or economy simply in the divine mind which Christ came into the world to serve in an outward and instrumental way. Every evangelical doctrine becomes different, as seen either from the one of these points of view or from the other. It is not enough that the articles of our faith may carry in any case separately an orthodox sound; all depends on the order in which they are bound together, the principle from which they proceed, their interior genealogy and connection as parts of a common whole. The most orthodox formula may be full

of heresy, if abstracted from the real ground of Christianity, and made to
stand before us as a naked word or thought in some other form. The true
order of the Christian faith is given in the Creed. All rests on the mystery
of the Incarnation. *That* is itself Christianity, the true idea of the gospel,
the new world of grace and truth, in which the discord of sin, the vanity
of nature, the reign of death, are brought forever to an end. Here is an
order of life which was not in the world before, the Word made flesh,
God and man brought into living union in the person of Jesus Christ, as
the nucleus and fountain of salvation for the race. He is the Mediator,
because God and man are thus in a real way joined together and made one
in his person. The primary force of his character in this view, the power
which belongs to him to make reconciliation and atonement, lies in the
fact that the parties between whom he mediates are in truth united first
of all in the very constitution of his own life. He is in this way the actual
medium of their conjunction. The mission of salvation which he came to
fulfill was not indeed at once completed by the mystery of the hypostatical union; his mediatorship involved a history, a work, the execution of
prophetical, priestly, and kingly offices, a life of suffering and trial, the
atonement, the resurrection, the sitting at the right hand of God, from
whence he shall come to judge the world; but all this only as the proper
and necessary result of the first mystery itself, the entrance of the divine
Word in a living way into the sphere of our fallen humanity. This
brought heaven and earth together in the very heart or center of the
world's life, and carried in itself the guaranty that all which was required
to make the union permanent and complete should in due order be triumphantly accomplished. Conceived by the Holy Ghost and born of the
Virgin Mary, Jesus Christ must necessarily suffer also and die, but only
that by doing so he might conquer death, and bring in everlasting righteousness and immortal life for the nature he came to redeem and save.
Forth from this sublime Fact proceeds the presence of the Holy Ghost,
the power of a new creation in the world, the mystery of the Church,
one, holy, and catholic, and the whole process of salvation from the remission of sins in baptism on to the resurrection of the last day. The sense
of Christ's Person, as the true bond that reconciles God and man, brings
along with it all this faith; and no article, we repeat it, deserves to be considered part of the Christian Creed, which comes not to be of force in this
order and on this ground. The early Church stood here on the true foundation. The Creed, as held from the beginning, forms the true and only
legitimate basis of Christian orthodoxy. It needs, in this view, no con-

descending indulgence, no apology, no qualification, no surreptitious foisting of a new and better sense into its ancient phraseology. Any modern system which finds it necessary, however creditable and plausible it may appear in other respects, stands convicted by the very fact of being itself in a false position. No doctrine can be valid and worthy of trust in the world that comes from Christ, which is not inwardly rooted in the Christological mystery of the old Creed. As an *abstraction*, a thing of mere thought and notion, supposed to hold in the relations of God and man out of Christ, and beyond the power of the concrete Fact embodied in his person, all pretended orthodoxy is reduced at last to a mere empty sham. Even as it regards the nature of God or the nature of man separately taken, our faith and science become truly *Christian* only when they are conditioned by a lively apprehension of what has come to pass in Christ. Where sympathy with the Creed is dull, and inward sense for its grandeur gone, there may still be much talk of God's attributes and works in a different view, of election and reprobation, of man's natural depravity, of justification by faith, regeneration, and other such high evangelical themes; but there can be no really sound and vigorous theology at any point. We will not hear, in such case, those who pretend to plant themselves on the authority of the *Bible*, while they are guilty of such palpable falling away from the mind of the Church in the age when the New Testament was formed; for the very point here to be settled is the true sense and meaning of the Bible; and what we maintain is that the early Church is more to be trusted than they are in regard to what constitutes the primary conception of Christianity, which must serve as a rule to guide us in the proper study of the Scriptures. The Bible rests on Christ. Light is not more necessary for seeing the world than the idea of Christ is for reading the true mind of God in his written word. The indwelling Creed, in this view, must underlie our use of the Bible, if it is to be at all just and safe. To say otherwise is to subordinate the Bible to that which is *not* original Christianity, the thinking of this man or that, or the thinking of a sect in no union with the Fact of the Christian faith as it stood in the beginning; and surely when it comes to this, there ought to be no great difficulty, one would think, in deciding which alternative it is the part of wisdom, not to say faith, to choose. However grating it may sound to some ears, the truth needs to be loudly and constantly repeated: the Bible is not the *principle* of Christianity, neither its origin, nor its fountain, nor its foundation. For the opposite imagination is not by any means an innocent or powerless error. It strikes at the essence of Christi-

anity, which is neither doctrine nor law but living grace, and tends to resolve it into a mere abstraction, a theory, that has its being in the world in
men's thoughts mainly, and not in any more substantial form; which, carried out to its legitimate end, is just what we are to understand by rationalism. It is of the utmost account to see, on the contrary, that the principle of Christianity is the Lord Jesus Christ himself, the Word made flesh,
the Christological fact underlying, as in the Creed, the new heavens and
the new earth. With the sense of this old faith in the mind, no difficulty
whatever is found in recognizing it as the true voice also of the Bible. It
springs into view from all sides; and the only wonder is how it should be
possible for any, under the power of the uncatholic theory, *not* to perceive and acknowledge its force. Christ *is* always, in the New Testament,
the sum and substance of his own salvation; the way, the truth, the life;
the divine . . . reconciliation or atonement, in whom God appears
reconciling the world to himself (2 Cor. 5:18, 19), the victory over death
and hell, the true ladder of Jacob's vision, by which the heavens are
brought into perpetual free and open communion with the earth. He is
the Peace of the world, the deepest and last sense of man's life, by which
all its other discords are harmonized, in the deep-toned diapason of its real
union with God.

II. This conception implies that the sense and power of man's life universally considered come to view only in Christ, on which account the
mystery of the Incarnation, as revealed in his person, is no isolated
portent or prodigy, but a fact that holds in strict *organic and historical
continuity and unity with the life of the human world as a whole.* In no
other view can the mystery be regarded as real. Christ is indeed the entrance of a *new* life into the world, the Word clothing itself with flesh;
but he is this, at the same time, in the way of an actual, and not simply
apparent, entrance into the world. He was no theophany, but a real and
proper man, bone of our bone and flesh of our flesh. In this character,
however, he could not be merely a common man, one of the race as it
stood before. Such a supposition would belie the other side of his being.
As the beginning of a new and higher creation, his entrance into the
world must be of universal force, a fact of force for humanity in its collective view. In no other way can the mystery be apprehended as real.
Make Christ either a common man, sharing humanity with Moses, David,
Peter, and Paul, or, in lieu of this, a man wholly on the outside of this
humanity as it belongs to others; and in both cases the conception of his
mediatorial character is gone, lost in Ebionitism on the one side or lost in

fantastic Gnosticism on the other. The person of Christ, as Mediator, is of universal human significance and force. So the Scriptures teach when they call him the *second Adam*, a title plainly implying that he is to be regarded in some way as the root of the race, in a deeper sense even than this can be affirmed of the first Adam. It is accordingly a vast mistake, contradicting alike the letter and the spirit of the gospel, and leading to consequences of enormous mischief, when the Christian salvation is taken to be in its primary purpose and plan for a part of the race only, a certain number of individuals as such, and not for humanity as a whole. It must terminate on individuals, indeed, and this involves an "election of grace"; but like all *Life*, it is universal before it becomes thus particular and single, and the single Christian is saved only by receiving it into himself under this character. To conceive of Christ's redemption as having regard either to all men numerically and outwardly considered, according to the Pelagian theory, or to a given number only in the same outward view, according to at least one kind of Calvinism, involves in the end the same error: this, namely, that Christ did not really assume our human nature at all, in his mediatorial life, but only stood on the outside of it, and wrought a work beyond it, in the semblance of our common manhood, for the benefit of such as are brought individually and separately to avail themselves of his grace. This is to make Christ a mere instrument or means, for the accomplishment of an end which is supposed to have its existence and necessity under a wholly different form — than which it is hard to conceive of anything more derogatory to the true dignity of his person. Gloriously above all this is the form under which he appears in the gospel. He is himself there the salvation of the world, not simply as a true mediation between heaven and earth is reached in his own life separately considered, but as this life also, on its human side, is found to be the comprehension in truth of man's life as a whole, the actual lifting up of our fallen nature from the ruins of the fall, and its full investiture with all the glory and honor for which it was originally formed. Humanity, as a single universal fact, is redeemed in Christ, truly and really, without regard to other men, any farther than as they are made to partake of this redemption by being brought into living union with his person. . . .

Such a collective existence in the case of our race, not the aggregate of its individual lives but the underlying substance in which all these are one, is everywhere assumed in the Bible, as a fact entering into the whole history of religion. The race starts in Adam. It is recapitulated again, or gathered into a new center and head, in Christ. . . .

The universalness of Christ's life does not consist in the assumption of the lives of all men into himself, but in the assumption of that living law or power which, whether in Adam alone or in all his posterity, forms at once the entire fact of humanity, irrespectively of the particular human existences in which it may appear. These are always a finite *All*, the other is a boundless *Whole* — two conceptions which are as wide as the poles apart. Christ, in this view, is organically and historically joined, we say, with the universal life of man as its only true ground, and center, and end. The child, it is sometimes said, is father to the man, inasmuch as the first foreshadows the coming of the second; although, in truth, that which is second here, when we look to inward reality, must be counted first. It is only in full manhood that the tendencies and powers of childhood are made complete at last, through the actualization of their own sense. Analogous with this is the relation of our general human nature to the coming of Christ. It looks to this event from the beginning as the proper completion of its own meaning, and in such view may be regarded as opening the way for it in the order of time; although as regards the order of actual being the mystery of the Incarnation must be considered first as that which lies at the ground of our whole human life in its true form. Christ thus is the deepest sense, the most urgent want of humanity, as it stood previously to his coming, or still stands where his coming is not owned. The universal constitution of the world looks towards him as its necessary center. All the lines of history converge towards him as their necessary end. He is the "desire of all nations," the dream of the Gentile as well as the hope of the Jew. If there be any wholeness in our human life whatever, any rational unity in history, and if the Incarnation be at the same time a real putting on of humanity, a real entrance of the Word into the process of our existence, and not a mere Gnostic vision or Hindu avatar instead, how is it possible to escape the truth of this proposition? Those who seek to cut off Christ from all organic, inwardly historical connection with the world in its natural form, as though his credit must be endangered by his being made to appear a true *birth* of mankind, the veritable *seed* of the woman which should bruise the serpent's head [Gen. 3:15], know not surely what they are about. As an abstraction, in no natural union with the life of man universally considered, how could his pretensions ever be legitimated or made sure?

III. The *Humanity* of Christ is the repository and medium of salvation for the rest of mankind. The truth of this proposition flows inevitably from what has been already said of his mediatorial nature, and its relation to the universal or whole life of the race. Christ has redeemed the world, or the nature of man as fallen in Adam, by so taking it into union with his own higher nature as to deliver it from the curse and power of sin, meeting the usurpation of this false principle with firm resistance from the start, triumphantly repelling its assaults, and in the end leading captivity captive, by carrying his man's nature itself, through the portals of the resurrection, to the right hand of God in glory. The process holds primarily altogether in his own person. In his own person, however, as the Second Adam, the bearer and root of our whole human nature, now lifted thus into actual union with the Godhead, and so made answerable to its true idea, as we find this labored after by its whole creation from the beginning. Thus perfected, he has become the captain and author of salvation for others (Heb. 2:10, 5:9); and through his glorification, the way is open for the Spirit to carry forward the work of Christianity in the hearts and lives of his people (John 7:39). Such is the order of the Creed: manhood glorified first in Christ, then by the Spirit in the Church, which is his Body, the true fullness or completion of his life in the world. The beginning of the new creation, then, the primary and original seat of our actual salvation, is the *human nature* of Christ; for this is the real ground and foundation of the universal conception of humanity in its highest form, the central orb through relation to which only this can ever change its character from darkness to light. True, the power of Christ to save rests in his person as a whole and falls back specially on his Divinity; it is the life of the Word which becomes the light of men. But it is this Life still only as it "comes into the world," and appears clothed in the habiliments of *flesh;* and so we say the flesh of Christ, or the Word which has come in the flesh, and not the Word out of the flesh, is the door or fountain by which the whole grace of the gospel comes to its revelation in the world. Starting in eternity, it finds here the only outlet for its entrance into time. As an accomplished fact upon the earth, in living union with man's life, and not a mere decree or thought in the mind of God, the entire gospel begins in Christ, and proclaims itself as something to be seen, felt, and handled (1 John 1:1–3), in the power of his true Man's nature. Whatever of power there is in Christ for salvation, it is lodged for the use of the world in his *Flesh,* as the necessary medium of communication with the human race, the only bond of his brotherhood and fellowship with those he came to save. To imagine any saving union possible with Christ apart from his flesh, aside from that glorified humanity by which only his mediation stands in real contact with the world, is virtually to deny the mystery of the Incarnation itself, by making it to be of no meaning or force. It is the mark of Antichrist, we are told (1 John 4:1–3), to place the coming of Christ *out of the flesh*.

This idea meets us everywhere in the ancient Church. "The mixture of Christ's bodily substance with ours," says Hooker, "is a thing which the ancient Fathers disclaim. Yet the mixture of his flesh with ours they speak of, to signify what our very bodies, through mystical conjunction, receive from that vital efficacy which we know to be in his; and from bodily mixtures they borrow divers similitudes rather to declare the truth, than the manner of coherence between his sacred [body?] and the sanctified bodies of saints." [5] So with the Church of the Reformation, the sense of the same mystery, as set forth in the Creed, wrought powerfully on all sides. Luther's faith and zeal here are well known. Calvin, in his way, is no less strong. With all his opposition to a crass Capernaitic view of Christ's flesh, he insists continually on the great idea that the Christian salvation starts from the humanity of Christ in a real way, and that we participate in it only by entering really into the new order of life of which this is the fountain and seat. His language on this subject has been pronounced mystical and unmeaning, but it is so only for those who have become estranged in their thinking from the true and proper sense of the mystery with which it is concerned. In itself it is uncommonly lucid and clear, and admirably answerable to the form under which the subject meets us in the gospel. The Word is the source of life; to recover man, this has entered into union with his nature by becoming flesh; *in which form alone,* Christ is now the author of salvation to all who believe in his name. "The very flesh in which he dwells is made to be vivific for us, that we may be nourished by it to immortality. I am the living bread, he says, which came down from heaven; and the bread that I will give is my flesh, which I will give for the life of the world (John 6:48, 51). In these words he teaches, not simply that he is Life, as the Everlasting Word descending to us from heaven, but that in thus descending he has infused this virtue also into the flesh with which he clothed himself, in order that life might flow over to us from it continually." [6] Calvin speaks, of course, not of Christ's flesh materially considered, but of his real human nature, through which only it is possible for this same nature in other men to be raised from death to immortality. The vivification of humanity begins in *his* manhood. His flesh is truly thus *life-giving*, not as the origin of life, but as its necessary

5. [ED.] *Laws of Ecclesiastical Polity*, Book V, LVI, 9, adapted.
6. [ED.] Calvin, *Institutes*, IV.17.8 (McNeill ed., 1369).

and only medium for our fallen race. The manhood of Christ is the reservoir or depositary in which all grace dwells first (the Spirit without measure), for the use of the whole world besides. *"Christi caro instar fontis est divitis et inexhausti, quæ vitam a divinitate in seipsam scaturientem ad nos transfundit."* [7] It would be hard to express the same thought more beautifully, or more clearly, in the same compass. . . .

IV. The participation of Christ's benefits, in the case of his people, turns on a *real communication with his human nature* in the way of life. This is the idea of the "mystical union," which all evangelical Christians are willing to admit, while they are too prone, however, in many cases, to make it of no force by carefully excluding from it the very mystery from which it draws its name. Because it holds only through the Spirit or Holy Ghost, they will have it that it is altogether spiritual, in such sense as to have no relation to Christ's manhood whatever — pleasing themselves, under his name, with the fancy of a life-union with Christ in his divine nature, as though this only might be regarded as the fountain of such high grace in a separate and independent view. But this would imply the very consequence from which they pretend to shrink, without reason, on the other side, an actual partnership of believers with Christ in the awful mystery of the Incarnation itself; for what less is it, if every single Christian be joined in the way of real life directly with the Word absolutely taken, and not with the Word only *through* the flesh which it has already assumed in Christ? There is but one Incarnation (*one* Mediator between God and man, the *Man* Christ Jesus), but he is of such constitution, carrying our universal nature in his person, that all men may be joined with God also through him, by receiving into themselves the power of his life. This implies in their case no hypostatical union with Deity, no new theanthropy in the sense of Christ's person, but just the reverse; since the only medium of union with the Godhead is Christ's manhood, as something that must necessarily intervene between the Divine Word and all other men.

The law of such relation is by no means confined to this case, but finds analogies and exemplifications throughout the universal economy of our life; only we have here the absolute truth of what in all other cases comes before us relatively only and in the way of remote approximation. Men never stand separately, and with fully co-ordinate personality, in the

---

7. [ED.] "The flesh of Christ is like a rich and inexhaustible fountain that pours into us the life springing forth from the Godhead into itself." *Institutes*, IV.17.9 (McNeill ed., 1369).

union of society, but always in organic groups that cluster around some common center, and find support in this as the bond or medium of communion with a life that is higher and more general than their own. Every *hero*, in the broad sense of this word as denoting one who is qualified and called to go before others in the mission of humanity, stands actually between those who follow him and the superior world from which this mission proceeds; he is for them the real organ of its revelation, and through him, at the same time, they gain strength and power to master it as their own, although without such central support this would be wholly impossible. In this case the personality of every follower is completed, like that of the leader himself, by union with the higher life which fills his soul; but this only, let it be observed, not by taking his place as the primary organ of such communication, but by acknowledging rather his central position, and leaning upon him as the necessary medium of the benefit thus gained. Such is the universal law of our life. And what does it teach? Clearly this, that our human personality can never become absolutely complete, till it comes to be joined in a real way at last with the life of God itself, which alone needs no ground beyond itself; and that such conjunction requires (not a general deification of the race as the Hegelians dream), but a Central Person, in whom Divinity may be actually united with humanity, and who may be qualified thus to communicate the fellowship of the "divine nature" mediately to all who trust in his name. This is just the mystery which meets us in Christ. In him alone among men dwelleth the fullness of the Godhead bodily, and we are complete in him, as the head of all principality and power (Col. 2:9, 10). Christ's person is the bearer of our persons. We are complete, as regards intelligence and will, only as we live not by and from ourselves, but through faith in him, as the center and end of our whole existence.

There is no room, then, to object to the idea of the mystical union as now stated, that it implies a continuation of the hypostatical mystery over into the life of the Church. The ancients do indeed speak at times of our being deified in Christ, as sharers of his nature; but they mean not by this, of course, any deification aside from Christ himself. Through the medium of his humanity, it is the privilege of believers, without losing their own separate individuality, to fall in on the fullness of his person as the true central ground of their own lives, and thus to participate in the grace of which he alone is the repository and fountain, and which is accessible to others only as they are joined to him in this way. . . .

v. As the medium of such living grace the *human nature* of Christ, and not simply his Divinity, is actively *present* always in the world. The mediation of the Saviour, since his Ascension, holds towards God in his Intercession, while towards man it may be summed up in the single term of his *presence*. This was his great promise, on going away: "I will not leave you comfortless, I will come to you" [Jn. 14:18]. The promise plainly regards the restoration of what was about to be lost, the presence of our Lord, namely, according to his human nature, only under a new and higher form. In this view, it is a spiritual and not a carnal presence, a presence accomplished not in the way of place and material contact, but by the intervention of the Holy Ghost, while, however, as regards efficiency and force, it is not for this reason less real, but rather we may say more real, than it could be in any other way. . . .

The Mediation of Christ, then, is not something past and gone, nor yet something that lies wholly beyond the actual order of the world, with which we are to communicate only in the way of memory or thought; it lives always, with perennial force, in the actual presence of Christ's manhood in the world. This thought reigns throughout the Epistle to the Hebrews. His *one* sacrifice is once for all, not as a transient event, but as an ever-during fact in the power of his indissoluble mediatorial life. His intercession is going forward *now* in real union with the daily course of the world, as truly as the sun enters into the same economy from day to day. . . . To separate the action of Christ in the world now from his man's nature, and to refer it only to his Divinity, is just to say that he no longer acts as a man at all, in other words *is* no longer really man, as in the days of humiliation. . . . The Incarnation cannot be held as real, if the being and working of the Mediator in the world be not apprehended as the presence in it still of the living power of his true Human Life. This should be plain to all.

vi. Christ's presence in the world is in and by his Mystical Body, the *Church*. As a real human presence, carrying in itself the power of a new life for the race in general, it is no abstraction or object of thought merely, but a glorious living Reality, continuously at work, in an organic and historical way, in the world's constitution. Christ communicates himself to his people, and lives in them, not by isolated favor in each case, but collectively. His relation is at once to the whole family of the redeemed, and single Christians accordingly have part in him only as they are comprehended at the same time in this whole. To be in Christ, is to be a member also necessarily of his Mystical Body, as dependence on a natural center implies comprehension in the universal orb or sphere holding in the same relation. This is the idea of the Church. It comes from within and not from without. It grows out of the mystery of the Incarnation, apprehended as an abiding fact, and comes before us in the Creed accordingly, not as a notion or speculation merely, but as an article of *faith*. So too it has its attributes from itself and not from abroad. It is by an *a priori* necessity [that] it claims to be one, holy, and catholic. To deny or question this necessity is at once a heresy, which strikes in the end at the very foundation of Christianity itself. "That the Church is one body results from organization, not from enactment," much less from human policy and agreement. "Neither is the profession of the Church's unity the mere admission of an external appearance, but the belief of an inward verity"; [8] facts may or may not accord with it at any given time, but it still remains unalterably certain in its own nature, until Christianity itself be found to be false. Christ's *one* mediation, as related to men and reaching them through his glorified humanity, always present for this purpose in the world by the Spirit, is carried forward through the intervention of the Church, his Body Mystical, the fullness of what he is otherwise by distinction only in its single members. The Church, in this view, does indeed stand between Christ and the believer, but only as the body of a living man is between one of his limbs and the living soul by which it is quickened and moved.

VII. The idea of the Church, as thus standing between Christ and single Christians, implies of necessity visible *organization*, common *worship*, a regular public *ministry* and *ritual*, and to crown all, especially, grace-bearing *sacraments*. To question this is to give up to the same extent the sense of Christ's Mediation as a perennial fact, now and always taking effect upon the economy of the world through the Church as his Mystical Body. Let it be felt that the Incarnation is a mystery not simply past, and not simply beyond the world, but at this time in full force for the world, carrying in itself the whole value of Christ's sacrifice and resurrection as an undying *"once for all"* — the true conception of the Mediatorial Supremacy, as the real headship of Christ's manhood over all in behalf of the Church and for its salvation; let it be felt, at the same time, that this mystery touches men in and by the Church, which itself is made to challenge their faith for this reason as something supernatural and divine; and it becomes at once impossible to resist the feeling, that the "powers of the world to come" [Heb. 6:5] are actually at hand in its

8. [ED.] R. I. Wilberforce, *Doctrine of the Incarnation*, 247.

functions and services, with the same objective reality that attaches to the powers of nature under their own form and in their own place. To see no more in the ministry and offices of the Church, in this view, than a power of mere outward declaration and testimony, such as we might have in any secular school, betrays a rationalistic habit of mind, which only needs to be set free from the indolence of uninquiring tradition, that it may be led to deny altogether that Christ has ever or at all come in the flesh.

It sounds well, and falls in well, too, with *natural* reason and popular sense, to magnify what is called spiritual religion as compared with a religion of outward ordinances and forms, and to make Christianity turn on individual exercises transacted directly with God, in the sanctuary of the mind, aside from all regard to sacramental or other intervening media. But it ought to be borne in mind that Christianity is not mere nature, and that to throw ourselves here on simply natural conceptions and impulses is in truth to substitute for it another theory of religion altogether. It comes to us as a system of redemption and salvation by a Mediator. It is throughout a mediatorial economy. The grace it reveals is offered in Christ, not from a different quarter. It is offered in Christ again as man, by the intervention of his flesh, through the door of his humanity, in the most real and true way. Under this form it is not something to be thought of merely, with however much devotion, on the part of the believer; the case calls for an actual participation in its life and power. Christianity is so constituted, accordingly, as to be dependent always on means, which have for their object this union and communion in a real way. Salvation in these circumstances is still a personal and inward or spiritual interest; *mere* relations and forms save no man; but it is made to hang on the medium of a special economy in the Church as the Mystical Body of Christ, serving to bind the subject in living union with his natural flesh or humanity, which is embraced and rested upon by faith accordingly for this purpose. Not to acknowledge this, but to insist on having access to God independently of any such special economy, by virtue simply of the relation in which all souls stand to him as the "Father of the spirits of all flesh," is not Christianity but rationalism under the Christian name. . . .

There is no opposition between Christ and the Church, or between individual piety on the one hand and sacramental grace on the other, but just the reverse. Christ becomes full only in and by the Church, and personal experience is made solid and real only as it rests on grace offered and appropriated from abroad. . . .

With this view of the significance of Christian worship generally, the peculiar sense and power of the holy sacraments are apprehended as a necessary consequence, the rejection of which must do violence to the whole Creed. They are "not only badges of profession" but also "certain sure witnesses and effectual signs of grace" [Thirty-nine Articles, xxv]. They exhibit objectively the realities they represent. So we have it asserted very distinctly in the New Testament. Such was the faith, from the beginning, of the universal ancient Church. Such also is the original Protestant faith, as held by the two great confessions, Lutheran and Reformed, on the Continent, as well as by the Episcopal Church in England. . . .

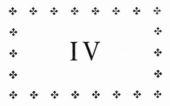

JOHN WILLIAMSON NEVIN

Antichrist and the Sect

Editor's introduction.

Most glorious and blessed God, who through the Holy Ghost, hast made thy one Catholic Church to be the Body of Christ, the fullness of him that filleth all in all; we humbly beseech thee to grant unto us, and to all thy people, such strong and steadfast faith in this great mystery of grace, that being safely defended from all heresy and schism, we may ever abide in the unity of the Spirit, and so grow up into him in all things which is the Head, even Christ: to whom, with thee and the Holy Ghost, ever one God, be all honor and praise, world without end. Amen.[1]

The Mercersburg views of the Incarnation and the New Humanity may be defined more sharply by contrast with their opposition. The movement was not, like its transatlantic counterparts, a reaction to the intervention of the civil power. It was, rather, the polemical response to what its adherents saw as the chaos of arbitrary subjectivism in American church life. As evangelical catholics, the Mercersburg men deplored sectarianism and schism above all.

Before leaving Germany Schaff had identified sectarianism, heathenism, and Roman error as the evils he was to combat in America. In *The Principle of Protestantism* he made a detailed analysis of sectarianism as the characteristic defect of Anglo-American Protestantism. Nevin, during the *Anxious Bench* controversy of 1843–44, had identified as the chief danger the manipulative revivalism of the "new measures," which assumed or promoted Arminian views of grace. But after his churchly conversion he shifted his guns to those movements which lacked respect for the institutions, the sacraments, and the Creed of the historic Church as

1. Collect for Whitmonday, *Order of Worship for the Reformed Church* (Philadelphia, 1866), 110.

the appointed medium of salvation. Some differences remained between Schaff's state-church presuppositions and Nevin's Presbyterian jealousy for the "Crown Rights of the Redeemer."

Just as the Church was best understood in relation to Christology, so the sect, in Nevin's thought, was characteristically associated with Christological heresy, docetic or Ebionite. The closing passage of *The Church* (see above, 75f.) argued, in an exposition of 1 John 4:1–3, that the denial of a divine historical Church was by implication a denial of the Incarnation and thus the badge of Antichrist. A sermon by Nevin on this theme was expanded to a tract, published in 1848 as *Antichrist, or the Spirit of Sect and Schism.* The Antichrist thus was metamorphosed from the papacy of "Catholic Unity" to the evil sectarian genius attendant upon Protestantism.

Nevin specified many symptoms of the sectarian spirit. He asserted in *The Mystical Presence* that the sect tended to a low doctrine of the Eucharist and to a rejection of infant baptism and baptismal grace. Similarly, he noted, the sect lacked respect for historical tradition and specifically for the historic Creed. The sect found uncongenial the theological context of the Creed, and what it did with doctrines out of this context — for example, with justification by faith and the authority of Scripture — caricatured their original meaning.

More than once Nevin attempted a rather elaborate characterization of the sectarian mind and tendency. The analysis in *Antichrist* is somewhat abstract. A more concrete discussion was occasioned by the appearance in 1848 of John Winebrenner's *History of All the Religious Denominations in the United States: containing authentic accounts of the rise, progress, faith and practise, localities and statistics, of the different persuasions: written expressly for the work, by fifty-three eminent authors belonging to the respective denominations.* Nevin was so impressed by this "Catlin's Indian Museum" of American sects that he devoted two articles to it. Entitled "The Sect System," they appeared in *The Mercersburg Review* in 1849. Over half of their text is reprinted below.

Winebrenner was a camp-meeting revivalist who had taken a following out of the German Reformed Church to set up his own "Church of God." For Nevin this body, and Jacob Albright's "Evangelical Association," were archetypical sects. Nevin had, in fact, already had an exchange of letters with Winebrenner,[2] which began with the latter's pro-

2. Published in *The Gospel Messenger*, October-December 1843.

test against Nevin's presentation of revivalist "new measures" in *The Anxious Bench.*

To be sure, the Mercersburg men were not primarily opposed to particular sects. What they deplored was the "sect mind," or sect feeling, which might be found in churchly denominations as well as in schismatic bodies. Not every confession or denomination was necessarily sectarian, although some bodies were sectarian and schismatic by constitution. And the denominational system itself, as soon as it was acquiesced in as satisfactory, approximated to sectarianism. Not to feel the ecumenical passion was thus a symptom of the sect mind. "Our sects, as such, do not love each other, and are not inwardly bound together." And the sect consciousness was in most of these denominations deeper than the Church consciousness.

In "Catholic Unity" Nevin had offered some criticism of proposed methods of achieving Church unity, as had Schaff in *What is Church History?* "The Remedy," the last section of *The Antichrist,* which is reprinted below, defines three bootless types of ecumenical strategy. First is the "restorationist" program, as proposed, e.g., by Alexander Campbell, of scrapping all existing structures in order to begin again with the New Testament. A second, the "liberal" proposal to relinquish all distinctive peculiarities to form a lowest-common-denominator Christianity, was more fully discussed by Nevin in an article entitled "Bible Christianity." [3] The third program, federation, was exemplified by Samuel Schmucker's proposed consensus creed, and later by the Evangelical Alliance.

❖ ❖ ❖ ❖

The Sect System

I

. . . This professed regard for the Bible . . . distinguishes the sects in general; and just here is one important lesson offered for contemplation by the pages of this work. The Adventists or Millerites (p. 41) own "no other creed or form of discipline than the written word of God, which they believe is a sufficient rule both of faith and duty." The Baptists (p. 49) "adhere rigidly to the New Testament as the sole standard of Christianity," and take the Holy Scripture for "the only sufficient, certain, and

3. *The Mercersburg Review,* II (1850), 353–67.

infallible rule of saving knowledge, faith, and obedience, the supreme
judge by which all controversies of religion are to be determined, &c." So
the Freewill Baptists (p. 78); the Free Communion Baptists (p. 85); the
Old School Baptists (p. 87), who oppose "modern missionism and its
kindred institutions" as unscriptural; the Six Principle Baptists (p. 90);
the German Baptists (p. 92); the Seventh Day Baptists, "who have no
authentic records by which they can ascertain their origin other than the
New Testament" (p. 95), and who tell us that the church can never contend successfully "with Catholicism, even in our own country," till the
lesson is fairly learned that the "Bible *alone* is the religion of Protestants"
(p. 103); the German Seventh Day Baptists, who (p. 110) "do not admit
the least license with the letter and spirit of the Scriptures, and especially
of the New Testament — do not allow one jot or tittle to be added or rejected in the administration of the ordinances, but practice them precisely
as they are instituted and made an example by Jesus Christ in his word."
The sect of the Bible Christians, as their name imports, "believe it to be
the duty of every one, in matters of faith (p. 124), to turn from the
erring notions, and false [?] traditions that are to be found in most of the
denominations of professing Christians, and to draw their principles directly from the Bible." The "Christians," constituted about the beginning
of this century by the confluence of three different streams of independ-
ency, reject all party names to follow Christ, take the Bible for their
guide (p. 166) and carry the principle of shaping their faith by it so far
that a doctrine which cannot be expressed "in the language of inspiration
they do not hold themselves obligated to believe"; and a strange *system*, it
must be allowed, they make of it in their way. The "Church of God," as
called into being by Mr. Winebrenner (p. 176), "has no authoritative
constitution, ritual, creed, catechism, book of discipline, or church standard, but the Bible" — with a short manifesto or declaration simply,
showing what the Bible, according to Mr. Winebrenner's mind, must be
taken clearly to mean. The Congregationalists, of course, appeal to the
Scriptures (p. 281) "as their only guide in all matters both of faith and
polity," though they do but speak in the name of all the sects when they
say, somewhat curiously in such company, speaking of creeds and confessions: "By the Bible they are to be measured, and no doctrine which cannot be found in it is to be received, however endeared to us by its associa-
tions, or venerable by its antiquity. This strict adherence to the Scriptures, as the only rule of faith and practice, must necessarily prevent
many of those erroneous opinions, and that credulous reliance upon tradi-

tion, which are too apt to characterize those who follow the Bible only at second hand." In the enterprise of Alexander Campbell to reconstruct the Church, an. 1810, which has given rise to the Disciples of Christ (or Campbellite Baptists), it was laid down as a fundamental maxim (p. 224) "that the revelations of God should be made to displace from their position all human creeds, confessions of faith, and formalities of doctrine and church government, as being not only unnecessary, but really a means of perpetuating division." The Albright Sect, an. 1803, "unanimously chose the sacred Scriptures for their guide in faith and action (p. 275), and formed their church discipline accordingly, as any one may see who will take the pains to investigate and examine the same." So in other cases. However they may differ among themselves in regard to what it teaches, sects all agree in proclaiming the Bible the only guide of their faith; and the more sectarian they are, as general thing, the more loud and strong do they show themselves in reiterating this profession.

All this is instructive. It sounds well to lay so much stress on the authority of the Bible as the only text-book and guide of Christianity. But what are we to think of it when we find such a motley mass of protesting systems, all laying claim so vigorously here to one and the same watchword? If the Bible be at once so clear and full as a formulary of Christian doctrine and practice, how does it come to pass that where men are left most free to use it in this way, and have the greatest mind to do so, according to their own profession, they are flung asunder so perpetually in their religious faith, instead of being brought together, by its influence apparently, and, at all events, certainly in its name? It will not do to reply, in the case, that the differences which divide the parties are small, while the things in which they agree are great, and such as to show a general unity after all in the main substance of the Christian life. Differences that lead to the breaking of church communion, and that bind men's consciences to go into sects, can never be small for the actual life of Christianity, however insignificant they may be in their own nature. Will it be pretended that the Bible is friendly to sects, that it is designed and adapted to bring them to pass, that they constitute, in short, the normal and healthy condition of Christ's Church? It is especially worthy of notice that one great object proposed by all sects, in betaking themselves, as they say, to the exclusive authority of the Scriptures, is to get clear of human dogmas and opinions, and so come the more certainly to one faith and one baptism. They acknowledge the obligation of such unity, and just for this reason call upon the Christian world to come with them to

the pure fountain of God's word, as having no doubt that it is to be secured in this way. Winebrennerism, Campbellism, Christianism, &c., are
all based (we doubt not, honestly) on a design to "restore the original
unity of the Church" and for the accomplishment of this object they hold
it most of all necessary "that the Bible alone should be taken as the authorized bond of union and the infallible rule of faith and practice," to
the full exclusion of every creed or formulary besides. This, however, as
we have seen, is just what all our sects are eternally admitting and proclaiming as their own principle. There is not one of them that is not disposed to take the lead, according to its own fancy, in such wholesome
submission to the Holy Scriptures, and the great quarrel of each with all
the rest is just this, that they are not willing like itself to sacrifice to this
rule all rules and tradition besides. How does it happen, then, that the sect
distraction has not been prevented or healed by this method, but is found
to extend itself perpetually in proportion to its free and untrammelled
use? When Congregationalism tells us (p. 201) that its principle of strict
adhesion to the Bible, in the sense now noticed, serves to shut out divisions, it tells us what is palpably contradicted by the whole history of the
sect system from beginning to end. However plausible it may be in
theory to magnify in such style the unbound use solely of the Bible for
the adjustment of Christian faith and practice, the simple truth is that the
operation of it in fact is, not to unite the church into one, but to divide it
always more and more into sects. The thing is too plain to admit any sort
of dispute. The work before us is a commentary in proof of it throughout. Clearly, then, the principle in question requires some qualification.
No one can intelligently study this book of sects without finding occasion
in it to distrust the soundness in full of a maxim, which all sects proclaim
with equal apparent sincerity, as lying at the foundation of their theology, and which is so plainly at the same time the main prop and pillar of
their conflicting systems. We must either admit a limitation in some form
to the principle, *No creed but the Bible,* or else make up our minds at
once to the hard requirement of accepting this array of sects as the true
and legitimate form of the Christian life, equally entitled to respect and
confidence in all its parts.

The full misery of the case becomes more evident when we connect
with it the idea of *private judgment,* in the full sense, as the necessary
accompaniment and complement of the exclusive authority thus attributed to the Scriptures. This, we may say, is always involved in the
maxim under its usual sectarian form, since the admission of any controlling influence whatever from beyond the individual mind must serve of

itself materially to qualify the maxim, changing it indeed into quite a new sense. It is easy enough to see, accordingly, throughout this book, that the supreme authority of the Bible, as it is made to underlie professedly the religion of all sects, is tacitly if not openly conditioned always by the assumption that every man is authorized and bound to get at this authority in a direct way for himself, through the medium simply of his own single mind. We have a somewhat rampant enunciation of the whole maxim (p. 512) in behalf of the Cumberland Presbyterians, in which, no doubt, however, the sects generally would without any hesitation concur. "The supremacy of the Holy Scriptures," it is there said, "and the right of private judgment, have long been the great governing principle of all evangelical Christians. These abandoned, and there is no excess, extravagance, or superstition, too monstrous for adoption. The Bible must be the supreme rule of faith and practice, or else it will be converted into fables and genealogies, unless we grant to the many the privilege of thinking for themselves, we must grant to the few, or one, the power of infallibility." An open Bible and private judgment, the only help against excess, extravagance, and superstition, in the name of religion! So say the Cumberland Presbyterians. So say the Baptists, through all the tribes of all their variegated Israel, from Maine to California. So the followers of Winebrenner, the Albright Brethren, and, in one word, every wild sect in the land. And why then are they not joined together as one? Why is Winebrenner's "Church of God" a different communion from Campbell's "Disciples of Christ," and why are not both merged in the broad fellowship of the "Christians," as the proper ocean or universe of one and the same Bible faith? Theory and fact here do not move by any means in the same line. The theory, however, still requires in these circumstances that the fact, such as it is, should be acknowledged to be right and good. Private judgment in religion is a sacred thing, which we are not at liberty to limit or restrain in any direction, but are bound to honor as the great palladium of piety, in every shape it may happen to assume. The Congregationalist, then, has no right to quarrel with the results to which it conducts the honest Baptist, and the honest Baptist again has just as little right to find fault with the use made of it by the Albright Brethren, or the African sect of the Bethelites. This principle of private judgment, the hobby of all sects, places all plainly on the same level, and unless men choose to play fast and loose with their own word, opens the door indefinitely for the lawful introduction of as many more as religious ingenuity or stupidity may have power to invent.

The principle, in truth, is absurd and impracticable, and such as always necessarily overthrows itself. We find, accordingly, that the glorification of it in the sect world is very soon resolved into mere smoke. Just here we encounter first, on a broad scale, the spirit of hypocrisy and sham which enters so extensively into the whole constitution of sectarian Christianity. Every sect is ready to magnify the freedom of the individual judgment and the right of all men to read and interpret the Bible for themselves, and yet there is not one among them that allows in reality anything of the sort. It is amusing to glance through the pages of this autobiography of religious denominations, and notice the easy simplicity with which so many of them lay down the broad maxim of liberty and toleration to start with, and then at once go on to limit and circumscribe it by the rule of their own narrow horizon — proving themselves generally to be at once unfree and illiberal, in proportion precisely to the noise they make about their freedom. The "Church of God," according to her V.D.M.[4] at Harrisburg, has no constitution, ritual, creed, catechism, book of discipline, or church standard, but the Bible. This she believes to be the only creed or text-book which God ever intended her to have. "*Nevertheless*, it may not be inexpedient," we are told (p. 176), "*pro bono publico*, to exhibit a short manifesto, or declaration, showing her views, as to what may be called leading matters of faith, experience and practice"; and so we have a regular confession of twenty-seven articles (pp. 176–181), all ostensibly supported by proof from the Bible as understood by Mr. Winebrenner, fencing in thus her "Scriptural and Apostolical" communion, and of course fencing out all who, in the exercise of their private judgment, may be so unfortunate as not to see things in precisely the same way. This is only a specimen of the inconsistency and contradiction which characterize sects in general. Their common watchword is: the Bible and private judgment! But in no case do they show themselves true to its demands. It is always, on their lips, an outrageous lie, of which all good men should feel themselves ashamed. What sect in reality allows the Bible and private judgment to rule its faith? Is it not notorious that every one of them has a scheme of notions already at hand, a certain system of opinion and practice, which is made to underlie all this boasted freedom in the use of the Bible, leading private judgment along by the nose, and forcing the divine text always to speak in its own way? It is of no account, as to the point here in hand, that sects agree to tolerate one another politically; the want of religious toleration is enough

4. [ED.] Winebrenner's self-description, by interpretation, "Minister of the Word of God."

of itself to falsify their pretended maxim of following simply the Bible and private judgment. It shows plainly that this maxim is *not*, at least, the measure of their religious life, but that some other rule is required to keep it to its particular form and shape.

But there is a vast chasm also in the political or outward toleration itself, as it may be called, to which the sect system affects in general to be so favorable. It is full of zeal, apparently, for human freedom in every shape, the rights of man, liberty of conscience, and the privilege of every man to worship God in his own way. The Independents claim the merit of opening, in regard to all these great interests, a new era in the history of the human race; but they had no toleration originally for the Quakers and Baptists; and both these bodies, accordingly, carry away the palm from them on this ground, as having by their patient testimony done far more signal service to the cause of religious freedom. Roger Williams is taken by his sect to be the father emphatically of our American independence (p. 57); and it is of the first Baptists in particular, we are told, that these words of Hume in favor of the Puritans stand good: "By these alone the precious spark of liberty was kindled, and to these America owes the whole freedom of her constitution." But, alas, the regular Baptists themselves have been found continually prone to assert, in one shape or another, the old tyranny over conscience, on which account it has been necessary for one new sect after the other to take a fresh start in the race of independence, so that one is left quite at a loss in the end to know to which of all the number the modern world should consider itself most deeply indebted for its full democratic emancipation in the affairs of religion. In Rhode Island itself, under the free charter of Roger Williams, the Seventh Day Baptists (p. 97) had to endure much for the right of differing from their more orthodox neighbors: "A hostile spirit was soon raised against the little band and laws were enacted severe and criminal in their nature; John Rogers, a member of the church, was sentenced to sit a certain time upon a gallows with a rope about his neck, to which he submitted." So the German Seventh Day sect in Pennsylvania protests loudly against all legislation that would force it in any way to keep a different Sabbath than its own, and claims the honor of standing with this question in the very Thermopylae of American freedom. "The great principle, we are told (p. 122), for which the Seventh Day People are contending — *unfettered religious liberty* — is alike dear to all the churches of the land; it belongs equally to all denominations, however large or however small." The "Christians" sprang from the same idea of independence.

One portion of them styled themselves at first characteristically "Republican Methodists" (p. 165); another grew out of "a peculiar travel [*sic*] of mind in relation to sectarian names and human creeds," on the part of one Dr. Abner Jones, a Baptist of Vermont; a third broke away from the Presbyterian Synod of Kentucky, at the time of the great revival, to escape "the scourge of a human creed." As a general thing, sects are loud for liberty, in the more outward sense, and seem to be raised up in their own imagination for the express purpose of asserting in some new way what they call liberty of conscience. But all history shows that they are bold for this liberty only in their own favor, and not at all in favor of others. It is not enough in their case that they acquiesce in the independence of other sects as already established; their maxim of private judgment, if they were honest, should lead them to throw no obstruction whatever in the way of new sects starting out of their bosom. Even if they might not feel bound to retain such divergent tendencies in their communion, they ought, at least, to recognize the perfect right they have to make their appearance, as legitimately flowing from the proper life of Christianity, and instead of laying a straw in their way, should assist them rather to develop their force, and stand out as new phases of religion in the general sect system to which they belong. Nothing short of this deserves to be considered true toleration, on the ground professedly occupied by private-judgment sects. Where, however, do we meet with any such sect, whose practice is governed by any such rule?

The truth is, as any one may see who has any familiarity at all with the character and history of sects, that no more unpropitious atmosphere for liberty and independence can well be conceived than that which they everywhere tend to create. Those precisely which make the greatest boast of their liberty are, as a general thing, the least prepared either to exercise it themselves or to allow its exercise in others. The sect habit, as such, is constitutionally unfree. All true emancipation in religion begins only where the power of this habit has begun to be broken, and the sense of a true catholic Christianity is brought to reign in its place. Each sect has its tradition, in most cases a very poor and narrow tradition, the fruit of accident or caprice in the history of its founder, conditioned more or less by the outward relations in which he was called to his apostolic mission — a certain scheme of notions and words, passing over always more and more to the character of dead mechanical gibberish and cant, to whose authority all are required to swear, within its communion, and whose little circle or ring none may transgress without losing caste. Take, for instance, the small community of the Albright Brethren. Is it not just as much bound, in this respect, full as servile and full as intolerant, to say the least, as the Church of Rome? Is it not, in its way and measure, a papacy, a would-be ecclesiastical domination, which seeks as far as possible to nullify and kill all independent thought and all free life? It is full indeed of professed zeal for Protestant liberty, free inquiry, an open Bible, universal toleration, the right of all men to think for themselves, and all such high-sounding phrases; but we must be simple enough if we can be led for a moment to take such professions for anything *more* than so much sound. The liberty of the sect consists at last in thinking its particular notions, shouting its shibboleths and passwords, dancing its religious hornpipes, and reading the Bible only through its theological goggles. These restrictions, at the same time, are so many wires that lead back at last into the hands of a few leading spirits, enabling them to wield a true hierarchical despotism over all who are thus brought within their power. All tends to crush thought, and turn the solemn business of religion into a sham. True spiritual independence must ever be an object of jealousy in such a communion, as much so fully as in any popish convent. Let a generous-minded man begin really to think for himself, by rising above the life of the mere sect, and it matters not how much he may have of the Spirit of Christ, or how truly he may reverence God's Word, he will fall into suspicion and condemnation; and if true to himself, must find it necessary in the end to quit the association altogether, the victim of reproach and persecution, for those very rights of conscience whose special guardianship the little brotherhood has been affecting to take almost exclusively into its own hands. This is only an instance, to exemplify a general fact. All sects, in proportion as they deserve the name, are narrow, bigoted, and intolerant. They know not what liberty means. They put out men's eyes, gag their mouths, and manacle their hands and feet. They are intrinsically, constitutionally, incurably popish, enslaved by tradition and prone to persecution. The worst of all schools for the formation of a true manly character is the communion of such a sect. The influence of sects is always illiberal, and it should be counted in this view a great moral calamity in the case of all young persons, especially, to be thrown upon it in any way for educational training.

The book before us illustrates instructively the *unhistorical* character of the sect system. The independence which it affects, in pretending to reduce all Christianity to private judgment and the Bible, involves of necessity a protest against the authority of all previous history, except so far as it may seem to agree with what is thus found to be true; in which case, of course, the only real measure of truth is taken to be, not this authority of history at all, but the mind, simply, of the particular sect itself. The idea of anything like a divine substance in the life of Christianity through past ages, which may be expected of right to pass forward into the constitution of Christianity as it now stands, is one that finds no room whatever in this system. A genuine sect will not suffer itself to be embarrassed for a moment, either at its start or afterwards, by the consideration that it has no proper root in past history. Its ambition is rather to appear in this respect *autochthonic,* aboriginal, self-sprung from the Bible, or through the Bible from the skies. "A Six Principle Baptist," we are told (p. 88), "who understands the true principles of his profession, does not esteem it necessary to have his tenets through the several ages of the Church. He is fully persuaded, however early or generally other opinions may have prevailed, that those principles which distinguish him from other professions of Christianity are clearly taught and enjoined by the great Head of the Church, in the grand commission to his Apostles." This language suits all sects. If the past be with them, here and there, it is all very well; but if not, it can only be, of course, because they are right, and the universal past wrong; for they follow (multifariously) the Bible, which is the only infallible rule of faith and practice. The Baptists glory in having no succession before the Reformation, except by occasional gleams and flashes athwart the darkness of the Middle Ages, here and there, in out-of-the-way crevices and corners, produced by sects and fragments of sects of whom almost nothing is known, and concerning whom, accordingly, all things may be the more easily *guessed.* But what of that? Every congregation has power to originate a new Christianity for its own use, and so may well afford to let that of all other ages pass for a grand apostasy, if need be, to keep itself in countenance. In the same spirit, one Baptist sect is continually rising after another, and setting in motion a new church, without the least regard to the "want of fellowship" proclaimed against it by the body it leaves behind. "It makes no difference to me who disowns me," cries Mr. Randall, in the face of such an exclusion (p. 75), "so long as I know that the Lord owns me; and now let that God be God who answers by fire, and that people be God's people, whom he owneth and blesseth." This, in his own words, "is the beginning of the now large and extensive connection called *Freewill Baptists.*" Hear another tribe: "Every denomination (p. 95) is proud of tracing its origin back to its founder. But not so with the Seventh Day Baptists. They have

no authentic records by which they can ascertain their origin, other than
the New Testament." Hear again the "Christians," self-started in Kentucky, A.D. 1803: "As they had taken the Scriptures for their guide, pedo-
baptism was renounced, and believers' baptism by immersion substituted
in its room. On a certain occasion, one minister baptized another minister,
and then he who had been baptized, immersed the others." So Roger Williams himself (p. 57), the father of American Anabaptism, "in March
1639 was baptized by one of his brethren and then he baptized about ten
more." Jacob Albright, of course, had quite as much right to originate a
new ministry (p. 275) in the same way — which, however, is very much
like a man pretending to lift himself up from the ground by his own
breeches or boot-straps. So throughout. The idea of a historical continuity in the life of the Church carries with it no weight whatever for the
sect consciousness. It is felt to be as easy to start a new church as it is to
get up a new moral or political association under any other name.

This turns, of course, at bottom, on a want of all true and steady faith
in the Church itself as such. . . .

II

Our sect system is exceedingly *irrational*. We can conceive of divisions
in the Church that might be in a certain sense rational and necessary, and
so capable of some scientific representation. The original distinction of
Protestantism from Catholicism, and the resolution of the first again into
the two great confessions, Lutheran and Reformed, have this character.
They have their ground in the Idea of Christianity itself; they form necessary *momenta*, or moving forces, in the process by which this Idea is
carried forward to its final completion; they can be studied accordingly,
and understood in the way, for instance, of comparative symbolism. But
nothing of this sort can be affirmed of our reigning modern sects. No Idea
underlies them by which they can be said to have a right to exist. Their
appearance is in defiance and scorn of all such objective reason. It is their
boast to be sprung for the most part of mere private judgment and private will. They start generally, by their own confession, in the most outward and accidental occasions. A Jacob Albright is awakened, and finding
no congenial religious connections immediately at hand, makes his subjectivity the basis of a new sect, which in due time swells into an evangelical church. A John Winebrenner takes it into his head that everybody
is wrong but himself, and being put out of the old church, complacently
offers himself to the world as the nucleus of a new one that may be ex-

pected to work better. Elder Randall is pushed aside by the Regular Baptists, and forthwith originates the Freewill Baptists. Mr. Cowherd (p. 124) is led to inculcate the doctrine of abstinence from the flesh of animals, as well as total abstinence from all intoxicating liquors, "on the testimony of the Bible," and has many other private fancies besides on the same testimony; and so we get the Bible Christian Church, still happily in the wilderness and out of sight. Dr. Abner Jones, of Vermont, has "a peculiar travel [sic] of mind in relation to sectarian names and human creeds," and to rectify the evil sets in motion a sect of his own, which falls in afterwards with two other equally providential accidents, and helps in this way to form the body calling themselves "Christians." And so it goes, to the end of the chapter. Can anything well be more accidental and capricious than the rise of sects in this way? Who does not see that we might as reasonably have five hundred in such form as fifty or sixty? Have there not been hundreds of men who had just as much vocation in their circumstances as Albright or Winebrenner to found new churches, that might have had just as much character and meaning, too, as theirs, or possibly a good deal more? It is the easiest thing in the world to moot new questions in religion, scores of them, that might just as fully justify division as half of those that have already led to it, provided only the proper zeal were got up in some quarter to push them out to such extreme, "for conscience' sake," and to put honor on the Bible. Will any pretend to reduce such a system to any sort of intelligible method or scheme? It has none. It is supremely irrational, so far as all inward reason goes, by its very constitution. We might as well pretend to systematize and genealogize the clouds, driven hither and thither by all conflicting winds. It is a chaos that excludes all science. Who will dream here of a sect symbolism, generically unfolding the inward sense of each upstart body, as related to all the rest and to the whole system, its historical necessity, its complemental contribution to the full idea of Protestantism? Who will find it needful for the right understanding of theology to pursue the history of its doctrines through the mazes of our present sectarianism, as held, for instance, by the United Brethren, the Cumberland Presbyterians, and all manner of Baptists, in the same way that all true theology does require undoubtedly such a prosecution of doctrines through the life of the ancient Greek Church, the life of the Roman Church, and that of the original Protestant Church under both its grand confessional distinctions? Take one wing only of the system, the Scotch Secession, which has been accustomed from the first to make the greatest account of its own theological significance, in this way; and what, after all, we ask soberly, is the value of all its witnessings put together, in this country, for the cause of universal Christianity, whether in theory or practice? Is there any inward reason in its divisions and subdivisions, its abortive unions and consequent new sections, till the whole has become a tangled web in the end which it is a perfect weariness of the flesh to pretend to unravel? Altogether we have some ten or twelve bodies in this country (possibly more) conscience-split for the glory of God, who stand united-ly, while severally excluding one another, not only on the Bible, the sure foundation of all sects, but on the Presbyterian sense of the Bible also as embodied in the Westminster Confession. *Can* there be any meaning or reason in such a phenomenon? Has historical theology any real interest whatever in the questions that lie between Old Covenanters, New Coven-anters, Associate Seceders, Associate Reformed Seceders, and Reformed Associate Reformed Seceders, clear out to the tip end of orthodoxy in the last wee Associate Presbytery of Pennsylvania? To ask the question is to provoke a smile. Who understands this field of Church history? Who cares to thrust himself into its briery waste? Do these sects understand themselves? Is there, in truth, anything in them *to be* understood, or that is likely to weigh a feather hereafter, under any separate view, in the mind of God's Universal Church? Alas for the *unreason* of our reigning sect system!

The evil just noticed is greatly aggravated by the consideration that very few sects remain *constant* at all to their own origins, or make it their business to understand and maintain them. If this change were the result of a true inward process, serving to develop the sense of some mission they had at first, it might be all very well; but everybody may easily enough see that this is not the case. The movement is altogether negative and outward, and amounts to nothing. Once formed, the body floats hither and thither according to circumstances, till finally its original moorings are lost sight of almost entirely; only it still carries its old name and has gradually accumulated a certain historical substance of its own, a body of recollections and traditions, shibboleths and hobbies, prejudices and pedantries, whereby all manner of selfish interests and ends are en-listed for its support, and room made for a few men in the saddle, by humoring its fancies, to rule and guide it almost at their pleasure. Thus the original irrationality of sects is made for the most part more irrational still, loses any little grain of reason it may have had at first, by the mean-ingless fluctuations of their subsequent history. The starters of a sect, fifty years afterwards, in many cases, would hardly recognize their own progeny. Happy is the sect that is able to define at all its own distinctive position, or that can give any show of reason whatever for its existence, under such form as it actually carries. In the great majority of cases this cannot be done even by the ministers themselves. And then as to the people, poor sheep in the hands of their leaders and pastors, what can *they* be expected to know of their own denominational "whereabouts," or of its rational necessity, in the general pellmell of conflicting "persuasions" with which they are surrounded? As a general thing they know nothing about it.

The system is constitutionally *tyrannical*. Every sect pretends, indeed, to make men free. But only consider what sects are — self-constituted ecclesiastical organizations, called forth ordinarily by private judgment and caprice, and devoted to some one-sided Christian interest, under perhaps the most superficial and narrow view, educated polemically to a certain fanatical zeal for their own separatistic honor and credit, and bent on impressing their own "image and superscription" on all that fall beneath their ghostly power. Are these the circumstances that favor liberality and independence? The man who puts his conscience in the keeping of a sect is no longer free. It might as well be in the keeping of a Roman priest. In many cases, indeed, this were far better. Have the Baptists no traditions? Is there no slavery of intellect and heart among the United Brethren? Pshaw! The very last place in which to look for true spiritual emancipation, the freedom of a divinely, self-poised catholic mind, is the communion of sects.

The narrowness and tyranny of the sect spirit, unfriendly to all generous Christian life, is of fatal force in particular against the cultivation of *theology*, without which in the end it is not possible for the Church to have any true prosperity. Theology can be no science except as it has to do with the whole of Christianity, and is thus at once both churchly and historical in the full sense of these terms. The sect life, by its very conception, kills it, by turning it into a petrifaction or causing it to evaporate in the way of thin abstraction. Facts here are very plain. Sects, as they actually exist, have no theology, save as now mentioned — the miserable residuum only, so far as it may have any value at all, of the church life they had to start upon in the beginning, carried along with them as a mere outward tradition. Sects have no pleasure in theology as a science. It has nothing to expect from this quarter. It is no libel on our American sects in particular, to say that they have not thus far contributed anything at all to the advance of this most noble and excellent of all sciences, and it needs no prophet's gift to say that they never will do so in time to come. If any service has been rendered to it in any quarter, it has been by such as have been able to surmount the system in some measure, forcing their way upwards into a more catholic region. No sectarian theology can ever be of any permanent value.

The sect plague has no tendency to work out its own *cure*, unless it be in the way of a deadly malady that ends itself by ending the life on which it has come to fasten. It is vain to look for a reduction of the number of sects by their voluntary amalgamation. No two have yet been able to make themselves one. The difficulty is not in their theological differences. These are for the most part of very little practical force — with the great mass of the people, we may say, indeed, of absolutely no force at all. In nine cases out of ten it is a matter of sheer accident that this man is an Albright and his neighbor a Cumberland Presbyterian, that one phase of the Baptist faith prevails here and another phase of it ten miles off. All this, however, makes no matter; and it would make very little matter, if it were brought to be never so clear that the causes of separation in any case had completely fallen away. There would still be no union. It is the curse of the system that it can never of itself break the chains it has thus forged for its own slaves. On the contrary, it tends perpetually from bad to worse. It is easier by far to divide one sect into two than it is to splice two sects into one. There is not the least reason to expect, accordingly, that the system will ever reform itself into any better shape. It is plain, moreover, that it has no necessary end; on the contrary, its capabilities and possibilities are indefinitely boundless. No multiplication of sects can exhaust the principle from which they spring.

It is well to note how generally the sect system adheres to the article of *justification by faith*, and how prone it is to run this side of Christianity out to a false extreme, either in the way of dead antinomianism or wild fanaticism. With many persons, at this time, the test of all soundness in religion is made to stand in the idea of salvation by grace as opposed to works, Christ's righteousness set over to our account in an outward way, and a corresponding experience more or less magical in the case of those who receive it, which goes under the name of evangelical conversion. But now it falls in precisely with the abstract mechanism of the sect mind to throw itself mainly on this view of religion, to the exclusion, or at least vast undervaluation, of all that is comprised in the mystery of Christianity as the power of a new creation historically at hand in the Church. It is common for sects, accordingly, to make a parade of their zeal, in such style, for the doctrines of grace and the interests of vital godliness; and this is often taken at once for a sufficient passport in their favor, as though any body of religionists professing faith in free justification and violent conversion must needs be part and parcel of Christ's Church, however unchurchly in all other respects. But surely, for a sober mind, it should be enough to expose the fallacy of such thinking to look over the array of sects which is here presented to our view, and see how easy it is for almost the whole of them, if need be, to legitimate their pretensions in this way. All fragments of the Scotch Secession, of course, are one here, however divided in their "testimonies" at other points. They make election the principle of Christianity, turn justification by faith into a complete abstraction, and so nullify the law in one form, only to come too generally under the yoke of it again in another. The Baptists, through all their divisions, meet here also as on common ground, with antinomian tendency in one direction, with a tendency to fanaticism in another direction, but with common intolerance, all round, to every view of religion that is not found to harmonize with their own abstract scheme. The Winebrennerians hold justification by faith without works (p. 177), and are great in their way for revivals and wholesale conversions. So, of course, the Albright Brethren (p. 277). So the United Brethren in Christ (p. 564). These and other sects, indeed, ambitiously strive to outdo one another in the business of saving souls in the most approved style, "getting them through," as it is called, according to the abstract scheme now noticed. The one grand requisite for fellowship in the Campbellite communion is (p. 225) "an entire reliance upon the merits of Christ alone for justification." It is founded, we are told (p. 223), "upon the two great distinguishing principles of the Lutheran Reformation, *viz.:* the Bible alone as the rule of faith, to the entire exclusion of tradition, and the relying only upon that justification that is obtained through faith in Jesus Christ." Even the "Christians," with no faith in Christ's divinity, and the Universalists too, when it suits, can go in for some sort of abstract magical justification, and on the strength of it bring into play the common revival machinery with quite good success. All this surely deserves to be well laid to heart. There are, it is but too plain, "depths of Satan" here, as well as in other quarters, against which we need to stand solemnly on our guard. Let no one feel that it is safe to go with a sect, simply because it may seem to be *evangelical* (O most abused word), in this quacksalvery style. What can it be worth, if it be dissociated wholly from the old Church consciousness embodied in the Creed?

For one who has come at all to understand the constitution of this abstract supernaturalism, it can produce no surprise to find the sect system marked universally by a *rationalistic* tendency. A rationalism that denies the supernatural altogether, and a supernaturalism that will not allow it to enter into any concrete union with the natural, are at bottom much of the same nature; and the last needs only the force of true consecutive thinking always, to pass over peacefully into the arms of the first. Sects start usually in abstract supernaturalism, with an affectation of hyper-spiritual perfection. But the rationalistic element comes at once into view, both in their thinking and practice. This is clearly exemplified in the Baptistic scheme, as already noticed: a divine statute book, outwardly certified to be from heaven, Christian *laws* drawn forth from it in a like outward way, the mechanism of salvation brought nigh to men all outwardly again, in the form of thought or credited report, its application magically affected by an outward impulsion from God's Spirit, carrying the soul through a certain process of states and feelings. No sacramental grace. No true union with the life of Christ. So with sects generally. Their idea of private judgment, their notion of religious freedom, their low opinion of the sacraments, their indifference to all earnest theology, their propensity to drive religion by might and by power, rather than by the still small voice of God's Spirit, all betray a rationalistic habit of mind, and lean inwardly to still more decidedly rationalistic consequences and results. When Mr. Campbell makes Christianity to be "simply and solely" (p. 233) the belief of certain testimony, and obedience to certain laws, outwardly offered to men in the Bible, what less is it, we ask, than the very genius of rationalism itself, although most of the other sects probably would accept the same definition as altogether satisfactory and sufficient? The sect life tends to destroy faith, as it is notoriously unfriendly also to everything like reverence. It is not strange at all to see it running out into "Christianism," or to hear, in certain quarters, of converts being taken into the church (so called) without baptism! There is too much reason to fear that the virus of a low vulgar insensibility to the divine fact of Christianity has come to pervade the popular mind in some sections of our country, under the forms and shams of this unchurchly religionism far beyond what most persons have ever been led to imagine or suspect.

It is encouraging, however, as well as curious, to see how the sect sys-

tem is made to lend *testimony* throughout, against itself, to the idea of the
holy catholic Church, not unlike the devils in the New Testament, who
were forced to acknowledge Christ while fighting against him or fleeing
from his presence. Every sect, in spite of itself, is forced to acknowledge,
at least indirectly, the necessary attributes of the Church, as one, holy,
catholic, and apostolical. It cannot be a *mere* particular corporation, society, or persuasion, however much in some views it may seem disposed to
be nothing more. To stand at all, it must put on the character of a church,
and then carry out as it best can what this character is felt by a sort of
inward necessity to imply and require. Some sects openly claim the
prerogatives and powers of the Universal Church, as belonging to themselves alone in such a way as to exclude all that is not of their own communion, and this certainly is the most consistent course. Generally, however, no such claim is made; but the sect professes to look upon itself only
as a tribe of the true Israel, a section or wing in the sacramental host of
God's elect. And yet it goes on, in these circumstances, to arrogate to itself within its own bounds full church powers, such powers as have no
meaning except as conditioned by the idea of a catholic or whole church,
powers which cannot be fairly asserted without virtual limitation upon
the equal independence of sister sects. The inward ecclesiastical economy
of every sect, as to its ordinations, admission of members, church censure,
supervision of both faith and practice, &c., is so ordered as to involve
throughout the assumption of an absolute and final and exclusive supremacy in matters of religion. The idea of the Church, however dimly and
obscurely present, will not allow it to be otherwise. It *must* be one and
universal, the *whole*, that of necessity excludes all beyond its own sphere.
In this way every sect, so far as it can be called a church at all, becomes
necessarily a caricature of the catholicity with which it pretends to make
war, and so, like every other caricature, bears witness to the truth, which
is thus distorted by it and brought into contempt. In some cases we have
surprising confessions in favor of the true idea of the Church, where they
might seem to be wholly out of place. Mr. Winebrenner (p. 175) insists
on visibility, unity, sanctity, universality, and perpetuity as the necessary
attributes of the Church. "An invisible church that some divines speak
of," he tells us, "is altogether an anomaly in Christian theology." So
again: "The union of sects into one general Evangelical Alliance, or into
one human organization diverse in character, faith, and practice, from the
one true Church of God, as characterized in the Bible, we have no belief
in nor sympathy for." So we meet in Mr. Alexander Campbell many

traces of a sound and right feeling here, which we may well regret to find overwhelmed again, and made of no effect, by the power of the unhistorical sect mind which is allowed after all to prevail in his system. . . .

The Remedy

After this review of the general misery comprehended in our reigning sect system, we are prepared to notice in conclusion its proper *remedy*.

It will be seen at once, of course, that we have no sympathy whatever with those who imagine that all which is wanted here is the violent overthrow in any way of outward denominational distinctions as they now stand. We wage no crusade against sects in this form. Of what avail would it be to strike all of them dead at a single blow, if the sect life be left still in force, ready to sprout forth into new similar creations the next day? Such merely negative destructional opposition to sects is itself necessarily sectarian also in its very constitution, and can only issue at best, accordingly, in some new *no-sect* sect, which is likely to be as narrow and rabid in its own way as any of the rest.

Just as little can we make common cause with those who make the idea of catholicity to consist in a certain liberality which shows itself indifferent at last to all religious distinctions, and overcomes the sect-consciousness by bringing it to dissolve simply in the sense of our life as a mere natural whole. Here, as before, the process of reconciliation is wholly negative and destructional; it surrenders, so far as it may prevail, the positive substance of Christianity, and lands us in a unity which is the mere show of truth and faith without their power. Against such spurious catholicity, often like an angel of light, we have need to stand constantly upon our guard. Caricature as the sect life always is of the true life of the Church, it still involves at bottom some apprehension of a positive new creation in Christ Jesus, which as such must needs be exclusive in order to be really catholic; and this, in any case, is something better than the "liberal Christianity" that, in giving up the caricature, parts also with the idea of the Church itself, and becomes universal only by including nothing.

Equally plain is it, however, that no faith is to be reposed in the dream of anything like a free construction of catholic unity by counsel and compact among the different sects themselves. To think of their ever consenting to merge their existence in a new common church organization would be, of course, perfectly extravagant. Every sect has power to multiply its own bad life, like the polypus, by new sections and slips; but no single two of them, it seems, have power to come together again in the way of full organic union. In this aspect, the system offers no hope for the future, but a prospect only of blank despair. The most to be expected from it, then, would be an outward federal union of sects, leaving each to its present independence, with some loose covenant and creed to represent the whole. But such a confederation, could it be made real, would be no Church; so far as this conception might continue to have force, it would remain bound only to the separate sects as such. And who may not see that in the very nature of any such transaction the sect-consciousness is left to assert throughout its own supremacy over the sense of the Church, something more wide than itself? It is just like the French Convention of Jacobin memory, after the prostration of throne and altar, legislating into authority the existence of a "Supreme Being"! The sects here, in solemn parliament assembled, each fully persuaded of its own indefeasible sovereignty and power, undertake to create a universal Church; not fully sure, indeed, whether there *be* any holy catholic Church, in the sense of the ancient Creed, but honestly minded, at all events, to bring something of the sort to pass, if God so please, and then see how it will work. But what is all this, less than an impudent affectation of mastering the Church-consciousness into base subordination to the sect-consciousness, and making the *whole* thus to be the mere creature of its own parts? Every such pretension is systematically [?] uncatholic in its very nature, and so far as it may ever prevail, runs out necessarily into the same merely indifferentistic liberalism which we have already noticed. Nothing is more easy or common than the union of such false catholicity, in one aspect, with the full bigotry of sect in another. They belong to the same general sphere — different sides only, of the antichristian life, the Gentile consciousness and that of the Jew playing into each other for self-support, with equal wrong on both sides to the mystery of the one universal Church, as constituted and revealed in Jesus Christ.

We have no hesitation, then, in saying that all redemption from the power of the sect plague must begin with a revival of true and hearty faith in the ancient article of one holy catholic Church.

The idea of the Church, in the first place, is the only effective measure of schism. It is to this precisely what the moral law is to the conception of sin. Where there is no law, we are told, there is no sin; the sense of the last springs only from the sense of the first. So, where there is no Church there can be no schism — no proper apprehension of it, at least, where it may prevail in fact. As long as men are disposed to deny the existence of one catholic Church, or to place it in the clouds merely as an invisible abstraction, or to substitute for it the negation and shadow of a simply ethnic brotherhood, it must be in vain to preach to them the evils of division and schism. They can have, at best, only a partial conception of their nature, and will not be engaged, of course, to put forth any strenuous desire or effort after deliverance.

This, plainly, is our prevailing state at the present time. We talk of the necessity of Christian love and union, and see to some extent the misery of our sectarianism; but still we seem satisfied in general, notwithstanding, to abide in the present system, as on the whole necessary and good. It is attended with no painful sense of schism, as necessarily involved in our divisions themselves. It is hard, oftentimes, to say precisely what this old ecclesiastical term signifies to our minds. No sect, as such, can make any effective protest against the position of any other, as schismatic; for, in the very nature of the case, it can have no objective rule or measure to appeal to that is any broader than its own sect-consciousness itself. But the consciousness of one sect, in this view, is just of as much authority as that of another. And so it comes to pass that men feel themselves, for the most part, free to act in church matters as they please. To quit a church connection, once viewed even in the Protestant world as a most solemn thing, is now regarded very much as a simple change of residence; it is simply to pass from one sect over to another, which belongs as much to the Church general as that which has been left behind. In the same way, ecclesiastical privileges are shorn of their value, and ecclesiastical penalties of their proper weight. It is hard to make anybody feel that there is the slightest danger of getting out of the Church, so as to have no true ministry and no true sacraments, in any sort of nominally Christian society. Such account of ordinances is treated as, at all events, no better than superstition. Few seem to have the least fear of schism, if only they can lay claim, in their own way, to the Bible and God's Spirit. And the reigning church sentiment, even with the more regular denominations, is such as to countenance in full this sad delusion. The sect mind, stopping short of all true church consciousness, can never, under its most respectable forms, administer any potent rebuke to the spirit in question. It is involved always in the same condemnation. It has no hearty faith itself in the Church, and how then can it so speak as to infuse any such faith into others?

The only help here, it should be clear, is in the general resuscitation of a sound church feeling, as something deeper and more comprehensive than the feeling of sect. Let this wake into life to some proper extent, and it would be of more force to stem the course of sectarian fanaticism in a short time than long years of argument and testimony exhibited in our present state. No one would think, then, of vindicating our sect system as the ultimate and normal order of Christianity, but all must feel themselves bound to condemn it, and to mourn over it, as a captivity to the iron reign of schism, with longing anticipation of the day when God shall happily bring it to an end.

And so again it is only by the force of such resuscitated faith in the Church, in the second place, that the way can be opened at all for any return out of this bondage into the land of true catholicity and peace. It requires, surely, no very deep reflection to perceive the force of this proposition. The sect-consciousness, as such, can never bring men beyond its own sphere, can never lead them into the clear knowledge of the Church, and, of course, still less into its full life. All this must come from a different quarter, the living apprehension, namely, of the idea of the Church itself as an objective reality in the world.

For it will be observed that we speak throughout of the catholic Church as an object of *faith,* which in this view must be regarded as something at once supernatural and real. So it is exhibited to us in the Creed. It is not a mere notion, or abstraction, or subjective creation of the human mind, in any form, but includes in itself an objective being, as we have seen, no less real and abiding than the person of Christ himself from which it starts. This it is, precisely, that makes the great difference between spurious ethnic catholicity, as exhibited to us in world conventions, or mere stage displays, and catholicity under its genuine form. The first holds only in the region of natural thought and feeling, and disturbs not necessarily, in the least, the inward habit of the sect mind from which it springs. To admit the existence of a holy catholic Church, in such a case, is no more than to admit the existence of a British Parliament, or an American Congress, or the authority of what is called the command of law in both countries. But the other stands in faith, whose very nature it is to mold the consciousness of its subject into the form of its object; and having this form, of course, it must necessarily require the sect mind to give way before the power of the deeper life which is thus made to take its place.

And here we may see at once the vanity of the plea which is sometimes urged against all faith in a real Church, that we are not able to point out clearly its external form, in the history of the world, in such a way as to cut off all cavil, as well as the falsehood of the position sometimes taken by sects, that the first step needed towards catholic unity is to make out satisfactorily some plan or scheme, to which the parties may then jointly agree as suited to secure this object. Every such thought, however plausible as it may appear, virtually denies the Church to be any object of faith whatever, and converts it from the start into an object of mere sense or natural ratiocination. *Show* us the Church, say the sects, and it sufficeth us; but to what can all homilies on the subject of catholicity and schism amount, so long as you are unable to mark out any door of escape from the present evil? Most plausible certainly, but at the same time sophistical and false. For is not this, palpably, to place in question the reality of the holy catholic Church altogether, as an objective supernatural fact, in the sense of the ancient Creed? The catholic Church is a *mystery*, in the sense of the Creed, just like its other articles, which as such is to be apprehended primarily by faith, and *not* in the way of intelligence. It does not, of course, exclude intelligence, as this is not done either by the article of the Incarnation. Faith is not blind here or slavish, but it is the necessary form of access, in the first place, to the object of knowledge. As springing not from ourselves, but from abroad, and under a supernatural character, this must be brought nigh to us, by faith, as a divine reality, before it can be understood. To put intelligence before faith, here as elsewhere, is just what we mean by rationalism. The conception of a Church to be manufactured by the sect mind, enthroned for the time as the higher power, called to sit in judgment on its claims, is itself an infidel absurdity. As well pretend to construct, in the same *ab extra* way, the mystery of the Incarnation, before surrendering the soul, by faith, to the power of the fact! Jesus Christ authenticates himself. And so it is with the mystery of the Church. It must overwhelm our inward consciousness first, with its own objective force as a necessary result from the great Christological fact itself, in order that it may come to right revelation subsequently in the sphere of thought and outward life. It is not necessary at all that the full contents of the article should be at once in our view, to allow the complete exercise of such faith. Peter's confession: "Thou art the Christ, the Son of the living God!" carried in itself in truth, potentially, the whole sense of the Apostles' Creed, though with no insight of his, at the time, into the several articles of this, as afterwards evolved from its bosom. And just so, we may have a true faith in the article of the one, holy, catholic

Church, while yet most incompetent in our own minds to estimate, in full, the terms and conditions under which it may be required to manifest itself in the world. Such faith does not turn primarily on the presence of the Church, as a given corporation accredited by outward seal, but on the idea of Christianity itself, as necessarily requiring this constitution to make itself complete. Not only the word of Christ, but his life, demands its presence. The article flows forth, with inward necessity, from the Christological mystery itself. To stand in the full sense of this, as the fact of a new order of life made originally permanent in the world, is to have the reality of the holy catholic Church, at the same time, actually at hand also as a part of our creed. The reality, in this case, is no mere notion or shadow, but a true divine object, apprehended by faith; and the consciousness which springs from it is something far more, accordingly, than the hollow, negative catholicity of Gentile unbelief; it is the sense of such wholeness as belongs to the positive life of Christianity itself.

With such objective, historical being in the world as this faith implies, the Church, of course, is no abstraction. Its existence is concrete, and its attributes are determined by its constitution. Still its revelation is a process, in the course of which wide room is found for the actual and the Ideal to fall asunder. In these circumstances, all may be said to turn on the presence of such a sound church-consciousness as is now described. It is from this alone that all catholic ideas must flow, and in virtue of it only can they ever be brought to take form in actual life.

Let no one say or think, then, that it amounts to little to insist upon faith in the Church itself as the most necessary remedy for the sect plague which now afflicts our Protestant Christianity. We come here at once to the ground-cause of the plague itself, which all may see to be the reigning want of such faith in the form now described; and it is plain that until this be in some measure removed, no other palliative or help can be of much avail. What can well be more preposterous, indeed, than to aim at catholic unity without being fully persuaded that it is anything more than a dream, or to treat the Church as a mere *hypothesis* in the first place, in order to test the possibility of bringing it to pass! Are the articles of the Creed, then, to be taken in the way of experiment? Are the great verities of the new creation so many problems to be solved, or theorems to be demonstrated, before we can yield to their authority as true? Can a genuine church-consciousness ever grow forth from the power of the sect-mind, however large and free in its own more narrow sphere? Take the ground that the sect-mind is itself a true Church-mind, that the Church, in any whole view, is an abstraction only, which need never become visible, or that we can have nothing to do with it properly, in any different light, till it has resolved itself into some tangible case whose merits we can then canvass and decide upon in an outward way; approach the subject, we say, in any such style as this, and it is clear that all the interest we may take in it must come to nothing in the end. What we need to start with is the sense of catholicity itself, "faith in the mystery of one universal historical Church," and the felt power of old catholic ideas as we find them reigning in the ancient Christian world. It cannot be disguised that a widespread hostility prevails towards these ideas themselves, and not simply towards the abuses into which they may have been run by the Church of Rome. So long as this is the case, there can be no honest care or concern for Church unity. These catholic ideas are not arbitrary or accidental; they form the necessary outbirth of a true Church life; and to refuse them their proper honor is of itself to do homage always to the spirit of sect as a higher power. Only as such feeling gives way before the sense of Christ's one universal Church, and room is made thus for true inward sympathy with catholic ideas, may we hope at all to understand or settle satisfactorily the questions involved in the restoration of our present captivity. Faith in the Church is not of itself all that the case requires; but it is the first and greatest thing, that must open the way for all ulterior counsel and action, and it is worse than idle to prate sentimentally of our good purposes in its absence. Half of our sects would be at once dissolved by it, like mists before the rising sun, while the field of division and debate among the rest would be narrowed to less than half its present dimensions; and, in the distance, at least, would be seen rising, to the fond vision of hope, the glorious one catholic *Church of the future*, as the praise, and joy, and glory of the whole earth.

PART TWO

❖

The Pattern of Historical Development of the New Creation

PHILIP SCHAFF

Theses for the Time

Editor's introduction.

Philip Schaff arrived in America at the age of twenty-five, eager to dispense the riches of German theological scholarship. After his inaugural address before the Synod at Reading on October 25, 1844, in which he did not find sufficient scope for a statement of his entire program, he elaborated it into *Das Princip des Protestantismus*, a work of 180 pages published early in 1845. In June of the same year, Nevin's translation appeared as *The Principle of Protestantism as Related to the Present State of the Church*, with an introduction by the translator and "Catholic Unity" as an appendix. A synopsis in the form of 112 "Theses" is the section given here. It was Schaff's evident wish to follow the German academic custom in this matter, although Nevin shuddered as he foresaw what the editors of the American religious press would make of the theses.

He was not mistaken in his forebodings — although in the hue and cry that followed, Nevin's own references in "Catholic Unity" to the Eucharistic Presence occasioned more scandal than anything else in the volume. Schaff was criticized primarily for his irenic attitude to Roman Catholicism and his qualified approval of Puseyism. One rather awkwardly translated sentence provoked especial attack. "I look upon Puseyism," Schaff had written, "as *an entirely legitimate and necessary reaction against rationalistic and sectaristic pseudo-Protestantism, as well as the religious subjectivism of the so-called Low Church Party*; with which the significance of the Church has been forgotten, or at least practically undervalued, in favor of personal individual piety, the sacraments in favor of faith, sanctification in favor of justification, and tradition in its right sense in favor of the holy Scriptures." [1] Schaff had argued that tradition

---

1. *The Principle of Protestantism* (Chambersburg, Pa., 1845), 122f.

as the agreed understanding of the scriptural message was indispensable. Opponents such as Dr. Berg denied that any tradition was indispensable; Scripture, they agreed, was its own interpreter.

Berg also disagreed thoroughly with the main historical argument of *The Principle of Protestantism*, but here the disagreement was less easy to formulate into a charge of heresy. Berg did not grant any idea of historical development of doctrine, but argued that the full and whole gospel had been maintained unchanged down the centuries into the present Reformed Church, and that Roman Catholicism had never been anything but apostasy. He had already, in 1844, presented this case in a sermon before the Synod, and after hearing Schaff's inaugural, he developed it into a full-scale reply: *The Old Paths, or a Sketch of the Order and Discipline of the Reformed Church before the Reformation, as maintained by the Waldenses prior to that Epoch, and by the Church of the Palatinate in the Sixteenth Century.* It is to this that Schaff's Thesis 31, reprinted below, refers.

Little if anything in Schaff's own book was original, as he himself protested with some amazement after its hostile reception. Running through the theses, one may identify them successively as characteristic of such German theologians as Kliefoth, Hegel, Schleiermacher, Schelling, Gerlach, Twesten, Ullmann, Stahl, and Baur. The work is a rather eclectic combination of philosophical idealism, the romantic theory of organism, Protestant orthodoxy, political conservatism, and high-church doctrine, set forth in a historical description of the rise and course of Protestantism. Schaff's is a triumphalist view of Church history — of history as theodicy, a demonstration of God's purposes in time.

Schaff's work resembled Newman's *Essay on Development*, published the same year, in that it acknowledged a genuine evolution of doctrines and institutions in the course of Christian history. But whereas Newman undertook only to show how modern Roman Catholicism might be accounted a legitimate "development" from apostolic Christianity, Schaff also portrayed the Reformation as the legitimate offspring of medieval Catholicism, and forecast that future developments in both would lead to an eventual ecumenical reunion. In this attitude to Roman Catholicism, characteristic of the entourage of the Prussian king, there was a sharp contrast even with Nevin's, as expressed in "Catholic Unity." In the fervor of Schaff's enthusiasm, nineteenth-century America became the appointed ecumenical stage for the coming of the millennium.

❖   ❖   ❖   ❖

Introduction

1. Every period of the Church and of theology has its particular problem to solve; and every doctrine, in a measure every book also of the Bible, has its classic age in which it first comes to be fully understood and appropriated by the consciousness of the Christian world.

2. The main question of *our* time is concerning the nature of the Church itself in its relation to the world and to single Christians.

1. *The Church in General*

3. The Church is the Body of Jesus Christ. This expresses her communion with her Head, and also the relation of her members to one another.

4. In the first respect, she is an institution founded by Christ, proceeding from his loins and animated by his Spirit, for the glory of God and the salvation of man; through which alone, as its necessary organ, the revelation of God in Christ becomes effective in the history of the world. Hence out of the Church, as there is no Christianity, there can be no salvation.

5. In the second respect, she is, like every other body, a living unity of different members; a communion in faith and love, visible as well as invisible, external as well as internal, of the most manifold individualities, gifts, and powers, pervaded with the same Spirit and serving the same end.

6. The definition implies farther that as the life of the parents flows forward in the child, so the Church also is the depository and continuation of the earthly human life of the Redeemer, in his threefold office of prophet, priest, and king.

7. Hence she possesses, like her Founder, a divine and human, an ideal and a real, a heavenly and an earthly nature; only with this difference, that in her militant stage, freedom from sin and error cannot be predicated of her in the same sense as of Christ; that is, she possesses the principle of holiness and the full truth, mixed, however, still with sin and error.

8. To the Church belong, in the wider sense, all baptized persons, even though they may have fallen back to the world; in the narrower sense, however, such only as believe in Jesus Christ.

9. The relation of the Church to the world, with its different spheres of science, art, government, and social life, is neither one of destruction on her part nor one of indifference; but the object of it is that she should transfuse the world with the purifying power of her own divine life, and thus bring it at last to its true and proper perfection.

10. The ultimate scope of history accordingly is this, that Christianity may become completely the same with nature, and the world be formally organized as the kingdom of Christ; which must involve the absolute identity of Church and state, theology and philosophy, worship and art, religion and morality; the state of the renovated earth, in which God will be All in all.

11. In relation to single Christians, the Church is the mother from which they derive their religious life and to which they owe therefore constant fidelity, gratitude, and obedience; she is the power of the objective and general to which the subjective and single should ever be subordinate.

12. Only in such regular and rational subordination can the individual Christian be truly free; and his personal piety can as little come to perfection apart from an inward and outward communion with the life of the Church, as a limb separated from the body or a branch torn from the vine.

13. Christianity in itself is the *absolute* religion, and in this view unsusceptible of improvement.

14. We must not confound with this, however, the *apprehension* and *appropriation* of Christianity in the consciousness of mankind. This is a progressive process of development that will reach its close only with the second coming of the Lord.

15. All historical progress, then, in the case of the Church, consists not in going beyond Christianity itself, which could only be to fall back to heathenism and Judaism, but in entering always more and more (materially as well as formally) into the life and doctrine of the Redeemer and in throwing off by this means, always more and more, the elements of sin and error still remaining from the state of nature.

16. It is possible for the Church to be in possession of a truth and to live upon it, before it has come to be discerned in her consciousness. So it was, for instance, with the doctrine of the Trinity before the time of Athanasius, with the doctrine of divine grace and human freedom before

Augustine, and with the evangelical doctrine of justification during the Middle Ages. Thus the child eats and drinks long before it has the knowledge of food, and walks before it is aware of the fact, much less *how* it walks.

17. The idea, unfolded in comprehensive and profound style particularly by the later German philosophy, that history involves a continual progress toward something better, by means of dialectic contrapositions (*Gegensätze*), is substantially true and correct.

18. It must not be forgotten, however, in connection with this, that there is a corresponding movement also on the part of evil toward that which is worse. Light and darkness, the wheat and the tares, grow together till their development shall become complete.

19. We must distinguish in the Church accordingly between Idea and manifestation. As to her Idea, or as comprehended in Christ, she is already complete; in the way of manifestation, however, she passes — like every one of her members — outwardly and inwardly, through different stages of life, until the Ideal enclosed in Christ shall be fully actualized in humanity and his body appear thus in the ripeness of complete manhood.

20. Such a process of growth is attended necessarily with certain diseases and crises, as well theoretical, in the form of heresies, as practical, in the form of schisms.

21. These diseases are to be referred partly to the remaining force of sin and error in the regenerate themselves, and partly to the unavoidable connection of the Church with the still unchristian world, by means of which the corrupt elements of this last are always forcing their way into her communion.

22. They can never overthrow, however, the existence of the Church. The Church may fall down, sore wounded, divided and torn, without ceasing for this reason to be the Body of Christ. Through her humiliation gleams evermore the unwasting glory of her divine nature.

23. In the wise providence of God, all heresies and schisms serve only to bring the Church to a more clear consciousness of her true vocation, a deeper apprehension of her faith, and a purer revelation of the power included in her life.

24. But the presence of disease in the body requires to the same extent a remedial or curative process, that is, a reformation.

25. Protestantism, consequently, in the true sense, belongs indispensably to the life of the Church, being the reaction simply of her proper vitality, depressed but not destroyed, in opposition to the workings of disease in her system.

II. *The Reformation*

26. Protestantism runs through the entire history of the Church, and will not cease till she is purged completely from all ungodly elements. So, for instance, Paul protested against Jewish legalism and pagan licentiousness as found insidiously at work in the first Christian communities, the Catholic Church of the first centuries against the heresies and schisms of Ebionitism, Gnosticism, Montanism, Arianism, Pelagianism, Donatism, etc.

27. The most grand and widely influential exhibition of Protestantism is presented to us under the formal constitution of a special church, in the Reformation of the sixteenth century, as originated, and in its most deep, inward, and truly apostolic form, carried out and consummated by the German nation.

28. It is a jejune and narrow conception of this event to look upon it as a restoration simply of the original state of the Church, or a renewal of Augustinianism against the Pelagian system by which it had been supplanted.

29. Such a view proceeds on the fundamentally erroneous supposition that the religious life revealed in the person of Christ primarily, and by derivation from him in his Apostles, has been fully actualized also from the beginning in the general mass of the Church.

30. Rather, the Reformation must be viewed as an actual advance of the religious life and consciousness of the Church, by means of a deeper apprehension of God's Word, beyond all previous attainments of Christendom.

31. As little is the Reformation to be regarded as a revolutionary separation from the Catholic Church, holding connection at best perhaps with some fractionary sect of the Middle Ages, and only through this and the help of certain desperate historical leaps besides, reaching back to the age of the Apostles.

32. This contracted view of Protestantism is not only unhistorical and unchurchly altogether, but conscious or unconscious treason at the same time to the Lord's promise that he would build his Church upon a rock, and that the gates of hell should not prevail against it [Mt. 16:18], as well as to his engagement: "Lo I am with you always, even to the end of the

world" [Mt. 28:20], and to the apostolic word: "The church is the pillar and ground of the truth" [1 Tim. 3:15].

33. Rather, the Reformation is the greatest act of the Catholic Church itself, the full ripe fruit of all its better tendencies, particularly of the deep spiritual law-conflicts of the Middle Period, which were as a schoolmaster toward the Protestant doctrine of justification.

34. The separation was produced, not by the will of the Reformers, but by the stiff-necked papacy, which like Judaism at the time of Christ, identifying itself in a fleshly way with the idea of the absolute Church, refused to admit the onward movement.

35. Thus apprehended, Protestantism has as large an interest in the vast historical treasures of the previous period as can be claimed rightfully by the Church of Rome. Hence the arguments drawn by Romanists from this quarter, and particularly from the Middle Ages — the proper cradle of the Reformation — have no application against our standpoint.

36. Equally false, finally, is the view, whether popular or philosophical, by which the Reformation is made to consist in the absolute emancipation of the Christian life subjectively considered from all Church authority, and the exaltation of private judgment to the papal throne.

37. This view confounds with the Reformation itself the foul excrescences that revealed themselves along with it in the beginning, and the one-sided character of its development since.

38. On the contrary, it is quite clear from history that the Reformers aimed only at such liberty of faith and conscience and such independence of private judgment as should involve a humble subjection of the natural will, which they held to be incapable of all good, to God's grace, and of the human reason to God's Word. Indeed their opposition to the Roman traditions was itself based on the conviction that they were the product of such reason sundered from the divine Word.

39. The material or life principle of Protestantism is the doctrine of justification by grace alone, through the merits of Jesus Christ, by means of living faith, that is, the personal appropriation of Christ in the totality of the inner man.

40. This does not overthrow good works; rather they are rightly called for and made possible only in this way — with dependence, however, on faith as being its necessary fruit, the subjective impression of the life of Christ, in opposition to Pelagianism, which places works parallel with faith, or above it even.

41. The formal or knowledge principle of Protestantism is the suffi-

ciency and unerring certainty of the holy Scriptures as the only norm of all saving knowledge.

42. This does not overthrow the idea of Church tradition, but simply makes it dependent on the written Word, as the stream is upon the fountain — the necessary, ever-deepening onward flow of the sense of Scripture itself, as it is carried forward in the consciousness of the Christian world; contrary to the Romish dogma, by which tradition, as the bearer of different contents altogether, is made coordinate with the Bible or even exalted above it.

43. These two principles, rightly apprehended, are only different, mutually supplementary sides of one and the same principle, and their living interpenetration forms the criterion of orthodox Protestantism.

44. Opposition to the Roman Catholic extreme, according to the general law of historical progress, led the Reformers to place the strongest emphasis on justification and faith, Scripture and preaching, whence the possibility of a one-sided development in which holiness and love, tradition and sacrament, might not be allowed to come to their full rights.

45. Respect for the Reformation as a divine work in no way forbids the admission that it included some mixture of error and sin; as where God builds a church, the devil erects a chapel by its side.

46. In any view, moreover, the Reformation must be regarded as still incomplete. It needs yet its concluding act to unite what has fallen asunder, to bring the subjective to a reconciliation with the objective.

47. Puritanism may be considered a sort of second Reformation, called forth by the reappearance of Romanizing elements in the Anglican Church, and as such forms the basis to a great extent of American Protestantism, particularly in New England.

48. Its highest recommendation, bearing clearly a divine signature, is presented in its deep practical earnestness as regards religion, and its zeal for personal piety, by which it has been more successful, perhaps, than any other section of the Church, for a time, in the work of saving individual souls.

49. On the other hand, it falls far behind the German Reformation by its revolutionary, unhistorical, and consequently unchurchly character, and carries in itself no protection whatever against an indefinite subdivision of the Church into separate atomistic sects. For having no conception at all of a historical development of Christianity, and with its negative attitude of blind irrational zeal towards the past in its own rear, it may be said to have armed its children with the same right and the same tend-

ency, too, to treat its own authority with equal independence and contempt.

III. *The Present State of the Church*

50. Protestantism has formed the starting point and center of almost all
important world movements in the history of the last three centuries, and
constitutes now also the main interest of the time.

51. The history of Protestantism in the spheres of religion, science, art,
and government, especially since the commencement of the eighteenth
century, may be regarded as the development of the principle of *subjectivity*, the consciousness of *freedom*.

52. In this development, however, it has gradually become estranged to
a great extent from its own original nature, and fallen over dialectically
into its opposite, according to the general course of history.

53. Its grand maladies at this time are *rationalism* and *sectarism*.

54. Rationalism is one-sided *theoretic religious subjectivism*, and its
fullest and most perfect exhibition has taken place accordingly in Germany — the land of theory and science — and in the bosom of the Lutheran Church.

55. Sectarism is one-sided *practical religious subjectivism*, and has
found its classic ground within the territory of the Reformed Church, in
the predominantly practical countries, England and America.

56. These two maladies of Protestantism stand in a relation to it similar
to that of the papacy to Catholicism in the Middle Ages; that is, they have
a conditional historical necessity and an outward connection with the system to which they adhere, but contradict, nevertheless, and caricature its
inmost nature.

57. The secular interests—science, art, government, and social life
— have become since the Reformation always more and more dissociated
from the Church, in whose service they stood, though with unfree sub-
jugation, in the Middle Ages, and in this separate form are advanced to a
high state of perfection.

58. This is a false position, since the idea of the kingdom of God requires that all divinely constituted forms and spheres of life should be
brought to serve him in the most intimate alliance with religion, that God
may be All in all.

59. The orthodox Protestantism of our day, with all its different char-

acter in other respects, is distinguished, in common with rationalism and sectarism, particularly in this country, by the quality of one-sided subjectivity — only with the advantage, of course, of a large amount of personal piety.

60. Its great defect is the want of an adequate conception of the nature of the Church and of its relation to the individual Christian, on the one hand, and the general life of man on the other.

61. Hence proceeds, first, indifference towards sectarian, or at least denominational divisions, which are at war with the idea of the Church as the Body of Christ.

62. Secondly, a want of respect for history, by which it is affected to fall back immediately and wholly upon the Scriptures, without regard to the development of their contents in the life of the Church as it has stood from the beginning.

63. Thirdly, an undervaluation of the sacraments as objective institutions of the Lord, independent of individual views and states.

64. Fourthly, a disproportionate esteem for the service of preaching, with a corresponding sacrifice in the case of the liturgy, the standing objective part of divine worship, in which the *whole congregation* is called to pour forth its religious life to God.

65. Fifthly, a circumscribed conception of the all-pervading leavenlike nature of the gospel, involving an abstract separation of religion from the divinely established order of the world in other spheres.

66. To this must be added in the case of a number of denominations the fancy of their own perfection, an idea that *their* particular traditional style of religion can never be improved into anything better, which is a rejection of the Protestant principle of mobility and progress, and a virtual relapse accordingly into the ground error of the Romish Church.

67. From all this it is clear that the standpoint, and with it the wants of our time, are wholly different from those of the sixteenth century.

68. Our most immediate and most threatening danger is not now from the Church of Rome, but from the, in part heterodox and antichristian, in part orthodox and pious, but always one-sided and false subjectivism, by which the rights of the Church are wronged in our own midst, which, however, must itself be considered again as indirectly the most alarming aspect of the danger that does in fact threaten us on the side of Rome, since one extreme serves always to facilitate the triumph of another.

69. The redeeming tendency of the age, therefore, is not such as looks directly to the emancipation of the individual and subjective from the

bonds of authority, as at the time of the Reformation, but it is that rather which regards the claims of the objective in the true idea of the Church.

70. Not until Protestantism shall have repented of its own faults and healed its own wounds, may it expect to prevail finally over the Church of Rome.

71. As this duty has been thus far in a great measure neglected, it is to be taken as a divine judgment in the case that popery has been enabled to make such formidable advances latterly, especially in England and the United States.

72. Puseyism (with which, of course, we must not confound the spurious afterbirth of fantastic, hollow-hearted affectation, always to be expected in such a case) may be considered in its original intention and best tendency a well-meant but insufficient and unsuccessful attempt to correct the ultra-subjectivity of Protestantism.

73. In this view we have reason to rejoice in its appearance, as indicating on the part of the Protestant world a waking consciousness of the malady under which it labors in this direction, and serving also to promote right church-feeling.

74. By its reverence for Church antiquity it exerts a salutary influence against what may be viewed as the reigning error of our time, a wild revolutionary zeal for liberty, coupled with a profane scorn of all that is holy in the experience of the past.

75. So also its stress laid upon forms exhibits a wholesome reaction against the irrational hyper-spiritualism so common among even the best Protestants, which the doctrine of the Resurrection alone, as taught in the Bible, is enough to prove fallacious.

76. Church forms serve two general purposes: first, they are for the lower stages of religious development conductors over into the life of the spirit; secondly, they are for the Church at large the necessary utterance or corporealization of the spirit, in the view in which Oetinger's remark holds good: "Corporeity is the scope of God's ways." [2]

77. All turns simply on this, that the form be answerable to the contents and be actuated by the spirit. A formless spiritualism is no whit better than a spiritless formalism. The only right condition is a sound spirit within a sound body.

78. The grand defect of Puseyism, on the other hand, is its unprotes-

2. [ED.] "Leiblichkeit ist das Ende der Werke Gottes." F. C. Oetinger, *Biblisches und Emblematisches Wörterbuch, dem Tellerischen und anderer falschen Schrifterklärungen entgegengesetzt* ([Frankfurt?] 1776), 407.

tant character in not recognizing the importance of the Reformation and the idea of progress in the life of the Church since.

79. It is for this reason only half-historical and half-catholic, since its sympathy and respect for the past life of the Church stop short with the sixteenth century.

80. Its view of the Church altogether is outward and mechanical, excluding the conception of a living development through the successive periods of its history.

81. This character appears particularly in its theory of episcopal succession, which is only a new form of the old pharisaic Judaism, and moreover makes the apostolicity of the Church dependent on a historical inquiry (in the case of which, besides, no absolute certainty is possible), resting it thus on a wholly precarious human foundation.

82. Puseyism is to be viewed then as nothing more than a simple reaction, which has served to bring to light the evils of ultra-pseudo-Protestant individualism, but offers no remedy for it save the perilous alternative of falling back to a standpoint already surmounted in the way of religious progress.

83. The true standpoint, all necessary for the wants of the time, is that of *Protestant Catholicism*, or genuine historical progress.

84. This holds equally remote from unchurchly subjectivity and all Romanizing churchism, though it acknowledges and seeks to unite in itself the truth which lies at the ground of both these extremes.

85. Occupying this conservative historical standpoint, from which the moving of God's Spirit is discerned in all periods of the Church, we may not in the first place surrender anything essential of the positive acquisition secured by the Reformation, whether Lutheran or Reformed.

86. Neither may we again absolutely negate the later development of Protestantism, not even rationalism and sectarism themselves, but must appropriate to ourselves rather the element of truth they contain, rejecting only the vast alloy of error from which it is to be extracted.

87. Rationalism and sectarism possess historical right, so far as the principle of subjectivity, individuality, singleness, and independence can be said to be possessed of right — that is, so far as this comes not in contradiction to the principle of objectivity, generality, the Church, authority, and law, so far, then, as it continues subordinate to these forces.

88. Rationalism was a necessary schoolmaster for orthodox theology, destroying its groundless prejudices and compelling it both to accept a more scientific form in general, and also in particular to allow the human,

the earthly, the historical, in the theanthropic nature of Christ and the Church, to come more fully to its rights.

89. Whilst, however, the earlier historico-critical rationalism has promoted a right understanding of the natural and historical in Christianity, this understanding in its case remains still but *half* true, since it has no organ for *ideas*, of whose inward life history after all is but the body.

90. The later speculative rationalism, or pantheistic mythologism, or the "Hegelingians" as they have been deridingly styled (Strauss and his colleagues), which from the Ebionitic standpoint of the old system has swung over to the opposite extreme of docetic Gnostic idealism, fails to apprehend the idea of Christianity in its full truth and vitality, and substitutes for it a phantom or mere shadow, since it has no organ for historical *reality*, the outward life without which after all the Idea must perish.

91. As in the first centuries the theology of the Catholic Church gradually developed itself through scientific struggles with the two ground heresies — Ebionism or christianizing Judaism, and Gnosticism or christianizing heathenism — so now also we are to look for a higher orthodoxy, overmastering inwardly both forms of Protestant rationalism, which shall bring the real and the Ideal into the most intimate union and recognize in full as well as the eternal spirit of Christianity as its historical body.

92. The germs of all this are at hand in the later movements and achievements of the believing German theology, and need only a further development to issue at last in a full dogmatical reformation.

93. Separation, where it is characterized by religious life, springs almost always from some real evil in the state of the Church, and hence sectarism is to be regarded as a necessary disciplinarian and reformer of the Church in its practical life.

94. Almost every sect represents in strong relief some single particular aspect of piety, and contributes to the more full evolution of individual religious activity.

95. Since, however, the truths of the gospel form an inseparable unity, and the single member can become complete only along with the whole body of which it is a part, it follows that no sect can ever do justice fully even to the single interest to which it is one-sidedly devoted.

96. Sects then owe it to themselves, as soon as they have fulfilled their historical vocation, to fall back again to the general Church communion from which they have seceded, as in no other way can their spiritual acquisitions be either completed or secured, and they must themselves oth-

erwise stiffen into monumental petrifactions, never to be revisited with the warm life pulse of the one universal Church.

97. It is a cheering sign of the time that in the most different Protestant lands, and particularly in the bosom of the Reformed Church, in which religious individualism both in the good and in the bad sense has been most fully developed, it is coming to be felt more and more that the existing divisions of the Church are wrong, and with this is waking more and more an earnest longing after a true union of all believers, in no communication whatever with the errors either of Oxford or Rome.

98. Finally, also, the liberation of the secular spheres of life from the Church since the Reformation, though not the ultimate normal order, forms notwithstanding — as compared with the previous vassalage of the world to a despotic hierarchy — an advance in the naturalization process of Christianity.

99. The luxuriant separate growth of these interests, as unfolded in the Protestant states, sciences, arts, and social culture, lays the Church under obligation to appropriate these advances to herself, and impress upon them a religious character.

100. The signs of the time, then, and the teachings of history, point us not backward, but forward to a new era of the Church that may be expected to evolve itself gradually from the present process of fermentation, enriched with the entire positive gain of Protestantism.

101. As the movement of history in the Church is like that of the sun from east to west, it is possible that America, into whose broad majestic bosom the most various elements of character and education are poured from the Old World, may prove the theater of this unitive reformation.

102. Thus far, if we put out of view the rise of a few insignificant sects and the separation of church and state, which, to be sure, has very momentous bearings, American church history has produced nothing original, no new *fact* in the history of the Church as a whole.

103. Nowhere else, however, is there at present the same favorable room for farther development, since in no country of the Old World does the Church enjoy such entire freedom, or the same power to renovate itself from within according to its own pleasure.

104. The historical progress of the Church is always conditioned by the national elements which form its physical basis.

105. The two leading nationalities, which are continually coming into contact in this country and flowing into one another with reciprocal action, are the English and the German.

106. The further advancement of the American Church, consequently, must proceed mainly from a special combination of German depth and *Gemütlichkeit* with the force of character and active practical talent for which the English are distinguished.

107. It would be a rich offering, then, to the service of this approaching reformation, on the part of the German churches in America, to transplant hither in proper measure the rich wealth of the better German theology, improving it into such form as our peculiar relations might require.

108. This their proper vocation, however, they have thus far almost entirely overlooked, seeking their salvation for the most part in a characterless surrendry of their own nationality.

109. In view of the particular constitution of a large part of the German immigration, this subjection to the power of a foreign life may be regarded indeed as salutary.

110. But the time has now come when our churches should again rise out of the ashes of the old German Adam, enriched and refined with the advantages of the English nationality.

111. What we most need now is, theoretically, a thorough intellectual theology, scientifically free as well as decidedly believing, together with a genuine sense for history, and, practically, a determination to hold fast the patrimony of our fathers and to go forward joyfully at the same time in the way in which God's Spirit by providential signs may lead, with a proper humble subordination of all we do for our own denomination to the general interest of the one universal Church.

112. The ultimate, sure scope of the Church, towards which the inmost wish and most earnest prayer of all her true friends continually tend, is that perfect and glorious unity, the desire of which may be said to constitute the burden of our Lord's last, memorable, intercessory prayer.

PHILIP SCHAFF

The Three Ages of Church History

Editor's introduction.

Philip Schaff's major literary achievement in his Mercersburg period was his *Geschichte der christlichen Kirche, Erster Band: Die apostolische Kirche* (1851), translated by E. D. Yeomans in 1853 as *History of the Apostolic Church with a General Introduction to Church History.* Several of Schaff's contributions to *Der Kirchenfreund* and *The Mercersburg Review* were studies prepared for this work.

In the introductory section may be found the schematic outline of the pattern of church history as a whole which follows. The idealist categories of objectivity and subjectivity, of corporate authority and individual freedom, of heteronomy and autonomy, are here carried through with more evident consistency than in *The Principle of Protestantism.*

❖ ❖ ❖ ❖

The most general mutual relation and difference of these three ages may be best described by means of the comprehensive philosophical distinction of *objectivity* and *subjectivity.*

The first age presents the *immediate union of objectivity* and *subjectivity;* that is, the two great moral principles on which the individual human life, as well as all history, turns, the *authority* of the general and the *freedom* of the individual, appear tolerably balanced, but still only in their first stage, without any clear definition of their relative limits. In the primitive Church we meet a highly productive activity and diversity of Christian life and Christian science, and a multitude of deformities, also, of dangerous heresies and divisions. But over all these individual and national tendencies, views, and characters, the mind of the universal Church holds sway, separating the false element with infallible instinct, and, in ecumenical councils, settling doctrines and promulgating ecclesiastical laws, to which individual Christians and nations submit. The prevailing tendency of this early Christianity, however, in doctrine, government, worship, and practical piety, is essentially Catholic, and prepares the way for that system which reached its full proportions in the Middle Ages.

Afterwards these two principles of objectivity and subjectivity, the outward and the inward, the general and the individual, authority and freedom, appear, each in turn, in disproportionate prominence. And, in the nature of the case, the principle of *objectivity* first prevails. In the Catholic Church of the Middle Ages, Christianity appears chiefly as law, as a pedagogical institution, a power from without, controlling the whole life of nations and individuals. Hence this may be termed the age of *Christian legalism*, of *Church authority*. Personal freedom is here, to a great extent, lost in slavish subjection to fixed, traditional rules and forms. The individual subject is of account only as the organ and medium of the general spirit of the Church. All secular powers, the state, science, art, are under the guardianship of the hierarchy, and must everywhere serve its ends. This is emphatically the era of grand universal enterprises, of colossal works whose completion required the co-operation of nations and centuries; the age of the supreme outward sovereignty of the visible Church. Such a well-ordered and imposing system of authority was necessary for the training of the Romanic and Germanic nations, to raise them from barbarism to the consciousness and rational use of freedom. Parental discipline must precede independence; children must first be governed, before they can govern themselves; the law is still, as in the days of Moses, a schoolmaster to bring men to Christ. This consciousness of independence awoke even before the close of the Middle Ages. The more the dominion of Rome degenerated from a patriarchal government into a tyranny over conscience and all free thought, the more powerfully was the national and subjective spirit roused to shake off the ignominious yoke.

All this agitation of awakened freedom was at last concentrated in a decisive historical movement, and assumed a positive religious character in the Reformation of the sixteenth century. Here begins the age of *subjectivity* and *individuality* — a name which may be given it both in praise and in censure. It is the characteristic feature of Protestantism, and its great merit, that it views religion as a *personal* concern, which every man, as an individual and for himself, has to settle with God and with his own conscience. It breaks down the walls of partition between Christ and the believer, and teaches every one to go to the fountain of the divine Word, without the medium of human traditions, and to converse, not through interceding saints and priests, but directly, with his Saviour, individually appropriating Christ's merit by a living faith, and rejoicing in his own personal salvation, while he ascribes all the glory of it to the divine mercy alone. Evangelical Protestantism, in its genuine form, moves throughout in the element of that freedom, into which Christ has brought us, and naturally calls forth vast individual activity in literary culture, social improvement, and practical piety. What Germany, Switzerland, Holland, England, Scotland, and the United States have accomplished during the last three centuries in religion, literature, and politics, is all more or less connected with the memorable Reformation of the sixteenth century. We ourselves are all involved in its development. Our present Protestant theology and piety breathe in its atmosphere. The Puritanism of the seventeenth century, the pietism and Methodism of the eighteenth, and most of the religious movements of our day, are but continued vibrations of the Reformation — essentially the same Protestant principle of religious subjectivity, variously modified and applied.

But, on the other hand, what thus constitutes the strength of Protestantism may be called also its weakness. Every right principle is liable to abuse. Every truth may be caricatured and turned into dangerous error by being carried to an extreme, and placed in a hostile attitude towards other truths equally important and necessary. Thus, together with its evangelical religious life, the Protestant movement includes also revolutionary and destructive elements, and dangerous tendencies to licentiousness and dissolution in church and state. True, the Reformers themselves aimed to free the Christian world only from the oppressive authority of human ordinances, and not by any means from the authority of God. On the contrary, they sought to make reason obedient to the Word of God, and the natural will subject to his grace. They wanted no licentiousness, but a freedom pervaded by faith, and ruled by the Holy Scriptures. Nay, so many churchly and catholic elements did they retain that much of our present Protestantism must be considered an apostasy from the position of Luther, Melanchthon, and Calvin. But as history, by reason of human sinfulness, which is always attended with error, proceeds only by opposites and extremes, the Protestant subjectivity gradually degenerated, to a fearful extent, into the corresponding extreme of division, arbitrary judgment, and contempt for every sort of authority. This has been the case especially since the middle of the last century, theoretically in *rationalism*, practically in *sectarianism*.

Rationalism has grown, indeed, into a learned and scientific system chiefly among the Germans, a predominantly theoretic and thinking people, and in the Lutheran Church, which has been styled the church of theologians. But, in substance, it exists also in other European countries, and in North America, under various forms, as Arminianism, Deism, Unitarianism, Universalism, Indifferentism, and downright infidelity; and it infects to some extent the theology even of the orthodox denominations. It places private judgment, as is well known, not only above the pope and the Church, but also above the Bible itself, receiving only so much of the Word of God as can be grasped by the natural understanding or reason . . .

The system of sect and denomination has sprung more from the bosom of the Reformed Church, the church of congregational life, and owes its form to the practical English character, which has a tendency to organize every new principle into a party, and to substitute sects for mere schools. In North America, under the banner of full religious freedom, it has reached its height; but, in its essence, it belongs properly to Protestant Christianity as a whole. All our Protestantism is sadly wanting in unity, at least in outward, visible unity, which is as necessary a fruit of inward unity as works are of faith. The sects, indeed, do not commonly reject the Bible. On the contrary, they stiffly adhere to it, in their own way. But they rely on it in opposition to all history, and in the conceit that they alone are in possession of its true sense. Thus their appealing to the Bible, after all, practically amounts in the end to rationalism; since by the Bible they always mean *their own sense* of it, and thus in fact follow merely their private judgment.

Finally, the principle of false subjectivity reveals itself in the fact that, since the Reformation, the various departments of the world's activity, science, art, politics, and social life, have gradually separated from the Church, and pursue their own independent course. In this wide-spread rationalism, in this frittering of the Church into innumerable party interests, and in her consequent weakness in relation to all the spheres of human life, and especially in relation to the state, we see the operation of a bad, diseased subjectivity, which forms just the opposite pole to the stiff, petrified, and burdensome objectivity of degenerate Catholicism.

But against these evils the deeper life of the Church, which can never be extinguished, again reacts. In opposition to rationalism there arises victoriously a new evangelical theology, which aims to satisfy the demands of science as well as of faith. And, on the other hand, against the sect system there comes up a more and more painful sense of its evils, which calls forth a longing for Church union. This practical want presses the question of the nature and form of the Church prominently into the foreground. The deeper though by no means the prevailing and popular tendency of the time is thus towards objectivity; not, indeed, towards that of the Middle Ages, or even of the Romanism of our day — for history can no more flow backwards than a stream uphill — but to an objectivity enriched with all the experience and diversified energies of the age of subjectivity, to a *higher union of Protestantism and Catholicism* in their pure forms, freed from their respective errors and infirmities. These yearnings of the present, when properly matured, will doubtless issue in a reformation far more glorious than any the Church has yet seen. And then will open a new age, in which human activity, in all its branches, shall freely come back into league with the Church; science and art join to glorify the name of God; and all nations and dominions, according to the word of prophecy, be given to the saints of the Most High.

We may find a parallel to this development of the Christian Church in the history of the Jewish theocracy, which is everywhere typical of the experience of Christ's people. The age of the Primitive Church corresponds to the patriarchal age, which already contained, in embryo, the two succeeding periods. Medieval Catholicism may be compared to the Mosaic period, when law and authority and the organization of the Jewish commonwealth were fully developed. And the modern or evangelical Protestant Church is not without resemblance to the age of the Old Testament prophets, in whom the evangelical element, the Messianic hope predominated, and who stood, to a certain extent, in a hostile attitude towards the unfaithful hierarchy, and towards the dead formalism and ceremonialism of the people. Law and prophecy, the two poles of the Old Testament religion, after having been separately developed, appeared at last united, and as it were incarnate, in the person of John the Baptist immediately before the first advent of Christ. Perhaps in this point also the analogy will hold; and then we might indulge the hope that a union, or at least a friendly approach of the two greatest principles of church history, and of the pious portions of the two most hostile sections of Christendom, will precede the second coming of our Lord, and the perfection of his kingdom, when there shall be one fold and one shepherd. Such private speculations, however, must not be too much trusted, and by no means permitted to influence the representation of facts. Philosophy, instead of presuming to dictate the course of history, and to accommodate it to a preconceived theory, must be made to depend upon it, and must draw her wisdom from its teachings.

III

PHILIP SCHAFF

German Theories of Development

Editor's introduction.

John Henry Newman's famous *Essay on Development* was published in the same year as Schaff's *The Principle of Protestantism*. The two books independently presented to the English-speaking world a new conception of history which had been maturing for more than a generation in Germany, and which was to revolutionize theology. In Germany, Schaff believed, the salient aspect of the theological thought of the preceding generation had been its preoccupation with history. All questions were now considered historically, and almost all theologians at least wrote historical introductions. The literary production in history was many times larger than that in dogmatic theology. The most influential figures in the great faculties were now the historians, such as Neander and Baur.

Schaff published two more extended discussions of the theme in his Mercersburg period. The introductory lecture of his Church history course in the fall of 1845 was enlarged into a little book, *What is Church History?*, which appeared the next year in Nevin's translation. In it Schaff at once surveyed the bibliography of Church history and set forth its presuppositions and theory. Half a decade later, he prefaced his *History of the Apostolic Church* with a "general introduction to Church history" of over one hundred pages, in which much of the same material was given under a somewhat modified organization.

The subtitle of *What is Church History?* was "A Vindication of the Idea of Historical Development." In identifying "the standpoint of organic development" as the common presupposition of German theology, Schaff was on firmer ground than he had been when, in the *History of the Apostolic Church*, he attempted further to identify organic development with the "period of evangelical catholicism." His own description

144

of the various concepts of development in German theology made it quite clear that many of them ought not to be classified under such a heading.

Schaff distinguished the standpoint of organic development from two earlier main conceptions of church history, with as well as certain transitional phases. Ancient, medieval, Reformation, and Tridentine Catholic historiography, from Eusebius through Bossuet and Flacius, could be described as that of unchanging orthodoxy. It was assumed that the orthodox church, however defined, had maintained unchanged the deposit of faith, and that all variant forms of Christianity were by definition error and heresy. The antithesis to this conception was to be found in the historiography of rationalism, as with Semler or Gibbon, which saw only indefinite and meaningless variation in the life of Christianity. The synthesis from the standpoint of organic development did justice at once to the continuities and discontinuities of church history, to the main stream of institutional orthodoxy, and to the sects and heresies as at least negative conditions of progress. Schaff asserted that history showed change, indeed, but an intelligible change, the "evolution of God's plan of redemption proceeding according to rational and necessary laws." [1] The new history was able to respect the variety and uniqueness of the individual phenomena of history, in part because the secret of their interrelations had been discovered.

The pattern or structure of the laws of development had been variously understood. Herder had conceived of the whole life of humanity in terms of the stages of individual growth — childhood, youth, manhood, and old age. With Hegel, on the other hand, the model of thought was one not of biology but of the inner relations of ideas in the perpetual process of defining, comparing, distinguishing, and synthesizing. The governing idea of one epoch would generate its own opposition. In this mode the historical process was seen as continual antagonism, whereas the biological analogy stressed continuity of type. There were numerous other possible ways of conceiving the laws of historical development, several of which Schaff himself utilized.

Four sections of the "General Introduction to Church History" are reprinted below. In the first Schaff briefly characterized the common features he had discerned in the German historical thought of the new era that had succeeded the Enlightenment. Then he devoted a section to each of the three leading "schools" or tendencies — those of Neander, of F. C.

---

1. *What is Church History?* (Philadelphia, 1846), 115.

Baur's Tübingen school, and of the conservative Hegelians as represented by Dorner and Rothe. Schaff acknowledged personal debts to the heads of all three, although he protested frankly against the "dangerous and anti-Christian extravagances" of the Tübingen school.

Several of the individual figures, such as Neander, Rothe, and Thiersch, had been sketched or discussed by Schaff in his *Kirchenfreund*. A whole gallery of portraits was to appear a little later in his *Germany, its Universities, Theology, and Religion, with Sketches of Distinguished German Divines of the Age* (Philadelphia, 1857).

The selection has been slightly trimmed at the beginning and end, and one or two sentences simply listing names have been deleted. About two-thirds of the original footnotes have also been omitted.

. . . With these explanations and qualifications, we proceed to point out those *general* features of the modern German historiography which give it a decided superiority over that of the preceding periods.

1. Its most prominent excellence, as to *form* and method, we take to be its *scientific* structure and that *spirited, lifelike* mode of representation, which springs from the idea of an *organic development*. History is no longer viewed as a mere inorganic mass of names, dates, and facts, but as *spirit* and *life,* and therefore as process, motion, development, passing through various stages, ever rising to some higher state, yet always identical with itself, so that its end is but the full unfolding of its beginning. This makes church history, then, appear as an organism, starting from the person of Jesus Christ, the creator and progenitor of a new race; perpetually spreading both outwardly and inwardly; maintaining a steady conflict with sin and error without and within; continually beset with difficulties and obstructions; yet, under the unfailing guidance of providence, infallibly working towards an appointed end. This idea of organic development combines what was true in the notion of something permanent and unchangeable in church history, as held by both the Catholic and the Old-Protestant Orthodoxy, with the element of truth in the rationalistic conception of motion and flow; and on such ground alone is it possible to understand fully and clearly the temporal life of Christianity. A permanent principle, without motion, stiffens into stagnation; motion, without a principle of permanence, is a process of dissolution. In neither case can there properly be any living history. The conception of such history is that, while it incessantly changes its form, never for a moment

standing still, yet through all its changes it remains true to its own essence; never outgrows itself; incorporates into each succeeding stage of growth the results of the preceding; and thus never loses anything which was ever of real value.

This idea of an organic, steadily improving development of humanity, according to a wise, unalterable plan of providence, is properly speaking as old as Christianity, meets us in many passages of the New Testament (Mt. 13:31,32; Eph. 4:12-16; Col. 2:19; 2 Pet. 3:18), and in occasional remarks of the early Fathers, such as Tertullian and Augustine, and was brought out in the eighteenth century with peculiar emphasis and freshness by the genial Herder, in his "Ideas for the Philosophy of the History of Humanity" (1784),[1] so highly valued by the gifted historian of Switzerland, John von Müller. The more mature and philosophical conception of it, however, and the impulse which it gave to a deeper and livelier study of history, are due especially to the philosophy of Schelling, and still more of Hegel. With Hegel, all life and thought is properly development, or a process of organic growth, which he calls *Aufhebung*; that is, in the threefold sense of this philosophical term so much used by him, (1) an abolition of the previous imperfect form (an *aufheben* in the sense of *tollere*), (2) a preservation of the essence (*conservare*), and (3) an elevation of it to a higher stage of existence (*elevare*). Thus as the child grows to be a man, his childhood is done away, his personal identity is preserved, and his nature raised to the stage of manhood. So, as Judaism passes into Christianity, its exclusive character, as a preparatory establishment, is lost; but its substance is transferred into the gospel, and by it completed. Christ is, on the one hand, the end of the law and the prophets, while, on the other, he says: "I am not come to destroy, but to fulfill" [Mt. 5:17]. This is no contradiction, but only the exhibition of the same relation in different aspects.

The general idea of development, however, takes very different forms from different standpoints; as faith, authority, freedom, nay, even Christianity itself are liable to the most contradictory definitions. How far apart, for example, are Neander and Baur, though both apprehend and represent church history as a process of life! How different again from both the Roman Catholic convert Newman, who has likewise a theory of development of his own! Hegel's development, in the hands of his infidel followers, is at bottom merely an intellectual process of logical thinking,

1. [ED.] *Ideen zur Philosophie der Geschichte der Menschheit* (4 v. in 2; Riga and Leipzig, 1785-92).

in which, in the end, the substance of the Christian life itself is lost. As once Platonism was for Origen, Victorinus, Augustine, Synesius, and others, a bridge to Christianity, while, at the same time, the Neo-Platonists and Julian the Apostate used it as a weapon against the Christian religion; so, also, the categories of modern philosophy (not only German but English too) have subserved purposes and tendencies diametrically opposite. *The right application of the theory of development depends altogether on having beforehand a right view of positive Christianity, and being rooted and grounded in it, not only in thought, but also in heart and experience.* With this preparation a man may learn from any philosophical system without danger, on the principle of Paul, that "all things are his" [2 Cor. 5:18]. Here, too, we may say: *Amicus Plato, amicus Aristoteles, sed magis amica veritas.*

But when this mode of viewing history is adopted, it cannot fail to have its influence on the *representation.* If history is spirit and life, and in fact rational spirit, the manifestation and organic unfolding of eternal, divine Ideas, its representation must likewise *be full of spirit and life,* an *organic reproduction.* A mechanical and lifeless method, which merely accumulates a mass of learned material, however accurately, is no longer enough. The historian's object now is to comprehend truly the events, leading ideas, and prominent actors of the past, and to unfold them before the eyes of his readers, just as they originally stood; to know not only *what* has taken place, but also *how* it has taken place. The old pragmatic method, too, of referring things merely to accidental subjective and psychological causes and motives, has become equally unsatisfying. A higher pragmatism is now demanded, which has paramount regard to the objective forces of history; traces the divine connection of cause and effect; and, with reverential wonder, searches out the plan of eternal wisdom and love.

2. With this view of history, as an inwardly connected whole, pervaded by the same life-blood and always striving towards the same end, is united the second characteristic, which we look upon as the greatest *material* excellence of the most important historians of modern Germany, *viz.,* the spirit of *impartiality* and *Protestant catholicity.* Here also, Herder, with his enthusiastic natural sensibility to the beautiful and the noble in all times and nations, was the mighty pioneer. By the recent development of theology and religious life in Germany the barriers of prejudice, which separated the Lutheran and Reformed churches, have been in a great measure surmounted, and by the Prussian Union (which

without such inward development would be an unmeaning governmental measure) these barriers have been, in a certain degree, also outwardly removed, and almost all the great theologians of the day in Germany now stand essentially upon the basis of the Evangelical Union. Nay more. Protestantism has also been forced to abandon forever her former one-sided posture towards Catholicism. The old view of the Middle Ages especially, whose darkness rationalism in its arrogant pretensions to superior light and knowledge (*Aufklärung*) could not paint black enough, has been entirely repudiated, since the most thorough research has revealed their real significance in poetry, art, politics, science, theology, and religion. It is now generally agreed that the Middle Ages were the necessary connecting link between ancient and modern times; that this period was the cradle of Germanic Christianity and modern civilization; that its grand, peculiar institutions and enterprises, the papacy, the scholastic and mystic divinity, the monastic orders, the Crusades, the creations of sacred art, were indispensable means of educating the European races; and that without them even the Reformation of the sixteenth century could not have arisen. Here, of course, the ultra-Protestant fanatical opposition to the Catholic Church must cease. The general disposition now is to break away from the narrow apologetic and polemic interest of a particular confession or party, the colored spectacles of which allow but a dim and partial view of the Saviour's majestic person. We wish to be guided solely by the spirit of impartial truth; and truth, at the same time, always best vindicates itself by the simple exhibition of its substance and historical course. Christianity can never be absolutely fitted to the last of a fixed human formula without losing her dignity and majesty; and her history may claim, for its own sake, to be thoroughly investigated and represented, *sine ira et studio*, without any impure or loveless designs. The greatest masters in this field become more and more convinced that the boundless life of the Church can never be exhausted by any single sect or period, but can be fully expressed only by the collective Christianity of all periods, nations, confessions, and individual believers; that the Lord has never left himself without a witness; that, consequently, every period has its excellencies, and reflects in its own way the image of the Redeemer. A Neander, for example, reverentially kisses the footprints of his Master, even in the darkest times, and bows before the most varied refractions of his glory. Hence, within the last thirty years, almost every nook of church history has been searched with amazing industry and zeal; the darkest portions have been enlightened; and a mass of treasures brought forth from primitive, medieval, and modern times, to be admired and turned to the most valuable account by present and future generations.

In short, the investigations of *believing* Germany in the sphere of church history are inwardly and irresistibly pressing towards an evangelical catholic, central, and universal position, which will afford a fair view of all parts of the vast expanse. They are making men see how the flood of divine light and life emanating from Jesus Christ, the central sun of the moral universe, has been pouring with unbroken effulgence on all past centuries, and will continue to pour upon the world in ever new variegations. For this reason, the study of our science is continually acquiring a greater practical importance. Church history is the field on which are to be decided the weightiest denominational controversies, the most momentous theological and religious questions. It aims to sketch forth from the old foundations of the Church the plan for its new superstructure. In truth, the spirit of the modern evangelical theology of Germany seems to have already risen, in principle, above the present sad divisions of Christendom; and to foretoken a new age of the Church. It can reach its aim and find complete satisfaction only in the glorious fulfillment of the precious promise of one fold and one shepherd.

Having noticed these general features, which, however, as already intimated, by no means belong to all the German church historians of our day, we must now characterize more minutely the most prominent authors; and in so doing we shall have occasion at the same time to explain our own relation to them, especially to Dr. Neander.

Among the latest German ecclesiastical historians who stand at the head of their profession, we must distinguish two widely different schools, which, as to their philosophico-theological basis, attach themselves to the names of the two greatest scientific geniuses of the nineteenth century, Schleiermacher and Hegel. They bear to each other, in some respects, the relation of direct antagonism, but partly also that of mutual completion; and are well matched in spirit and learning. They are: (1) The school of Schleiermacher and Neander, with Dr. Neander himself at its head, as the "father of modern church history." For Schleiermacher was, properly, no historian; and his posthumous lectures on church history amount to no more than a loose unsatisfactory sketch. But his philosophical views of religion, Christianity, and the Church have indirectly exerted a very important influence upon this department of theology, as well as upon almost all others. (2) The Hegelian school. This, however, falls again into two essentially different branches, *viz.:* (*a*) an *unchurchly* and *destruc-*

tive branch, the *Tübingen* school, as it is called, the chief representative of which is Dr. Baur, of Tübingen; and (*b*) a *conservative* branch, devoted to the *Christian faith,* among the leaders of which must be named with special prominence Drs. Rothe and Dorner. Since this later school, however, combines with the objective view of history and the dialectic method of the Hegelian philosophy the elements, also, of the Schleiermacherian theological culture, it may as well have an independent place, as a third school, intermediate between the two others.

§ 35. *Dr. Neander and His School*

Dr. Augustus Neander forms an epoch in the development of Protestant church historiography, as well as Flacius in the sixteenth century, Arnold at the close of the seventeenth, Mosheim and, somewhat later, Semler in the eighteenth; and was accordingly, by general consent, distinguished even before his death (1850) with the honorary title, "Father of (Modern) Church History." From him we have a large work, unfortunately not finished, on the general history of the Christian Church, extending from the death of the Apostles almost to the Reformation. Next a special work on the apostolic period, which together with one on the life of Christ (1837, 5th ed. 1849) serves as a foundation for the main work. Then, several valuable historical monographs on Julian the Apostate (1812), St. Bernard of Clairvaux (1813, 2nd ed. 1849), the Gnostic systems (1818), St. John Chrysostom (1821, 3rd ed. 1848), the Anti-Gnostic Tertullian (1825, 3rd ed. 1849). Finally some collections of smaller treatises, mostly historical, in which he presents single persons or manifestations of the Christian life, on the authority of original sources, indeed, but in a form better adapted to meet the practical religious wants of the public generally. The most important of these is his *Denkwürdigkeiten aus der Geschichte des christlichen Lebens* (3 vol., 1822; 3rd ed. 1845), a series of edifying pictures of religious life in the first eight centuries.[2]

Neander was fitted as few have been for the great task of writing the

2. [ED.] English versions of Neander's works are noted where they exist in the citations that follow: *General History of the Christian Religion and Church,* translated by J. Torrey (8 v., Edinburgh, 1847–52; 5 v., Boston, 1848–54); *History of the Planting and Training of the Christian Church,* translated by J.E. Ryland from the third German edition (Philadelphia, 1844); *Life of Jesus Christ,* translated by J. M'Clintock and C.E. Blumenthal from the fourth German edition (New York, 1848); *The Emperor Julian and His Generation,* translated by G.V. Cox (New York, 1850); *The*

history of the Church of Jesus Christ. By birth and early training an Israelite, and a genuine Nathanael too, full of childlike simplicity, and of longings for the Messianic salvation; in youth an enthusiastic student of the Grecian philosophy, particularly of Plato, who became, for him, as for Origen and other Church Fathers, a scientific schoolmaster to bring him to Christ — he had, when in his seventeenth year he received holy baptism, passed through, in his own inward experience, so to speak, the whole historical course by which the world had been prepared for Christianity; he had gained an experimental knowledge of the workings of Judaism and heathenism in their direct tendency towards Christianity; and thus he had already broken his own way to the only proper position for contemplating the history of the Church; a position whence Jesus Christ is viewed as the object of the deepest yearnings of humanity, the center of all history, and the only key to its mysterious sense. Richly endowed in mind and heart; free from all domestic cares; an eunuch from his mother's womb, and that for the kingdom of heaven's sake (Mt. 19:12); without taste for the distracting externals and vanities of life; a stranger in the material world, which, in his last years, was withdrawn even from his bodily eye — he was, in every respect, fitted to bury himself during a long and uninterrupted academical course, from 1812 to 1850, in the silent contemplation of the spiritual world, to explore the past, and to make his home among the mighty dead, whose activity belonged to eternity. In theology, he was at first a pupil of the gifted Schleiermacher, under whose electrifying influence he came during his university studies at Halle, and at whose side he afterwards stood as colleague for many years in Berlin. He always thankfully acknowledged the great merits of this German Plato, who, in a time of general apostasy from the truth, rescued so many young men from the iron embrace of rationalism, and led them at least to the threshold of the holiest of all. But he himself took a more positive course, rejecting the pantheistic and fatalistic elements which had adhered to the system of his master from the study of Spinoza, and which, it must be confessed, bring it in a measure into direct opposition to the simple gospel and the old faith of the Church. This was, for him, of the greatest moment. For only in the rec-

Life and Times of St. Bernard, translated by M. Wrench (London, 1843); Genetische Entwicklung der vernehmsten gnostischen Systeme (Berlin, 1818); Life of St. Chrysostom, translated by J. C. Stapleton (London, 1845); Antignostikus; or Spirit of Tertullian, translated by J. E. Ryland from the third German edition (London, 1851); Memorials of Christian Life in the Early and Middle Ages, translated by J. E. Ryland (London, 1852).

ognition of a personal God, and of the free agency of individual men, can history be duly apprehended and appreciated. But apart from this he was, in his own particular department, entirely independent. For Schleiermacher's strength lay in criticism, dogmatics, and ethics, far more than in church history, though by his spiritual intuitions he undoubtedly exerted on the latter science also a quickening influence.

Thus, from the beginning of his public labors, Neander appeared as one of the leading founders of the new evangelical theology of Germany, and its most conspicuous representative on the field of church and doctrine history.

His first and greatest merit consists in restoring the *religious* and *practical* interest to its due prominence, in opposition to the coldly intellectual and negative critical method of rationalism, yet without thereby wronging in the least the claims of science. This comes out very clearly even in the preface to the first volume of his great work, where he declares it to be the grand object of his life to set forth the history of Christ, "as a living witness for the divine power of Christianity; a school of Christian experience; a voice of edification, instruction, and warning, sounding through all ages, for all who will hear." True, he is second to none in learning. With the Church Fathers in particular, many years of intercourse had made him intimately familiar. And though, from his hearty dislike for all vanity and affectation, he never makes any parade with citations, yet by his pertinent and conscientious manner of quoting he everywhere evinces a perfect mastery of the sources: for the genuine scholar is recognized not in the number of citations, which, at any rate, may be very cheaply had from second or third hand, but in their independence and reliability, and in the critical discernment with which they are selected. With the most thorough knowledge of facts he united, also, almost every other qualification of a scientific historian; a spirit of profound critical inquiry, a happy power of combination, and no small talent for genetically developing religious characters and their theological systems. But he diffuses through all his theoretical matter a pious, gentle, and deeply humble, yet equally earnest spirit. Like Spener and Francke, Neander views theology, and with it church history, not merely as a thing of the understanding, but also as a practical matter for the heart; and he has chosen for his motto: *Pectus est quod theologum facit.*[3] This gives his works a great advantage over the productions of the modern Tübingen school, as well as over the text-book of Gieseler, which in

3. [ED.] "It is the heart that makes the theologian."

learning and keen research is at least of equal merit; though in the case of the latter work we are bound to consider that the author pursues a different object, and by his invaluable extracts from sources compensates in part for the lack of life in the dry skeleton of his text. Neander moves through the history of the Church in the spirit of faith and devotion, Gieseler with critical acumen and cold intellect. The one lives in his heroes, thinks, feels, acts, and suffers with them; the other surveys their movements from a distance, without love or hatred, without sympathy or antipathy. The former reverently kisses the footsteps of his Lord and Saviour wherever he meets them; the latter remains unmoved and indifferent even before the most glorious manifestations of the Christian life.

This spirit of Christian piety, which animates Neander's historical writings and rules his whole habit of thought, is further characterized by a comprehensive *liberality* and evangelical *catholicity*. Arnold and Milner, in their subjective and unchurchly pietism, had like regard, indeed, to practical utility; but they could find matter of edification, for the most part, only in heretics and dissenters. From these historians Neander differs not only in his incomparably greater learning and scientific ability, but also in that right feeling by which, notwithstanding his own disposition to show even too much favor to certain heretics, he still traces the main current of the Christian life in the unbroken line of the Christian Church. From the orthodox Protestant, rough, polemical historians of the seventeenth century, on the other hand, Neander differs in the liberal spirit with which, though constitutionally inclined rather to the German Lutheran type of religious character in its moderate, Melanchthonian form, he rises above denominational limits, and plants himself on the basis of the *Union*, where Lutheran and Reformed Protestantism became only parts of a higher whole. But his sympathies go far beyond the Reformation, and take in also the peculiar forms of *Catholic* piety. With him, in truth, the universal history of the Church is no mere fortuitous concourse of outward facts but a connected process of evolution, an unbroken continuation of the life of Christ through all centuries. He has won, in particular, the priceless merit of having introduced a more correct judgment respecting the whole Church *before* the Reformation; above all, of having presented to the Protestant mind, not in the service of this or that party, but in the sole interest of truth, and in an unprejudiced, living reproduction, the theology of the Church Fathers in their conflict with the oldest forms of heresy. This he did first in his monographs. In his

Tertullian he drew a picture of the African Church of the second and third centuries, and taught the true value, hitherto so much mistaken, of this rough but vigorous Christian, the patriarch of the Latin theology. In his *John Chrysostom* he portrayed the greatest orator, interpreter, and saint of the ancient Greek Church. In his *Bernard of Clairvaux* he described with warm though by no means blind admiration the worthiest representative of monkery, of the Crusades, and of the practical and orthodox mysticism, in the bloom of the Catholic Middle Ages, previously so little known and so much decried. He felt thus at home in all periods, because he met the same Christ in them all, only in different forms. By such sketches, drawn from life, and then by the connected representation in his large work, he contributed mightily to burst the shackles of Protestant prejudice and bigotry, and to prepare the way in some measure for a mutual understanding between Catholicism and Protestantism on historical ground. He adopted the significant words of the Jansenist Pascal, one of his favorite authors: "En Jésus-Christ toutes les contradictions sont accordées." [4] And in these great antagonisms in church history he saw no irreconcilable contradiction, but two equally necessary manifestations of the same Christianity; and he looked forward with joyful hope to a future reconciliation of the two, already typified, as he thought, in St. John, the apostle of love and of the consummation.[5]

These large views of history, however, and this candid acknowledgment of the great facts of the ancient and medieval church — views which may lead, in the end, to practical consequences even more weighty than he himself could foresee or approve — spring, in Neander's case, by no means from a Romanizing tendency. Such a disposition was utterly foreign to him. His liberality proceeds partly from his mild, John-like nature, and partly from his genuine Protestant toleration and high regard for individual personality; or from such a *subjectivity* as formed a barrier against ultra-Protestant and sectarian bigotry no less than against Romanism, where individual freedom is lost in the authority of the general. In this he is a faithful follower of Schleiermacher, who, though he based his philosophy on the pantheistic system of Spinoza, had nevertheless an uncommonly keen eye and a tender regard for the personal and individual.

4. [ED.] *Pensées*, fragment 683.
5. Cf. the closing words of his *History of the Apostolic Church*, and the dedication of the second edition of the first volume of his larger work to Schelling, where he alludes with approbation to that philosopher's idea of three stages of development answering to the three apostles Peter, Paul, and John.

What Schleiermacher thus asserted mainly in the sphere of speculation and doctrine, Neander carried out in history. He was fully convinced that the free spirit of the gospel could never be concentrated in any one given form, but could be completely manifested only in a great variety of forms and views. Hence his frequent remark that Christianity, the leaven which is to pervade humanity, does not destroy natural capacities, or national and individual differences, but refines and sanctifies them. Hence his partiality for diversity and freedom of development, and his enmity to constraint and uniformity. Hence his taste for monographic literature, which sets a whole age concretely before the eye in the person of a single representative; of which invaluable form of church history Neander is to be accounted the proper father. Hence the love and patience and scrupulous fidelity with which he goes into all the circumstances of the men and systems he unfolds, to whatever nation, time, or school of thought they may belong; setting forth their defects and aberrations, as well as their virtues and merits; though without neglecting the duty of the philosophical historian, to collect the scattered particulars again into one complete picture, and refer them to the one unchanging Idea. Finally this sacred reverence for the image of God in the persons of men, and for the rights of individuals, accounts for the esteem and popularity which this equally pious and learned Church Father of the nineteenth century commands, more than any other modern theologian, in almost all sections of Protestantism, not only in Germany, but also in France, Holland, England, Scotland, and America, nay, so far as difference of ecclesiastical ground at all allows, among liberal-minded scholars of the Roman Catholic Church itself. In this view he stands before us, amidst the present distractions of Christendom, as an apostle of *mediation,* in the noblest sense of the word; and as such he still has, by his writings, a long and exalted mission to fulfill.

To sum up what has now been said: the most essential peculiarity, the fairest ornament, the most enduring merit of Neander's church history consists in the *vital union of the two elements of science and Christian piety,* and in the exhibition of both in the form not of dead narrative or mechanical accumulation of material, but of *life and genetic development.* The practical element is not a mere appendage to the subject in the way of pious reflection and declamation, but grows out of it as by nature. It is the very spirit which fills and animates the history of Christianity as such. Neander is Christian not *although* but *because* he is scientific; and scientific, *because* he is Christian. This is the only form of edification which *can* be expected in a learned work; but such *must* be expected where the work has to do with Christianity and its history. And this gain, therefore, ought never to be lost. A church historian without faith and piety can only set before us, at best, instead of the living body of Christ, a cold marble statue, without seeing eye or feeling heart.

But a perfect church history calls for more than this. While we respect and admire in Neander the complete blending of the scientific element with the *Christian,* we miss, on the other hand, its union with the *churchly.* By this we mean, first, that he lacks decided *orthodoxy.* In his treatment of the life of Jesus and the apostolic period, we meet with views respecting the Holy Scriptures, their inspiration and authority, together with doubts respecting the strictly historical character of certain sections of the gospel history, and the genuineness of particular books of the sacred canon (the First Epistle to Timothy, the Second Epistle of Peter, and the Apocalypse), which, though by no means rationalistic, are yet rather too loose and indefinite, and involve, in our judgment, too many and sometimes too serious concessions to modern criticism. Of all his works, his *Leben Jesu* is perhaps, in this respect, the farthest from satisfying the demands of sound faith, however highly we must esteem the honesty and tender conscientiousness which usually give rise to his critical scruples and doubts. There is, it is true, in this difficult field, a skepticism more commendable than that hasty and positive dogmatism which, instead of seriously laboring to untie the Gordian knot, either refuses to see or carelessly cuts it. But the *full* and *unconditional* reverence for the holy word of God, in which the whole Schleiermacherian school is more or less deficient, requires, wherever science cannot yet clear away the darkness, an humble submission of reason to the obedience of faith, or a present suspension of decisive judgment, in the hope that farther and deeper research may lead to more satisfactory results.

Again, Neander must be called unchurchly in his views of theology and history, on account of his comparative disregard for the *objective* and *realistic* character of Christianity and the Church, and his disposition, throughout his writings, to resolve the whole mystery into something purely inward and ideal. In this respect he appears to us quite too little Catholic, in the real and historical sense of the word. True, he is neither a Gnostic, nor a Baptist, nor a Quaker, though many of his expressions, sundered from their connection, sound very favorable to these hyperspiritualistic sects. He by no means mistakes the objective forces of history, and can readily appreciate the realistic element in such men as Tertullian,

Athanasius, Augustine, Bernard, and even in the popes and schoolmen, up to a certain point. He in fact speaks frequently of general directions of mind which embody themselves in individuals; and the antitheses of idealism and realism, rationalism and supranaturalism, logical intelligence and mystic contemplation, and the various combinations of these tendencies, belong to the standing categories of his treatment of history. But in the first place he refers these differences themselves, for the most part, to a merely psychological basis, to the differences of men's constitutions — that is, to a purely subjective ground. His prevailing view is that the kingdom of God forms itself from individuals, and therefore, in a certain sense, from below upwards; that, as Schleiermacher once said, "the doctrinal system of the Church takes its rise from the opinions of individuals." Then, in the next place, it is plain that Neander himself is of the spiritualistic and idealistic turn, and does not always succeed in avoiding the dangers to which this tendency, in itself needful and legitimate, is exposed. Hence his predilection for the Alexandrian fathers, Clement and Origen. Hence his too favorable representation, as it appears to us, of Gnosticism, especially of Marcion, whose pseudo-Pauline hostility to the Catholic tradition he even makes to be a presage of the Reformation — which, if true, would do the Reformation poor service. Hence his overstrained love of equity towards all heretical and schismatical movements, in which he almost always takes for granted some deep moral and religious interest even where they clearly rest on the most willful insurrection against lawful authority; the love of justice, with him, though by no means so abused as by that patron of sects, the pietistic Arnold, still often running into injustice to the historical Church. Hence his undisguised dislike for all that he comprehends under the phrase, *re-introduction of the legal Jewish ideas* into the Catholic Church, including the special priesthood and outward service; this he thinks to be against the freedom advocated by St. Paul and the idea of the universal priesthood (which, however, even under the Old Testament, had place *along with* the special; comp. 1 Pet. 2:9 with Ex. 19:6); though he is forced to concede to this Catholic legalism at least an important office in the training of the Teutonic nations. Hence his indifference to fixed ecclesiastical organization, and his aversion to all restriction to confessions in the Protestant church; this, to him, savors of "bondage to the letter," "mechanism of forms," "symbol-worship." On this latter point we must, indeed, regard him as mainly in the right against those who would absolutely repristinate some particular confession of the past—the Form of Concord, perhaps,

with its rigid Lutheranism—utterly regardless of the enlarged wants of
the present. There was still more ground, also, for his zeal against the
philosophical tyranny of the Hegelian intellectualists and pantheists, who,
in the zenith of their prosperity, aimed to supplant a warm, living Christianity by dry scholasticism and unfruitful traffic in dialectic forms. Still
the theological school now in hand is plainly wanting in a just appreciation of the import of law and authority in general — a defect closely connected with the false view taken of the Old Testament in Schleiermacher's theology and philosophy of religion, and with his half-Gnostic ultra-
rationalism. The freedom for which Neander so zealously contends is of
quite a latitudinarian sort, running at times into indefiniteness and arbitrariness, and covering Sabellian, Semi-Arian, Anabaptist, Quakerish, and
other dangerous errors with the mantle of charity. Much as we respect
the noble disposition from which this springs, we must still never forget
the important principle that true freedom can thrive only in the sphere of
authority, the individual only in due subordination to the general; and
that genuine catholicity is as rigid against error as it is liberal towards the
various manifestations of truth.

Neander views Christianity and the Church not, indeed, as necessarily
opposed to each other, yet as two separate and more or less mutually exclusive spheres. In the mind, at least, of the whole ancient Eastern and
Western Church, these two conceptions virtually coincide, or at all
events are as closely related as soul and body; and the one is always the
measure of the other. This is abundantly proved by the examples of
Irenaeus, Tertullian, Cyprian, Ambrose, Augustine, Athanasius, Chrysostom, Anselm, Bernard, &c., even according to Neander's own representations of them. But the very title of his large work: "General History of
the Christian Religion and Church," seems to involve the idea, to which a
one-sided Protestant view of the world may easily lead, that there is a
Christian religion *out of* and *beside* the Church. On this point we venture
no positive decision; but we think that such a separation can hardly be
reconciled with Paul's doctrine of the church as the "body of Jesus
Christ," "the fullness of him that filleth all in all" [Eph. 1:23]. The future
must reveal whether Christianity can be upheld without the divine institution of the Church — that is, whether the soul can live without the
body; whether it will not, at last, resolve itself into a ghost or Gnostic
phantom, as certainly as the body without the soul sinks into a corpse.
Meanwhile we hold to the maxim: *Where Christ is, there also is the
Church, his Body; and where the Church is, there also is Christ, her*

Head, and all grace; and what God hath joined together, let not man put asunder.

With these principal faults of Neander's church history, which we have comprehended under the term "unchurchliness," in the wide sense — though, on the other hand, with its above-named merits too — are more or less closely connected several other subordinate defects. Neander is pre-eminently the historian, so to speak, of the *invisible* Church, and has therefore exhibited the development of Christian *doctrine* and Christian *life*, especially so far as these express themselves in single theologians and pious men, in the most thorough and original way. In this he has, in general, surpassed all his predecessors. On the contrary, in what pertains more to the outward manifestation of the Church, to its bodily form, his contemplative, idealistic turn allows him less interest. This appears at once in his sections on the *constitution* of the Church, where the subject is treated, even in the first period, in a very unsatisfactory manner, and under the influence of his antipathy to the hierarchical element; which, we may here remark, undeniably made its appearance as early as the second century, in the Epistles of Ignatius, too groundlessly charged by him with interpolation, even in their shorter form. For the worldly and political aspect of church history, with which the department of ecclesiastical polity has chiefly to do; the connection of the Church with the state; the play of human passions, which, alas! are perpetually intruding even into the most sacred affairs, the godly man, in his guileless, childlike simplicity and his recluse student life, had, at any rate, no very keen eye. But while he takes little notice of small and low motives, he enters the more carefully into the deeper and nobler springs of actions and events. For the superficial pragmatism of his instructor, Planck, who often derives the most important controversies from the merest accidents and the most corrupt sources, he thus substitutes a far more spiritual and profound pragmatism, which makes the interest of religion the main factor in church history. If he sometimes causes us almost to forget that the kingdom of God is *in* the world, it is only to bring out the more forcibly the great truth of that declaration of Christ, which he has characteristically taken as a motto for each volume of his larger work: "My kingdom is not *of* this world" [Jn. 18:36].

Equally lacking was the excellent Neander in a cultivated sense for the *esthetic* or *artistic* in church history; though this defect, again, appears as the shadow of a virtue, arising from the unworldly character of his mind. Had he lived in the first centuries, he, with Clement of Alexandria,

Tertullian, and others, would have looked upon art, so prostituted to the service of heathen idolatry, as a vain show, inconsistent with the humble condition of the Church, if not as an actual *pompa diaboli*.[6] This, indeed, is by no means his view. He is not puritanically, from principle, opposed to art. The all-pervading, leavenlike nature of the gospel is one of his favorite thoughts. He advocates even the use of painting "for the glorifying of religion; agreeably to the spirit of Christianity, which should reject nothing purely human, but appropriate, pervade, and sanctify all";[7] and in his account of the image controversies, he approves the middle course between the two extremes of worship of images and war upon them. But a full description of the influence of Christianity upon this sphere of human activity, a history of church sculpture, painting, architecture, music, and poetry, as well as of all that belongs to the symbolic show of the medieval Catholic worship, is not to be looked for in his work. In this respect he is far surpassed by the spirited though much less spiritual Hase, who was the first to interweave the history of Christian art into the general body of church history, with his elegant taste, in short but expressive and pointed sketches. But Neander's indifference to the beautiful as such is fairly balanced, to a great extent, by his merit in not allowing himself to be repelled, like polite wits and worldlings, by the homely and poor servant-form in which the divine on earth is often veiled; in discerning the real worth of the heavenly treasure in earthen vessels, of the rich kernel even under a rough shell; or, as he himself says of Tertullian, in "recognizing, and bringing out from beneath its temporal obscurity, the stamp of divinity in real life."[8]

From the same point of view we must judge, finally, Neander's style. His writing moves along with heavy uniformity and wearisome verbosity, without any picturesque alternation of light and shade, without rhetorical elegance or polish, without comprehensive classification, like a noiseless stream over an unbroken plain. Thus far it can by no means be recommended as a model of historical delineation. But, on the other hand, by its perfect naturalness, its contemplative unction, and its calm presentation of the subject in hand, it appeals to sound feeling, and faithfully reflects the finest features of the great man's character, his *simplicity and*

6. [ED.] Schaff apparently refers here to Tertullian's argument in *De Spectaculis*, 7, that the processions in the public games were idolatrous. An English translation of the work may be found in the Ante-Nicene Fathers series.

7. *Kirchengeschichte*, III, 400. [ED.] General History, III, §4.2: Gregory the Great on Images.

8. [ED.] Preface to *Antignostikus; or Spirit of Tertullian*.

his humility. The golden mean here appears to us to lie between the un-adorned and uncolored plainness of a Neander and the dazzling brilliancy of a Macaulay.

But in spite of all these faults, Neander still remains, on the whole, be-yond doubt the greatest church historian thus far of the nineteenth cen-tury. Great, too, especially in this, that he never suffered his renown to obscure at all his sense of the sinfulness and weakness of every human work in this world. With all his comprehensive knowledge, he justly re-garded himself as, among many others, merely a forerunner of a new creative epoch of ever-young Christianity; and towards that time he gladly stretched his vision, with the prophetic gaze of faith and hope, from amidst the errors and confusion around him. "We stand," says he, "on the line between an old world and a new, about to be called into being by the ever fresh energy of the gospel. For the fourth time an epoch in the life of our race is in preparation by means of Christianity. We therefore can furnish, *in every respect, but pioneer work* for the pe-riod of the new creation, when life and science shall be regenerated, and the wonderful works of God proclaimed with new tongues of fire." [9]

To the school of Schleiermacher and Neander, in the *wide* sense, be-longs the majority of the latest theologians of Germany, who have be-come known in the field of church and doctrine history by larger or smaller, general or monographic works . . .[10] From Hagenbach, for in-stance, we have a doctrine history, and in more popular style for the general reader, an interesting work on Protestantism, and another on the first three centuries; which, by their simple, clear vivacity, and freedom from technical pedantry, commend themselves even to English taste.[11] Hundeshagen and Schenkel have likewise bestowed their chief strength upon the nature and history of German Protestantism; the former at the same time touching, with the soundest discernment, upon many of its

9. [ED.] *Life of Jesus Christ,* xxii.

10. [ED.] Two sentences, listing some twenty historical authors, have been omitted from what follows.

11. [ED.] The works of Karl R. Hagenbach available in English include: *Compen-dium of the History of Doctrines,* translated by C. W. Buch from the second, much improved German edition (2 v., Edinburgh, 1850–52); *Textbook of the History of Doctrines,* a revision of the preceding with additions from the fourth edition and other sources by H. B. Smith (2 v., New York, 1869); *A History of Christian Doc-trines,* translated by E. H. Plumptre from the fifth German edition (3 v., Edinburgh, 1883–95); *History of the Reformation in Germany and Switzerland Chiefly* translated by E. Moore from the fourth German edition (2 v., Edinburgh, 1878–79); *History of German Rationalism,* translated by W. L. Gage and J. H. Stuckenberg (Edinburgh, 1865); *History of the Church in the Eighteenth and Nineteenth Centuries,* translated by J. F. Hurst (2 v., New York, 1869).

weaknesses, and the bad effects of a disproportionate literary activity, from which Germany has long suffered. But still more distinguished is Ullmann, professor in Heidelberg, whom we consider, next to Neander, the most eminent church historian of Schleiermacher's school. His monograph on Gregory Nazianzen (A.D. 1825), and still more his work on the Reformers before the Reformation (two volumes, 1841–42), are, for thorough learning, calm clearness, and classic elegance, real masterpieces of church historiography. From this mild and amiable author we may, perhaps, still look for a general church history, which as to form and style would undoubtedly greatly surpass that of Neander.[12]

Among the historians who, though not professional theologians, have yet made church history the subject of their study, we cannot omit to mention in this connection the celebrated Leopold Ranke, professor in Berlin, and author of the history of the popes in the sixteenth and seventeenth centuries, and of "German History in the Age of the Reformation." He is not a man of system, and seldom rises to general philosophical views; but he has an uncommonly keen eye for details and individuals, and is in this respect akin to the school of Schleiermacher, and still more to Dr. Hase. With this he combines fine diplomatic tact and shrewdness, the power to reveal the most secret springs of historical movements, and that, too, in part from original unprinted sources, especially from accounts of embassies and private correspondence. And he can present the results of his thoroughly original investigations with graphic perspicuity and lively elegance, affording his readers at the same time instruction and delightful entertainment. He might be termed, in many respects, the German Macaulay.[13]

§ 36. Dr. Baur, Pantheistic Rationalism and Modern Gnosticism

In direct opposition to the Neandrian style of church history stands the new Tübingen school, in close connection with the Hegelian philoso-

12. [ED.] Karl Ullmann, Reformers before the Reformation, translated by R. Menzies (2 v., Edinburgh, 1855); Gregory of Nazianzum, translated by G. V. Cox (London, 1851).

13. [ED.] Leopold Ranke, The Popes of Rome, translated by D.D. Scott (2 v., Glasgow, 1846–47); same, translated by S. Austin from the fourth German edition (3 v., London, 1866); The History of the Popes, translated by E. Foster (3 v., London, 1896); History of the Reformation in Germany, translated by S. Austin (3 v., London, 1845–47).

phy. This philosophy carries out in all directions, and brings into well-proportioned shape, the fundamental views of Schelling, though at the same time it is in a high degree independent, and a wonderful monument of comprehensive knowledge and of the power of human thought. Its original peculiarity, which distinguished it from the systems of Fichte and Schleiermacher, was its objective and so far historical spirit. It was, in a certain sense, a philosophy of restoration, in rigid antagonism to the revolutionary, self-sufficient Illuminationism of the last century. To arbitrary self-will it opposed stern law; to private individual opinion, the general reason of the world and the public opinion of the state. It regarded history not as the play of capricious chance, but as the product of the necessary, eternal laws of the spirit. Its maxim is: Everything reasonable is actual, and everything actual (all that *truly* exists) is reasonable. It sees in all ages of history the agency of higher powers; not, indeed, of the Holy Ghost, in the biblical sense, yet of a rational world-spirit, which makes use of individual men for the accomplishment of its plans. Hegel acknowledges Christianity as the absolute religion, and ascribes to the ideas of the Incarnation and the Trinity, though in a view very different from that of the Church doctrine, a deep philosophical truth, carrying the idea of Trinity into his view of the whole universe, the world of matter as well as of mind.

But these general principles were capable, in theology, of leading to wholly opposite views, according as the objective forces, by which Hegel conceived the process of history to be started and ruled, were taken to be real existences or mere abstract conceptions, according as the mind was guided by a living faith in Christianity or by a purely speculative and scientific interest. Thus arise from the Hegelian philosophy two very different theological schools, a positive and a negative, a churchly and an antichristian. They are related to one another as the Alexandrian Fathers, Clement and Origen, who brought the Hellenistic, particularly the Platonic philosophy into the service of Christianity, were related to the Gnostics, who by the same philosophy caricatured the Christian religion, and to the Neo-Platonists, who arrayed themselves directly against it. The notorious Strauss, one of the infidel Hegelians, has applied to these parties the political terms *right* wing and *left* wing, calling the neutral and intermediate party the center. The leaders of the Right are Marheineke, Daub, and Göschel (the last two, however, having nothing to do with church history); of the Left, Baur and his disciples, Strauss, Zeller, and Schwegler, all from Württemberg, and all students and afterwards teachers in Tübingen; so that they may be called the Tübingen school. As the Tübingen theologians have paid more attention to historical theology than the older Hegelians, who devoted themselves almost exclusively to systematic divinity, we turn our eye first to them, and more particularly to Baur, on whom they all depend.

Dr. Ferdinand Christian Baur, professor of historical theology in Tübingen, is a man of imposing learning, bold criticism, surprising power of combination, and restless productiveness; but, properly, too philosophical to be a faithful historian, and too historical to be an original philosopher; a pure theorist, moreover, and intellectualist, destitute of all sympathy with the practical religious interests of Christianity and the Church. He has founded, since the appearance of his article on the Christ-party in Corinth,[14] a formal historical, or rather unhistorical, school, which in the negation of everything positive, and in destructive criticism upon the former orthodox views of primitive Christianity, has far outstripped Semler and his followers. We might therefore have placed it in the fourth period, as a new phase of the rationalistic mode of treating history. But, in the first place, this would too much interrupt the chronological order; and then again there is, after all, a considerable scientific difference between the older and the later rationalism, although in their practical results, when consistently carried out, they come to the same thing, namely the destruction of the Church and of Christianity. The vulgar rationalism proceeds from the common human understanding (whence its name, *rationalismus communis* or *vulgaris*), and employs, accordingly, a tolerably popular but exceedingly dry, spiritless style. The more refined rationalism deals with the speculative reason, and clothes its ideas in the stately garb of a high-sounding scientific terminology and dexterous logic. The former is deistic, abstractly sundering the divine and the human, so as to allow no real intercommunion of both. The latter is pantheistic, confounding God and the world and deifying the human spirit. The one is allied to the Ebionistic heresy, the other to the Gnostic. The first holds fast the ideas of so-called natural religion, God, freedom, and immortality, and endeavors to keep on some sort of terms with the Bible. The last recognizes neither a personal God nor a personal immortality of man; denies the apostolic authorship of almost all the books of the New Testament; and resolves the most important historical statements of

14. "*Die Christuspartei in der Korinthischen Gemeinde, der Gegensatz des petrinischen und paulinischen Christenthums in der ältesten Kirche,*" in the *Tübinger Zeitschrift für Theologie,* 1831, No. 4.

the Bible into mythological conceits or even intentional impositions. Both give themselves out for legitimate products of the Protestant principle of free inquiry and resistance to human authority; but both keep entirely to the negative, destructive side of the Reformation; have no concern for its positively religious, evangelical character; and must, in the end, destroy Protestantism itself, as well as Catholicism.

Baur, in virtue of his predominant turn for philosophy, has applied himself with particular zest to the most difficult parts of doctrine history. These suit him much better than biographical monographs, which require a lively interest in individual persons. The extent of his productions since 1831 is really astonishing.[15] Besides a small text-book of doctrine history and several treatises in various journals, we have from him a number of larger works, of which we may mention particularly those on the Gnosis (1835), in which he wrongly and somewhat arbitrarily includes not only the proper Gnosticism of antiquity, but also all attempts at a philosophical apprehension of Christianity; on Manicheism (1831); on the historical development of the doctrine of the Atonement (1838), and of the dogma of the Trinity and Incarnation (three stout volumes, 1841–43); all characterized by extensive, thorough, and well-digested learning, great philosophical acumen, freshness of combination, and skillful description; forming epochs in their kind; but too much under the influence of his own false preconceptions [16] to claim justly the praise of invariable objective fidelity.

The Tübingen school, however, has made most noise with its investiga-

15. [ED.] Although the titles that follow are given in English, none of these works by F. C. Baur is available in an English translation. The original publications are: *Lehrbuch der christlichen Dogmengeschichte* (Stuttgart, 1847); *Die christliche Gnosis oder die christliche Religions-Philosophie in ihrer geschichtlichen Entwicklung* (Tübingen, 1835); *Das Manichäische Religionssystem nach den Quellen neu untersucht und entwickelt* (Tübingen, 1831); *Die christliche Lehre von der Versöhnung in ihrer geschichtlichen Entwicklung von der alteresten Zeit bis auf die neuste* (Tübingen, 1838); *Die christliche Lehre von der Dreieinigkeit und der Menschwerdung Gottes in ihrer geschichtlichen Entwicklung* (3 v., Tübingen, 1841–43).

16. True, this school, especially Strauss in his *Leben Jesu*, boasts of freedom from all philosophical or doctrinal prepossession. But, with Strauss, this consists in freedom from all leaning towards the Christian faith, and a full bias towards unbelief, which wholly unfits him for any right apprehension or representation of the life of Jesus. Absolute freedom from prepossession, in an author of any character, is a sheer impossibility and absurdity. The grand requisite for the theologian is not that he have no preconceptions, but that his preconceptions be just, and such as the nature of the case demands. Without being fully possessed, beforehand, with the Christian faith, a man can rightly understand neither the Holy Scriptures nor the history of the Church.

tions respecting the history of primitive Christianity; seeking to over-throw, in due form, the old views on this subject. This operation was publicly commenced by Dr. David Frederick Strauss — a younger pupil of Baur's, but rather more daring and consistent than his master — in his *Leben Jesu*, which astounded the world in 1835. In this book he reduces the life of the God-man, with icy, wanton hand, to a dry skeleton of everyday history, and resolves all the gospel accounts of miracles, partly on the ground of pretended contradictions, but chiefly on account of the offensiveness of their supernatural character to the carnal mind, into a mythical picture of the idea of the Messiah as it grew unconsciously from the imagination of the first Christians, thus sinking the gospels virtually to the level of heathen mythology. This, of course, puts an end to the idea of a divine origin of Christianity, and turns its apologetic history of eighteen hundred years into an air-castle built on pure illusions, a pleasing dream, a tragi-comedy entitled, "Much ado about nothing." [17]

The same crafty, sophistical criticism, which Strauss did not hesitate to employ upon the inspired biographies of the Saviour, Baur and several of his younger disciples have applied to the Acts of the Apostles, and to the whole Christian literature of the first and second centuries, gradually con-structing an entirely peculiar view of early Christianity. This philo-sophico-critical construction is most completely exhibited in Baur's *Paulus, der Apostel Jesu Christi* (1845),[18] and Schwegler's *Nachapos-tolischer Zeitalter* (two volumes, 1846). It makes Christianity proper only a product of the Catholic Church in the middle of the second century. In the minds of Jesus, of the twelve Apostles, and of the first Christian community, Christianity was only a perfected Judaism, and hence essen-tially the same as the Ebionism afterwards condemned as heresy. Paul, the Apostle of the Gentiles — no one knows how he came to be an apostle of Jesus Christ — was the first to emancipate it from the bondage of Jewish particularism, and to apprehend it as a new and peculiar system; and that too, in violent, irreconcilable opposition to the other Apostles, particu-larly to Peter, the leading representative of Jewish Christianity. Of this the Epistle to the Galatians and the well-known collision at Antioch (Gal. 2:11 sqq.) give authentic proof; while the Acts of the Apostles through-out, and especially in its description of the apostolic council at Jerusalem,

17. [ED.] *The Life of Jesus*, translated from the fourth German edition by Marian Evans (3 v., London, 1846).

18. [ED.] *Paul, the Apostle of Jesus Christ*, translated by A. Menzies (2 v., London and Edinburgh, 1875–76).

intentionally conceals the difference. This latter production, falsely attributed to Luke, was not written till towards the middle of the second century, and then not from a purely historical interest, but with the two-fold apologetic object of justifying the Apostle of the Gentiles against the reproaches of the Judaizers, and reconciling the two parties of Christendom. These objects the unknown author accomplished by making Peter, in the first part, come as near as possible to Paul in his sentiments, that is, approach the free Gentile-Christian position; and in the latter part, on the contrary, assimilating Paul as much as possible to Peter, or, which is the same thing, to the Ebionites and Judaizers. A similar pacific design is ascribed to the epistles of Peter and the later epistles of Paul, which all come from the second century; for, of all the epistles of the New Testament, Baur holds as genuine only those of Paul to the Galatians, Corinthians, and Romans; and even from the Epistle to the Romans he rejects the last two chapters. At length, after a long and severe struggle, the two violent antagonists, Petrinism and Paulinism, or properly Ebionism and Gnosticism, became reconciled, and gave rise to the orthodox catholic Christianity. The grand agent in completing this mighty change was the Fourth Gospel, which, however, is of course not the work of the apostle John — though the author plainly enough pretends to be that apostle — but of an anonymous writer in the middle of the second century. Thus the most profound and spiritual of all productions comes from an obscure nobody; the most sublime and ideal portrait of the immaculate Redeemer, from an impostor!! And it is not a real history but a sort of philosophico-religious romance, the offspring of the speculative fancy of the Christians after the time of the Apostles!! Here this panlogistic school, with its critical acumen and *a priori* construction, reaches the point where, in its mockery of all outward historical testimony, its palpable extravagance, and violation of all sound common sense, it confutes itself. "Professing themselves to be wise, they became fools" [Rom. 1:22]. The notion, in itself true and important, of a difference between the Jewish Christianity of Peter and the Gentile Christianity of Paul, is pushed so far that it becomes a caricature, a Gnostic fable. The process of sound criticism is tasked to its utmost by the Tübingen school. The most genuine and reliable testimony of the apostolic and old Catholic Church is rejected or suspected; and on the other hand, the self-contradictory, heretical productions of the second century, Ebionistic and Gnostic whims and distortions of history, are made the sources of the knowledge of primitive Christianity! Such a procedure can, of course, amount to nothing but theological romancing, a venturesome traffic in airy hypotheses. And in fact the books of Baur and Schwegler form, in this respect, fit counterparts to the pseudo-Clementine Homilies and Recognitions, which charge the apostles James and Peter with a Gnostic Ebionism, and bitterly attack the apostle Paul under the name of Simon Magus, clothing their theory in the dress of a historical romance.

Generally speaking, this whole modern construction of primitive Christianity is substantially but a revival, with some modification, of the ancient Gnosticism; and of that, too, mainly in its heathen, pseudo-Pauline form. In truth, Baur and his followers are, in the principles of their philosophy and criticism, the Gnostics of German Protestantism.[19] The only difference is that they are pure theorists and scholars of the study, while at least the more earnest of their predecessors joined with their fantastic speculations a rigid asceticism — seeking, by an unnatural mortification of the body, to work out the salvation of the soul. It was not, therefore, a mere accident that Baur, in the very beginning of his theological course, paid so much attention to the Gnostic and Manichean systems. His affinity with the anti-Judaistic and pseudo-Pauline fanatic Marcion is particularly striking. In criticism he seems to have taken this man for his model, only going beyond him. Marcion retained in his canon at least ten of Paul's Epistles and the Gospel of Luke, though he mutilated the latter in a very arbitrary way, to cleanse it of pretended Jewish interpolations. But Baur rejects all the Gospels, the Acts, all the General Epistles, and all but four of Paul's; and then these four he either arbitrarily clips (condemning, for instance, the last two chapters of the Epistle to the Romans as a later addition by another pen), or wrests, to suit his own preconceived hypotheses. This Tübingen school will no doubt meet the fate of the old Gnostic heresies. Its investigations will act with stimulating and fertilizing power upon the Church, calling forth especially a deeper scientific apprehension and defense of the historical Christianity of antiquity; and for itself, it will dry up like the streams of the desert, and figure hereafter only in the history of human aberrations and heresies.

The fundamental defect of this destructive method is the *entire want of faith*, without which it is as impossible [truly?] to understand Christianity, its inspired records, and its inward history, as to perceive light and

19. Had the late Dr. Möhler lived to see the subsequent course of his former colleague and opponent in Tübingen, he would have found in him a strong confirmation of the parallel between Protestantism and Gnosticism which he draws in his able *Symbolik*, §27. [ED.] In English, *Symbolism*, translated by J. B. Robertson (New York, 1844).

color without eyes. Here this school is on the same footing with the older rationalism. But it differs from the latter in having a philosophical ground-work. It rests not, like the works of Semler, Henke, Gibbon, &c., on an abstract Deism, which denies the presence of God in history, but upon a *logical Pantheism,* or a denial of the *personality* of God, which necessar-ily brings with it an entire misconception of the personality of man. Baur finds fault with Neander for recognizing merely the individual, nothing general, in doctrine history; and claims for himself the merit of having advanced this branch of history from the empiric method to the specula-tive, and of having found, in the idea of the *spirit,* the motive power of history.[20] What, then, is this "spirit," this "dogma," which according to his ever recurring, high-sounding but pretty empty terminology, "comes to terms with itself," "unfolds itself in the boundless multiplicity of its consciousness"? Is it the personal, living God, the Father of our Lord Jesus Christ? Of this that philosophy has at best but the name, making it the vehicle of an entirely different conception. The objective forces which Baur justly declares to be the factors of history — are they sub-stantial things, living realities? No! They amount to nothing but bare formulas of the logical understanding, abstract categories, Gnostic phan-toms. The entire history of doctrines is, according to this school, a mere fruitless process of thinking, which thinks thought itself; a tedious mech-anism of dialectic method; the "reeling off of a fine logical thread," which invariably runs out at last into Hegelian pantheism. The labor of the most profound and pious minds for centuries upon the mystery of the Incarna-tion, the Trinity, the Atonement, results merely in the philosophical formula of the identity of thought and being, the finite and the infinite, the subject and the object! Thus withers, beneath the simoom of a purely dialectic process, that glorious garden of the Lord, the history of the Church and her doctrines, with its boundless wealth of flowers, with its innumerable fruits of love, of faith, of prayer, of holiness. All becomes a sandy desert of metaphysics, without a green oasis, without a refreshing fountain.[21] This method fails most, of course, in those parts of Church history where the leading interest is that of practical religion, as in the apostolic period and the one immediately following. Here, under the pre-

---

20. Baur, *Lehrbuch der christlichen Dogmengeschichte,* 52, 53. Cf., also the conclu-sion of his latest work, *Die Epochen der kirchlichen Geschichtschreibung,* 247 sqq.

21. Here apply, in their full force, the words of the poet [ED. Goethe, *Faust* I]:

> Ich sag' es dir: ein Kerl, der speculirt,
> Ist wie ein Thier, auf dürrer Heide
> Von einem bösen Geist im Kreis herum geführt,
> Und rings umher liegt schöne grüne Weide.

tense of objective treatment, it falls into the most wretched subjectivity of a hyper-criticism which has no solid ground, and sets at defiance all the laws of history. But even the purely doctrinal investigations of Baur, highly as we are willing to rate their other scientific merits, need complete revision. For, interested only in speculation, he turns even the Church Fathers, the schoolmen of the Middle Ages, Calvin and Schleiermacher, into critics and speculators "upon the arid heath"; sunders their thinking from its ground in their religious life; and hence frequently loads them with opinions of which they never dreamed.

This is true even of his celebrated reply to Möhler's *Symbolik* (1834), though written before his Gnosticism had fully developed itself.[22] The Protestantism which he seeks to guard from the ingenious assaults of Möhler is by no means the faith of the Reformers in its purity, but corrupted by elements of modern pantheism and fatalism. Such assistance the true evangelical Christian is compelled to decline; and he often feels tempted to join hands with the pious Catholic, in common opposition to modern skepticism and infidelity. Baur has since gone much farther from the proper ground and limits of history. He justly regards the grand antagonists, Catholicism and Protestantism, as the two poles around which the entire history of the Church now turns. But he looks at Protestantism almost exclusively in its negative aspect. "Protestantism," says he, "is the principle of individual freedom, freedom of faith and conscience, in which a person is a law unto himself, in opposition to all the outward authority involved in the Catholic idea of the Church." Catholicism, he owns, was indispensable, as the only basis on which this freedom could arise, and so far has great significance and full historical authority, but only for the past. "The Reformation is the grand turning-point whence the whole tendency of the idea of the Church seems to be to unravel again the web which itself had woven. If the development of the Church previously moved only forward, it now appears to have suddenly veered, to have turned backwards, and to have bent back into itself. Opposition and protestation, hostility, negation of what exists; this is the spirit which now animates the Church" (255).[23] Though he immediately adds that this negation is, on the other hand, a deepening, which will lead to a new affirmation of what is true and permanent, yet in his system this is saying very little or nothing. According to the whole texture of his views, as

22. [ED.] *Der Gegensatz des Katholizismus und Protestantismus* (Tübingen, 1835).
23. *Die Epochen der kirchlichen Geschichtschreibung* [Tübingen, 1852], 257, 255. See 260: "Protestantism must itself remain an inexplicable riddle, if, to be what it has become, it could think of itself in any other way than by having its consciousness of itself mediated by papacy and Catholicism."

above explained, the history of Protestantism is a progressive dissolution of the Church as such; till at last even the Holy Scriptures, on which the Reformers planted themselves in protesting against human additions, are, by a shameless, profane, conceited hyper-criticism, snatched from under our feet, and nothing is left us but our own natural, helpless selves, with that empty notion of likeness to God with which the fearful tragedy of the Fall began. This is the legitimate and necessary result of this negative Protestantism of the extreme Left.

This extensive literature of modern philosophical and critical antichristianity would be absolutely disheartening, and would awaken the most gloomy anticipations for Protestantism, which embosoms it, and even tolerates some of its champions in her chairs of theology, were we not assured, by the cheering testimony of many centuries of history, that God, in his infinite wisdom and love, can bring good out of all evil, and make all the aberrations of the human mind aid the triumph of the truth. Like all previous enemies of Christianity, this most learned, most ingenious, and therefore most dangerous form of ultra, false, infidel Protestantism, which appears in the exegetical and historical productions of the Tübingen school, will also surely miss its aim. Nay, it has already involuntarily given a mighty impulse to the productive energy of the positive, evangelical, churchly theology. As Strauss' *Leben Jesu* has already been philosophically refuted by the counter productions of Tholuck, Neander, Lange, Ebrard, Hoffman, Lücke, Ullmann, &c., so also the speculations of Baur, Schwegler, and Zeller on the age of the Apostles and the succeeding period have been directly or indirectly assailed with the invincible weapons of thorough learning, and their inward weakness exposed, by the investigations of Dorner (in his history of Christology), Lechler (on the apostolic and postapostolic periods), Weitzel (on the paschal controversies of the first three centuries), Wieseler (on the chronology of the Acts of the Apostles), Neander (in the last edition of his history of the planting and training of the Church), Bunsen (on the Ignatian Epistles, and on Hippolytus), Thiersch (on the formation of the New Testament canon, and on the apostolic Church), and others. But certainly no work has yet appeared which fully sets forth the whole history of the early Church in its organic connection, with steady reference to these modern errors.

§ 37. Marheineke, Leo, Rothe, Dorner, Thiersch; Recapitulation

The *right* or *conservative* wing of the Hegelian school sought to reconcile this philosophical system with the faith of the Bible and the Church, though it must be confessed that in so doing they often too much spiritualized the articles of faith, and unwittingly did them more or less violence by their logic, resolving them pretty much into unsubstantial notions and metaphysical abstractions. Their case was even worse than that of Origen, in whom Platonism, instead of always bending to Christianity, sometimes gained the mastery over it. The older Hegelians of this class, moreover, have confined their labors almost entirely to the philosophical and systematic branches of theology. Marheineke alone († 1847) was at the same time a historian. His General Church History of Christianity (first part, 1806) is the first attempt to construct a history on the basis of the modern speculations, and to set up a more objective method against the rationalistic subjectivism. But the work is very defective, and at all events unfinished. Of far more permanent value is his History of the German Reformation,[24] drawn from the sources, and presented in a purely objective way, but without the learned apparatus, and intended more for the general reader. This work, unsurpassable in its kind, is fortunately free from all that heavy dialectic accouterment in which his *Dogmatik* is clothed, and is distinguished for its genuine national, old German style and spirit, peculiarly appropriate to the character of its leading hero, the thoroughly German Luther. Marheinecke has also won laurels in doctrine history and symbolism, and especially by his extended and on the whole faithful exhibition of the system of Catholicism (3 vols., 1810–13).

As to orthodoxy, this theologian, though a member and advocate of the United Evangelical Church of Prussia, was predominantly of the Lutheran doctrinal stamp. This confession, with its closer affinity to Catholicism, speculation, and mysticism, suited the Hegelian mode of treating history better than the genius of the Reformed Church, which recedes farther from the previous traditions, gives larger scope to subjectivity, and concerns itself more with practice than with theory. With the

24. Four volumes, 2nd ed. Berlin, 1831–34.

younger Wiggers, author of a work on ecclesiastical statistics (1842–43); still more with Martensen, a Danish divine, but of purely German education, and a very spirited, original theologian; with Theodore Kliefoth, the excellent author of an extended philosophical introduction to doctrine history; with Kahnis, who has published a work on the history of the doctrine concerning the Holy Ghost (1847), and another on the doctrine of the Eucharist (1851); and with the jurist Göschel, only an amateur, however, in theology, a confused compound of heterogeneous elements, Hegel, Goethe, and Christianity — with all these the Hegelian philosophy has become a bridge to strict symbolical Lutheranism.

But on the same ground the method of history, started by Hegel, may be considered as involving also, to some extent, a tendency towards Catholicism. By its objective character it is better fitted than the more subjective method of the school of Schleiermacher and Neander to appreciate and do full justice to the heroes of the Roman Church, and especially to the Middle Ages. We have an example of this in F. R. Hasse's monograph on Anselm of Canterbury, a model of purely objective and minute, yet living and clear historical representation, superior to Neander's *Bernard*.

This Catholicizing tendency is still more visible in Heinrich Leo, and assumes with him an almost Romanizing form. Though not a theologian, he has yet, in his Universal History, carefully noticed religion and the Church, and we cannot here omit his name. Leo, a man of great originality and native force, but rough, unsparing, and prone to extravagance, altogether threw off, it is true, in later life, the strait-jacket of the Hegelian logic and dialectics; but the influence of this philosophy still appears in his making the subject entirely subordinate to the objective powers; the individual, to the general. Since he exchanged his youthful free-thinking, however, which vented itself in his worthless history of the Jewish commonwealth, for positive Christianity, he has meant by these objective forces, not dialectic forms and notions, but concrete realities, laws, and institutions of the personal, Christian God, which to resist is sin and guilt, which to obey is man's true freedom, honor, and glory. He regards history as proceeding from above; the will of God, not the popular will, and least of all the individual, as its motive power. Hence his favorable view of the Middle Ages, and his unfavorable, nay, one-sided and unjust judgment of the Reformation; though his fault here may well be excused as a reaction against the blind eulogies of that movement. Leo's view of history is thoroughly ethical, churchly, conservative, absolutely anti-revolutionary, even to the favoring of despotism. He feels it to be his duty, amidst the distractions and instability of modern Europe, to lay the strongest emphasis on law, the necessity of the principle of authority and the general will. In this respect he goes undoubtedly too far; he overlooks the real wants of the people and gets into conflict with the progressive spirit of the age. Yet in a polemical character so harsh, violent, irritable and uncompromising as Leo, who often falls like a bulldog on what displeases him,[25] we cannot always take single expressions in their strict sense, any more than in the case of Luther, whom he much resembles in temperament, though his wrath is directed towards entirely different enemies. Hence, we are not to understand from his catholicizing tendency that he would hold the restoration of an antiquated state of things — say of the Middle Ages — as possible, or even desirable; but, with many of the profoundest minds of our time, he doubtless has in his eye a new age, which will embody what is true in the past, and yet at the same time stand on peculiar and higher ground.

Anticipations of such an advancement appear also in the works of the two professors of theology in Bonn, Dr. R. Rothe, and Dr. J. A. Dorner, whom we consider the most important speculative divines of the day. They have confined themselves chiefly, it is true, to the dogmatic and ethical fields (especially Rothe); but they merit the most honorable mention, also, as historians. The philosophical principles of their theology, and through these their conceptions of history, have plainly received powerful impulse and direction from the philosophy of Hegel. But at the same time they have appropriated all the elements of Schleiermacher's theology. These two ingredients they have compounded with genuine originality, and wrought into a peculiar shape. Rothe's "Theological Ethics"[26] stands forth as a thoroughly original work, and, in fact, as a masterpiece of speculative divinity, with which very few works of ancient or modern times can compare. On account of this relation of both Rothe and Dorner to Hegel and Schleiermacher, and their essential agreement in a positively Christian and yet genuinely speculative theology, we here put the two together, though in many other respects they differ.

25. Particularly in his occasional articles in the *Evangelische Kirchenzeitung* of his friend Hengstenberg, who is, like himself, completely anti-democratic, anti-republican, and absolutistic in his views of both Church and state, and in this respect wholly at variance with the Anglo-American taste, with which, in other points in his orthodoxy, especially his views of inspiration and his exegesis, he accords better than most other German theologians.

26. [ED.] *Theologische Ethik* (3 v., Wittenberg, 1845–48). The work is not available in English.

Dr. Rothe, in 1837, published the first volume of a work on the begin-nings of the Christian Church, and its constitution,[27] which in our view has not yet received the attention it merits. It consists chiefly of an ex-ceedingly thorough and acute investigation of the origin and development of the episcopal constitution, and (what is closely connected with this) of the Catholic doctrine concerning the historical, visible Church, its unity, holiness, catholicity, apostolicity, and exclusiveness. It comes to the con-clusion that the episcopate, as a necessary substitute for the apostolate in maintaining and promoting unity, reaches back even to the days of St. John, and thus has the apostolic sanction; and that the above-named idea of the Church arose by an inward necessity in the first centuries, particu-larly through the influence of Ignatius, Irenaeus, Cyprian, and Augustine, and lay at the bottom of the whole conception of Christianity in those days. This conclusion, if true, must have a powerful bearing on the final solution of the Church question, which is now pressing so heavily on Protestant Christendom. But while Rothe puts the whole weight of antiquity into the scale of Catholicism, where all the Church Fathers in their prevailing spirit belong, he is, in so doing, far from giving up Protes-tantism. His position in this respect he sets forth in language which we particularly commend to the consideration of our fanatical anti-Catholics: "There is no more effectual way of defending Protestantism than by just acknowledging, nay, expressly asserting, that *in the past* Catholicism *had*, in its essence, full historical reality and authority; that it *contained* deep inward truth, high moral glory and power." He also supposes, however, that the Reformation of the sixteenth century was a shock to the whole institution of the Church in its previous form, a serious breach in its unity and catholicity; and, at the same time, he rejects the distinction of a visi-ble and invisible Church as a mere shift of the older Protestant theologi-ans to save the catholic idea of the Church, whose visible, historical real-ity had disappeared. He therefore vindicates Protestantism on the hy-

---

27. [ED.] *Die Anfänge der christlichen kirche und ihrer verfassung: Beilage über die Echtheit der Ignatianischen Briefe* (Wittenberg, 1837). Rothe, Schaff noted, had described his work (Preface, ix) as a Protestant counterpart to Möhler's *Einheit in der Kirche* (Tübingen, 1825). Rothe admired and on the whole accepted Möhler's account of the self-consciousness of the primitive Church. The visible unity and universality which were essential to that Church, however, were lost, he believed, at the Reforma-tion (103). The Protestants, unwilling to relinquish the idea of a Church altogether, produced the self-contradictory notion of an invisible Church, a "pure fiction" in Rothe's judgment (109). Schaff did not consider Rothe's argument easy to refute, but was unwilling to give up wholly the old distinction between a visible and an invisible Church.

pothesis, which he unfolds at large in his philosophical introduction, that the Church is but a temporary vehicle and a transient form of Christianity, through which it passes into the more perfect form of the kingdom of God, that is, according to Rothe, an ideal *state*, a theocracy. This result, moreover, is not fully attained till the end of the historical development; and thus the institution of the Church is still, for a time, even in Protestantism, of relative authority and necessity along with the state, in its present imperfect form, until the latter shall become wholly penetrated and transformed by Christianity. Rothe here starts from Hegel's overstrained idea of the state; idealizing it, however, even far more than Hegel; considering it, not indeed as it now is, but as it will one day be(?), the most suitable form of moral society; and identifying it with the idea of the kingdom of God itself. This is not the place to go more minutely into this remarkable theory. But we must here repeat the observation, previously made respecting Neander, that such a separation between the kingdom of God and the Church seems to us to have sufficient ground neither in exegesis nor in history; and that we very much doubt whether Christianity could perpetuate itself without the Church, which, St. Paul tells us, is the Body of Christ, the fullness of him that filleth all in all [Eph. 1:23]. True, we too believe that Catholicism in its former condition can never be restored, that Protestantism is preparing the way for a new outward form of the kingdom of God, and that Church and state will at last be united in one theocracy; not, however, by the Church merging in the state, but rather conversely, by the state being taken up and glorified in the Church, as art in worship, as science in theosophy, as nature in grace, as time in eternity. Of the indestructible permanence of the Church we are assured by the express promise of our Lord that the gates of hell shall not prevail against her [Mt. 16:18]. Even from her present shattered and apparently ruined condition, therefore, she will rise, phoenix-like, in loftier beauty and new power; convert the whole world to Christ; and thenceforth, as his bride, reign blissfully over the new heavens and new earth forever.

From Dr. Dorner we have a very valuable (but, in its new, enlarged form, not yet finished) history of the doctrine of the Incarnation of God and the Person of Christ (1845).[28] He here traces the development of this central doctrine of Christianity, on which the solution of all other theological problems depends, and which is justly, therefore, again claim-

28. [ED.] *History of the Development of the Doctrine of the Person of Christ,* translated by W. L. Alexander and D. W. Simon (5 v., Edinburgh, 1866–70).

ing the serious attention of our age. He sets forth the history with exemplary thoroughness, keen penetration, perfect command of the copious material, and in dignified, happy language, though not entirely without a certain scientific pretension and stiffness. At the same time he makes it bear throughout, and triumphantly, against Baur's investigations on the same subject. He is not a whit behind his opponent in speculative talent, while he far excels him in sound comprehension, and writes in the service not merely of science, but also of the Church. Similar in spirit and contents, but not so full and satisfactory, is the work of George Augustus Meier on the history of the doctrine of the Trinity (1844), in part, also, a successful positive refutation of Baur's work on the Trinity and Christology.

In this connection we must mention, finally, a younger theologian, Dr. Henry W. J. Thiersch, one of the most learned opponents of Dr. Baur and the Tübingen school. He has already written several interesting works — Lectures on Catholicism and Protestantism, a kind of conciliatory symbolism (1846); a book on the Formation of the New Testament Canon, against the modern hyper-critics and dealers in hypotheses (1845); and a History of the Christian Church in Primitive Times, the first volume of which, embracing the apostolic period, appeared in 1852.[29] Thiersch has no sympathy whatever with the Hegelian philosophy, and as little with Schleiermacher's theology, but fights against both with a zeal which reminds one of Tertullian's war against Gnosticism. In his doctrinal persuasion he was at first decidedly Lutheran, with a strong leaning to an ascetic pietism. But of late he has fallen out with the present state of Protestantism at large, and in honorable disinterestedness and impatient haste has resigned his professorship at Marburg and joined the Irvingites. Of all Protestant sects this is the most churchly, catholic, hierarchical, sacramental, and liturgical. It arose in England A.D. 1831, and has of late made some little progress also in Germany and in the United States. It has in view the restoration of the apostolic Church, with its peculiar supernatural offices, particularly the apostolate, and with its miraculous powers, as speaking with tongues and prophecy; the collection of all the vital forces of the Catholic and Protestant churches into this community, to save them from the approaching judgment; and

---

29. [ED.] *Vorlesungen über Katholizismus und Protestantismus* (Erlangen, 1846); *Versuch zur Herstellung des historischen Standpunckts für die Kritik der neutestamentlichen Schriften* (Erlangen, 1845); *The Church in the Apostolic Age*, translated by T. Carlyle (London, 1852).

preparation for the glorious return of the Lord. Thiersch is related to this so-called "Apostolic Community" as the essentially catholic and orthodox and yet schismatic Tertullian was to the kindred sect of the Montanists in the second and third centuries. He is the theological representative of Irvingism, and stands mediating between it and Protestantism, especially in Germany. But the proper value of his historical works depends not so much, or not exclusively, on these Irvingite peculiarities and extravagances. It consists, rather, in his clear, elegant, and noble style, which everywhere evinces the classical scholar and worthy son of the celebrated Greek philologian of Munich; in his extensive and thorough acquaintance with patristic literature; in the lovely spirit of deep and warm though sometimes enthusiastic and visionary piety which breathes in all his writings; and in his mild, irenic, conciliatory posture towards the great antagonism of Catholicism and Protestantism. Even his latest work, the history of the apostolic Church, is, as he himself says, "not a part of his new activity, as pastor in the Apostolic Community, but a sequel to his former labors as teacher of theology." Besides, Irvingism contains many elements of truth, well worthy of the most serious consideration; and it is to be expected that, through the writings of Thiersch, it will exert some influence on German theology. So Montanism wrought, through Tertullian, on the Catholic Church, though the system itself shared the inevitable fate of sects, death without the hope of resurrection. Only the universal, historical Church has the promise that the gates of hell shall not prevail against her.

We have now traced the history of our science down to the labors of our contemporaries. It runs parallel with, and reflects in an interesting manner, the development of the Church itself in its different ages. We have seen how, in the abounding historical literature of Germany since the appearance of Neander, is mirrored the whole confused diversity of the elements of modern culture; now repelling, now attracting one another, and now striving towards a higher position of union; at one time bound, entirely or in part, in the fetters of a philosophical system; at another, with free, untrammelled spirit endeavoring to apprehend and do justice to everything according to its own peculiar nature. We have observed, too, that the most profound and earnest students in this department become more and more convinced of the high practical office of this science, to set forth faithfully and candidly the whole undivided fullness of the life of Jesus Christ, as it has continuously unfolded itself in time; to aid hereby in understanding the present; to animate for the work of the future; and gradually to effect the final, satisfactory solution of the question of all questions, that of *Christ and his Church*, in relation as well to the unbelieving world as to the various parties in Christendom itself, especially to the colossal, all-comprehending antagonism of Catholicism and Protestantism. . . .

IV

JOHN WILLIAMSON NEVIN

The Meaning of Protestantism in Ecumenical Christianity:
Answer to Professor Dorner

Editor's introduction.

Isaak Dorner was probably the weightiest theologian with whom Mercersburg entered into debate. At the time Schaff heard him on dogmatics and apologetics at Tübingen, Dorner was finishing the first edition (1839) of his *History of the Development of the Doctrine of the Person of Christ.* It was probably of the second edition of 1845 that Nevin wrote Henry Harbaugh in 1847: "Since my return I have got Dorner's First Part of *Lehre von der Person Christi* (three volumes) and am now devouring it with vast interest. . . . How clear it is to my mind that the whole sense and power of Christianity turn at last on the fact of the Incarnation, as embodied with perennial life in the consciousness of the Church." [1] Both Schaff and Nevin undoubtedly owed much to Dorner for their idealistic reading of patristic Christology. Schaff was to take especial pleasure in securing Dorner's attendance at the New York meeting of the Evangelical Alliance in 1873.

With regard to what seemed to him the necessary implications of the Incarnation for the Church, however, Nevin found Dorner quite unsatisfactory — as he did even Stahl and Gerlach. He wrote of Germany in 1848, "I know no writer there, whose views in full I would be willing to accept on this subject." [2]

Twenty years later the tension was aired in a public debate, which began when Dorner published, in his *Jahrbücher für Deutsche Theologie* for 1867, an article on the liturgical controversy in the German Re-

---

1. Letter of May 18, 1847. (Library of the Historical Society of the Evangelical and Reformed Church, Franklin and Marshall College, Lancaster, Pa.)
2. *The Weekly Messenger,* July 19, 1848.

formed Church in America. Although Dorner's grasp of the American situation was seriously defective, he had nevertheless identified the basic divergencies. Nevin answered him in a series of articles which first appeared in *The Weekly Messenger* during the summer of 1868, and were then collected into one comprehensive essay in *The Mercersburg Review*. Besides this "Answer to Professor Dorner," [3] the same volume of the *Review* also contained two articles by Nevin on Dorner's *History of Protestant Theology*, which had appeared in Munich the preceding year.

In these interchanges a number of issues were raised. The two men differed sharply on the Church and the ministry. To Dorner's charge of "Puseyizing," Nevin granted that as regarded the Church, "Our theology is more Anglican than German." [4] He was not shaken by Dorner's charge that the Ordination Service had been made in effect a "third sacrament." Dorner's whole standpoint in these matters, Nevin replied, was Erastian and false.

Dorner also objected to the acceptance at Mercersburg of the ancient Creed as regulative for all theology. This he called a Greek Orthodox position. The issue involved divergent conceptions of the relation of Protestantism to the patristic age, and thus of the historical relation between objective and subjective as it had developed in Christianity. The portion of Nevin's "Answer" reprinted below is from the tenth and twelfth articles in his series, entitled respectively "Ecumenical or Whole Christianity" and "The Principle of Protestantism." The excerpt begins with a passage from the preface to H. Martensen's *Christliche Dogmatik* (Kiel, 1856), which Nevin found "admirable" to "express my whole view on this subject."

❖   ❖   ❖   ❖

x. *Ecumenical or Whole Christianity*

"It has been objected to this system of theology from different sides," [Dr. Martensen] writes, "even by theologians of my native country, that it contains elements which cannot be joined with the practical nature of Protestantism. Sin and redemption, it is said, and the plan of salvation connected with them, are the cardinal points that determine all in the

3. *The Mercersburg Review*, XX (1868), 534–646.   4. *Ibid.*, 632.

Evangelical Church, and a system in which so many objective and speculative elements are taken up, and which gives such wide room, for example, to the doctrines of the Trinity and the Logos, has not maintained the
Protestant standpoint. This objection, we see at once, if it has any force
at all, reaches not simply to my work, but to the speculative tendency at
large in our Evangelical theology.

"But to judge of the relation of a system of theology to Protestantism,
it is not enough to take the Protestant scheme of doctrine as once for all
finished and complete; rather we must place ourselves at the point where
the doctrinal productivity of Protestantism took its start, and consider the
principle by which this productivity was ruled. The Reformation did not
aim to form a new separate Church, but sought to purify the holy, universal Church from the errors which, in the course of centuries, had
come to obscure its true form. It intended no purely subjective Christianity, but the ecumenical, original Catholic Christianity in renovated form;
for which reason it went back not only to the apostolical tradition in the
Sacred Scriptures, but to the first Christian centuries generally, whose
ecclesiastical testimonies show traces of the original purity and freshness
of the new life. Was this return now to original Christianity completely
carried out in the sixteenth century? Did the Protestant scheme of doctrine attain to full catholicity, so that all parts of the Christian faith were
revived and renewed in *like proportion?* It was natural that the consciousness of redemption should come first to its representation, not only
because this forms the heart of Christian religious experience, but because
also the Reformation had to take stand immediately in opposition to the
Roman Church, which had assumed more and more the character of a
perverted Judaism, had more and more left the true way of salvation, and
become a legalistic church. It was not strange thus that the Protestant
doctrinal system, on its first appearance, should take the Pauline type,
especially as we have it in the Epistles to the Romans and to the Galatians, and that it was made to center in justification by faith, and its
kindred topics, in the plan of salvation. Can we say, however, that the
system attained by this to full catholicity? It is plain as day, rather, that
although the Reformation denied no single article of Christian revealed
truth, but on the contrary sought to make all its own, essential parts of
this revealed truth nevertheless were appropriated as a traditional heritage
simply, without coming to any true inward reproduction. The sense of
revelation (*Offenbarungsbewusstsein*) did indeed make itself strongly
felt, no less than the sense of redemption; there was controversy, for ex-

ample, not only about the effects of the sacraments, but also about the nature of them, about the objective presence of Christ. But the sense of revelation was not developed by any means in the same measure with the sense of redemption. If we compare the Protestant theology here with the doctrinal consciousness of the first three centuries, we discover a great difference. We find, indeed, that the Fathers of the first three centuries, like the teachers of the Reformation period, live and breathe in the element of redemption; but we do not find that they *reflect* with the same care on the experience of the redeemed; their reflection is not turning back always upon their justification by faith; they enter into no fine psychological analysis of the order of salvation, of the struggle of conviction and conversion, of sanctification and mystical union with God. On the contrary, we find another circle of doctrines determining the character of that period; we find in Irenaeus, for example, the most important representative of the period, earnest and profound thought on the great truths of the Word made flesh and the Holy Trinity, on the connection of the mystery of Creation with the Incarnation, on the presence of the Lord in the sacrament, on the resurrection of the body and the consummation of all things. Those old teachers feel themselves drawn also especially to the writings of St. John, and this on account of their anti-Gnostic testimony to the coming of Christ in the flesh; while among the Epistles of St. Paul they are most of all attracted by those to the Ephesians and to the Colossians, through their grand thoughts on the cosmical significance of Christ — Epistles from which the period of the Reformation was not able at all to derive any similar benefit. Those old teachers, furthermore, take deep interest in the eschatological discourses of our Lord, in the apocalyptic sections of St. Paul's Epistles, and in the Revelation of St. John; which exercised a fructifying influence over their course of thought, altogether beyond any like experience on the part of the Protestant Fathers. For who can deny that the doctrine of the Last Things is one of the weakest and most poorly handled topics belonging to the Protestant divinity?

"If now we are aware of this difference (and all deeper historical inquiry here has but served to place it in clearer light), we cannot, of course, think for a moment of giving up one iota of what has been gained by the Reformation, or of not going forward in the Pauline Augustinian direction. But just as surely as we know that the problem of the Reformation was of universal Church character, and believe our confession to be the most perfect one, because it is the most ecumenical expression of

Christianity, so surely must this demand for Church universality, for true catholicity, reveal itself also in theology. To express the object of theology, then, in church-historical form, it is not enough, in my opinion, to say that it is to reproduce only the *redemption-consciousness* of the age of the Reformation, in a form answerable to the present need of the Church, as Schleiermacher, for example, apprehended the subject; but it is to reproduce at the same time, in new form, the *revelation-consciousness* of the first centuries, whose contents the Reformation period took up mainly in a merely traditional way; or rather to *recapitulate both scientifically in a higher synthesis*, a synthesis which would then gather up into itself also all that was right in the theology of the Middle Ages. A theology which in our times does not propose to itself this object, but aims at nothing more than to reproduce the Augustinian element of Protestantism, can have no promise of progress, and shows a want of power to comprehend the present need of the Church."

So Martensen; defending his theology here from the very same charge that is preferred against ours. The only wonder is that such a man as Dorner should now seem to be countenancing at all the opposite view. For does he not also himself tell us, in plain terms, that the only order of theology at this time which has the promise of the future, is that which neither ignores primitive Christianity nor ignores the Reformation, but is *truly historical* in the sense of doing justice to both; or in such way that the original wholeness of the Christian faith shall be maintained, by such an apprehension of Protestantism as may serve to place it in harmonious agreement at the same time with what was the life of the Church in the beginning? And what is this, I ask, but that very idea of the "recapitulation or gathering up of both in a higher synthesis," which Martensen insists upon as the proper object of all right theological science at the present time, and which, I will add, has been the animating soul of the entire church movement which is now at work among ourselves? All our theology aims at this — not a giving up of the Reformation, nor yet such a blind starting with it, as would infer that there had been no historical Christianity before that modern time, but a free inward conjunction of the Reformation life with the older life of the early Church. This, we know, means something more than the raking up simply of the dead bones and dust of either period; something more than a mere mechanical repristination of the buried past in any view; it can be reached only through a revivification of the true actuating spirit of both periods, which, as being in both the effluence and birth of the same One Spirit of Christ, must be capable, it is believed, of appearing in full concord with itself. Such a view implies, of course, that Protestantism has not from the first carried along with it the full and complete sense of all that was comprehended originally in Christianity. As Dorner himself says,[5] there may be much left behind it yet in the old communions, Greek and Latin, which it needs still to take up into itself as the necessary ultimate complement of its own higher life; and there is no question but that Martensen is right also when he tells us that what is wanted particularly is the bringing up of what he calls the old *Offenbarungsbewusstsein* (sense of revelation — the powers of the world to come objectively considered) to some sort of parallelism with the *Erlösungsbewusstsein* (sense of redemption — the processes of the Christian salvation subjectively considered), which has come to be so generally all in all for Protestant thinking. Now this is precisely what is aimed at in our liturgy. There is not in it anywhere the slightest undervaluation of Christ's sacrifice and death. On the contrary, the altar feeling pervades all its services, and gives them their universal tone and force. But it seeks to carry along with all this, at the same time, the lively sense of the great Christian facts, *in the bosom of which only the ideas of atonement and justification can be kept from evaporating finally into sheer rationalistic dreams.* Hence its intonation of the Trinity, of the Word Incarnate, of the Life which has become the Light of men, of Christ's Resurrection and Ascension, of the Pentecostal Gift, of the Holy Catholic Church, and of the Second Advent — of all the grand ideas, in a word, that meet us in the Christological and liturgical productions of the ancient Greek Church. Hence its unison throughout with the sublime old hymns and Creeds, that hold us in communion still with the Christian life of the first ages. . . .

XII. *The Principle of Protestantism*

The different points of controversy which have thus far claimed our attention, as may be easily seen, refer themselves throughout, more or less directly, to one great radical subject of inquiry, *the principle of Protestantism and its right relation to the principle of Christianity.* Here the controversy between Dr. Dorner and myself, the divergency, as he calls it, of our Christological ways, comes to what is, after all, its main mean-

5. [ED.] Quoted, *The Mercersburg Review*, XX (1868), 262f.

ing. The subject is large and difficult. I can only, of course, glance at it briefly in this closing article of our present discussion.

We have seen how in various ways Dr. Dorner takes occasion to insinuate, or openly assert, that my Christological views, and the reigning spirit of our liturgy also, are not in harmony with the essential genius of the Evangelical Church (meaning by this, Protestantism in its German form), but involve, if not a conscious, at least an unconscious falling back upon a standpoint anterior to the Reformation — not just Roman Catholic perhaps — but then all the more certainly Oriental or Greek, as we find it in the first Christian ages. Let us now try to understand exactly what this German Evangelical theory of the Reformation is in its modern form, which is thus made to be the measure of all true and sound Protestantism in such sweeping style.

Dorner, as we have seen, sets out in his criticism, by charging me in a polite way with overlooking the fact that for Protestantism all turns on faith and the right relation of the soul to God — as if my idea of a Christocentric theology implied somehow that the mere theoretical knowledge of Christ is to be considered the source of true Christianity for us (either as theology or as practical religion), apart from all personal experience of what Christ is for us as the power of salvation. No misapprehension could well be more total or complete. The central place assigned to Christ in my theology has always been under the view of an actual apprehension of his person, first of all, through the exercise of faith; and it is only wonderful how Dr. Dorner could ever have got himself into any other imagination. Certainly all true Christianity has its ground for us in faith, the power of saying with Peter, *Thou art the Christ, the Son of the Living God.* But no such faith can exist without embracing its object; and in such view the object apprehended is still more the ground of what is thus brought to pass (although object and subject in the case go both together) than is the simple act of apprehension by which it is taken up into our subjective life. Dr. Dorner knows that, and admits it freely, although at times he seems to forget it, and talks as if the mere subjective exercise of faith (without regard to its contents) were to be considered in some way of independent authority in the Protestant system. This we know is the view that has come to be taken practically of the Protestant principle, by a very considerable part of our modern sectarian religion. Faith itself, or mere personal feeling and conviction, is made to be with it the source of justification; and the freedom of the Reformation is taken to be the right of determining, from within simply, what is true Christianity, without regard to any objective authority whatever. But such is not Dr. Dorner's view. Faith, with him, is of no account, and can have no real existence in fact, without being filled with the positive substance of divine truth. Here too he sees (though sometimes a little confusedly) that this truth is not just the documentary form in which it is presented to us in the Bible, but the living fact of revelation itself, as it lies behind the Bible and looks forth upon us through its inspired pages. Faith has to do in the case, not primarily with the inspiration of the book but with the substantive matter which the book makes known; with this, in its own immediate self-authenticating form. But now, all revelation centers in Christ; and so Dorner is willing to admit in the end that the last ground of certitude for faith is found in the direct apprehension of the Saviour himself, who is the alpha and omega of all that God has been pleased to make known of himself in this way. This, as I have remarked before, seems to be equivalent to making the Person of Christ the root and principle in full of the whole Christian salvation. But here it is now that Dr. Dorner refuses, after all, so far as I can understand him, to carry out this great thought to what seems to me to be its necessary theological consequences, as we have them set forth comprehensively in the Apostles' Creed. On to this point, our ways would appear to be in general harmony, since it is a pure mistake to suppose that I make any less account than he does of the factor of faith in the Protestant principle. How is it, then, that just here the material principle of Protestantism becomes with him, all at once, something different from what it is in my system, to such an extent that I am charged with being unfaithful to it altogether? The subject is of fundamental account for this whole discussion, and deserves certainly our most close attention.

The peculiarity of Dorner's view of justifying faith (the material principle of Protestantism) shows itself in this, that the feeling of a rectified relation to God (the sense of guilt met with the sense of pardon through the righteousness of Christ) is regarded by him as going before the apprehension of Christ in any wider view, and as mediating, so to speak, our full access to his person. His interest is in maintaining the absolute autonomy of the believing subject, which he thinks cannot be done effectually without making the subjective side of the process of salvation in this way the *primum mobile* of the whole movement. Faith must be free of all outward authority, all coercion from beyond itself. It is independent thus of the Church, of course, but that is not all; it is independent also of the Bible, and in the end, it would really seem, is to be considered independent also of the objective presence of Christ himself, except as a certain inward experience comes in first to make him intelligible and apprehensible in his whole character to the awakened soul.

I am blamed for making the objective Christ primordial for the Christian salvation. This position, he will have it, belongs in the Evangelical Church only to faith, which is (*per se*, it would seem) the "Divine assurance of salvation," and in which, as the consciousness of redemption, "is implanted principially, and as with one stroke, the consciousness of the Redeemer, and of his dignity and truth." That is, while the sense of subjective redemption and the apprehension of Christ's objective presence go in fact together, it is the sense of redemption, nevertheless, which, properly speaking, makes room for such embracing of the actual Christ, and which is thus the true principle of all that is reached in the process.

Thus, criticizing the Reverend S. Miller on what he says of the power of Christianity to make itself evident to faith,[6] Professor Dorner remarks: "Faith so described is, unfortunately, however, not faith in personal salvation by Christ, but only in objective Christianity; its certainty, thus, does not rest on the experienced certainty of salvation, but on the blindly received authority of the Church, and is promised only as the reward of such blind, willful obedience. The author comes to this by looking away from the ethical side of the faith process, from the eye of the moral consciousness which recognizes both its own sin and the righteousness of Christ."

This is clear. Faith, as the experience of subjective right-setting in relation to God, must go before all other evidence in Christianity. Except as mediated and illuminated by this, all other evidence, as being "only objective Christianity," must be necessarily *heteronomic*, a foreign outward law, for the proper freedom of the human spirit, and the faith engendered by it no better than blind, willful obedience to external authority (*Autoritätsglaube*, called also sometimes *Köhlerglaube*). The "objective Christianity" which Dr. Dorner has first in his mind, as thus heteronomic for faith, is that of the Church, though he does not shrink, as we have seen, from speaking of the authority of the Bible also in the same way. But what shall we say when we find his language here virtually bringing the glorious Person of the Redeemer himself under the terrible operation of the same

---

6. [ED.] A reference to Samuel Miller, *A Treatise on Mercersburg: or Mercersburg and Modern Theology Compared* (Philadelphia, 1866). Since the Mercersburg faculty did not hold themselves responsible for this popular exposition, Dorner had taken it more seriously than it deserved.

Procrustean rule? *"Only* in objective Christianity," he says of all faith, for which its object has not *first* found the seal of its truth in the believer's own mind! But is such objective Christianity found only in the Church or in the Bible? Where have we it in full, if not in our Lord Jesus Christ himself? And shall we say now that bowing implicitly to the authority of *his* presence is blind, willful obedience to a heteronomic rule? Can we ever, by our subjective experiences, verify Christ sooner or farther than he, through the blessed vision of his own Person, offered to the eyes of our faith, verifies *us* by the light of truth, showing us at once what we are, where we are, and whither we must turn for salvation? Subject and object in all such faith of course flow together; but it is a strange way of looking at the matter, surely, to subordinate the objective to the action of the subjective; to make the last primordial for the process, and the first secondary only and relatively dependent.

So far, however, does this inversion prevail with Dr. Dorner, that he insists on conditioning by it the universal sense of the gospel, in such sort that the gospel must be considered as having been only imperfectly developed before the Reformation, because the principle of justifying faith, in the form here described, had not before been advanced to its proper autonomic dignity and independence. The great significance of Protestantism, he thinks, lies in the bringing out of this principle. Here is the signature of its being the work of God. This constitutes it a new creation, not in the sense of a full rupture with older Christianity (for Dorner, as we have seen, is historical, and requires a continuity of Christian life between the sixteenth century and the first ages), but in the sense of such a re-ordering of Christianity as makes its whole previous history from the beginning to have been relatively defective and wrong, as not flowing strictly from the true idea of the gospel. The standpoint of the primitive Church, therefore, needs rectification from the retroactive force of the new position which was gained for faith in the age of Luther and Calvin. In other words, the principle of Protestantism here is made to be the only true principle of Christianity in its widest view; and we are given to understand that we have no right (evangelically) to go back of it, in quest of any other more general root or ground in which it may be supposed to be comprehended.

Our theology, Dorner tells us, must be genuinely historical, by breaking neither with the ancient Church nor with the Reformation. But this requires, he adds, that as "children of the Reformation" we proceed from its special standpoint, the free personal laying hold of Christian salvation and truth, an end, he goes on to say significantly, *which, in the manner of all teleology, must work back into what goes before it, so as to preclude whatever is not consonant with its own nature.* That is, it would seem, the true teleology of the gospel is reached in the standpoint of the Reformation; and therefore the sense of all earlier Christianity must suffer itself to be righted retroactively from this, instead of being called in ever as itself a principle of rectification for the later period. The beginning, thus, must be construed into conformity with the end, and not the end into harmony with the beginning. Such is Dorner's idea here of historical Christianity.

Now, it is true that the end, in God's ways, actuates and rules the beginning. But, as I have taken occasion to say before, it is only the absolute end that does this, and not any merely partial intermediate end. It is an utter wrong done to the full sense of Christianity, therefore, when Dr. Dorner presumes to circumscribe it by the special article of justification by faith, as we have this brought out in the sixteenth century. The full gospel embraces far more than that in its ultimate teleology, and we are bound, accordingly, to include far more than that in its original principle or germ. For the very reason that the end must give us the sense of the beginning, I insist on seeing in the beginning *more* than the special mind simply of the sixteenth century, which cannot by any means be taken for the consummation of all Christian truth. Original Christianity is a deeper and wider fact than Protestantism, and in the relation of one to the other, the only true order unquestionably is that by which Protestantism is taken to have its root in Christianity, and not Christianity to have its root in Protestantism. The Protestant principle of justification by faith then is valid only as it falls back on the general principle of Christianity, which is none other than Christ himself, and this in such a way that Christ is not brought in as the instrument simply of our justification, but is apprehended as being at once in himself the whole fullness of our salvation.

Here it is that Dr. Dorner's doctrine of Protestantism appears to me to be sadly at fault. It is not fully Christological in the sense of making Christ the absolute ground and beginning of Christianity. He acknowledges a falling away of Protestantism itself from its own original principle, which calls now for a reconstruction and righting of its whole present status (both as Lutheran and Reformed) by a proper historical recurrence again to this principle in its true sense. But he is not willing to see that the Protestant principle itself may need to be righted, or at least secured in its only right sense by a similar historical recurrence to the older and more general principle of Christianity as it comes before us in the first ages of the Church. For want of this his idea of historical Protestantism is lame, and his theory of what he calls the Evangelical Church very much of one sort in the end, I must be allowed sorrowfully to say, with the radicalism of our most unhistorical and unchurchly American sects. We see at once why he is not on good terms with primitive Christianity, why he is not satisfied with the Christological construction of the Creed — why, in a word, he cannot abide its article of the *Church*, or the idea of an objective authority for faith belonging to the Church in any form.

To this it comes necessarily at last with the primacy of faith, as it is made to be the distinguishing basis of Protestantism by Dorner and other great German theologians. The old dualism between subject and object in religion, it is assumed, has been for theological science, since the time of Schleiermacher, effectually surmounted; by seeing in the supernatural only the necessary complement or filling out of the natural (as man's intelligence and will), which then the natural again, that is, the rational nature of man, has the power of taking into itself through its own free activity and apprehension. In this way the law is supposed to be maintained, that nothing can enter the mind as objectively binding for its intelligence or will, which is not first authenticated for it as true and right by its independent, spontaneous (not approval simply, but) actual production, as it were, from the depths of its own nature. This is that *autonomy* of faith, which is here put forward now as the true principle of the Reformation (over against all merely outward objectivity, whether of Church or Bible, Dorner makes no difference); which our original Protestantism, it seems, did not itself thoroughly understand, and so drifted away by devious course into the neology and general rationalism finally of the eighteenth century, and which it is the business of the nineteenth century at last, we are told, to re-inaugurate in right form as our only reasonable hope for the welfare and prosperity of Protestantism in time to come.

Now I make no question but that there is a deep truth in Schleiermacher's idea of a necessary correlation and synthesis of the natural and the supernatural in religion. But I have dreadful misgivings, I confess, with regard to much that I meet with among modern German theologians, in their way of carrying out the idea to its practical applications. There is no one of them whom I admire more than the late Dr. Richard Rothe, author of that wonderful structure of speculative thought which he has entitled *Theological Ethics,* himself a sort of Schleiermacher over again, and at the same time no less remarkable for what seems to be the simplicity of his piety than for the greatness of his learning and the profundity of his genius; and yet who can feel safe altogether in his guidance? With him, the synthesis of the human and the divine in Christianity amounts to a resolution of all at last into a simple completion of the world process in its ultimate ethical form. The idea of the Church loses itself thus finally in the idea of the State! Dr. Dorner, with all his regard for Rothe, would join here, I suppose, in the condemnation of his system. But one cannot help feeling that his own way of looking at Christianity involves much also which would appear to run precisely in the same direction — as Rothe himself, indeed, charges the new *Evangelical* theology of Germany generally with not speaking out here fully its own necessary sense, and predicts that it must yet come openly to his ground. Is this whole scheme, after all, any other than the arch-heresy of our fallen life, *Humanitarianism,* in its most subtle and refined form, all the more dangerously adapted to deceive the very elect through such gorgeous semblance to an angel of light? I merely ask the question, without pretending to answer it now, for the purpose of bringing into view the very deep solemnity of the subject with which it is concerned.

It is as coming within the sweep of this general humanitarian tendency that Dorner's doctrine of justifying faith in particular, regarded as the subjective material side of the principle of Protestantism, becomes to my mind unsound and unsafe. In his zeal for the full moral freedom of the believer (the autonomy of the human subject), he will have it that all merely objective authority must be held in secondary relation to the exercise of this subjective factor or force. So in the Bible, and so in the Church, and so then, in spite of himself, it would seem necessarily to follow, in the Person of our Lord Jesus Christ also. For is not *he,* as already said, the fullness of all objective Christianity, before it becomes otherwise objective, either in the Bible or in the Church? Hence the weakness of Dorner's Christological hypothesis, by which he allows himself to invert the true relation of Christ's work to his person, and so of course the true order of faith in regard to it — subordinating, in fact, the wholeness of the Mediator to one function simply of his mediatorial office. Hence his persistence in the strange opinion that to lay emphasis on the Incarnation and to magnify the life of Christ is necessarily to wrong the claims of the Atonement, and to make small account of the death of Christ. Hence his confessed divergency from the Christology of the Creed, and the religious thinking generally of the first Christian ages. Hence his opposition at large to the idea of the Church as it stands in the Creed, and was for this old thinking unquestionably the object of universal faith.

Now, against all this I maintain that the authority of Christ's presence and person (objective Christianity exhibited to us in Christ) is the ground of all subjective Christianity. Faith, in its last and deepest sense, is simply submission (free, but yet unseeing also, and implicit) to such objective authority. The gospel to which it bows is primarily an external gospel. So the Apostles believed in response to the word, *Follow me*. So the apostolic commission runs: "He that believeth and is baptized," that is, comes under the yoke of entire self-surrendry to Christ through baptism, "shall be saved" [Mk. 16:16]. And so it must be through all ages. The Christianity which was originally in Christ, must be for the Christian world an objective authority till the end of time. It is so in the Bible, but it is so also in the Church, and without its actualization for faith under this last form, it can never make itself fully actual in the first form. In some way the general life of Christianity (which is the Church) must come between all individual faith and the letter of Scripture, to make the relation either Christian or Protestant in any true sense of these terms. The very idea of faith implies a relation of dependence and need toward an object, which is thus for it an outward authority (not indeed heteronomic, but still) absolutely binding for its whole action, just as all natural vision holds in the objective power of outward light, without which there can be no exercise of the visual faculty whatever. . . .

❖

PART THREE

The Reformed Eucharist: Communion through the Glorified Humanity

JOHN WILLIAMSON NEVIN

The Mystical Presence: Reformed Doctrine of the Lord's Supper

Editor's introduction.

The view of the Church which Nevin had set forth in "Catholic Unity" and in other writings was intimately related to, if not governed by, a conception of the Eucharist as its most representative activity. As he saw it, our participation in the second Adam and the New Creation is focussed and actualized most forcefully in the Lord's Supper. It was for this idea that Nevin was accused of heresy, the summer after his "Catholic Unity" [1] appeared along with Schaff's *The Principle of Protestantism*. The debates which followed led to the publication in 1846 of *The Mystical Presence: A Vindication of the Reformed or Calvinistic Doctrine of the Holy Eucharist*.

Nevin acknowledged that he taught, as charged, the "spiritual Real Presence."

> To my own mind, all that is great and precious in the gospel may be said to center in this doctrine. Without it, I must feel that the whole Christian salvation would be shorn of its glory and force. I have no hope, save on the ground of a living union with the nature of Christ as the resurrection and the life. Both for my understanding and my heart, theology finds here all its interest and attraction. For no truth am I more willing to suffer contradiction and reproach, if such be the will of God. . . . The fact that the Christian life holds in an actual communication with the humanity of Christ, and that this, in particular, forms the soul of the Lord's Supper, may never be relinquished.[2]

1. See 35–55, above.
2. "The Mystical Union," *The Weekly Messenger*, October 8, 1845.

Such a view was so far from being heretical in the Reformed tradition, he asserted, that "the whole Church, in Switzerland, France, Germany, Holland, Scotland, and England, united in maintaining a real communication of the whole substantial humanity of Christ to the believer in the sacrament of the Lord's Supper." [3]

This was apparently for Nevin the article of the standing or falling Church. It was, he noted, a "gross error" of F. D. Maurice [4] to identify as Calvin's the subjectivism of modern evangelicalism; but, he went on,

> Whether this standpoint is to be held itself responsible for the apostasy is another question, perfectly legitimate and of immense practical importance, which it becomes the friends of the Reformed Church to look steadily in the face. If Calvinism — the system of Geneva — *necessarily* runs here into Zwinglianism, we may indeed well despair of the whole interest. For most assuredly no church can stand, that is found to be constitutionally *unsacramental*.[5]

The exposition of Eucharistic theology and piety in *The Mystical Presence* is thus shaped primarily by a reference to the acknowledged standards of the "Calvinist" wing of the Reformation. There is also a brief sketch of patristic views of the subject, and it was noted that the Reformers themselves honored the ancient Fathers and claimed their authority in considerable measure. But since the opposition deprecated this appeal to post-biblical tradition, the weight of the demonstration must fall upon the theologians and confessions of the sixteenth century, and upon the Scriptures.

The polemic pressure was almost entirely from the exponents of a "low" or anti-sacramental outlook, and the exposition was therefore oriented primarily in this direction, in the form of a vigorous counterattack. Nevin charged that Protestantism, especially in America, had very generally shifted ground concerning the Lord's Supper from the position of its official confessions and catechisms. The change was most striking in Eastern Lutheranism, where *The Lutheran Observer*, a powerful though unofficial organ, had wholly abandoned Luther for Zwingli, and from that position was attacking Calvinism as papist. The Baptists, the largest Protestant body in the country, were of course unsacramental on principle, and Baptist attitudes were widely influential in other denominations that retained infant baptism. Methodism, the next largest body, did almost

3. "Pseudo-Protestantism," *Ibid.*, August 27, 1845.
4. *The Kingdom of Christ*, II, 105.   5. *The Mystical Presence*, 74.

as much wrong to the understanding of the Church and sacraments as the Baptists.

Among the Reformed churches, which concerned Nevin most immediately, the defection from the standards was only slightly less material than among the Lutherans. The transformation could be documented by the preaching, the exposition of Scripture, the systematic theology, and the general attitudes and feelings of the laity toward the sacraments. Among Congregationalists, the Reformed Dutch, and the various Presbyterian bodies, the old doctrine of the spiritual Real Presence was almost lost; it was not believed that the Reformed Church had ever taught such a conception, or if some conceded its presence in Calvin and other theologians it was dismissed as an obsolete relic of medieval superstition. The Protestant Episcopal Church retained a greater sacramental emphasis, but even here the majority would no longer accept the view taught by Richard Hooker and Calvin.

In prevailing American opinion the whole subject was a rather marginal one. That very fact, Nevin believed, was evidence of a dangerously pervasive rationalistic and unchurchly drift.

> As the Eucharist forms the very heart of the whole Christian worship, so it is clear that the entire question of the Church, which all are compelled to acknowledge the great life-problem of the age, centers ultimately in the sacramental question as its inmost heart and core. Our view of the Lord's Supper must ever condition and rule in the end our view of Christ's person and the conception we form of the Church. It must influence at the same time, very materially, our whole system of theology, as well as all our ideas of ecclesiastical history.[6]

The historical argument then consisted of an exposition of the classical Reformed doctrine, chiefly as found in Calvin and in the official confessions of the chief Reformed churches, Swiss, French, Dutch, German, Scots, and English, followed by systematic contrast with the views of the representative spokesmen of American Reformed theology. These were chiefly New England Congregationalists, such as Jonathan Edwards and his most famous disciples, Samuel Hopkins and Joseph Bellamy, and at the turn of the century President Dwight of Yale, or among the Presbyterians, Ashbel Green for the Old School, and for the New, Albert Barnes, the most widely read American biblical commentator. John Dick, himself a Scot, had written the theology text-book which was probably

6. *The Mystical Presence*, 3.

most widely used in America. Taken together, these men represented "modern Puritanism" in contrast to the "old Reformed view."

But Mercersburg was not content merely to establish its own position by bringing to light the true views of the Reformation. Nevin believed that Calvin's doctrine could be effectively recast in the categories of a more up-to-date psychology and thus freed from some apparent difficulties. He redefined the categories and presented a reconstructed statement which he could then fit into his organic incarnational theology. Even if the reformulation were to prove unacceptable, Nevin would still plead for the substance of the Reformed doctrine, "the fact of a real life-union in the case of the believer with the whole person of Christ, through the force of which the vivific virtue of his true human flesh is carried over in the sacrament particularly into our persons, soul and body, by the power of the Holy Ghost, for our nourishment unto eternal life." [7]

The selection below consists of five sections, one from each of the first two chapters, and the first three sections of Chapter III.

❖   ❖   ❖   ❖

SECTION I. *Statement of the Doctrine* [8]

To obtain a proper view of the original doctrine of the Reformed Church on the subject of the Eucharist, we must have recourse particularly to Calvin. Not that he is to be considered the creator, properly speaking, of the doctrine. It grew evidently out of the general religious life of the Church itself, in its antagonism to the Lutheran dogma on the one hand and the low Socinian extreme on the other. Calvin, however, was the theological organ by which it first came to that clear expression, under which it continued to be uttered subsequently in the symbolical books. His profound, far-reaching, and deeply penetrating mind drew forth the doctrine from the heart of the Church, exhibited it in its proper

7. "Our Union with Christ," *The Weekly Messenger*, January 14, 1846.
8. [ED.] This section in the original text is liberally documented. About a third of the citations are from "The True Partaking," available in English in the Library of Christian Classics, Volume XXII. Another third came from Calvin's Second Defense against Westphal, which is summarized below, 253–259. Of the remainder, half are from the *Institutes*, either from Section 17 of Book IV or from Book III, 11.10. There is one citation each from the Exposition of the Consensus, the Last Admonition to Westphal, and the *Commentary on Ephesians*, 5:30. The first two of these are available only in the Latin (*Opera*, Amsterdam edition, VIII). These references have all been omitted from the text as reprinted here.

relations, proportions, and distinctions, gave it form in this way for the understanding, and clothed it with authority as a settled article of faith in the general creed. He may be regarded, then, as the accredited interpreter and expounder of the article for all later times. A better interpreter in the case we could not possibly possess. Happily, too, his instructions and explanations here are very full and explicit. He comes upon the subject from all sides, and handles it under all forms, didactically and controversially, so that we are left in no uncertainty whatever, with regard to his meaning, at a single point.

Any theory of the Eucharist will be found to accord closely with the view that is taken at the same time of the nature of the union generally between Christ and his people. Whatever the life of the believer may be as a whole in this relation, it must determine the form of his communion with the Saviour in the sacrament of the Supper as the central representation of its significance and power. Thus, the sacramental doctrine of the primitive Reformed Church stands inseparably connected with the idea of an inward living union between believers and Christ, in virtue of which they are incorporated into his very nature, and made to subsist with him by the power of a common life. In full correspondence with this conception of the Christian salvation as a process by which the believer is mystically inserted more and more into the person of Christ till he becomes thus at last fully transformed into his image, it was held that nothing less than such a real participation of his living person is involved always in the right use of the Lord's Supper. The following distinctions may serve to define and explain more fully the nature of the communion which holds between Christ and his people, in the whole view now mentioned, as taught by Calvin and the Reformed Church generally in the sixteenth century.

1. The union of *believers* with Christ is not simply that of a common humanity, as derived from *Adam*. In this view, all men partake of one and the same nature, and each may be said to be in relation to his neighbor bone of his bone and flesh of his flesh. So Christ took not on him the nature of angels but of men. He was born of a woman, and appeared among us in the likeness and fashion of our own life, only without sin. But plainly our relation to his nature, and through this to his mediatorial work, as Christians, is something quite different from this general consanguinity of the human race. Where we are said to be of the same life with him, "members of his body, of his flesh and of his bones" [Eph. 5:30], it is not on the ground merely of a joint participation with him in the nature of Adam, but on the ground of our participation in his own nature as a

higher order of life. Our relation to him is not circuitous and collateral only; it holds in a direct connection with his person.

2. In this view, the relation is more again than a simply *moral* union. Such a union we have where two or more persons are bound together by inward agreement, sympathy, and correspondence. Every common friendship is of this sort. It is the relation of the disciple to the master whom he loves and reveres. It is the relation of the devout Jew to Moses, his venerated lawgiver and prophet. It holds also undoubtedly between the believer and Christ. The Saviour lives much in his thoughts and affections. He looks to him with an eye of faith, embraces him in his heart, commits himself to his guidance, walks in his steps, and endeavors to become clothed more and more with his very mind itself. In the end the correspondence will be found complete. We shall be like him in all respects, one with him morally in the fullest sense. But Christianity includes more than such a moral union, separately considered. This union itself is only the result here of a relation more inward and deep. It has its ground in the force of a common life, in virtue of which Christ and his people are one even before they become thus assimilated to his character. So in the sacrament of the Lord's Supper; it is not simply a moral approach that the true worshipper is permitted to make to the glorious object of his worship. His communion with Christ does not consist merely in the good exercises of his own mind, the actings of faith, and contrition, and hope, and love, the solemn recollections, the devotional feelings, the pious resolutions, of which he may be himself the subject during the sacramental service. Nor is the sacrament a sign only, by which the memory and heart may be assisted in calling up what is past or absent, for the purposes of devotion; as the picture of a friend is suited to recall his image and revive our interest in his person, when he is no longer in our sight. Nor is it a pledge simply of our own consecration to the service of Christ, or of the faithfulness of God as engaged to make good to us in a general way the grace of the new covenant, as the rainbow serves still to ratify and confirm the promise given to Noah after the flood. All this would bring with it in the end nothing more than a moral communication with Christ, so far as the sacrament itself might be concerned. It could carry with it no virtue or force more than might be put into it in every case by the spirit of the worshipper himself. Such, however, is not the nature of the ordinance. It is not simply an occasion by which the soul of the believer may be excited to pious feelings and desires; but it embodies the actual presence of the grace it represents in its own constitution; and this grace is not simply the promise of God on which we are encouraged to rely, but the very life

of the Lord Jesus Christ himself. We communicate, in the Lord's Supper, not with the divine promise merely, not with the thought of Christ only, not with the recollection simply of what he has done and suffered for us, not with the lively present sense alone of his all-sufficient, all-glorious salvation, but with the living Saviour himself, in the fullness of his glorified person, made present to us for the purpose by the power of the Holy Ghost.

3. The relation of believers to Christ, then, is more again than that of a simply *legal* union. He is indeed the representative of his people, and what he has done and suffered on their behalf is counted to their benefit, as though it had been done by themselves. They have an interest in his merits, a title to all the advantages secured by his life and death. But this external imputation rests at last on an inward, real unity of life, without which it could have no reason or force. Our interest in Christ's merits and benefits can be based only upon a previous interest in his person; so, in the Lord's Supper, we are made to participate not merely in the advantages secured by his mediatorial work, the rewards of his obedience, the fruits of his bitter passion, the virtue of his atonement, and the power of his priestly intercession, but also in his true and proper life itself. We partake of his merits and benefits only so far as we partake of his substance.

4. Of course, once more, the communion in question is not simply with Christ in his *divine nature* separately taken, or with the *Holy Ghost* as the representative of his presence in the world. It does not hold in the influences of the Spirit merely, enlightening the soul and moving it to holy affections and purposes. It is by the Spirit, indeed, we are united to Christ. Our new life is comprehended in the Spirit as its element and medium. But it is always bound in this element to the person of the Lord Jesus Christ himself. Our fellowship is with the Father and with his son Jesus Christ, *through* the Holy Ghost. As such it is a real communion with the Word made flesh, not simply with the divinity of Christ but with his humanity also, since both are inseparably joined together in his person, and a living union with him in the one view implies necessarily a living union with him in the other view likewise. In the Lord's Supper, accordingly, the believer communicates not only with the Spirit of Christ, or with his divine nature, but with Christ himself in his whole living person, so that he may be said to be fed and nourished by his very flesh and blood. The communion is truly and fully with the *man* Christ Jesus, and not simply with Jesus as the Son of God.

These distinctions may serve to bound and define the Reformed doctrine of the Eucharist on the side towards *rationalism*. All pains were taken to guard it from the false tendency to which it stood exposed in this direction. The several conceptions of the believer's union and communion with Christ which have now been mentioned, were explicitly and earnestly rejected as being too low and poor altogether for the majesty of this great mystery. In opposition to all such representations, it was constantly affirmed that Christ's people are inserted by faith into his very life; and that the Lord's Supper, forming as it does an epitome of the whole mystery, involves to the worthy communicant an actual participation in the substance of his Person under this view. The participation is not simply in his Spirit, but in his flesh also and blood. It is not figurative merely and moral, but *real, substantial* and *essential*.

But it is not enough to settle the boundaries of the doctrine on the side of rationalism. To be understood properly, it must be limited and defined, in like manner, on the side of *Romanism*.

1. In the first place, then, it excludes entirely the figment of *transubstantiation*. According to the Church of Rome, the elements of bread and wine in the sacrament are literally transmuted into the actual flesh and blood of Christ. The accidents, outward properties, sensible qualities only, remain the same, while the original substance is converted supernaturally into the true body of the glorified Saviour, which is thus exhibited and received in an outward way in the sacramental mystery. This transmutation, too, is not limited to the actual solemnity of the sacramental act itself, but is held to be of permanent force, so that the elements continue afterwards to be the true body of Christ, and are proper objects of veneration and worship accordingly. This theory was rejected as a gross superstition, even by the Lutheran Church, and of course found still less favor in the other section of the Protestant communion. The Reformed doctrine admits no change whatever in the elements. Bread remains bread, and wine remains wine.

2. The doctrine excludes, in the second place, the proper Lutheran hypothesis of the sacrament, technically distinguished by the title *consubstantiation*. According to this view, the body and blood of Christ are not actually substituted supernaturally for the elements; the bread and wine remain unchanged, in their essence as well as in their properties. But still the body and blood of Christ are in their very substance *present*, where the supper is administered. The presence is not, indeed, bound to the elements apart from their sacramental use. It holds only in the moment and form of this use as such; a mystery in this respect, transcending all the

common laws of reason and nature. It is, however, a true, corporal presence of the blessed Saviour. Hence his body is received by the worshipper *orally*, though not in the form and under the quality of common food; and so not by believers simply, but by unbelievers also, to their own condemnation. The dogma was allowed in the end to involve also, by necessary consequence, the ubiquity of Christ's glorified body. Bread and wine retain their own nature, but Christ, who is in virtue of the *communicatio idiomatum* [sharing of attributes] present in his human nature in all places where he may please to be, imparts his true flesh and blood *in*, *with*, and *under* the outward signs to all communicants, whether with or without faith, by the inherent power of the ordinance itself.

In opposition to this view, the Reformed Church taught that the participation of Christ's flesh and blood in the Lord's Supper is *spiritual* only, and in no sense corporal. The idea of a local presence in the case was utterly rejected. The elements cannot be said to comprehend or include the body of the Saviour in any sense. It is not *there*, but remains constantly in heaven, according to the Scriptures. It is not handled by the minister and taken into the mouth of the communicant. The manducation of it is not oral, but only by faith. It is present in fruition accordingly to believers only in the exercise of faith; the impenitent and unbelieving receive only the naked symbols, bread and wine, without any spiritual advantage to their own souls.

Thus we have the doctrine defined and circumscribed on both sides, with proper distinction from all that may be considered a tendency to rationalism in one direction, and from all that may be counted a tendency to Romanism in the other. It allows the *presence* of Christ's person in the sacrament, including even his flesh and blood, so far as the actual participation of the believer is concerned. Even the term *Real Presence*, Calvin tells us, he was willing to employ if it were to be understood as synonymous with *true* presence, by which he means a presence that brings Christ truly into communion with the believer in his human nature, as well as in his divine nature. The word *real*, however, was understood ordinarily to denote a local, corporal presence, and on this account was not approved. To guard against this, it may be qualified by the word *spiritual*, and the expression will then be quite suitable to the nature of the doctrine as it has been now explained. A *real* presence, in opposition to the notion that Christ's flesh and blood are not made present to the communicant in *any* way. A *spiritual* real presence, in opposition to the idea that Christ's body is in the elements in a local or corporal manner. Not real simply, and not spiritual simply, but real and yet spiritual at the same time. The body of Christ is in heaven, the believer on earth; but by the power of the Holy Ghost, nevertheless, the obstacle of such vast local distance is fully overcome, so that in the sacramental act, while the outward symbols are received in an outward way, the very body and blood of Christ are at the same time inwardly and supernaturally communicated to the worthy receiver, for the real nourishment of his new life. Not that the material particles of Christ's body are supposed to be carried over, by this supernatural process, into the believer's person. The communion is spiritual, not material. It is a participation of the Saviour's life — of his life, however, as human, subsisting in a true bodily form. The living energy, the vivific virtue, as Calvin styles it, of Christ's flesh, is made to flow over into the communicant, making him more and more one with Christ himself, and thus more and more an heir of the same immortality that is brought to light in his person.

Two points in particular, in the theory now exhibited, require to be held clearly in view.

The first is that the sacrament is made to carry with it an *objective* force, so far as its principal design is concerned. It is not simply suggestive, commemorative, or representational. It is not a sign, a picture, deriving its significance from the mind of the beholder. The virtue which it possesses is not put into it by the faith of the worshipper in the first place, to be taken out of it again by the same faith, in the same form. It is not imagined, of course, in the case that the ordinance can have any virtue *without* faith, that it can confer grace in a purely mechanical way. All thought of the *opus operatum*, in this sense, is utterly repudiated. Still faith does not properly clothe the sacrament with its power. It is the condition of its efficacy for the communicant, but not the principle of the power itself. This belongs to the institution in its own nature. The signs are bound to what they represent, not subjectively simply, in the thought of the worshipper, but objectively, by the force of a divine appointment. The union, indeed, is not natural but sacramental. The grace is not comprehended *in* the elements, as its depository and vehicle outwardly considered. But the union is none the less real and firm on this account. The grace goes inseparably along with the signs, and is truly present for all who are prepared to make it their own. The signs in this view are also *seals*, not simply as they attest the truth and reality of the grace in a general way, but as they authenticate also its presence under the sacramental exhibition itself. This is what we mean by the objective force of the institution, and this, we say, is one point that must always be kept in view, in looking at the doctrine that is now the subject of our attention.

The other point to be steadily kept in sight is that the invisible grace of the sacrament, according to the doctrine, is the substantial life of the Saviour himself, particularly in his human nature. He became flesh for the life of the world, and our communion with him involves a real participation in him as the principle of life *under this form*. Hence in the mystery of the Supper, his flesh and blood are really exhibited always in their essential force and power, and really received by every worthy communicant.

Such is the proper sacramental doctrine of the Reformed Church as it stood in the sixteenth century. It is easy to show that it labors under serious difficulties. With these, however, at present, we have no concern. They can have no bearing, one way or another, upon the simply historical inquiry in which we are now engaged. My object has been thus far only to describe and define the doctrine itself. . . .

SECTION II. *Systems Contrasted* [9]

1. In the old Reformed view, the communion of the believer with Christ in the Supper is taken to be *specific* in its nature, and *different* from all that has place in the common exercises of worship. The sacrament — not the elements, of course, separately considered, but the ordinance as the union of element and Word — is held to be such an exhibition of saving grace as is presented to the faith of the Church under no other form. It is not simply the Word brought to mind in its ordinary force. The outward is not merely the occasion by which the inward, in the case, is made present to the soul as a separate existence; but inward and outward, by the energy of the Spirit, are made to flow together in the way of a common life, and come thus to exert a peculiar and altogether extraordinary power, in this form, to the benefit of the believer. "There is a peculiar communion with Christ," says Dr. Owen, "which we have in no other ordinance"; and this, he adds, has been the faith of the whole Church in all ages. "A way of receiving Christ by eating and drinking, something peculiar that is not in prayer, that is not in the hearing of the Word, nor in any other part of divine worship whatsoever; a peculiar

9. [ED.] The original text of this section contained three footnotes by the author, which have been omitted here.

participation of Christ, a peculiar acting of faith towards Christ." [10] In the modern Puritan view, on the contrary, this specific peculiar virtue of the sacraments is not recognized. Christ is present, we are told by Dr. Dick, in all ordinances, "and he is present in the same manner in them all, namely, by his Spirit, who renders them effectual means of salvation." [11] So with Dr. Dwight the entire force of the institution is made to consist in the occasion it affords for the affections and exercises of common religious worship. The idea of a peculiar sacramental power, belonging to this form of worship as such, seems to have no place at all in his system.[12]

2. In the old Reformed view the sacramental transaction is a *mystery*, nay, in some sense an actual *miracle*. The Spirit works here in a way that transcends not only the human understanding, but the ordinary course of the world also in every other view. There is a form of action in the sacraments which now belongs, indeed, to the regular order of the life that is comprehended in the Church, but which as thus established still involves a character that may be denominated *supernatural*, as compared with the ordinary constitution not only of nature, but even of the Christian life itself. "Not without reason," says Calvin, "is the communication which makes us flesh of Christ's flesh and bone of his bones, denominated by Paul *a great mystery*. In the sacred Supper, therefore, we acknowledge it a *miracle*, transcending both nature and our own understanding, that Christ's life is made common to us with himself and his flesh given to us as aliment." [13] This *mystery* of our coalition with Christ," says the Gallic Confession, "is so sublime that it transcends all our senses and also the whole course of nature." [14] "The mode is such," according to the Belgic Confession, "as to surpass the apprehension of our mind, and cannot be understood by any." [15] "The *mysteriousness*," we are told by Dr. Owen, "is beyond expression, the *mysterious* reception of Christ in this peculiar way of exhibition." [16]

10. [ED.] John Owen, *Works*, ed. T. Russell (London, 1826), XVII, 268: Sacramental Discourse xxv.

11. [ED.] John Dick (1764–1832), *Lectures on Theology* (Philadelphia, 1836), II, 414: Lecture xcii.

12. [ED.] Timothy Dwight, *Theology* (Middletown, 1819), V; Sermon clxi.

13. [ED.] The clear explanation of . . . the true partaking, *Calvin: Theological Treatises*, Library of Christian Classics, XXII, 328 (Nevin's translation and italics).

14. [ED.] Art. xxxvi. Cf. Schaff, *Creeds of Christendom*, 4th ed., III, 380 (Nevin's translation).

15. [ED.] Art. xxxv. *Ibid.*, 429, 430 (Nevin's translation).

16. [ED.] *Works*, XVII, 270 (Nevin's italics).

Contrast with this now the style in which the ordinance is represented, from the proper Puritan standpoint, in the extracts already quoted. We find it spoken of, it is true, with great respect, as full of interest, significance, and power. But it is no mystery, much less a miracle — as little so, it would seem, in the view of Dr. Dwight, as a common Fourth of July celebration. The ends contemplated in the one case are religious, in the other patriotic, but the institutions as related to these ends are in all material respects of one and the same order. The ends proposed in the Supper [are] "the enlargement and rectification of our *views* . . . the purification of our *affections* . . . the amendment of our *lives*. The means . . . are . . . efficacious and desirable, at the same time simple, *intelligible to the humblest capacity*, in no respect burdensome, lying within the reach of all men, incapable of being misconstrued without violence, and therefore not easily susceptible of *mystical* or superstitious perversion. In their own proper, undisguised nature, they appeal powerfully to the *senses*, the *imagination*, and the *heart*, and at the same time enlighten in the happiest manner, the *understanding*." All this is said to show "the *wisdom* of this institution." [17] "There seems to have been a disposition in that age," says Dr. Dick, with reference to the sixteenth century, "to believe that there was a presence of Christ in the Eucharist *different* from his presence in the other ordinances of the gospel; an undefined something, which corresponded to the strong language used at the institution of the Supper: *This is my body — this is my blood.* Acknowledging it to be figurative, many still thought that a *mystery* was couched under it." [18] Dr. Dick himself, of course, finds no mystery in the case. Calvin's doctrine accordingly is rejected as *incomprehensible*, not understood by himself (as the great theologian indeed humbly admits), and beyond the understanding also of his readers. "Plain, literal language is best, especially on spiritual subjects, and should have been employed by Protestant churches with the utmost care, as the figurative terms of Scripture have been so grossly mistaken." [19] To this we may add that the very reason why *such* plain, simple language as might have suited Dr. Dick has *not* been employed by the Protestant churches in their symbolical books, is to be found in the fact that these Protestant churches believed and intended to assert the presence of a mystery in the sacrament, for the idea of which no place is allowed in *his* creed, and that could not

17. [ED.] Dwight, *Theology*, V, 381 (condensed).
18. [ED.] Dick, *Lectures*, II, 411: Lecture XCI. 19. [ED.] *Ibid.*, 414: Lecture XCII.

be properly represented therefore by any language which this creed might supply.

3. The old Reformed doctrine includes always the idea of an *objective force* in the sacraments. The sacramental union between the sign and the thing signified is real, and holds in virtue of the constitution of the ordinance itself, not in the faith simply or inward frame of the communicant. Without faith, indeed, this force which belongs to the sacrament cannot avail to the benefit of the communicant; faith forms the indispensable condition, by whose presence only the potential in this case can become actual, the life that is present be brought to take effect in the interior man. But the condition here, as in all other cases, is something different from the thing itself, for which it makes room. The grace of the sacrament comes from God; but it comes as such under the sacrament as its true and proper form, not inhering in the elements, indeed, outwardly considered, but still mysteriously lodged, by the power of the Holy Ghost, in the sacramental transaction as a whole. The grace is truly present, according to Calvin, even where it is excluded from the soul by unbelief, as much so as the fertilizing qualities of the rain that falls fruitless on the barren rock. Unbelief may make it of no effect, but the intrinsic virtue of the sacrament itself still remains the same. The bread and wine are the sure pledge still of the presence of what they represent, and "a true exhibition of it on the part of God." [20] "The symbols," say Beza and Farel, "are by no means naked; but, so far as God is concerned, who makes the promise and offer, they always have the thing itself truly and certainly joined with them, whether proposed to believers or unbelievers." [21] "We do utterly condemn the vanity of those who affirm that the sacraments are nothing else but mere naked signs." — Old Scotch Confession. [22] "Those signs, then, are by no means vain or void." Belgic Confession. [23] "We teach that the things signified are together with the signs in the right use exhibited and communicated." — Ursinus. [24] The sacrament, in this view, not only signifies, but *seals* to believers, the grace it carries in its constitution. It is not simply a pledge that the blessings it represents are

---

20. [ED.] Calvin, *Opera Omnia* (Amstelodami 1667–71), VIII, 699d.

21. [ED.] R. Hospinian, *Historiae Sacramentariae Pars altera* (Tiguri, MDCII) 251b.

22. [ED.] Article XXI. See Schaff, *Creeds*, III, 467, 468. (Nevin gives another translation.)

23. [ED.] Article XXXIII. See Schaff, *Creeds*, III, 424. (Nevin gives another translation.)

24. [ED.] *Summe of Christian Religion by Zacharias Ursinus*, trans. Henry Parry (London, 1645?), 718.

sure to them, in a general way, apart from this particular engagement itself; as when a man by some outward stipulation binds himself to fulfill
the terms of a contract in another place and at another time. The sacramental transaction certifies and makes good the grace it represents, as
actually communicated at the time. So it is said to *exhibit* also the thing
signified. The thing is *there*, not the name of the thing only, and not its
sign or shadow, but the actual substance itself. "The sacrament is no picture," says Calvin, "but the true, veritable pledge of our union with
Christ." [25] To say that the body of Christ is adumbrated by the symbol
of bread, only as a dead statue is made to represent Hercules or Mercury,
he pronounces profane. The signs, Owen tells us, "*exhibit* that which
they do not contain. . . ." It is no "empty, painted feast . . . Here is
something really exhibited by Jesus Christ unto us, to receive, besides the
outward pledges of bread and wine." [26]

How different from all this, again, the light in which the subject is presented in our modern Puritan theology. Here, too, the sacraments are
indeed said to seal, and also to exhibit, the grace they represent. But
plainly the old, proper sense of these terms in the case is changed. The *seal*
ratifies simply a covenant in virtue of which certain blessings are made
sure to the believer, on certain conditions, under a wholly different form.
Two parties in the transaction, Christ and his people, stipulate to be faithful to each other in fulfilling the engagements of a mutual contract, and
in doing so, they both affix their seal to the sacramental bond. Such is the
view presented very distinctly by Edwards, Hopkins, and Bellamy. The
contract of salvation according to this last, is in the Lord's Supper, "externally and visibly sealed, ratified, and confirmed, on both sides, with as
much formality as any 'written instrument' is mutually sealed by the parties in any covenant among men. And now if both parties are sincere in
the covenant thus sealed, and if both abide by and act according to it, the
communicant will be saved." [27] So the sacrament is allowed to be exhibi-
tional, not, however, of any actual present substance, as the old doctrine
always held, but only in the way of figure, shadow, or sign. A picture or
statue may be said to exhibit their original to the same extent. The sacramental elements are Christ's *proxy*. "Or the matter may be more fitly
represented by *this* similitude: it is as if a prince should send an ambassador to a woman in a foreign land, proposing marriage, and by his

25. [ED.] Calvin, *Opera Omnia* (Amstelodami 1667–71), VIII, 667; *cf.* 727.
26. [ED.] Owen, *Works*, XVII, 211.
27. [ED.] Joseph Bellamy, *Works* (New York, 1812), III, 166.

ambassador should send her his *picture*, &c." [28] With Dr. Dwight the sacrament is reduced fully to the character of a mere occasion by which religious affections are excited and supported in the breast of the worshipper. He seems to have no idea at all of an objective force belonging to the institution in its own nature. All is subjective and subjective only. All turns on the adaptation of the rite to instruct and affect. He measures its wisdom and power wholly by this standard. It is admirably *contrived* to work upon "the senses, the imagination, and the heart," as well as to "enlighten the understanding." [29] Its whole force, when all is done, is the amount simply of the good thoughts, good feelings, and good purposes, that are brought to it, and made to go along with it, on the part of the worshippers themselves.

4. According to the old Reformed doctrine the invisible grace of the sacrament includes a real participation in his *person*. That which is made present to the believer is the very life of Christ himself in its true power and substance. The doctrine proceeds on the assumption that the Christian salvation stands in an actual union between Christ and his people, mystical but in the highest sense real, in virtue of which they are as closely joined to him as the limbs are to the head in the natural body. They are in him, and he is in them, not figuratively but truly, in the way of a growing process that will become complete finally in the resurrection. The power of this fact is mysteriously concentrated in the Holy Supper. Here Christ communicates *himself* to his Church, not simply a right to the grace that resides in his person, or an interest by outward grant in the benefits of his life and death, but his person itself, as the ground and fountain from which all these other blessings may be expected to flow. This idea is exhibited under all forms in which it could well be presented, and in terms the most clear and explicit. Christ first, and *then* his benefits. Calvin will hear of no other order but this. The same view runs through all the Calvinistic symbols. Not a title to Christ *in* his benefits, the efficacy of his atonement, the work of his Spirit, but a true property in his life itself, out of which only that other title can legitimately spring. "We are quickened by a real participation of him, which he designates by the terms *eating* and *drinking* that no person might suppose the life which we receive from him to consist in simple knowledge." [30] We communicate with Christ's *substance*. "A substantial com-

28. [ED.] *The Works of President Edwards* (New York, 1830), Vol. IV. "Qualifications for Communion," Part II, Section IX, 371.

29. [ED.] Dwight, *Theology*, V, 381.

30. [ED.] Calvin, *Institutes*, IV.17.5 (McNeill ed., 1365).

munication is affirmed by me everywhere." [31] "He nourishes and vivifies us by the substance of his body and blood." — Gallic Confession.[32] "It is *not only* to embrace with a believing heart all the sufferings and death of Christ, and thereby to obtain the pardon of sin and life eternal; but also *besides that* to become more and more united to his sacred body, by the Holy Ghost, &c." — Heidelberg Catechism.[33] "We teach that he is present and united with us by the Holy Ghost, albeit his body be far absent from us." — Ursinus.[34] "In the Supper we are made partakers, not only of the Spirit of Christ, and his satisfaction, justice, virtue, and operation; but also of the very substance and essence of his true body and blood, &c." [35] "*Christ* crucified, *and* all benefits of his death." — Westminster Confession.[36] "It is on all sides plainly confessed . . . that this sacrament is a true and a real participation of Christ, who thereby imparteth himself, even his whole entire person, as a mystical head, unto every soul that receiveth him, and that every such receiver doth incorporate or unite himself unto Christ as a mystical member of him." — Hooker.[37] A peculiar exhibition of Christ under outward signs, "and a mysterious reception of him in them really, so as to come to real substantial incorporation of our souls." — Owen.[38]

As the modern Puritan theory eviscerates the institution of all objective force, under any view, it must, of course, still more decidedly refuse to admit the idea of any such virtue belonging to it as that now mentioned. The union of the believer with Christ it makes to be moral only, or at least a figurative incorporation with his Spirit! The sacred Supper forms an occasion by which the graces of the pious communicant are called into favorable exercise, and his faith in particular is assisted in apprehending and appropriating the precious contents of the Christian salvation, as wrought out by the Redeemer's life and death! He participates in this way in the fruits of Christ's love, the benefits of his mediatorial work, his imputed righteousness, his heavenly intercession, the influences of his Spirit, &c., but in the substantial life of Christ himself he has no part whatever. "A mutual solemn profession of the two parties transacting the

31. [ED.] Calvin, *Opera Omnia* (Amstelodami, 1667–71), VII, 732.
32. [ED.] Cf. note 14, above.
33. [ED.] Ans. to Q. 76. Cf. Schaff, *Creeds*, III, 332, 333 (Nevin's italics).
34. [ED.] Parry, *Summe*, 718.   35. [ED.] *Ibid.*, 730.
36. [ED.] Chap. XXIX, 7. Cf. Schaff, *Creeds*, III, 666 (Nevin's italics).
37. [ED.] *Laws of Ecclesiastical Polity*, Book V, LXVII: Of the sacrament of the body and blood of Christ, par. 7.
38. [ED.] *Works*, XVII, 270.

covenant of grace, and visibly united in that covenant." — Edwards.[39] So
also Hopkins and Bellamy. "Sensible impressions are much more powerful
than those which are made on the understanding, &c." — Dwight.[40] "The
ends proposed in the institution of the Lord's Supper are, the enlargement
and rectification of our views concerning the noblest of all subjects, the
purification of our affections and the amendment of our lives." [41] "Stript
of all metaphorical terms, the action must mean that in the believing and
grateful commemoration of his death, we enjoy the blessings which were
purchased by it, in the same manner in which we enjoy them when we
exercise faith in hearing the gospel." — Dick.[42] "No man who admits
that the bread and wine are only signs and figures can consistently suppose the words, 1 Corinthians 10:16, to have any other meaning than that
we have communion with Christ in the fruits of his sufferings and death;
or that receiving the symbols we receive by faith the benefits procured
by the pains of his body and the effusion of his blood." [43] Christ's "*doctrine* is truly that which will give life to the soul." — Barnes.[44] "To dwell
or abide in him, is to remain in the belief of his doctrine and in the participation of all the benefits of his death." [45] "The whole design of the
sacramental bread is by a striking emblem to call to *remembrance*, in a
vivid manner, the dying sufferings of our Lord." [46]

5. In the old Reformed view of the Lord's Supper, the communion of
the believer in the true person of Christ, in the form now stated, is supposed to hold with him especially as the Word made flesh. His humanity
forms the medium of his union with the Church. The life of which he is the
fountain flows forth from him only as he is the Son of Man. To have part
in it at all, we must have part in it as a real human life; we must eat his
flesh and drink his blood, take into us the substance of what he was as
man, so as to become flesh of his flesh and bone of his bones. "The very
flesh in which he dwells is made to be vivific for us, that we may be
nourished by it to immortality." — Calvin.[47] "This sacred communication of his flesh and blood, in which Christ transfuses his life into us, just
as if he penetrated our bones and marrow, he testifies and seals also in the

---

39. [ED.] Jonathan Edwards, *Works*, IV, 369.

40. [ED.] Timothy Dwight, *Theology*, V, 345: Sermon CLX.

41. [ED.] *Ibid.*, 381.

42. [ED.] John Dick, *Lectures on Theology*, II, 413: Lecture XCII.   43. [ED.] *Ibid.*

44. [ED.] Albert Barnes, *Notes, Explanatory and Practical, on the Gospels* (New
York, 1850), II, 259: *In re* Jn. 6:55 (Nevin's italics).

45. [ED.] *Ibid., In re* Jn. 6:56.

46. [ED.] *Ibid.*, I, 301: *In re* Mt. 26:26 (Nevin's italics).

47. [ED.] *Institutes*, IV.17.8 (McNeill ed., II, 1368).

Holy Supper." [48] "I do not teach that Christ dwells in us simply by his Spirit, but that he so raises us to himself as to transfuse into us the vivific vigor of his flesh." [49] "The very substance itself of the Son of Man." — Beza and Farel.[50] "That same substance which he took in the womb of the Virgin, and which he carried up into heaven." — Beza and Peter Martyr.[51] "As the eternal deity has imparted life and immortality to the flesh of Jesus Christ, so likewise his flesh and blood, when eaten and drunk by us, confer upon us the same prerogatives." — Old Scotch Confession.[52] "That which is eaten is the very, natural body of Christ, and what is drunk is his true blood." — Belgic Confession.[53] "Flesh of his flesh and bone of his bone. . . . We are as *really* partakers of his true body and blood . . . as we receive these holy signs." — Heidelberg Catechism.[54] "We are . . . in such sort coupled, knit, and incorporated into his true, essential human body, by his Spirit dwelling both in him and us, that we are flesh of his flesh and bone of his bones." — Ursinus.[55] "They that worthily communicate in the sacrament of the Lord's Supper, do therein feed upon the body and blood of Christ . . . truly and really." — Westminster Catechism.[56]

All this the modern Puritan view utterly repudiates as semi-popish mysticism. It will allow no real participation of Christ's person in the Lord's Supper, under any form, but least of all under the form of his humanity. Such communion as it is willing to admit, it limits to the presence of Christ in his divine nature, or to the energy he puts forth by his Spirit. As for all that is said about his body and blood, it is taken to be mere figure, intended to express the value of his sufferings and death. With his body in the strict sense, his life as incarnate, formerly on earth and now in heaven, we can have no communion at all, except in the way of remembering what was endured in it for our salvation. The *flesh* in any other view profiteth nothing; it is only the Spirit that quickeneth. The language of the Calvinistic confessions on this subject is resolved into bold, violent metaphor, that comes in the end to mean almost nothing. "If

48. [ED.] *Ibid.*, IV.17.10 (McNeill ed., II, 1370).
49. [ED.] Calvin, *Omnia Opera* (Amstelodami, 1667–71), VIII, 669.
50. [ED.] Beza and Farel at Worms, 1557. Cf. R. Hospinian, *loc. cit.*
51. [ED.] Beza and Peter Martyr at Poissy, 1561. Cf. Hospinian, *op. cit.*, 301a.
52. [ED.] Art. XXI. Cf. Schaff, *Creeds*, III, 469.
53. [ED.] Art. XXXV. Cf. Schaff, *Creeds*, III, 430. (Nevin supplies another translation).
54. [ED.] *Ans.* 76, 79. Cf. Schaff, *Creeds*, III, 333, 335.
55. [ED.] Ursinus, *Summe*, 731.
56. [ED.] Westminster Larger Catechism, Ans., Q. 170.

he (Calvin) meant that there is some mysterious communication with his human nature, we must be permitted to say the notion was as incomprehensible to himself as it is to his readers." — Dick.[57] "There is an absurdity in the notion that there is any communion with the body and blood of Christ, considered in themselves." [58] "Justly does our Confession of Faith declare . . ." that "the body and blood of Christ are as *really*, but spiritually present to the faith of believers," &c. . . . . "What blessed visions of faith are those, in which this precious grace creates an *ideal* presence of the suffering, bleeding, dying, atoning Saviour! Then Gethsemane, and Pilate's hall, and the cross, the thorny crown, the nails, the spear, the hill of Calvary, are in present view!" — Green.[59] "This broken bread shows the manner in which my body will be broken; or this will serve to call my dying sufferings to your *remembrance*." — Barnes.[60]

Let this suffice in the way of comparison. The two theories, it is clear, are different throughout. Nor is the difference such as may be considered of small account. It is not simply formal or accidental. The modern Puritan view evidently involves a material falling away, not merely from the form of the old Calvinistic doctrine, but from its inward life and force. It makes a great difference, surely, whether the union of the believer with Christ be regarded as the power of one and the same life, or as holding only in a correspondence of thought and feeling; whether the Lord's Supper be a sign and seal only of God's grace in general, or the pledge also of a special invisible grace present in the transaction itself; and whether we are united by means of it to the person of Christ, or only to his merits; and whether, finally, we communicate in the ordinance with the whole Christ, in a real way, or only with his divinity. Such, however, is the difference that stares us in the face, from the comparison now made. All must see and feel that it exists, and that it is serious. . . .

57. [ED.] *Theology*, II, 412: Lecture XCI.   58. [ED.] *Ibid.*, 413: Lecture XCII.
59. [ED.] Ashbel Green, *Lectures on the Shorter Catechism* (Philadelphia, 1841), Vol. II, 399: Lecture LXX (Nevin's italics).
60. [ED.] *Op. cit.*, I, 300: *In re* Mt. 26:26 (Nevin's italics).

An Attempt to Place the Doctrine in its Proper Scientific Form

SECTION I. *Preliminary Positions* [1]

Calvin's theory seems to labor particularly at three points, all connected with a false psychology, as applied either to the person of Christ or the persons of his people.

In the *first* place he does not make a sufficiently clear distinction between the idea of the organic law which constitutes the proper identity of a human body, and the material volume it is found to embrace as exhibited to the senses. A true and perfect body must indeed appear in the form of organized matter. As a *mere* law, it can have no proper reality. But still the matter, apart from the law, is in no sense the body. Only as it is found to be transfused with the active presence of the law at every point, and in this way filled with the form of life, can it be said to have any such character; and then it is, of course, as the medium simply, by which what is inward and invisible is enabled to gain for itself a true outward existence. The principle of the body as a system of life, the original salient point of its being as a whole, is in no respect material. It is not bound, of course, for its identity, to any particular portion of matter as such. If the matter which enters into its constitution were changed every hour, it would still remain the same body, since that which passed away in each case would have no more right to be considered a part of the man than it had before entering the law of life in his person, and the demands of this law would always be abundantly satisfied by the matter that might fill it at each moment. A real communication, then, between the body of Christ and the bodies of his saints, does not imply necessarily the gross imagination of any transition of his flesh as such into their persons. This would be, indeed, of no meaning or value. For how could the flesh of Christ as something sundered from the law of life, in the presence of which only it can have any force, and in this form supernaturally inserted into my flesh under the like abstract view, bring with it any advantage or profit? In such sense as this, we *may* say, without wresting our Saviour's

1. [ED.] One footnote occurring in the original text of this section has been omitted here.

words, "the flesh profiteth nothing" [Jn. 6:63]. And here precisely comes
into view one of the most valid and forcible objections to the dogma of
the Roman Church, as well as to the kindred doctrine of Luther, in both
of which so much is made to hang on a sort of tactual participation of the
matter of Christ's body in the sacrament, rather than in the law simply of
his true human life. This is urged in fact by Calvin himself, with great
force, against the false theories in question. This shows, of course, that he
was not insensible to the idea of the distinction now mentioned, a point
abundantly manifest besides from his whole way of representing the subject in general. Still it seems to have been a matter of correct feeling with
him, rather than of clear scientific apprehension. Hence he never brings it
forward in a distinct way, and never turns it to any such account in the
service of his theory, as in the nature of the case he might have done.
Thus too much account is made, perhaps, of the flesh of Christ under a
local form (here confined to the right hand of God in heaven), as the seat
and fountain of the new life which is to be conveyed into his people; and
the attempt which is then made to bring the two parties together, notwithstanding such vast separation in space, must be allowed to be somewhat awkward and violent. No wonder that men of less dialectic subtlety
than the great theologian himself were at a loss to make anything out of
such a seeming contradiction in terms. In this case he may be said to cut
the knot which his speculation fails to solve. Christ's body is altogether in
heaven only. How then is its vivific virtue to be carried into the believer?
By the miraculous energy of the Holy Ghost, which, however, cannot be
said in the case so much to bring his life down to us as it serves rather to
raise us in the exercise of faith to the presence of the Saviour on high.
The result, however, is a real participation always in his full and entire
humanity. But the representation is confused, and brings the mind no
proper satisfaction. If for the "vivific virtue" of Christ's flesh Calvin had
been led to substitute distinctly the idea of the organic law of Christ's
human life, his theory would have assumed at once a much more consistent and intelligible form. For, in this view, it cannot be said that local,
material contact is necessary to sustain a true and strict continuity of
existence, either in the sphere of nature or in that of grace.

A *second* point of difficulty in the case of Calvin's theory is that he fails
to insist, with proper freedom and emphasis, on the absolute *unity* of
what we denominate *person*, both in the case of Christ himself and in the
case of his people. Hence he dwells too much on the life-giving virtue of
Christ's *flesh* simply, as if this were not necessarily and inseparably knit to

his soul, and to his divinity, too, as a single indivisible life, so that where the latter form of existence is present in a real way, the other must be really present, too, so far as its inmost nature is concerned, to the same extent. When I travel, whether by the eye or in thought simply, to the planet Saturn, the act includes my whole person, not the body as such, of course, but just as little the soul under the like abstraction; it is the act of that single and absolutely one life which I call myself, as the unity of both soul and body. And if it were possible in any way that the thought which carries me to Saturn could be made to assume there a real concrete existence, holding in organic connection with my own life, it must as a *human* existence appear under a human form, which in such a case would be as strictly a continuation of my bodily as well as spiritual being as though it had sprung immediately from the local presence of my body itself. So the acts of the incarnate Word belong to his person as a whole. Not as though his humanity separately considered could be said to exercise the functions of his divinity, for this is a false distinction in the case, and we have just as little reason to say that the divinity thus separately considered ever exercises the same functions. They are exercised by the theanthropic Person of the Mediator, as one and indivisible. If, then, Christ's life be conveyed over to the persons of his people at all, in a real and not simply figurative way, it *must* be so carried over under a human form, including both the constituents of humanity, body as well as soul, and the new bodily existence, thus produced, must be considered, independently of all local connection, a continuation in the strictest sense of Christ's life under the same form. This point does not appear to have been apprehended with sufficient distinctness by Calvin and the Reformers generally. Hence more or less confusion, and at times some apparent contradiction, in tracing the derivation of Christ's human life into the person of the believer. Bound as he felt himself to be to resist everything like the idea of a local presence, he found it necessary to resolve the whole process into a special supernatural agency of the Holy Ghost, as a sort of foreign medium introduced to meet the wants of the case. Thus the view taken of Christ's human nature becomes altogether too abstract, and it is made difficult to keep hold of the idea of a true organic connection between his life in this form and that of his people. It is not easy then, of course, to maintain a clear distinction between such a communication of the substance of Christ's life, and an influence in the way of mere spiritual power, to which conception Calvin's thory was in fact always made to sink by his high-toned Lutheran adversaries; although he never failed to protest against this as grossly perverse and unjust, and has taken the greatest pains indeed to save himself at this point from misconstruction. But his theory, it must be allowed, carries here a somewhat fantastic character. So, on the other hand, the relation of soul and body in the person of the believer appears too abstract also, according to his view. He will hear of no translation of the material particles of Christ's body into our bodies. The vivific virtue of his flesh can be apprehended on our part only by faith, and in this form, of course, by the soul only, through the power of the Holy Ghost. Still it extends to the body also, in the end: but all this, it would seem, in a way transcending all known analogies, in virtue of an extraordinary divine power present for the purpose, rather than as the natural and necessary result of the new life lodged in the soul itself. This is not satisfactory. Christ's Person is one, and the person of the believer is one; and to secure a real communication of the whole human life of the first over into the personality of the second, it is only necessary that the communication should spring from the center of Christ's life and pass over to the center of ours. This can be only by the Holy Ghost. But the Holy Ghost in this case is not to be sundered from the Person of Christ. We must say rather that this, and no other, is the very form in which Christ's life is made present in the Church, for the purposes of the Christian salvation.

The *third* source of embarrassment belonging to the form in which Calvin exhibits his theory is found in this, that he makes no clear distinction between the individual personal life of Christ and the same life in a *generic* view. In every sphere of life the individual and the general are found closely united in the same subject. Thus, in the vegetable world, the acorn, cast into the ground, and transformed subsequently into the oak of a hundred years, constitutes in one view only a single existence. But, in another, it includes the force of a life that is capable of reaching far beyond all such individual limits. For the oak may produce ten thousand other acorns, and thus repeat its own life in a whole forest of trees. Still, in the end, the life of the forest, in such a case, is nothing more than an expansion of the life that lay involved at first in the original acorn; and the whole general existence thus produced is bound together, inwardly and organically, by as true and close a unity as that which holds in any of the single existences embraced in it, separately considered. So among men, every parent may be regarded as the bearer not only of a single individual life, that which constitutes his own person, but of a general life also, that reveals itself in his children. Thus especially, in an eminent sense, the first

man Adam is exhibited in our view always under a twofold character. In
one respect he is simply *a* man, to be counted as one amongst men since
born, his sons. In another he is *the* man, in whose person was included
the whole human race. Thus he bears the name (in Hebrew) of the race
itself, and it is under this generic title particularly that he is presented to
our notice in the sacred history of the Bible. His individual personality, of
course, was limited wholly to himself. But a whole world of like separate
personalities lay involved in his life, at the same time, as a generic principle or root. And all these, in a deep sense, form at last but one and the
same life. Adam lives in his posterity as truly as he has ever lived in his
own person. They participate in his whole nature, soul and body, and
are truly bone of his bone and flesh of his flesh. So, in the case before us,
the life of Christ is to be viewed also under the same twofold aspect. Not,
indeed, as if the individual and general here might be supposed to hold
under the same form, exactly, as in the cases which have been mentioned.
The relation of the single oak to its offspring forest is not the same fully
with that of the first man to his posterity. Nor is this last at all commensurate with the relation of Christ to his Church. This will appear hereafter. Still, however, for the point now in hand the cases are parallel. The
distinction of an individual and a general life in the person of Christ is just
as necessary as the same distinction in the person of Adam; and the
analogy is at all events sufficient to show that there may be a real communication of Christ's life to his people, without the idea of any thing like a
local mixture with his person. In one view the Saviour is *a* man, Jesus of
Nazareth, partaking of the same flesh and blood with other men, though
joined at the same time in mysterious union with the everlasting Word.
But in another view he is again *the* man, in a higher sense than this could
be said of Adam, emphatically the Son of Man, in whose person stood revealed the true idea of humanity, under its ultimate and most comprehensive form. Without any loss or change of character in the first view, his
life is carried over in this last view continually into the persons of his
people. He lives in himself, and yet lives in them really and truly at the
same time. This distinction between the individual and the general in the
life of Christ, Calvin does not turn to account as he might have done.
That the force of it was in some measure present to his mind seems altogether clear. But it is not brought out in a distinct, full way, and his system is made to labor under some unnecessary difficulty on this account.

It is easy to see that the three scientific determinations to which our
attention has now been directed, when taken together and clearly

affirmed, must serve to modify and improve very materially the Calvinistic doctrine of Christ's union with his people, so far as the mode of its statement is concerned, relieving it in fact from its most serious difficulties, and placing it under a form with which even the abstract understanding itself can have no good right to find fault. For the positions here applied to the case are in no sense arbitrary or hypothetical. They belong to the actual science of the present time, and have a *right* to be respected in any inquiry which has this question for its object. No such inquiry can deserve to be considered scientific if it fail to take them into view. At the same time it is equally clear that in all this the true and proper substance of the old doctrine is preserved. Here we stand divided from rationalism and modern Puritanism. We agree with them that the doctrine under its old form has difficulties with which the understanding had a right to quarrel. But, to get clear of these, *they* have thought good to cast away the whole doctrine, substance and form together — a process of pure negation and destruction which, in such a case, can *never* be right. *We* hold fast to the substance, while, for the very sake of doing so, we endeavor to place it in a better form. Of this none can have a right to complain, and least of all those who have given up the whole doctrine. They are negative only in the case. We are positive. We cling to the old, in its life, however, rather than by slavish adhesion to its letter. So it must be, indeed, in the case of all religious truth, dogmatically considered. It cannot hold in the form of dead tradition. But neither can it be disjoined from the life of the past. Its true form is that of *history*, in which the past, though left behind in one view, is always in another taken up by the present, and borne along with it as the central power of its own life.

When we speak, however, of putting the doctrine in question into a form more satisfactory to the understanding, it is not to be imagined, of course, that we consider it to be any the less a mystery, on this account, in its own nature. The mystical union of Christ with his Church is something that, in the very nature of the case, transcends all analogies drawn from any lower sphere of life, which it is vain to expect, therefore, that the finite understanding as such can ever fathom or grasp. Still, however, much depends on the statement, even of what is incomprehensible, for its being brought to stand at least in a right relation to the understanding. The understanding may be reconciled, relatively, to that which it cannot comprehend absolutely. It may be set right in relation to a mystery negatively, where it has no power still to grasp it in a positive way, but can only fall back for relief at last on the *reason*, as a deeper and more comprehensive power. But it is much that false conceptions be taken out of the way, and that no room be given for objections that lie in the end not against the truth itself, but only against the form of its representation. It is much also that this last be made to stand in true correspondence with known analogies in other spheres of life, and especially with the organic idea of the new creation itself, which, with all its supernatural character as a whole, must always be regarded as a continuation still of the natural creation in its highest form, and as such most perfectly symmetrical and self-consistent in all its parts. It is only in such view that we may be allowed to speak of bringing the doctrine before us nearer to the understanding by any improvement that may be possible in the mode of its exhibition.

Taking advantage, then, of the scientific truths which have been already mentioned and which Calvin failed at least to apply to the subject in their full force, and keeping in view always the authority of God's most holy revelation (not so much single abstract texts as the life and power of the Word rather as a whole), I will now endeavor to throw the doctrine comprehensively into the form which the nature of the case seems to me to require. The way will then be open for the actual trial of the doctrine, by the Scriptures themselves. These form, of course, the last and only conclusive measure of truth in the case. But before we make our appeal to them, it is important that we should have clearly in view the precise object for which they are to be consulted.

The subject may be exhibited to the best advantage, perhaps, in the way of successive theses or propositions, accompanied with such illustration as each case may seem to require in order to be made clear. These will have respect first to the Mystical Union, and then to the question of the Eucharist.

SECTION II. *The Mystical Union* [1]

1. *The human world in its present natural state, as descended from Adam, is sundered from its proper life in God by sin, and utterly disabled in this character from rising by itself to any higher position.* The fall of Adam was the fall of the race, not simply because he represented the race, but because the race was itself comprehended in his person. The terrible fact of sin revealed itself in him as a world-fact that was now incorpo-

---

1. [ED.] One footnote occurring in the original text has been omitted here, and two others have been shortened.

rated with the inmost life of humanity itself, and became from this point onward an insurmountable law in the progress of its development. The ruin under which we lie is an organic ruin, the ruin of our nature, universal and whole, not simply because all men are sinners, but as making all men to be sinners. Men do not make their nature, their nature makes them. To have part in the human nature at all, we must have part in it primarily as a fallen nature, a spiritually impotent nature, from whose constitution the principle of life has departed in its very root. Not by accident or bad example only, as the Pelagians vainly dream, are we all in the same condemnation. There is a law of sin at work in us from our birth. The whole Pelagian view of life is shallow in the extreme. It sees in the human race only a vast aggregation of particular men, outwardly put together, a huge living sand-heap and nothing more. But the human race is not a sand-heap. It is the power of a single life. It is bound together, not outwardly but inwardly. Men have been one before they became many, and as many, they are still one. We have a perfect right, then, to say that Adam's sin is imputed to all his posterity. Only let us not think of a mere outward transfer in the case. Against *such* imputation the objection commonly made to the doctrine has force. It would be to substitute a fiction for a fact. No imputation of that sort is taught in the Bible. But the imputation of Adam's sin to his posterity involves no fiction. It is counted to them simply because it is theirs in fact. They are born into Adam's nature, and for this reason only, as forming with him the same general life, they are born also into his guilt.

2. *The union in which we stand with our first parent, as thus fallen, extends to his entire person, body as well as* soul. He did not fall in his soul simply, nor in his body simply, but in both at once. The *man* fell. So the humanity of which he was the root fell in him and with him, to the same extent. The *whole* became corrupt. And now, as such, it includes in all his posterity a real and true perpetuation of his life under both forms on to the end of time. They partake of his body as well as of his soul. Both are transmitted by ordinary generation, the same identical organic life-stream, from one age onward always to another. We are bone of his bone, and flesh of his flesh, and blood of his blood. And still there is no material communication, no local contact. Not a particle of Adam's body has come into ours. The identity resolves itself at last into an invisible law, and it is not one law for the body, and another law for the soul; but one and the same law involves the presence of both, as the power of a common life. Where the law works, there Adam's life is reproduced,

body and soul together. And still the individual Adam is not blended with his posterity in any such way as to lose his own personality or swallow up theirs. His identity with his posterity is generic, but none the less real or close on this account. We are all familiar with the case, and if we stop to think of it at all can hardly feel perhaps that it calls for any explanation. And yet of a truth, it is something very wonderful. A mystery, in fact, that goes quite beyond the region of the understanding.

3. *By the hypostatical union of the two natures in the person of* Jesus Christ, *our humanity as fallen in Adam was exalted again to a new and imperishable divine life.* That the race might be saved, it was necessary that a work should be wrought not beyond it but in it, and this inward salvation to be effective must lay hold of the race itself in its organic, universal character, before it could extend to individuals, since in no other form was it possible for it to cover fully the breadth and depth of the ruin that lay in its way. Such an inward salvation of the race required that it should be joined in a living way with the divine nature itself, as represented by the everlasting Word or Logos, the fountain of all created light and life. The Word, accordingly, became flesh, that is, assumed humanity into union with itself. It was not an act whose force was intended to stop in the person of one man, himself to be transplanted soon afterwards to heaven. Nor was it intended merely to serve as the necessary basis of the great work of atonement, the power of which might be applied to the world subsequently in the way of outward imputation. It had this use, indeed, but not as its first and most comprehensive necessity. The object of the Incarnation was to couple the human nature in real union with the Logos, as a permanent source of life. It resulted from the presence of sin only (itself no part of this nature in its original constitution), that the union thus formed called the Saviour to suffer. As the bearer of a fallen humanity he must descend with it to the lowest depths of sorrow and pain, in order that he might triumph with it again in the power of his own imperishable life. In all this he acted for himself and yet for the race he represented at the same time. For it was no external relation simply that he sustained to this last. He was himself the race. Humanity dwelt in his person as the second Adam, under a higher form than ever it carried in the first.

4. *The* value *of Christ's sufferings and death, as well as of his entire life, in relation to men, springs wholly from the view of the Incarnation now presented.* The assumption of humanity on the part of the Logos involved the necessity of suffering, as the only way in which the new life

with which it was thus joined could triumph over the law of sin and death it was called to surmount. The passion of the Son of God was the world's spiritual crisis, in which the principle of health came to its last struggle with the principle of disease, and burst forth from the very bosom of the grave itself in the form of immortality. This was the Atonement, Christ's victory over sin and hell. As such it forms the only medium of salvation to men. But how? Only as the value of it is made over in each case to the subject who is to be saved. This, we are told, is by imputation. But does the act of imputation reckon to us as ours that which is not ours in fact? Does it proceed upon a fiction in the divine mind? Just as little as in the case of our relation to the sin of Adam. This last is not a foreign evil arbitrarily set over to our account. It is immanent to our nature itself. Just so here. The Atonement, as a foreign work, could not be made to reach us in the way of a true salvation. Only as it may be considered *immanent* in our nature itself, can it be imputed to us as ours, and so become available in us for its own ends. And this is its character in truth. It holds in humanity, as a work wrought out by it in Christ. When Christ died and rose, humanity died and rose at the same time in his person, not figuratively but truly, just as it had fallen before in the person of Adam.

5. *The Christian Salvation, then, as thus comprehended in Christ, is a new Life, in the deepest sense of the word.* Not a doctrine merely for the mind to embrace. Not an event simply to be remembered with faith, as the basis of piety in the way of example or other outward support, the sense of some, who have much to say of Christianity as a *fact* in their own shallow way. Not the constitution, only, of a new order of spiritual relations, or a new system of divine appliances, in the case of fallen, helpless man. But a new Life introduced into the very center of humanity itself. In this view, though bound most closely with the organic development of the world's history as it stood before, it is by no means comprehended in it, or carried by it, as its proper product and fruit. Christianity is more than a continuation simply of Judaism. It claims the character of a *creation*, by which old things in the end must pass away, and all things become new. This indicates, however, its relation to the old order. That is not to be annihilated by it, but taken up into it as a higher life. The Incarnation is supernatural — not magical, however, not fantastic or visionary, not something to be gazed at as a transient prodigy in the world's history. It is the supernatural linking itself to the onward flow of the world's life, and becoming thenceforward itself the ground and principle of the entire

organism, now poised at last on its true center. In this sense Christianity is indeed a *fact,* even as the first creation was a Fact, a Fact for all time, a World-Fact.

6. *The new Life of which Christ is the Source and Organic Principle, is in all respects a true* Human *Life.* It is in one sense a divine life. It springs from the Logos. But it is not the life of the Logos separately taken. It is the life of the Word made flesh, the divinity joined in personal union with our humanity. It was not in the way of show, merely, that Christ put on our nature, as many of the old Gnostics believed, and as the view that multitudes still have of the Christian salvation would seem to imply. He put it on truly and in the fullest sense. He was Man more perfectly than this could be said of Adam himself, even before he fell; humanity stood revealed in his person under its most perfect form, not a new humanity wholly dissevered from that of Adam, but the humanity of Adam itself, only raised to a higher character, and filled with new meaning and power, by its union with the divine nature. The new creation in Christ Jesus appeared originally only in this form, and can hold in no other to the end of time.

7. *Christ's life, as now described, rests not in his separate person, but passes over to his people, thus constituting the* Church, *which is his body, the fullness of him that filleth all in all* [Eph. 1:23]. This is involved in the view already taken of his Person, as the principle of the new creation. The process by which the whole is accomplished is not mechanical but organic. It takes place in the way of history, growth, regular living development. Christ goes not forth to heal the world by outward power as standing beyond himself, he gathers it rather into his own person, that is, stretches over it the law of his own life, so that it is made at last to hold in him and from him altogether, as its root. As individuals, we are inserted into him by our regeneration, which is thus the true counterpart of that first birth that makes us natural men. We are not, however, set over into this new order of existence wholly at once. This would be magic. We are apprehended by it in the first place only, as it were, at a single point. But this point is central. The new life lodges itself, as an efflux from Christ, in the inmost core of our personality. Here it becomes the principle or seed of our sanctification, which is simply the gradual transfusion of the same exalted spiritual quality or potence through our whole persons. The process terminates with the resurrection. All analogies borrowed from a lower sphere to illustrate this great mystery are necessarily poor, and always more or less perilous. Perhaps the best is furnished in the action of a

magnet on iron. The man in his natural state centers upon himself, and is thus spiritually dead. In his regeneration, he is touched with a divine attraction that draws him to Christ, the true center of life. The tendency and motion here come not of himself, grow not out of what he was before. They are in obedience simply to the magnetic stream that has reached him from without. The old nature still continues to work. The iron is not at once made free from its *gravity*. But a new law is producing at every point an inward nisus in the opposite direction, which needs only to be filled with new force continually from the magnetic center to carry all at last its own way. "I, if I be lifted up," says Christ, "will draw all men unto me" [Jn. 12:32].

8. *As joined to Christ, then, we are* one *with him in his life, and not simply in the way of a less intimate and real union.* The new birth involves a substantial change in the center of our being. It is not the understanding or the will, simply, that is wrought upon in a natural or supernatural way. Not this or that power or function of the man is it, that may be called the seat of what is thus introduced into his person. Life is not thinking, nor feeling, nor acting, but the organic unity of all these, inseparably joined together. In this sense, we say of our union with Christ that it is a new *life*. It is deeper than all thought, feeling, or exercise of will: not a quality only; not a mere relation; a relation in fact, as that of the iron to the magnet, but one that carries into the center of the subject a form of being which was not there before. Christ communicates his own life substantially to the soul on which he acts, causing it to grow into his very nature. This is the *mystical union*, the basis of our whole salvation, the only medium by which it is possible for us to have an interest in the grace of Christ under any other view.

9. *Our relation to Christ is not simply parallel with our relation to Adam, but goes* beyond it, *as being immeasurably more intimate and deep.* Adam was the first man; Christ is the archetypal man, in whom the true Ideal of humanity has been brought into view. Adam stands related to the race as a simple generic head, Christ as the true center and universal basis of humanity itself. Our nature took its start in Adam, it finds its end and last ground only in Christ. It comes not with us to the exercise of a free, full personality till we are consciously joined to the person of the divine Logos in our nature. In a deep sense, thus, Christ is the universal Man. His *Person* is the root, in the presence and power of which only all other personalities can stand, in the case of his people, whether in time or eternity. They not only spring from him, as we all do from Adam, but

continue to stand in him, as an all present, everywhere active personal Life.[2] In this way, they all have part in his divinity itself, though the hypostatical union, as such, remains limited, of course, to his own person. The whole Christ lives and works in the Church, supernaturally, gloriously, mysteriously, and yet really and truly, "always, to the end of the world" [Mt. 28:20]. Glory be to God!

10. *The mystical union includes necessarily a participation in the entire humanity of Christ.* Will any one pretend to say that we are joined in *real* life-unity with the everlasting Logos, apart from Christ's manhood, in the way of direct personal mutual inbeing? This would be to exalt ourselves to the same level with the Son of God himself. The mystical union then would be the hypostatical union itself, repeated in the person of every believer. Such a supposition is monstrous. Those who think of it only impose upon themselves. For the conception of a *real* union they substitute in their thoughts always one that is moral in fact. The Word became flesh in Christ for the very purpose of reaching us in a real way. The Incarnation constitutes the only medium by which, the only form under which, this divine life of the world can ever find its way over into our persons. Let us beware here of all Gnostic abstractions. Let us not fall practically into the condemnation of Nestorius. But allowing the humanity of Christ to be the indispensable medium of our participation in his person as divine, will any dream only of his human soul as comprehended in the case? Then the whole fact is again converted into a phantom. The life of Christ was *one*. To enter us at all in a real way, it must enter us in its

2. Personality is constituted by self-consciousness. This includes, in our natural state, no reference whatever to an original progenitor. Adam forms in no sense the center of our life, the basis of our spiritual being. But the *Christian* consciousness carries in its very nature such a reference to the person of Jesus Christ. It consists in the active sense of this relation, as the true and proper life of its subject. The man does not connect with Christ the self-consciousness which he has under a different form, in the way of outward reference merely, but this reference is comprehended in his self-consciousness itself, so far as he has become spiritually renewed. Christ is felt to be the center of his life, or rather this feeling may be said to be itself his life, the form in which he exists as a self-conscious person. It is with reason, therefore, that Schleiermacher speaks of the communication which Christ makes of himself to believers, as molding the *person*, since he imparts, in fact, a new higher consciousness that forms the basis of a life that was not previously at hand, the true center of our personality under its most perfect form. In this case the person of Christ is the ground and fountain of all proper Christian personality in the Church. It is only as he is consciously in communication with Christ as his life center (which can be only through an actual self-communication — *Wesensmittheilung* — of Christ's life to him for this purpose), that the believer can be regarded as a *Christian*, or new man in Christ Jesus. . . .

totality. To divide the humanity of Christ is to destroy it, to take it away, and lay it no one can tell where. What God has joined together, we have no right thus to put asunder. Christ's humanity is not his soul separately taken; just as little as it is his body separately taken. It is neither soul nor body as such, but the everlasting, indissoluble union of both.

11. *As the mystical union embraces the whole Christ, so we too are embraced by it, not in a partial but* whole *way.* The very nature of life is that it lies at the ground of all that may be predicated besides of the subject in which it is found, in a way of quality, attribute, or distinction. It is the whole at once of the nature in which it resides. A new life, then, to become truly ours, must extend to us in the totality of our nature. It must fill the understanding, and rule the will, enthrone itself in the soul and extend itself out over the entire body. Besides, the life which is to be conveyed into us, in the present case, we have just seen to be in all respects a true human life before it reaches us. It is the life of the *incarnate* Son of God. But as such, how can it be supposed in passing over to us, to lodge itself exclusively in our *souls,* without regard to our bodies? Is it not a contradiction to think of a *real* union with Christ's humanity, which extends at least only to one half of our nature? In the person of Christ himself, we hold with the ancient Church the presence of a *true body* as well as of a reasonable soul. Shall this same Christ, as formed in his people, be converted into an incorporeal, docetic, Gnostic Christ, as having no real presence except in the abstract soul? Or may his bodily nature continue to hold in this case in the soul simply, separately taken? Incredible! Either Christ's human life is not formed in us at all, or it must be formed in us as a *human* life, must be corporeal as well as incorporeal, must put on outward form, and project itself in space. And all this is only to say, in other words, that it must enter into us, and become united to us, in our bodies as truly as in our souls. In this way, the mystical union becomes real. Under any other conception, it ends in a phantasm, or falls back helplessly to the merely moral relation that is talked of by Pelagians and rationalists.

12. *The mystery now affirmed is accomplished, not in the way of two different forms of action, but by one and the same single and undivided process.* Much of the difficulty that is felt with regard to this whole subject arises from the inveterate prejudice by which so commonly the idea of human life is split for the imagination into two lives, and a veritable dualism thus constituted in our nature in place of the absolute unity that belongs to it in fact. The Bible knows nothing of that abstract separation

of soul and body which has come to be so widely admitted into the religious views of the modern world. It comes from another quarter altogether, and it is as false to all true philosophy as it is unsound in theology and pernicious for the Christian life. Soul and body, in their ground, are but one life, identical in their origin, bound together by mutual interpenetration subsequently at every point, and holding for ever in the presence and power of the self-same organic law. We have no right to think of the body as the prison of the soul, in the way of Plato, nor as its garment merely, nor as its shell or hull. We have no right to think of the [body?] in any way as a form of existence of and by itself, into which the soul as another form of such existence is thrust in a mechanical way. Both form *one* life. The soul, to be complete to develop itself at all as a soul, *must* externalize itself, throw itself out in space, and this externalization is the body.[3] All is one process, the action of one and the same living organic principle, dividing itself only that its unity may become thus the

3. To some, possibly, this representation may seem to be contradicted by what the Scriptures teach of the separate existence of the soul between death and the resurrection, and it must be admitted that we are met here with a difficulty which it is not easy, at present, to solve. Let us, however, not mistake the true state of the case. The difficulty is not to reconcile Scripture with a psychological theory, but to bring it into harmony with itself. For it is certain that the Scriptures teach such an identification of soul and body in the proper human personality, as clearly at least as they intimate a continued consciousness on the part of the soul between death and the resurrection. The doctrine of *immortality* in the Bible is such as to include always the idea of the resurrection. . . . The whole argument in the 15th chapter of 1st Corinthians, as well as the representation in 1 Thessalonians 4:13–18, proceeds on the assumption that the life of the *body*, as well as that of the soul, is indispensable to the perfect state of our nature as human. The soul, then, during the intermediate state, cannot possibly constitute, in the biblical view, a complete man, and the case requires besides, that we should conceive of its relation to the body as still in force, not absolutely destroyed but only suspended. The whole condition is interimistic, and by no possibility of conception capable of being thought of as complete and final. When the resurrection body appears, it will not be as a new frame abruptly created for the occasion, and brought to the soul in the way of outward addition and supplement. It will be found to hold in strict organic continuity with the body, as it existed before death, as the action of the same law of life, which implies that this law has not been annihilated, but suspended only in the intermediate state. In this character, however, it must be regarded as resting in some way (for where else *could* it rest?) in the separate life, as it is called, of the soul itself, the slumbering power of the resurrection, ready at the proper time, in obedience to Christ's powerful word, to clothe itself with its former actual nature, in full identity with the form it carried before death, though under a far higher order of existence. Only *then* can the salvation of the soul be considered complete. All at last is *one* life, the subject of which is the totality of the believer's person, comprehending soul and body alike, from the beginning of the process to its end.

more free and intensely complete. There is no room to dream, then, of a
bodily communication with Christ on the part of believers as something
distinct from the communication they have with him in their souls. His
flesh cannot enter our flesh under an abstract form, dissevered from the
rest of his life, and in no union with our souls as the medium of such
translation. This would be the so-called Capernaitic communion in full,
not mystical but magical, incredible, and useless at the same time. The
process by which Christ is formed in his people is not thus twofold but
single. It lays hold of its subject in each case, not in the periphery of his
person but in its inmost center, where the whole man, soul and body, is
still one undivided life. As in the case of the mind it is neither the understanding nor the will that is apprehended by it, so in the case of the person also, it is neither the soul nor the body, separately considered, that is
so apprehended; it is the totality which includes all; it is the *man* in the
very center and ground of his personality. Christ's life as a *whole* is borne
over into the person of the believer as a like *whole*. The communication is
central, and central only, from the last ground of Christ's life to the last
ground of ours, by the action of a single, invisible, self-identical, spiritual
law. The power of Christ's life lodged in the soul begins to work there
immediately as the principle of a new creation. In doing so, it works organically according to the law which it includes in its own constitution.
That is, it works as a *human* life, and, as such, becomes a law of regeneration in the body as truly as in the soul.

13. *In all this of course then there is no room for the supposition of
any* material, *tactual approach of Christ's body to the persons of his people.* It is not necessary that his flesh and blood, materially considered,
should in any way pass over into our life and become locally present in us
under any form, to make us partakers of his humanity. Even in the sphere
of mere nature, the continuity of organic existence, as it passes from one
individual to another—mounting upwards, for instance, from the buried
seed, and revealing itself at last, through leaves and flowers, in a thousand
new seeds after its own kind — is found to hang in the end not on the
material medium as such, through which the process is effected, but on
the presence simply of the living force, immaterial altogether and impalpable, that imparts both form and substance to the whole. The presence of the root in the branches of the oak is not, properly speaking,
either a local or material presence. It is the power simply of a common
life. And why then should it be held impossible for Christ's life to reach
over into the persons of his people, whole and entire, even without the

intervention of any material medium whatever — belonging as it does pre-eminently to the sphere of the Spirit? Why should it seem extravagant to believe that the *law* of this life, apart from all material contact with his person, may be so lodged in the soul of the believer by the power of the Holy Ghost, as to become there the principle of a new moral creation, that shall still hold in unbroken organic continuity with its root, and go on to take full possession of its subject, soul and body, under the same form?

14. *Such a relation of Christ to the Church involves no* ubiquity *or idealistic dissipation of his body, and requires no* fusion *of his proper personality with the persons of his people.* We distinguish between the simple man and the universal man, here joined in the same person. The possibility of such a distinction is clear in the case of Adam. His universality is not indeed of the same order with that of Christ. But still the case has full force for the point now in hand. Adam was at once an individual and a whole race. All his posterity partake of his life and grow forth from him as their root. And still his individual person has not been lost on this account. Why then should the life of Christ in the Church be supposed to conflict with the idea of his separate, distinct personality, under a true human form? Why must we dream of a fusion of persons in the one case more than in the other? Here is more, it is true, than our relation to Adam. We not only spring from Christ, so far as our new life is concerned, but stand in him perpetually also as our ever-living and ever-present root. His *Person* is always thus the actual bearer of *our* persons. And yet there is no mixture, or flowing of one into the other, as individually viewed. Is not God the last ground of all personality? But does this imply any pantheistic dissipation of his nature into the general consciousness of the intelligent universe? Just as little does it imply any like dissipation of Christ's personality into the general consciousness of the Church when we affirm that it forms the ground, out of which and in the power of which only, the whole life of the Church continually subsists. In this view Christ is personally present always in the Church — this, of course, in the power of his divine nature. But his divine nature is at the same time *human* in the fullest sense, and wherever his presence is revealed in the Church in a real way, it includes his person necessarily under the one aspect as well as under the other. With all this, however, which is something very different from the conception of a proper ubiquity in the case of Christ's body, we do not relinquish the thought of his separate human individuality. We distinguish between his universal humanity in the

Church, and his humanity as a particular man whom the heavens have received till the time of the restitution of all things. His glorified body, we doubt not, is possessed of qualities, attributes, and powers that transcend immeasurably all we know or can think of a human body here. Still it is a body, a particular body having organized parts and outward form. As such, of course, it must be defined and circumscribed by local limits and cannot be supposed to be present in different places at the same time.

15. *The mystical union, holding in this form, is more intimate and real than any union which is known in the world besides.* Even in nature, the most close connection is not that which holds in the way of mere local contact or outward conjunction. There may be an actual transfusion of one substance into another, with very little union in the end. A simply *mechanical* unity, one thing joined to another in space, is the lowest and poorest that can be presented to our thoughts. Higher than this is the *chemical* combination, which, however, is still comparatively outward. The *organic* union, as it holds, for instance, between the root and topmost branches of the tree, is far more inward and close. Though they do not touch each other at all, they are one, notwithstanding, in a sense more true than can be affirmed either of the different parts of a crystal, or of the elements that are married in the constitution of atmospheric air. Of vastly higher character still is the union of head and members in the same human body. But even this is a poor image of the oneness of Christ with his people. There is nothing like this in the whole world, under any other form. It is bound by no local limitations. It goes beyond all nature, and transcends all thought.

16. *The union of Christ with believers is wrought by the power of the* Holy Ghost. The new birth is from the Spirit. It is by the Spirit the divine life is sustained and advanced in us, at every point, from its commencement to its close. There is no other medium by which it is possible for us to be in Christ, or to have Christ in ourselves. The new creation holds absolutely and entirely in the powerful presence of the Holy Ghost. Hence it is said, "He that is joined to the Lord is one *Spirit*" [1 Cor. 6:17], and the indwelling of Christ and his Spirit in believers is spoken of as the same thing. But for this very reason, we have no right to dissolve this unity again in our thoughts by making the presence of the Spirit a mere substitute for the presence of Christ himself. Where the one is, there the other is truly and really at the same time. The Spirit, proceeding from the Father and Son and subsisting in everlasting union with both, constitutes the form in which and by which the new creation in

Christ Jesus upholds itself, and reveals itself, in all its extent. It is not *Nature*, but *Spirit*. So in the Person of Christ himself, the root of this creation. The Spirit was never brought near to men before, as now through the incarnate Word. It dwelt in him without measure. Humanity itself was filled completely with its presence, and appears at last translucent with the glory of heaven itself by its means. Forth from the person of Christ, thus "quickened in the Spirit," the flood of life pours itself onward continually in the Church, only, of course, by the presence and power of the Holy Ghost, for it holds in no other form. Not, however, by the presence and power of the Holy Ghost as abstracted from the presence of Christ himself, as though he were the fountain only, and not the very life-stream too, of the new creation, nor could he be supposed to be in it and with it by the intervention only of a presence not involving at the same time and to the same extent his own. "The Lord is that Spirit" [2 Cor. 3:17]. He reveals himself in his people, dwells in them and makes them one with himself in a real way, by his Spirit. In this view, the new life formed in them is *spiritual*, not natural or physical, as belonging simply to the first creation. But this does not imply at all that it is limited to the soul as distinguished from the body. There is no absolute opposition here between the idea of body and the idea of Spirit. Here is a spiritual *body*, as well as a body natural, according to the Apostle. The Spirit of Christ, in his own person at least, fills the whole man, soul and body. All is spiritual, glorious, heavenly. His whole humanity has been taken up into the sphere of the Spirit, and appears transfigured into the same life. And why then should it not extend itself, in the way of strict organic continuity, as a *whole* humanity also, by the active presence of Christ's Spirit, over into the persons of his people? A spiritual life no more excludes the thought of the body in the one case than it does in the other.

17. *Christ's life is apprehended on the part of his people only by* faith. The life itself comes to us wholly from Christ himself, by the power of his Spirit. The magnetic stream is poured upon us from abroad. If we move at all, it is only in obedience to the divine current thus brought to bear upon our souls. To live in this at all, however, it is necessary that we should surrender ourselves spontaneously to its power. This is faith, the most comprehensive, fundamental act of which our nature is capable. The man swings himself, in the totality of his being, quite off from the center of self, on which hitherto his consciousness has been poised, over upon Christ, now revealed to his view, as another center altogether: the birth of a new *life*, in the strictest sense, as we have already seen. Faith, of

course, is not the principle of this life. It is only the medium of its introduction into the soul, and the condition of its growth and development when present. But as such it is indispensable. The process of our sanctification is spiritual, and not mechanical or magical.[4]

18. *The new life of the believer includes degrees, and will become complete only in the* resurrection. Only in this form could it have a true human character. All life, in the case of man, is actualized, and can be actualized, only in the way of process or gradual historical development. So in the case before us, there is the seed; and when it springs, "first the blade, then the ear; and after that, the full corn in the ear" [Mk. 4:28]. The new life struggles with the old, like Jacob and Esau in the same womb! The Christian carries in himself two forms of existence, a "law of sin and death" on the one hand, and "the law of the spirit of life in Christ Jesus" [Rom. 8:2] on the other; and the power of the last is continually opposed and restrained by the power of the first. From its very start, however, the life of Christ in the believer is a whole life, and in all its subsequent progress it reveals its power continually under the same character. From the first it includes in itself *potentially* all that it is found to become at the last. The life of the tree is only the same life that was comprehended originally in the seed from which it has sprung. So it is with all life. All that belongs, then, to the new life of the Christian, conceived as complete at the last day, must be allowed to be involved in it as principle and process from the beginning. In every stage of its progress it is a true human life, answerable to the nature of its organic root, and to the nature also of the subject in which it is lodged. It is always, as far as it prevails, the law of a new nature for the body as well as for the soul. The full and final triumph of the process is the resurrection, which is reached in the case of the individual only in connection with the consummation of the Church as a whole. The bodies of the saints in glory will be only the last result, in organic continuity, of the divine life of Christ implanted in their souls at their regeneration. There is nothing abrupt in Christianity. It is a supernatural constitution indeed, but as such it is clothed in a natural form, and involves in itself as regular a law of historical development as the old creation itself. The resurrection body will be simply the ultimate outburst of the life that had been ripening for immortality under cover of the old Adamic nature before. The winged psyche has its elemental organization in the worm, and does not lose it in the tomb-like chrysalis. Let us not be told that this is to suppose two bodies in the person of the

---

4. "Living faith in Christ," says Schleiermacher, "is nothing but the self-consciousness of our union with Christ." [ED. *The Christian Faith*, II, § 14.]

believer at one time. Does the new life, abstracted from the body, involve the supposition of two *souls?* The cases are precisely parallel. The man is one, soul and body. But a new organic law has become lodged in the inmost center of his personality, and is now gradually extending its force over the entire constitution of his nature as a whole. It does not lay hold of one part of his being first, and then proceed to another in the way of outward territorial conquest, as though a hand or foot could be renovated before the head, or the understanding apart from the will, or the soul in no connection with the body. The whole man is made the subject of the new life at once. The law of revolution involved in it extends from the center to the extreme periphery of his person. The old body becomes itself, in a mysterious way, the womb of a higher corporeity, the life-law of Christ's own glorious body, which is, at last, through the process of death and the resurrection, set free from the first form of existence entirely, and made to supersede it for ever in the immortality of heaven.

SECTION III. *The Lord's Supper*

19. *"A sacrament is a holy ordinance instituted by* Christ; *wherein, by sensible signs,* Christ *and the benefits of the new covenant are represented,* sealed, *and* applied *to believers."* Thus the Westminster Shorter Catechism,[1] echoing the voice of the whole Reformed Church, as it had sounded throughout Christendom for a century before. The *signs,* as such, make not the sacrament. They are only one part of it. The other part is found in the invisible grace that is sacramentally or mystically joined with the signs. To be complete, that is to be at all a true sacrament, the ordinance must comprehend both. In other words, the invisible grace enters as a necessary constituent element into the idea of the sacrament, and must be, of course, *objectively* present with it wherever it is administered under a true form. Whether it shall become available to the benefit of the participant must depend on the presence of the conditions that are needed to give it effect. All turns here at last on the exercise of faith. But the objective presence of the grace itself, as an essential part of the sacrament, is none the less certain and sure on this account. It belongs to the ordinance in its own nature, which, in this view, is not a picture or remembrancer simply for the mind, but a true and real exhibition of that which it represents. The sign and the thing signified are, by Christ's insti-

1. [ED.] Ans. 92. Schaff, *Creeds,* III, 696 (Nevin's emphases).

tution, mysteriously bound together, so as to form in the sacramental transaction one and the same presence. Not as though the last were in any way included in the first, as its local or material receptacle. The conjunction is in no sense such as to change at all the nature of the sensible sign, in itself considered, or to bring it into any physical union with the grace it represents. But still the two form one presence. Along with the outward sign is exhibited always at the same time the represented grace. The union of the one with the other is mystical, and peculiar altogether to the nature of a sacrament; but it is not for this reason *less* real, but only a great deal *more* real, than it could be possibly under any natural and local form. The invisible grace thus made present by sensible signs in the sacraments is "Christ *and* the benefits of the new covenant." Not the *benefits* of the new covenant only, but Christ himself also, in a real way, as the only medium of a real communication with the benefits. Christ first, and *then* and *therefore* all his benefits, as inhering only in his person, and carrying with them no reality under any different view.

20. "*The Lord's Supper is a sacrament, wherein, by giving and receiving bread and wine according to Christ's appointment, his death is showed forth, and the worthy receivers are, not after a corporal and carnal manner, but by faith, made partakers of his body and blood, with all his benefits, to their spiritual nourishment and growth in grace.*" Thus again the Westminster Shorter Catechism.[2] Here are sensible signs, bread and wine solemnly given and received. Here also we have the invisible grace, Christ and his benefits. To make the case clearer, it is Christ's "body and blood, with all his benefits," the first, of course, as the basis and medium of the last. The visible and invisible are different, and yet, in this case, they may not be disjoined. They flow together in the constitution of one and the same sacrament. Neither of the two is the sacrament, abstracted from the other. The ordinance holds in the sacramental *transaction*, which includes the presence of both, the one materially, for the senses, the other spiritually, for faith. Christ's body is not in or under the bread, locally considered. Still, the power of his life in this form is actually exhibited at the same time in the mystery of the sacrament. The one is as truly and really present in the institution as the other. The elements are not simply significant of that which they represent, as serving to bring it to mind by the help of previous knowledge. They are the pledge of its actual presence and power. They are bound to it in mystical, sacramental union, more intimately, we may say, than they would be if they

2. [ED.] Ans. 96. Schaff, *Creeds*, III, 697 (Nevin's emphases).

were made to include it in the way of actual local comprehension. There is far more, then, than the mere commemoration of Christ's death. Worthy receivers partake also of his body and blood, with all his benefits, through the power of the Holy Ghost, to their spiritual nourishment and growth in grace.

21. *The sacrament of the Lord's Supper has reference directly and primarily to the* atonement *wrought out by Christ's death on the cross.* So in the words of institution, it is his body *broken,* and his blood *shed* for the remission of sins, that are held up to view. It is not simply of Christ but of the "body and blood" of Christ, that is of Christ as sacrificed and slain for the sins of the world, that worthy receivers are made to partake in the holy ordinance. Not as though the sacrament were itself a sacrifice, or included in its own nature any expiatory force, in the way dreamed of by the Church of Rome. It serves simply to ratify and advance the interest, which believers have already, by their union with Christ, in the new covenant established through his blood. Only under this form can the salvation of the gospel stand us in stead. We are sinners and as such need redemption. Only through the medium of Christ's sufferings and death can we come to have any part in his glory. He must be our righteousness in order that he may be our life. Hence our first relation to him as believers is that which is formed in our justification, that "act of God's free grace, wherein he pardoneth all our sins, and accepteth us as righteous in his sight, only for the righteousness of Christ imputed to us, and received by faith alone." [3] And so our whole subsequent Christian life, as it grows forth from this objective righteousness, may be said to involve a constant return to it, and dependence upon it, on to the end of our course. We need no new atonement, but we do need to fall back perpetually on the one sacrifice for sin, which Christ has already made upon the cross, appropriating the power of it more and more to our souls, as the only ground of our salvation. The Lord's Supper accordingly, concentrating in itself as it does, in some sense, the force and meaning of the whole Christian life, has regard to this sacrifice always as the great object of its representation. It is the sacrament of Christ's death, the communion of his body and blood.

22. *As the medium, however, by which we are thus made partakers of the new covenant in Christ's death, the Holy Supper involves a real communication with the* person *of the Saviour, now gloriously exalted in heaven.* Our justification, as we have seen, rests on the objective merit of

3. [ED.] Ans. 33. Schaff, *Creeds,* III, 683.

Christ, by whose blood alone propitiation has been made for the sins of the world. But this justification, to become ours in fact, must insert us into Christ's life. It reaches us from abroad, the "act of God's free grace"; but *as* God's act, it is necessarily more than a mere declaration or form of thought. It makes us to be in fact what it accounts us to be, *in Christ*. The ground of our justification is a righteousness that *was* foreign to us before, but is *now* made to lodge itself in the inmost constitution of our being. A real life-union with Christ, powerfully wrought in our souls by the Holy Ghost, is the only basis on which there can be any true imputation to us of what he had done and suffered on our behalf. And so, in the whole subsequent progress of our Christian life, our interest in his merits can be renewed and confirmed only in the same way. We must have Christ himself formed in us more and more in a real way, in order that "he may be made unto us of God, wisdom, and righteousness, and sanctification, and redemption" [1 Cor. 1:30]. The Eucharistic communion, then, as serving to confirm our interest in the one sacrifice accomplished on the cross, must include a true participation in the life of him by whom the sacrifice was made. We can make no intelligible distinction here between the crucified body of Christ and his body as now glorified in heaven. Both at last are one and the same life. To partake of the "broken body" and "shed blood" of the Redeemer, if it meant a real participation in his person at all, must be to communicate with him as now exalted at the right hand of God. For it is not a dead contract or a dead sacrifice we have to do with in this case; the "new covenant in Christ's blood" can hold only in the power of that indissoluble life by which Jesus, once put to death in the flesh, is now quickened forever in the Spirit. The virtue of this covenant is not only represented, but *sealed* also and applied, to believers; which means not merely that they have in the sacrament a general pledge that God will be faithful to his own promises, but that the grace which it exhibits is actually made over to them, at the time, in this very transaction itself. The grace, however, namely the merit of Christ's sufferings and death, has a real character only as rooted in a living way in Christ's person, and it can become ours by new application, accordingly, no farther than Christ himself is made over to us at the same time. "To eat the crucified body and drink the shed blood of Christ," then, in the language of the Heidelberg Catechism, "is *not only* to embrace with a believing heart all the sufferings and death of Christ, and thereby to obtain the pardon of sin and life eternal; *but also, besides that*, to become more and more united to his sacred body by the Holy Ghost, who dwells both in Christ and in us; so that we, though Christ is in heaven and we on earth, are notwithstanding flesh of his flesh and bone of his bone; and that we live, and are governed forever, by one Spirit, as members of the same body are by one soul." [4]

23. *The real communication which believers have with Christ in the Holy Supper, extends to his whole person.* To be real, and not simply moral, it *must* be thus comprehensive. We may divide Christ in our thoughts, abstracting his divinity from his humanity, or his soul from his body. But no such dualism has place in his actual person. If, then, he is to be received by us at all, it must be in a whole way. We partake not of certain rights and privileges only, which have been secured for us by the breaking of his body and shedding of his blood, but of the veritable substantial life of the blessed Immanuel himself, as the fountain and channel by which alone all these benefits can be conveyed into our souls. We partake not of his divinity only, nor yet of his Spirit as separate from himself, but also of his true and proper humanity. Not of his humanity in a separate form, his flesh and blood disjoined from his Spirit, but of the one life which is the union of both, and in virtue of which the presence of the one must ever involve in the same form, and to the same extent, the presence of the other.

24. *Christ communicates himself to us, in the real way now mentioned, under the form of the sacramental mystery as such.* It is not as the object of thought simply, or lively recollection, that he is made present in the ordinance. Nor is it by the activity of our faith, merely, that he is brought nigh. His presence is identified objectively with the sacrament itself, and we receive him in the sacrament as the bearer of his very life itself, in the form in which it is here presented to our view. This implies no *opus operatum*, no mechanical or magical force in the use of the elements. All is by the Spirit, and for the communicant himself, all hangs upon the condition of faith. But still the grace exhibited, the action of the Spirit as here present, belongs to the sacrament in its own nature, and where the way is open for it to take effect at all, by the presence of the proper conditions on the part of the communicant, it serves in itself to convey the life of Christ into our persons. Such is the sound *feeling* of Dr. Owen, the great Puritan divine, when he tells us: "This is the greatest mystery of all the practicals of our Christian religion, a way of receiving Christ by eating and drinking, something peculiar, that is not in the hearing of the word nor in any other part of divine worship whatsoever; a peculiar par-

4. [ED.] Ans. 76. Schaff, *Creeds*, III, 332-33 (Nevin's emphases).

ticipation of Christ, a peculiar acting of faith towards Christ." [5] The presence of which we speak is not in the bread and wine materially considered, but in the sacramental mystery as a whole. This consists of two parts, the one outward and visible, the other inward and invisible. These, however, are not simply joined together in time, as the sound of a bell, or the show of a light, may give warning of something with which it stands in no farther connection. They are connected by a true inward bond, so as to be different constituents only of one and the same reality. This union is not mechanical nor local, but as the old divines say, *mystical* or *sacramental*, that is, peculiar to this case and altogether incomprehensible in its nature, but only all the more real and intimately close, on this very account.

25. *Christ communicates himself to us in the sacrament only in a spiritual, central way.* Not his body by one process, and his Spirit by another, but his whole life, as a single undivided form of existence, by one and the same process. Not by the mechanical transplantation of some portion of his glorified body into our persons, to become there the germ of immortality in a physical view, but by the conveyance of his life in its inmost substance, by the power of the Holy Ghost, over into the very center of our souls. The communication is in this view wholly independent of all material contact or conjunction. It holds altogether in the sphere of the Spirit. Christ reveals his presence in us centrally, as the power of the new spiritual creation which is comprehended in his person, and which in this way is made to extend itself out organically over the entire living man, as the life of the vine is reproduced, with all its properties and qualities, in every branch to which it extends.

26. *The Lord's Supper is the medium of a real communication with Christ only in the case of* believers. The object of the institution is to confirm and advance the new life where it has been already commenced. It has no power to convert such as are still in their sins. The grace which it exhibits can be apprehended only by faith. Those who come to the Lord's table unworthily, as to a common meal, without being in a state to discern the Lord's body, eat and drink only judgment to themselves. They receive in no sense Christ's flesh and blood, but the bare signs only, by which they are exhibited for the benefit of those who come in a right way. Nor is it enough that the communicant be a regenerated person; he must be in the exercise of faith at the time. A gracious state, accompanied with gracious affections in the transaction itself, is the indispensable condition of a profitable approach to the Lord in the holy sacrament. And yet, as before said, it is not our faith at all that gives the sacrament its

5. [ED.] Owen, *Works* (London, 1826), XVII, 268.

force, nor does this consist at all in the actings of our faith, or penitence, or love, or any other gracious affection that may be called into exercise at the time. These constitute not, and create not, the presence of Christ in the case. On the contrary, this presence forms itself the ground from which all such affections draw their activity and strength. The force of the sacrament is in the sacrament itself. Our faith is needed only as the condition that is required to make room for it in our souls. "Thy faith hath made thee whole," said the blessed Saviour to the woman who came behind him in the crowd, and touched the hem of his garment [Mk. 5:34]. But the healing virtue went forth in fact wholly from his own person, and was present there, as an ample remedy for all diseases, independently altogether of any application that might be made to him for relief. The woman's faith formed the necessary condition only on her own part, for her becoming the recipient of the grace which was thus at hand. So in the case before us. The virtue of Christ's mystical presence is comprehended in the sacrament itself, and cannot be said to be put into it in any sense by our faith. This serves only to bring us into right relation to the life that is thus placed within our reach. Faith puts not into the sacrament what it has power instrumentally to draw from it for our use.

27. *Christ's mystical presence in the Eucharist, as now affirmed, leaves no room for the idea of* transubstantiation *or* consubstantiation. According to the first of these errors, the bread and wine are changed into the actual substance of the Saviour's body and blood. According to the other, the proper Lutheran view, the Saviour's true body and blood are so contained and carried in the elements, that the reception of these even on the part of the impenitent and unbelieving is supposed to involve the reception also of the other. Both these views are chargeable with the error of supposing an identification of Christ's presence in the Eucharist with the elements as such. According to the Roman theory, this is permanent; the bread remains Christ's body, even when carried away afterwards to another place. By the Lutheran doctrine, the relation which binds them together holds only in the sacramental transaction itself, but while it holds, it is such that the *elements* in some way bear the divine life which they represent, so that it is received along with them in an oral, corporeal manner. This seems to imply a communication of the bodily life of Christ, not physically, of course, but supernaturally, to the body of the believer, in an immediate and direct way; in which case, the sacramental fruition, as something different from the oral reception of the elements on the one hand, and the spiritual participation of Christ's body and blood on the other, becomes no better than an empty word, to which we can attach no

meaning, unless it be as we think of mere blind magic. But the presence here affirmed is not such as to identify the body of Christ in any way with the sacramental symbols, separately considered. It is not bound to the bread and wine, but to the act of eating and drinking. In the service of the Eucharist, and by its means, the believer is made to partake of Christ's body and blood. The outward transaction, where faith is at hand, involves this inward fruition, and forms the vehicle or channel by which it is accomplished. But the outward is not itself the form or mode in which the inward here takes place. The participation of Christ is wholly spiritual. He communicates himself, by the Spirit, to the soul of the believer, in a central way, according to the general law of the new creation to which this mystery belongs. No room is left here for the supposition of a mere corporeal communication, the transference of Christ's life directly into the bodies of his people, even though conceived to be in a wholly hyperphysical way. This, it is felt, would be only a mechanical and outward union in the end, the action at best of the power of the Spirit on nature as such, by which a magical character must necessarily be imparted to the ordinance, as in the Church of Rome. It would imply, besides, a dualism in our proper life, that must overthrow its reality altogether. As the life itself is one, so it is to be renovated and sanctified through the provisions of the gospel as a single whole, from its ground or center, and not by influences exerted in any way upon its organic volume apart from this. The new nature, to be real, must spring perpetually from the inmost being of its subject in the form of spirit; and every fresh impulse, accordingly, which it is made to receive from its fountain in Christ, in whatever way, can be communicated to it only in this general form. So the participation of Christ's life in the sacrament is in no sense corporeal, but altogether spiritual, as the necessary condition of its being real. It is the soul or spirit of the believer that is immediately fed with the grace which is conveyed to it mystically in the holy ordinance. But this is in fact a fruition that belongs to the entire man, for the life made over to him under such central form becomes at once, in virtue both of its own *human* character, and of the *human* character of the believer himself, a renovating force that reaches out into his person on all sides, and fills with its presence the undivided totality of his nature. In whatever sense the communication may be *real* at all, as distinguished from figurative, imputative, or simply moral, it must be real for the whole man, and not simply for a part of the man.

II

JOHN WILLIAMSON NEVIN

The Doctrine of the Reformed Church on the Presence of Christ in the Lord's Supper

Editor's introduction.

The Mystical Presence was generally either attacked or ignored by the American press, but the reaction of Reformed churchmen in Germany was quite different. Krummacher, for example, wrote Schaff [1] that he found it "historically and exegetically impregnable throughout." The American opponents perforce retreated in chagrin to what Nevin called a "theological nativism," demonstrating the anomalous character of the predominant American view when set in the wider perspective of world Christianity.

The most massive support for Nevin's views came with the history of Eucharistic theology [2] by J. H. A. Ebrard (1818–88). Ebrard led Nevin to revise somewhat his negative assessment of Zwingli, and persuaded him that the corrections of Calvin's theory proposed in *The Mystical Presence* were largely unnecessary, that Calvin's psychology was not open to so many difficulties as he had thought.

What Nevin considered "the only respectable or tolerable attempt" to refute his exposition in *The Mystical Presence* was an article by Charles Hodge in the *Princeton Review* for April 1848. This was an unexpected turn for the Mercersburg men, who had looked for at least benevolent neutrality from what was generally supposed to be the more churchly wing of American Presbyterianism. Not all Old School Presbyterians, in fact, were happy with Hodge's handling of the doctrines of Church and sacraments, but his influence in American church life was more weighty

1. *The Weekly Messenger*, August 11, 1847.
2. *Das Dogma vom Heiligen Abendmahl und seine Geschichte* (2 v., Frankfurt/a/ Main, 1845–46).

than that of any German. Over the summer of 1848 Nevin made his rebuttal in several numbers of *The Weekly Messenger*. That he appeared to have been boycotted by the chief theological quarterlies was a major factor in the decision to launch *The Mercersburg Review*, which from 1849 onward became the chief outlet of the school. In 1850 it carried a monograph of over 100 pages, "The Doctrine of the Reformed Church on the Lord's Supper," consisting largely of a rearrangement and expansion of the historical portions of the articles in *The Weekly Messenger*. The title used here is that of a later separate reprinting.

Hodge had concentrated on Nevin's treatment of the Reformed confessions and the theologians of the Reformation. He argued that what Nevin called the "modern Puritan theory" had rather been the dominant view from the beginning, and backed this assertion from early Zwinglian documents. He largely conceded Calvin and the French, Dutch, and Scots confessions to Nevin, but argued that the Heidelberg Catechism, the Zurich Consensus, and the Second Helvetic Confession were to be interpreted in a Zwinglian sense. An outline of Nevin's reply to this argument, without his discussion of the several documents, is given below.

"The Doctrine of the Reformed Church on the Lord's Supper" was essentially an expansion of the section of *The Mystical Presence* which dealt with the Reformation. As an historical monograph, it remained without a rival in English until the twentieth century. The Princeton position had been shown to be indefensible in terms of the classic Reformed confessions. Nearly twenty years later, Nevin was able to refer to his essay as "an argument which no one has ever yet pretended to meet, and whose historical force, at least, never can be overthrown." [3]

The second of the selections given below is an ingenious passage from the debate in which Nevin replied to Hodge's exegesis of the Zurich Consensus, using an imagined dialogue based on Calvin's second reply to Westphal. The Zurich Consensus, as the agreement between Calvin and Zwingli's successor Bullinger, was a crucial document in the definition of Reformed Eucharistic doctrine.[4] Westphal, the ultra-Lutheran controversialist of Hamburg, had in effect argued, like Hodge, that Calvin could scarcely be supposed to mean what he said.[5]

3. "Theology of the New Liturgy," *The Mercersburg Review*, XIX (1867), 64.

4. An English translation by I. Bunting appears in the *Journal of Presbyterian History*, March 1966.

5. A score of citations from the Latin text of Calvin's Second Defense, as found on

. . . Two phases of thought, it is admitted, come together to a certain extent in the early history of the Reformed doctrine: one which lays all stress on the *sacrifice* of Christ, as an atonement for sin, and another, specially insisted upon by Calvin, which carries back our salvation to the idea of Christ's *life,* as its necessary perpetual source and ground. This latter view, it is allowed also, made the *human* side of Christ's life to be in some mysterious way the depositary and seat of the grace now mentioned, and so the medium of its communication to our souls. The sacramental manducation was held to bring into the soul of the true worshipper a vivific power or virtue from the Saviour's *flesh,* once slain on Calvary, but now gloriously exalted at the right hand of God in heaven. This thought, however, if we are to believe Princeton, though in the Reformed doctrine for a time, was never of it in any inward way; it was a relic only of the old traditional superstition, which it was found hard at once to lay entirely aside; it lingered, accordingly, while it lasted, only as a foreign element in the system, with which it vainly sought assimilation; and so finally forsook the doctrine altogether, leaving it in the bald puritanic form in which it has come to prevail generally in modern times. Calvin himself, it is argued, could not have seriously intended here what his language seems to mean, for he held constantly that the Old Testament saints had the same communion with Christ which it is the privilege of believers to enjoy now — which could not have been the case if his flesh and blood are to be taken as the medium of life in a real way, since the Incarnation had not then taken place. The notion of a life-giving virtue from Christ's body, then, must be given up, as no part of the Reformed faith. We have to do in the sacrament only with the value of his death as a propitiation for sin. This is set before us as a fact, under fit memorials and symbols, and by the help of these we are required to embrace it with our intelligence or thought, in the exercise of faith, firmly believing that Christ's blood is sufficient to remove all guilt, and looking for righteousness and salvation only in his name. This grace is not lodged objectively even in the actual humanity of the Son of Man, much less in any mystical exhibition to which this may be supposed to come in the Holy Eucharist, but only and wholly in the Divine Mind, from which the plan of salvation proceeds and which imparts to it at last all its efficacy and force. The ob-

---

pages 666–72 of Volume VIII of the Amsterdam edition of Calvin's *Opera,* have been omitted here, along with three references to the Exposition of the Consensus, from pages 657–61 of the same volume, a citation from the *Commentary on Ephesians* at 5: 32, another from that on 1 Corinthians, 15:44, and one from Calvin's 1557 letter to Schalling.

ject to be embraced, thus, is a truth simply of general force, based on a past event which the sacrament commemorates, but in no way necessarily bound now to any such representation. It is not in the transaction in any sense, but out of it and beyond it altogether, so that this serves only as a stepping stone, or ladder, by which the mind of the worshipper is engaged and assisted to enter into direct correspondence with it under another form. It turns, of course, then wholly on the worshipper's mind at last, whether the relation between the sign and the thing signified shall be of any force whatever in the transaction; if his faith be so exercised as to bring the general truth of the Atonement into connection with what is going forward, the truth will be there, otherwise the institution will stand shorn of its celestial significance altogether. An objective force must be allowed, indeed, to attend the sacrament, where it is rightly used; but it is simply the influence of the Holy Ghost, as he is active also at other times in bringing the faith of the truly pious into felt communication with God's truth and grace. Where faith is at hand, it may be expected that this heavenly agency will fall in concurrently with the use of the sacrament; just as it has power to make itself felt (to "blow where it listeth") in connection with any other outward occasion or spectacle. The Spirit may work on men's minds, exciting pious thoughts or feelings of devotion, by the presence of a majestic cataract, or a whirlwind, or a smiling beautiful landscape; and why not then with equal ease through the graphic and affecting representation of the blessed Eucharist? In one case, however, as in the other, the relation between the earthly object and the grace thus made to go along with it is wholly external. The sacrament, like the storm or the landscape, is in no sense an actual embodiment of the presence of this last, but an *occasion* merely, in its own nature accidental, though here of divine appointment, by which it is brought to reveal itself under an independent and wholly different form. No *specific* force is to be imagined in the institution as such; it serves only to bring to mind a general grace which is always just as near at hand without it, where faith is prepared to embrace it, for the accomplishment of the same end. No peculiar *mystery*, of course, is to be regarded as entering into its constitution. The working of God's Spirit is indeed universally something mysterious, the action of a higher world on the sphere of our common natural life; but the grace of the sacrament in this respect is just like all other grace. To dream of it as mystically present at all in the sacraments themselves is a superstition that ends legitimately at last in Rome.

Such in a general light, we say, is the shape given to the sacramental theory of the Reformed Church in this Princeton analysis, by way of counter statement to the view taken of it in *The Mystical Presence*. It will be seen that the two representations are indeed materially different, and that the difference regards points of no common interest and consequence. The statement and counter statement are fairly and completely at issue on the following particular heads, the one denying what is by the other affirmed.

1. The analysis before us grounds itself, as we have seen, in the assumption that the Calvinistic conception of a life-giving virtue extending itself from Christ's body to the souls of his people never entered constitutionally into the Reformed doctrine of the Lord's Supper, as distinguished from the Lutheran and Roman; that it is at war intrinsically with the general Protestant creed, and particularly with the doctrine of justification by faith; that Calvin himself, in his better moments, treated it as a practical nullity; that it was always only an outward and foreign element in the theology of the Reformed Church generally, kept up to save appearances towards those without, rather than to satisfy the heart and soul of the Church itself; and that it gradually fell away, therefore, from the doctrine altogether, died out of it, and thus left it in its proper pure original and distinctive form, as held by the Puritan world at the present day. All this we broadly and firmly deny. There is no inward contradiction between the two views of the Christian salvation which are here taken to stand in such relation. The life of Christ is the true and real basis of his sacrifice, and so the natural and necessary medium of communion with it for the remission of sins. This Calvin saw clearly, and urged accordingly the vivific side of the Christian mystery always as the proper complement of the sacrificial. From this order of thought he never swerved in the least, and so far was he from dropping it to please the Swiss, as here pretended, that we find this very order, and no other, settled with general consent, under his auspices, as a true and right expression of the Reformed faith universally. We meet it in all the standard confessions of this faith in the latter part of the sixteenth century. It is distinctly recognized in the whole sacramental controversy of the same period, under such symbolical view. That a change has taken place in later times is not denied. But this, we contend, has been for the worse and not for the better, so far as the idea of Christ's life in the sacrament has come to be divorced from the idea of his death. It is no growth, no development of the true sense and import of the doctrine as it stood in the beginning, but the distortion of it rather into a different import altogether. The two sides in

question entered organically into the contents of the old doctrine. With their divorce, the idea of the sacrament itself is no longer the same. We have in truth under this name a different conception generally from what it is made to be by the older view. Here is the root of all the other variations and issues that enter into this historical controversy.

2. According to the same analysis again, the Reformed doctrine excluded the reality of Christ's presence from the sacrament (save as he is everywhere present in his divine nature separately considered), resolving it altogether into a simply mental presence, as distinguished from every sort of local or material contact. This we deny. The Reformed doctrine did indeed reject the last, but not in such a way as to make the other its only and necessary alternative. It asserted always a real presence, not simply as an object of thought or intelligence on the part of men, but in the way of actual communication on the part of Christ; a presence not conditioned by the relations of space, but transcending these altogether in a higher sphere of life, a presence not material but dynamic, like that of the root in its branches, and only the more intimate and deep by its distance from all that belongs to the experiment of sense.

3. The Reformed doctrine, we are told still farther, recognized especially no participation of believers in the human side of Christ's life; the reference to his flesh and blood has no significance in this view, but must be taken as a bold metaphor simply, setting forth the thought of our participation in the benefits procured by his bloody death upon the cross. This again we deny. The doctrine in question never set aside the true meaning of the Incarnation in any such Gnostic style. It made Christ to be a fountain of life for the world, and the immediate seat of this grace it represented always to be his human nature. Here it was regarded as coming to its primary revelation for the use of the race at large, in which view his flesh is taken to be the medium truly of life as well as righteousness (life we may say in order to righteousness), for all his people. They participate in the vivific virtue of his humanity, and in such high mysterious sense may be said actually to eat his flesh and drink his blood, as the antidote of death and pabulum of immortality.

4. The Princeton analysis finds in the intervention of the Holy Ghost, as constantly affirmed in the Reformed doctrine of the Eucharist, a full exclusion of Christ's proper presence, especially of his presence under any human view; the stress laid on the agency of the Spirit is taken to mean clearly that no communication is to be thought of in the case with the true and proper life of the Saviour himself. But this whole construction,

we contend, is false and wrong. The intervention of the Spirit, in the old Reformed doctrine, stands opposed only to the idea of all action that falls within the sphere of mere nature, and was never designed to be set in this way over against the reality of Christ's presence. On the contrary, the mystery of the transaction is taken to lie especially in this, that in a mode transcending the experience of sense, by the mirifical power of the Holy Ghost, the life-giving virtue of his flesh and blood is made to be dynamically at hand, in a real and true way, for the use of his people.

5. According to Princeton, the sacramental doctrine of the Reformed Church knows nothing of an efficacious virtue in the holy sacraments themselves; the relation between them and the grace that may go along with them in another form is taken to be altogether outward and loose; they point to it only like dead finger-boards, or as signs in algebra, giving notice of truth which is not in themselves, and that can have no presence save by the mind and will of those who are led to think of it in this way. We affirm, on the contrary, that the Reformers, with the whole ancient Church, acknowledge a real conjunction between the outward form of sacraments and their inward grace. The latter was taken to belong to their very constitution as truly as the first. That the union between them could not be regarded as physical or magical was not felt to set aside at all its actual force. It was still held to be mystically sure and firm. The idea of a sacrament embraced both, the terrene side having its necessary complement always in the celestial. Sacramental grace thus was no fiction. It lay with objective force in the solemnity itself, not, of course, in the outward elements or signs in themselves considered, but in the transaction taken as a whole. How far it might take effect on the subject would depend still on the posture in which it should be received, but this posture was not to be confounded with the grace itself. This must be held to have an actual exhibition in the divine transaction, whether met with a right reception or not.

6. In robbing the Reformed doctrine of this conception of objective grace in the sacraments, the analysis before us finally strips it at the same time of all mystical character, since in such view no significance belongs to any institution of the sort, other than what the truth of the gospel carries with it in its general form. But this, we contend, is to wrong the doctrine as it comes before us in the sixteenth century. The faith of the Reformed Church in the beginning, no less than the faith of the Lutheran Church, saw in the Lord's Supper the presence of a heavenly mystery, something more in this respect than the high nature of the truth here rep-

resented under its general form, something different from the Word in
no connection with such solemnity. An inward bond was acknowledged
to hold, by the power of the Holy Ghost, between the visible and invisible sides of the holy transaction. It was allowed to carry in it thus a mystical force, a meaning above sense and natural reason, to which especially
faith was encouraged and required to have regard in using it as a medium
of worship.

. . . To see at a glance the difference between the two representations,
as well as to estimate their comparative claims to regard, in the light of
the examination through which we have now gone, we have only to repeat the recapitulatory paragraph of the Princeton article, which we have
before quoted, adding to its several clauses at the same time what is
needed in the way of supplement to complete their sense. To make the
contrast between the two forms of statement more immediately plain, the
supplementary parts are presented in a different type, and of course without quotation marks.

"Christ is really present to his people, in this ordinance, not bodily, but
by his Spirit," *as the medium of a higher mode of existence,* "not in the
sense of local nearness, but of efficacious operation," *nullifying mirifically
the bar of distance and bringing the very substance of his body into union
with their life.* "They receive him, not with the mouth, but by faith," *as
the organ by which only the soul is qualified to admit the divine action
now noticed;* "they receive his flesh, not as flesh, not as material particles," *but dynamically in the inward power of its life (so that the clause
"nor its human life," is not correct),* "his body as broken and his blood as
shed," *the value of that sacrifice carried in the vivific virtue of the same
body now gloriously exalted in heaven.* "The union thus signified and
effected between him and them is not a corporeal union, nor a mixture of
substances," *in the Roman or Lutheran sense,* "but spiritual and mystical"; *not merely mental, but including the real presence of Christ's whole
life under an objective character, and reaching on our side also through
the soul into the body,* "arising from the indwelling of the Spirit," *not as
the proxy only of an absent Christ, but as the supernatural bond of a true
life-connection, by which his very flesh is joined to ours, more intimately
far than the trunk to its branches, or the head to its members, in the natural world.* "The efficacy of this sacrament, as a means of grace, is not in
the signs," *separately taken,* "nor in the service," *outwardly considered,*
"nor in the minister, nor in the Word, but solely in the attending influence of the Holy Ghost," *as the necessary complement or inward side of*

the divine mystery itself, of whose presence the outward signs are the
sure guaranty and pledge, and whose mirific action can never fail to take
effect objectively where the subject is in a state to admit it by faith.
"This we believe," *so filled out with positive contents,* "to be a fair statement of the doctrine of the Reformed Church." . . .

Calvin and Westphal

. . . One of the very best replies to Princeton, so far as Calvin is concerned, would be simply a full republication, in clear intelligible English,
of his memorable Second Defense "adversus Joachimi Westphali *calum-*
nias." As a substitute for this, we can offer here only a most cursory
glance over the leading points of crimination and reply. This may be
done best, perhaps, in the form of a regular dialogue between the parties
themselves.

Westphal. Here we have it at last. An open confederation with the
Helvetians! What is this Consensus Tigurinus but a barefaced transition
to the camp of the accursed Zwinglians, a crafty compromise with Bullinger, which goes to undermine the whole cause of Lutheran Protestantism in favor of its enemies? And yet you have professed to stand in the
bosom of Lutheran Protestantism, and to be a true friend to the faith of
the Augsburg Confession. Before all Germany, I proclaim you, John Calvin, a hypocrite and a traitor.

Calvin. Your charge is false. I am guilty in this case of no duplicity nor
change. My relation to Lutheranism remains what it was ten years ago.
To one part of his sacramental theory, I never could assent; while the
mystery itself which it sought to maintain had my full faith; as for the
person of the great Reformer also, I have ever cherished the most profound reverence and regard. I might easily prove, moreover, that Luther
himself looked upon my views with favor. Let Philip Melanchthon, however, be my one voucher, in place of all others. We have been of one
mind here, and are of one mind still. I *did* subscribe the Augsburg Confession at Strassburg, taking it in its generally acknowledged sense, as settled by the authority of its illustrious framer, the excellent Melanchthon
himself; and to this subscription I still adhere, without any sort of mental
reservation whatever.

Westphal. A fine story truly, when we see you walking arm in arm with the Zwinglians, and passing yourself off as one of their own kidney.

Calvin. All turns again on your own hasty construction. I have always set my face openly against the view commonly laid to Zwingli's charge, by which the idea of an actual communication with Christ's life is excluded from the mystery of the Lord's Supper. This I have not hesitated heretofore to stigmatize as absolutely profane, and I trust I shall never cease to regard it in the same light. The Consensus Tigurinus, however, proceeds on the supposition throughout that the proper Helvetic faith involves nothing really of this sort; and it is an effort simply to carry it out, by suitable explanation and definition, to such a full statement as might serve to relieve it from this reproach, and set it in a correct light before the Christian world. The statement is no act of subscription, of course, to the system of Luther strictly so called. I have always rejected that, and it is openly rejected also in this Consensus. But the instrument is not for this reason a simple falling over to the contrary extreme. It is fairly and truly a bond of union and peace, between the Helvetic churches and the faith of the Augsburg Confession.

Westphal. Nonsense! You do not pretend that this Consensus agrees with the Confession of Augsburg!

Calvin. Take the tenth article of this last in the sense of its author, without any popish perversion or gloss, and I contend that the sacramental doctrine of the two instruments is in truth the same.

Westphal. You can hardly expect the world to give you credit for honesty and plain dealing in this business. You have been playing a game. You carry two faces.

Calvin. God knows that this is not the case. I have had no worldly interest to serve, and I have used no concealment or reserve. On the contrary, I have tried always to be both candid and clear, as far as language would admit; and it will be found, I think, that few men have taken more pains to let their position be known, or have less differed from themselves with the onward progress of time. My views now are just what they were clearly stated to be twenty years ago, in the first edition of my *Institutes.*

Westphal. Be it so then. It only shows that you have been all along a false teacher. For only look at this Consensus Tigurinus. It evacuates the sacraments of their mystical force, and turns them thus into mere void signs.

Calvin. That is a gross slander. Both the Consensus and the Exposition attached to it most distinctly affirm the contrary.

Westphal. You make the elements mere *signs.*

Calvin. Signs certainly; but by no means naked and empty signs. Christ uses here no false colors. The verities represented by the power of God are made to go along with the signs. The last divinely certify the presence of the first. The things represented are at the same time *exhibited*, or made to be actually at hand.

Westphal. Exhibited, you mean, in the way of image or picture, but not as they are in their own nature; for you explicitly deny, in the case of the Lord's Supper, the actual presence in any way of Christ's body and blood, materially considered, along with the bread and wine by which they are represented.

Calvin. Certainly I have always rejected, and reject still most firmly, the idea of every sort of presence here that is to be regarded as local or material, or that may be said to fall within the experience and measure of mere nature as such. But this by no means implies that the realities signified by the symbols are absent, or that they are at hand only in the way of picture. When I acknowledge their exhibition or presentation in the sacrament, my meaning is always that they are made to be actually present in the whole power of their own proper nature, only not in the way of sense, but in a higher way.

Westphal. All is made to depend at last, however, on the exercises of the worshipper. The verities exhibited are present only in thought and contemplation, as these enter into the action of faith.

Calvin. I mean not so. The verities are at hand objectively — the inward grace in the outward transaction. Faith is only the condition, not the cause, of our mystical participation of Christ in the Holy Supper. God forbid that I should think of turning the process into a mere mental exercise of any kind.

Westphal. Still you will have it that the process is altogether spiritual, and any objective force you may allow to the transaction will be found to resolve itself thus into the mere agency of the Holy Ghost, exciting faith, love, and other graces.

Calvin. Spiritual the process is, as distinguished from your crass conception of an oral manducation. The mystery centers in the soul, and is wrought by the vivific power of the Holy Ghost under a mode of existence that transcends all natural experience and conception. But it is not a mere influence. The Spirit actually binds Christ and his people into one life, not as a river may join two cities which are many miles apart, by merely flowing through both, but as being the very form and medium (*modus habitationis Christi in nobis* [mode of Christ's dwelling in us]), under and by which the life of the first is made to pass over into the last.

Westphal. The communion you think of in this way must be regarded as holding at last only with the *divine* nature in Christ, if it be allowed to have any reality at all; for your theory completely excludes the presence of his body.

Calvin. It does so only in a local or material view, but not at all as regards living power and force. The communication which we have with Christ in the sacrament is by no means limited to his divine nature, but extends to his humanity also, as the real seat and fountain of salvation for our dying world; in which sense it is, we are said to eat his flesh and drink his blood unto everlasting life.

Westphal. You take the word *body* in an ambiguous sense, for all that you allow in the end is that we partake of Christ's benefits — which, as they were procured by his sufferings in the body, may be spoken of under the name of his flesh and blood. But all runs out in this way into a bold metaphor. You substitute in your mind an imagination merely, for the true and proper body of our blessed Lord.

Calvin. I never confound the benefits which we have by Christ with the idea of his life. It is idle to remind us, then, that his merits and benefits are not his body. The insinuation that this is all I mean by the communion of his flesh and blood is purely gratuitous and does me gross injustice. I own no fiction or metaphor whatever in the case. The body of which we partake in the blessed sacrament is the same that once hung upon the cross, and is now glorified in heaven.

Westphal. And yet you will not hear of this being present in the sacrament, but hold it to be absent from us by an immense distance. How then can we be said to partake of it in any real way?

Calvin. The whole is a mystery, as I have said before, in the sphere of the Spirit. Dynamically and organically things may be joined together in the most intimate unity, which are at the same time wide apart in space. Christ's body remains indeed always in heaven, but by the power of the Holy Ghost, as something which transcends all local and mechanical relations, not only his divine life, as this is present in all places, but the proper life of his body also, the quickening vigor of his flesh and blood, is made to pass into the souls of his people, as a true aliment of immortality.

Westphal. You confess this, however, to be only for the soul or mind of the communicant, not for his body.

Calvin. Not for the body, indeed, in a direct and outward way, as your theory requires, but just as little either for the mind separately considered. Soul and mind are not the same thing. I mean by the soul, the central principle of our whole life, which in the end reaches out to the body also no less than the spirit. In this way, Christ is the true food, by which our whole nature is nourished unto immortality.

Westphal. A purely spiritual transaction thus, and nothing more, is made to stand for the whole mystery. The flesh of Christ, with you, is not present in the supper. You do not allow an actual giving and receiving of his body.

Calvin. The presence is spiritual, allow me to repeat, only as it is not material and local, but not at all in any such sense as may be taken to overthrow its reality. As regards this, there is no difference nor debate. I freely allow here what the sacrament requires, an actual participation in Christ's flesh and blood, and this without any sort of metaphor or rhetorical fiction. Only I cannot yield to your view of the *mode* in which this is brought to pass, for it seems to me to be at war with the very object of the mystery itself; and I see no reason in the Bible or elsewhere for its being made to hang exclusively on so gross a conception, but every reason rather for insisting on a higher view. You seem to have no idea of presence in the case save in the way of physical contact and transfusion. To my mind, I confess, it is something far more real, in the form of a *living* entrance into the inmost sanctuary of the believer's life.

Westphal. You take away the donation of the true and proper body, and give us what you are pleased to call its virtue and vigor merely in its stead.

Calvin. When I say that Christ reaches us with the virtue of his life, I deny that any substitute is brought in that sets aside at all the donation of his body. I only explain the mode of the donation.

Westphal. It is a plain case, however, that what is given and taken in the sacrament, as you hold it, is not the real matter of Christ's body, but something else. You will not allow that we partake of his *substance.*

Calvin. Not of the outward material of his nature certainly in any way, but still of its actual substantial life, the vivific virtue of his true flesh and blood. Put away the crass thought of a manducation of the flesh, as though it were to enter the stomach by the mouth like common food, and there is no reason to deny that we are fed with Christ's flesh *substantially.* His body remains in heaven, while nevertheless life flows out from its very substance, and reaches down into the persons of his people, just as the substance of the head passes over continually to the members in the natural body.

Westphal. You are a perfect eel, sir, as all the world may see, slimy and slippery to the very tail. There is no such thing as holding you fast. Your "virtue" and "vigor" of Christ's body resolve themselves, when all is said, into the idea of a mere influence proceeding from him through the Spirit, and mean simply the efficacy and value of his death, made available for our benefit by God, and so appropriated on our side by faith.

Calvin. Miserable misrepresentation. How often must I protest against your trick of turning my words into a sense which they openly disown? Have I not said in all possible ways that Christ must be distinguished from the fruits he brings to pass, and that he must go before them also in the way of actual and real appropriation on the part of his people? Christ *first*, and only *then* his merits and benefits. By "virtue" or "efficacy" here, I understand always the essential living force of the Redeemer's body, once slain and now in heaven, as I use the word "vigor" also to express its actual power and substance, the very sap of its heavenly constitution. This in its glorified state is all "life and spirit" — a body, of course, still, but not such as belongs to our present mortal condition. It is capable thus of reaching over, by the Spirit, and we may say also *in* the Spirit, into the souls of his people on earth, as the head is able to live itself, in a lower sphere, into its members, or the root into its branches, independently of all local contact.

Westphal. Clouds! clouds! Spare us, if you please, these transcendental flights. We have no wings to soar behind you into regions so high and *thin.* Seriously, we want no philosophy in this matter. Let us stick to the plain sense of the Bible. What is the voice of reason, with its carnal perplexities and plausibilities, over against the voice of Christ?

Calvin. I would a hundred times rather die than weigh the smallest single word of Christ against the whole world of philosophy. My theology comes from another quarter. It is not philosophy which teaches either that human flesh is endowed with life-giving virtue, or that this life breathes from heaven, or that we come into possession of it efficaciously under the outward symbol of bread; nothing of this sort falls in with common sense, or comes forth from the philosophical schools. The word of him who founded the sacrament is held up to us in opposition. But what is it that he says? That he gives us his own body. This promise I reverently embrace, not stopping in what is before the eyes only, the mere bread and wine, but accepting by faith the life itself, which proceeding from Christ's flesh and blood, is secretly conveyed into our very souls. The charge of substituting philosophy for God's Word, holds in truth only against the other side. It is Westphal that *theorizes* here, not Calvin.

Westphal. It is fine for you to talk in that style! Your theory is made up of speculation, and is so full of riddles and contradictions that a plain Bible Christian like myself must puzzle himself in vain to say what it means. It may be questioned whether you understand your own meaning.

Calvin. God knows the simplicity and honesty of my faith, while I am not ashamed freely to acknowledge here the helplessness of my poor understanding. St. Paul himself pronounces the whole subject a "great mystery." So I feel it to be in my inmost soul. My faith bows before it with childlike homage.

Such we conceive to be a fair representation of Calvin's doctrine, as it may be extracted from this controversy with Westphal, as well as from his writings in general. . . .

AN EVANGELICAL CATHOLIC LITURGY

Editor's Introduction.

What made the liturgical movement there remarkable was not the *Order of Worship*, despite its high degree of liturgical skill. It was rather the fact that it was the first liturgy in the Reformed Church to articulate a theology. Indeed, it was at Mercersburg that there was worked out, often in the heat of battle, for the first time in the Reformed Churches what could be called a theology of the liturgy.[1]

In the liturgical history of the Reformed churches of the English-speaking world, the decade of the eighteen-fifties was probably the most productive of the century. One of the most distinctive and influential of its achievements was informed by Mercersburg theology. This was the *Liturgy, or Order of Christian Worship*, presented to the Eastern Synod of the German Reformed Church in 1857. The chairman of the liturgical committee, and the chief architect of its work, was Philip Schaff.

The "Provisional Liturgy," as it came to be called, needs to be understood against the prevailing tradition of "non-liturgical" Puritan worship in the American churches. Presbyterians, Congregationalists, and Baptists jointly inherited the concept of the Westminster Directory, and except for the sacraments they were virtually indistinguishable in their practice. Methodist services, again apart from the sacraments, were assimilated to the same tradition. The spontaneous excitement of Puritan worship in the earlier seventeenth century had given way in the Restoration period to the routine formula of cant phrases, into which in the eighteenth century a recurrent intensity had been injected by revivalism.

The closely related Dutch and German Reformed churches faced common problems when they found it necessary to make English the language of their worship. Should they translate their traditional liturgies

1. H. G. Hageman, *Pulpit and Table* (Richmond, 1962), 92.

into English? If so, what adaptations would be called for? Or should their congregations simply adopt the patterns of "free" worship prevailing in the English-speaking churches about them? The Dutch had formally adopted an English liturgy, although in practice the pastors used it at their own discretion. But the German Reformed churches were just at the point of decision on this matter when Mercersburg took the theological leadership of the denomination. The English-language congregations had gone over almost entirely to the free-prayer system for the regular services. For the sacraments and special occasions some borrowed from the Dutch liturgy, some from the Episcopalian, some compiled their own forms, and others depended on the inspiration of the moment.

The committees appointed to deal with this situation faced a number of alternatives. Probably a majority of pastors in the English-speaking congregations desired a collection of forms for the sacraments and special occasions, but for the regular Lord's Day service they preferred full freedom, or at most a few specimen prayers to be utilized if and as they pleased.

For this kind of proposal, which found some support in most of the American Reformed churches, a considerable volume of usable published materials were now available. The historians had uncovered a number of Reformed liturgical texts. In 1849, Calvin's *Form of Prayers* was published in an English translation. The Scottish *Book of Common Order*, often called "Knox's Liturgy," had been published by Dr. Cumming in 1840, and extensive portions of the Palatinate liturgy in an English translation by J. H. A. Bomberger had appeared in *The Mercersburg Review* (1850, 1851). The old Huguenot church of Charleston, South Carolina, published in 1853 an English translation of its service book, which was essentially Osterwald's revision of the Neuchatel service, as *The Liturgy, or Forms of Divine Service of the French Protestant Church*. Baird's *Eutaxia: or the Presbyterian Liturgies* (1855), which appeared while the German Reformed liturgical committee was at work, attempted a comprehensive description and history of the worship practice of the chief Reformed churches. To most American Reformed pastors and laymen this work must have been a startling revelation, though for Schaff, a professional church historian familiar with the discussions occasioned by the liturgy imposed on the Evangelical Church by the king of Prussia, there was probably little in it that was new. Ebrard had already attempted a compilation of classical Reformed prayers in his 1847 *Reformirtes Kirchenbuch,* and Baird published an English counterpart, under the title of *A*

Book of Public Prayer, in the same year as the "Provisional Liturgy." The evidence was overwhelming that all the Reformed churches had originally possessed and regularly used liturgical books.

The proposals of most of the American liturgical reformers were modest. Baird wished only to restore the congregational "Amen," the two Scripture chapters of the *Westminster Directory,* and the use of the Creed, the Lord's Prayer, and the Ten Commandments in worship. At St. Peter's Church in Rochester, a kind of Presbyterian proprietary chapel, these suggestions were followed, and also there were chanted prose psalms in place of metrical singing, but still no venture away from free prayer. Baird's and Ebrard's collections were designed to furnish resources to the pastor, but not to the layman in the pew.

Again, few of the reformers ventured to challenge the current American resistance to recognizing such festivals as Christmas and Easter. The Continental Reformed churches had always observed these, but the Scottish and Puritan rejection of them prevailed generally in America. Ebrard, of course, included them, but in the proposals of Baird and the Dutch they were ignored. The Palatinate Liturgy contained half a dozen festival prayers, and the German Reformed churches, whose parishes were often in close contact with those of German Lutherans, were readier than most others to accept suggestions in this matter.

In these circumstances, the principles for the liturgical committee accepted in 1852 by the Synod of Baltimore were bold indeed. The committee wished their liturgy to be in the hands not of the ministers only, but of every member of the Church, so that the congregation might follow the minister and respond at least at the end of each prayer with an audible "Amen."

Again, while particular regard was to be had to the old Palatinate and other sixteenth-century Reformed liturgies, their over-didactic and doctrinal tone was not to be generally emulated. The language and style was to be scriptural and devotional as far as possible. The "general basis," moreover, was to be the liturgical worship of the primitive Church up through the third and fourth centuries, as "the source from which the best portions of the various liturgies of the sixteenth century were derived." On this general basis some new forms might be added, and the old adapted to the peculiar wants of the denomination and the age. Room was to be left also for extemporaneous prayer, although not in the services for the Lord's Day or the sacraments. It was hoped to produce a liturgy which would be "a bond of union both with the ancient Catholic Church and the Reformation, and yet be the product of the religious life of our denomination in its present state." [2]

The order for the Holy Communion owed its final stabilization to the liturgy of the Catholic Apostolic Church, by which Schaff had been profoundly impressed in London in 1854. Cardale, who was apparently the chief liturgist of the "Irvingites," had preceded Mercersburg in the study and exploitation of patristic liturgical materials. These two liturgies were to play a significant role during the following century in the Reformed churches, in Scottish and American Presbyterianism, and among the Reformed Dutch in America.

In 1866, after a decade of experiment, the "Provisional Liturgy" was replaced by a revised *Order of Worship*. This second version of the order for Holy Communion is reprinted below. The revision was controlled by the same conceptions as the book of 1857. Indeed, the most heated controversy was still to come.

❖ ❖ ❖ ❖

Preparation for the Holy Communion

Having taken his place at the altar, the congregation also standing up, the minister shall say:

The Lord is in his holy temple: let all the earth keep silence before him. *Amen.*

God spake all these words, saying, I am the Lord thy God, which have brought thee out of the land of Egypt, out of the house of bondage.

Thou shalt have no other gods before me.

Thou shalt not make unto thee any graven image, or any likeness of any thing that is in heaven above, or that is in the earth beneath, or that is in the water under the earth: thou shalt not bow down thyself to them, nor serve them; for I the Lord thy God am a jealous God, visiting the iniquity of the fathers upon the children unto the third and fourth generation of them that hate me; and shewing mercy unto thousands of them that love me, and keep my commandments.

Thou shalt not take the name of the Lord thy God in vain; for the Lord will not hold him guiltless that taketh his name in vain.

Remember the sabbath day, to keep it holy. Six days shalt thou labor,

2. Schaff, "The New Liturgy," *The Mercersburg Review*, X, (1858), 218–20.

and do all thy work: but the seventh day is the sabbath of the Lord thy God: in it thou shalt not do any work, thou, nor thy son, nor thy daughter, thy manservant, nor thy maidservant, nor thy cattle, nor thy stranger that is within thy gates: for in six days the Lord made heaven and earth, the sea, and all that in them is, and rested the seventh day: wherefore the Lord blessed the sabbath day, and hallowed it.

Honor thy father and thy mother: that thy days may be long upon the land which the Lord thy God giveth thee.

Thou shalt not kill.

Thou shalt not commit adultery.

Thou shalt not steal.

Thou shalt not bear false witness against thy neighbor.

Thou shalt not covet thy neighbor's house, thou shalt not covet thy neighbor's wife, nor his manservant, nor his maidservant, nor his ox, nor his ass, nor any thing that is thy neighbor's.

Congregation. Lord, have mercy upon us, and incline our hearts to keep all these laws.

Minister. Hear also what our Lord Jesus Christ saith:

Thou shalt love the Lord thy God with all thy heart, and with all thy soul, and with all thy mind. This is the first and great commandment. And the second is like unto it: Thou shalt love thy neighbor as thyself. On these two commandments hang all the law and the prophets.

M. Let us pray.

O Lord God, who didst at first deliver thy commandments from the mount which burned with fire, amid blackness, and darkness, and tempest, at which terrible sight even Moses said, I exceedingly fear and quake: we thank thee that this same law is now published unto us from mount Zion, through the Mediator of a new and better covenant; and we humbly beseech thee to put these words into our minds, and write them in our hearts, that we may delight in thy law after the inward man, and serve thee in newness of spirit, through Jesus Christ our Lord; who with Thee and the Holy Ghost liveth and reigneth, ever one God, world without end. *Amen.*

Then all shall kneel, and join in the Litany as follows:

M. O God the Father in heaven; have mercy upon us.

C. Have mercy upon us.

M. O God the Son, Redeemer of the world; have mercy upon us.
C. Have mercy upon us.

M. O God the Holy Ghost, proceeding from the Father and the Son; have mercy upon us.
C. Have mercy upon us.

M. O holy, blessed, and glorious Trinity, three Persons and one God; have mercy upon us.
C. Have mercy upon us.

M. Remember not, Lord, our offenses, nor the offenses of our forefathers; neither take Thou vengeance of our sins: spare us, good Lord, spare Thy people, whom thou hast redeemed with thy most precious blood, and be not angry with us for ever.
C. Spare us, good Lord.

M. From all evil and harm; from the power of sin, and the snares of the devil; from thy wrath, and from everlasting damnation;
C. Good Lord, deliver us.

M. From all blindness of heart; from pride, vainglory, and hypocrisy; from envy, hatred, and malice and all uncharitableness;
C. Good Lord, deliver us.

M. From all impure lusts and desires; and from all the deceits of the world, the flesh, and the devil;
C. Good Lord, deliver us.

M. From lightning, tempest, and earthquake; from plague, pestilence, and famine; from all disasters by land and by water; from battle and murder, and from sudden death;
C. Good Lord, deliver us.

M. From tumult and riot; from sedition and rebellion; from heresy and schism; from hardness of heart, and contempt of thy word and authority;
C. Good Lord, deliver us.

M. By the mystery of thy holy incarnation; by thy holy nativity and circumcision; by thy baptism, fasting, and temptation;
C. Good Lord, deliver us.

M. By thine agony and bloody sweat; by thy cross and passion; by thy precious death and burial; by thy glorious resurrection and ascension; and by the coming of the Holy Ghost;

C. Good Lord, deliver us.

M. In all time of our tribulation; in all time of our wealth; in the hour of death, and in the day of judgment;

C. Good Lord, deliver us.

M. We sinners do beseech thee to hear us, O Lord.

C. Son of God, we beseech thee to hear us.

M. That it may please thee to keep us in all time of temptation and heaviness; to comfort and help all the weak-hearted; to raise up them that fall, and finally to beat down Satan under our feet;

C. We beseech thee to hear us, O Lord.

M. That it may please thee to succor, help, and comfort all that are in danger, necessity, and tribulation;

C. We beseech thee to hear us, O Lord.

M. That it may please thee to preserve all travellers and strangers, all women in the perils of childbirth, all sick persons, and young children, and to show thy pity upon all prisoners and captives;

C. We beseech thee to hear us, O Lord.

M. That it may please thee to defend and provide for the fatherless children, and widows, and all that are desolate and oppressed;

C. We beseech thee to hear us, O Lord.

M. That it may please thee to have mercy upon all men;

C. We beseech thee to hear us, O Lord.

M. O Son of God, Redeemer of the world;

C. Have mercy upon us.

M. O Lamb of God, that takest away the sin of the world;

C. Have mercy upon us.

M. O Lamb of God, that takest away the sin of the world;

C. Grant us thy peace.

O God, merciful Father, who despisest not the sighing of the contrite, nor rejectest the desire of the sorrowful; be favorable to our prayers which in our afflictions that continually oppress us, we pour out before thee; and graciously hear them, that those things which the craft of the devil or man worketh against us, may be brought to nought, and by the counsel of thy goodness be dispersed; so that being hurt by no persecutions, we may evermore give thanks unto thee in thy holy Church, through Jesus Christ our Lord. *Amen.*

O God, from whom all holy desires, all good counsels, and all just works do proceed; give unto thy servants that peace which the world cannot give; that our hearts may be set to obey thy commandments, and also that we, being defended from the fear of our enemies, may by thy protection pass our time in peace and quietness; through Jesus Christ our Lord. *Amen.*

A suitable psalm or hymn shall now be sung.

Then the minister, having taken his place in the pulpit, shall proceed to deliver a brief sermon or exhortation.

After the sermon, the minister, at the altar, shall address the communicants, and say:

Beloved in the Lord: Our Blessed Saviour Jesus Christ, when he was about to finish the work of our redemption, by making himself a sacrifice for our sins upon the cross, solemnly instituted the Holy Sacrament of his own Body and Blood; that it might be the abiding memorial of his precious death; the seal of his perpetual presence in the Church by the Holy Ghost; the mystical exhibition of his one offering of himself made once, but of force always, to put away sin; the pledge of his undying love to his people; and the bond of his living union and fellowship with them to the end of time.

The same night, we are told, in which he was betrayed, he took bread; and when he had given thanks, he brake it, and said, Take, eat; this is my body, which is broken for you; this do in remembrance of me. After the same manner also he took the cup, when he had supped, saying, This cup is the new testament in my blood; this do ye, as oft as ye drink it, in remembrance of me.

It has not been without reason, therefore, that the celebration of the Holy Eucharist has ever been regarded by the Church as the inmost sanctuary of the whole Christian worship. We have to do here, not with outward signs only, but with the heavenly realities themselves which these signs represent. Our Lord himself calls the bread his body, and the cup his blood, or the new testament in his blood. The cup of blessing which we bless, says St. Paul, is it not the communion of the blood of Christ? The bread which we break, is it not the communion of the body of Christ? And it is the same Apostle who utters, in another place, the solemn warning: Let a man examine himself, and so let him eat of that bread, and drink of that cup; for he that eateth and drinketh unworthily, eateth and drinketh judgment to himself, not discerning the Lord's body.

Being of such high and awful character, it is plain that the Lord's Supper can be rightly and safely approached only by those who are of a truly devout and religious mind. These holy mysteries are not for the irreverent, the worldly, or the profane. All who are impenitent and unbelieving, and who refuse to obey the gospel of our Lord Jesus Christ, have no right to partake of this Christian altar. They can do so only at their own peril; for coming to it thus in the spirit of hypocrisy and wickedness, they turn the blessing of the Sacrament into a curse, and that which should be a savor of life unto life is made to be for them only a savor of death unto death. They eat and drink damnation or judgment to themselves; not because they are sinners, but because they are impenitent sinners; not because they are unworthy, but because they eat and drink unworthily, not discerning the Lord's body.

If any of you who are here present, then, know yourselves to be the willing servants of sin, being without repentance and faith, and yielding yourselves to the power of worldly affections and lusts, we solemnly warn and admonish you, that ye presume not, so long as this is your character, to come to the table of the Lord. Do not pretend in this way, to join righteousness with unrighteousness, and light with darkness. Ye cannot drink the cup of the Lord, and the cup of devils; ye cannot be partakers of the Lord's table, and of the table of devils.

On the other hand, we cordially invite to this table all who are truly grieved and penitent for their sins, who look to the Lord Jesus Christ for righteousness and salvation, who abide in the fellowship of his Church, and who earnestly desire to possess his Spirit and to walk in his steps. To all such the voice of the infinitely compassionate Redeemer himself speaks: Come unto me, all ye that labor, and are heavy laden, and I will give you rest. Fear not, therefore, as many of you as have this mind, to embrace the joyful and glorious privilege which is here offered for your use. Having, brethren, boldness to enter into the holiest by the blood of

Jesus, by a new and living way, which he hath consecrated for us, through the veil, that is to say, his flesh; and having an High Priest over the house of God; let us draw near with a true heart, in full assurance of faith, having our hearts sprinkled from an evil conscience, and our bodies washed with pure water.

Only ye must take good heed, that your particular preparation for the Sacrament at this time be sincere and whole, according to God's command; so that no let or bar may be found in yourselves to its proper comfort and benefit. See that ye have grace, not only in general habit, but also in present exercise and power. Renew your repentance and faith. Be in perfect charity with all men. Put away from you the leaven of malice and wickedness. Remember earnestly your past offenses and shortcomings, that ye may humble yourselves, with true hearty confession, under the mighty hand of him, who alone has power to exalt you in his own good time. Thus, clothed in the robes of salvation, you will be able to compass God's holy altar with thankfulness and joy, and to share the full benefit of its one offering for sin, while you feed on the sacrifice at the same time as the bread of everlasting life. For in this most comfortable sacrament of the body and blood of our Saviour Jesus Christ, we have exhibited to us at once, both the forgiveness of sins through his death, and the gift of immortality through his glorious resurrection; according to his own word: Verily, verily, I say unto you, Except ye eat the flesh of the Son of Man, and drink his blood, ye have no life in you. Whoso eateth my flesh, and drinketh my blood, hath eternal life; and I will raise him up at the last day. For my flesh is meat indeed, and my blood is drink indeed. He that eateth my flesh, and drinketh my blood, dwelleth in me, and I in him. As the living Father hath sent me, and I live by the Father; so he that eateth me, even he shall live by me. This is that bread which came down from heaven: not as your fathers did eat manna, and are dead; he that eateth of this bread shall live for ever.

Ye then, beloved brethren in the Lord, who have looked earnestly into your own hearts, and who find in yourselves these good dispositions of penitence and faith, with the sincere desire and purpose of forsaking all sin and following after all Christian holiness, approach with me now to the throne of grace, and make your humble confession to Almighty God.

All kneeling.

Almighty God, Father of our Lord Jesus Christ, Maker of all things, Judge of all men; we cast ourselves down at thy feet, with deep humilia-

tion and heartfelt penitent grief, in view of our manifold sins and great
unrighteousness, whereby we have provoked against ourselves most justly
thine indignation and wrath. We have sinned against thee in thought,
word, and deed. We have broken thy holy laws. We have come short of
thy righteousness and glory, in all our ways. Our lives bear testimony
against us, and our own hearts condemn us, as being prone to all evil, and
backward to all good. We have abused thy mercies, and made light of thy
judgments. We have turned aside from thy covenant; and have not been
faithful and diligent, as we ought to have been, in using the helps of thy
grace for our eternal salvation. We acknowledge and bewail before thee,
the corruption of our nature, the vanity of our minds, the waywardness
of our hearts, the wanderings and apostasies of our whole fallen life.
Righteousness belongeth unto thee, O Lord; and unto us only confusion
of face. But unto thee, O Lord our God, belong also mercies and forgive-
nesses, though we have rebelled against thee. For thou, Lord, art good, and
ready to forgive, and plenteous in mercy unto all them that call upon
thee. Look upon us, therefore, O righteous and holy Father, with an eye
of pity and compassion, as we now humble ourselves, with sincere confession, before the throne of thy heavenly grace; and for the sake of thy
Son Jesus Christ, speak pardon and peace to our souls. Let thy mercy be
upon us, O Lord, according as we hope in thee. And with the full pardon
of our past sins, be pleased also to quicken us, we beseech thee, in the way
of righteousness, and uphold us with thy free Spirit; that we may walk
worthy henceforth of the vocation wherewith we are called, and ever
hereafter serve and please thee in newness of life, to the honor and glory
of thy holy name, through Jesus Christ our Lord. Amen.

Then shall the minister rise, and pronounce to the congregation, still kneel-
ing, the following declaration of pardon.

Hearken now unto the comforting assurance of the grace of God,
promised in the Gospel to all that repent and believe: As I live, saith the
Lord God, I have no pleasure in the death of the wicked, but that the
wicked turn from his way and live. God so loved the world, that he gave
his only begotten Son, that whosoever believeth in him should not perish,
but have everlasting life.

Unto as many of you, therefore, beloved in the Lord, as have now
made confession of your sins unto God with hearty repentance and sincere faith, being resolved to turn from them, and to follow after righteousness and true holiness in time to come, I declare, by the authority of
the Gospel, that all your sins are remitted and forgiven, through the per-

fect satisfaction of the most holy passion and death of our Lord Jesus Christ. *Amen.*

Then shall the congregation rise, and join in singing a doxology; after which the service shall be concluded with this benediction:

The God of peace, who brought again from the dead our Lord Jesus, the great Shepherd of the sheep, through the blood of the everlasting covenant, make you perfect in every good work, to do his will, working in you that which is well-pleasing in his sight, through Jesus Christ: to whom be glory for ever and ever. *Amen.*

The Holy Communion

[The sacrament of the Lord's Supper shall be administered publicly in the church, in every congregation, at least twice a year, and if possible oftener.]

HAVING taken his place at the altar, the congregation also standing up, the minister shall say as follows:

In the name of the Father, and of the Son, and of the Holy Ghost. *Amen.*

Dearly Beloved in the Lord: If we say that we have no sin, we deceive ourselves, and the truth is not in us; but if we confess our sins, God is faithful and just to forgive us our sins, and to cleanse us from all unrighteousness. Let us therefore humble ourselves before the throne of Almighty God, our heavenly Father, and confess our manifold sins and transgressions with lowly and contrite hearts, that we may obtain forgiveness of the same through the merits of our Lord Jesus Christ.

Then the minister and congregation shall kneel, and repeat the following confession.

Almighty God, our heavenly Father, who dost admit thy people unto such wonderful communion, that partaking of the body and blood of thy dear Son, they should dwell in him, and he in them; we unworthy sinners, approaching to thy presence, and beholding thy glory, do abhor ourselves, and repent in dust and ashes. We have sinned, we have sinned, we have grievously sinned against thee, in thought, in word, and in deed, provoking most justly thy wrath and indignation against us. The remembrance of our transgressions and shortcomings fills us with sorrow and shame. Yet now, O most merciful Father, have mercy upon us; for the sake of Jesus Christ, forgive us all our sins; purify us, by the inspiration of thy Holy Spirit, from all inward uncleanness; enable us heartily to forgive others, as we beseech thee to forgive us; and grant that we may ever here-after serve and please thee in newness of life; to the honor and glory of thy name, through Jesus Christ our Lord. Amen.

Then shall the minister rise, and pronounce to the congregation, still kneel-ing, the following declaration of pardon.

Hearken now unto the comforting assurance of the grace of God, promised in the Gospel to all that repent and believe: As I live, saith the Lord God, I have no pleasure in the death of the wicked, but that the wicked turn from his way and live. God so loved the world, that he gave his only begotten Son, that whosoever believeth in him should not perish, but have everlasting life.

Unto as many of you, therefore, beloved brethren, as truly repent of your sins, and believe in the Lord Jesus Christ, with full purpose of new obedience, I announce and declare, by the authority and in the name of Christ, that your sins are forgiven in heaven, according to his promise in the Gospel, through the perfect merit of Jesus Christ our Lord.

Here, and at the end of every collect and prayer, the congregation shall say:

Amen.

The congregation shall now rise, and join with the minister in repeating the Nicene Creed; immediately after which shall be sung, chanted, or recited, the Gloria in Excelsis; all in the following order.

We believe in one God, the Father Almighty, Maker of heaven and earth, of all things visible and invisible:

And in one Lord Jesus Christ, the only begotten Son of God, begotten of the Father before all worlds, God of God, Light of Light, very God of very God; begotten not made; of one substance with the Father, by whom all things were made: who for us men and for our salvation came down from heaven, and was incarnate by the Holy Ghost of the Virgin Mary, and was made man: who was also crucified for us under Pontius Pilate, and suffered, and was buried; and the third day rose again accord-ing to the Scriptures; and ascended into heaven, and sitteth at the right hand of the Father; and shall come again with glory to judge the quick and the dead; of whose kingdom there shall be no end.

And we believe in the Holy Ghost, the Lord, the Giver of life, who proceedeth from the Father and the Son, who with the Father and the

Son together is worshipped and glorified, who spake by the prophets; in one holy catholic and apostolic Church. We confess one baptism for the remission of sins; we look for the resurrection of the dead, and the life of the world to come. Amen.

Minister. Praise ye the Lord.
Congregation. The Lord's name be praised.

Glory be to God on high, and on earth peace, good will toward men. We praise thee, we bless thee, we worship thee, we glorify thee, we give thanks to thee for thy great glory, O Lord God, heavenly King, God the Father Almighty.

O Lord, the only begotten Son, Jesus Christ; O Lord God, Lamb of God, Son of the Father, that takest away the sin of the world, have mercy upon us. Thou that takest away the sin of the world, have mercy upon us. Thou that takest away the sin of the world, receive our prayer. Thou that sittest at the right hand of God the Father, have mercy upon us.

For thou only art holy; thou only art the Lord; thou only, O Christ, with the Holy Ghost, art most high in the glory of God the Father. Amen.

Then shall the minister read the proper Gospel and Epistle for the day.

After the reading, the service shall proceed thus, the congregation rising:

M. Glory be to the Father, and to the Son, and to the Holy Ghost:

C. As it was in the beginning, is now, and ever shall be, world without end. Amen.

M. The Lord be with you.

C. And with thy spirit.

M. Let us pray.

Here shall be offered the collect for the day and the festival prayer.

A suitable psalm or hymn shall then be sung.
After this, the minister having taken his place in the pulpit, shall proceed to deliver a brief sermon. Or, instead of this, he may read a lesson of moderate length, taken from the Holy Gospels, on the history of Christ's passion and death.

Then shall follow a collection of the offerings of the people, to be devoted to the service of the poor, or to some benevolent purpose; during which the minister, standing at the altar, shall read some of the following sentences from the Holy Scriptures.

He which soweth sparingly shall reap also sparingly; and he which soweth bountifully shall reap also bountifully.

Every man according as he purposeth in his heart, so let him give; not grudgingly, or of necessity: for God loveth a cheerful giver. As it is written, he hath dispersed abroad; he hath given to the poor: his righteousness remaineth forever.

Charge them that are rich in this world, that they be not high-minded, nor trust in uncertain riches, but in the living God, who giveth us richly all things to enjoy; that they do good, that they be rich in good works, ready to distribute, willing to communicate; laying up in store for themselves a good foundation against the time to come, that they may lay hold on eternal life.

To do good and to communicate forget not: for with such sacrifices God is well pleased.

Whoso hath this world's good, and seeth his brother have need, and shutteth up his bowels of compassion from him, how dwelleth the love of God in him?

He that hath pity upon the poor lendeth unto the Lord; and that which he hath given will he pay him again.

I have shewed you all things, how that so laboring ye ought to support the weak, and to remember the words of the Lord Jesus, how he said, It is more blessed to give than to receive.

The collection shall be brought by the deacons, in a proper vessel provided for the purpose, to the minister; who shall then reverently place it upon the altar, as an oblation presented unto God.

After this, the minister shall uncover and expose to view the vessels containing the bread and wine for the use of the Holy Sacrament, and proceed as follows:

M. Let us pray.

Almighty and everlasting God, who by the blood of thy dear Son hast consecrated for us a new and living way into the holiest of all; cleanse our minds, we beseech thee, by the inspiration of thy Holy Spirit, that we, thy redeemed people, drawing near unto thee in these holy mysteries, with a true heart and undefiled conscience, in full assurance of faith, may offer unto thee an acceptable sacrifice in righteousness, and worthily magnify thy great and glorious name; through Jesus Christ our Lord. *Amen.*

Then shall the minister pronounce, slowly and solemnly, either the whole, or some part, of the following selection of passages from the Holy Scriptures.

Surely he hath borne our griefs, and carried our sorrows: yet we did esteem him stricken, smitten of God, and afflicted. But he was wounded for our transgressions, he was bruised for our iniquities: the chastisement of our peace was upon him; and with his stripes we are healed. All we like sheep have gone astray; we have turned every one to his own way; and the Lord hath laid on him the iniquity of us all.

In this was manifested the love of God toward us, because that God sent his only begotten Son into the world, that we might live through him. Herein is love, not that we loved God, but that he loved us, and sent his Son to be the propitiation for our sins.

Abide in me, and I in you. As the branch cannot bear fruit of itself, except it abide in the vine; no more can ye, except ye abide in me. I am the vine, ye are the branches: he that abideth in me, and I in him, the same bringeth forth much fruit: for without me ye can do nothing.

I am the living bread which came down from heaven. If any man eat of this bread, he shall live for ever: and the bread which I will give is my flesh, which I will give for the life of the world. The Jews therefore strove among themselves, saying, How can this man give us his flesh to eat? Then Jesus said unto him, Verily, verily, I say unto you, except ye eat the flesh of the Son of man, and drink his blood, ye have no life in you.

Whoso eateth my flesh, and drinketh my blood, hath eternal life; and I will raise him up at the last day. For my flesh is meat indeed, and my blood is drink indeed. He that eateth my flesh, and drinketh my blood, dwelleth in me, and I in him. As the living Father hath sent me, and I live by the Father: so he that eateth me, even he shall live by me. This is that bread which came down from heaven: not as your fathers did eat manna, and are dead: he that eateth of this bread shall live for ever.

Then, the whole congregation rising, the service shall proceed:

M. The Lord be with you.
C. And with thy spirit.

M. Lift up your hearts.
C. We lift them up unto the Lord.

M. Let us give thanks unto the Lord our God.
C. It is meet and right so to do.

It is very meet, right, and our bounden duty, that we should at all times, and in all places, give thanks unto thee, Lord God Almighty, Father, Son, and Holy Ghost.

Before the mountains were brought forth, or ever thou hadst formed the earth and the world, even from everlasting to everlasting, thou art God.

Thou didst in the beginning create all things for thyself. By thy word were the heavens made, and all the host of them by the breath of thy mouth. The armies of the invisible world, angels and archangels, thrones, dominions, principalities and powers; the glorious firmament on high, sun, moon and stars; the earth and the fullness thereof; all are the work of thy hands, and all are upheld by thee continually in their appointed order and course.

Thou also at the first didst make man in thine own image, and after thine own likeness, and didst set him over the works of thy hands, endowing him with the excellent gift of righteousness, and forming him for immortality. And when afterwards, through the fraud and malice of Satan, he fell by transgression from that first estate, thou didst not leave him still to perish utterly in his fall, but wast pleased to raise him up again and to restore him to the joyful hope of everlasting life, by the promise of redemption through Jesus Christ; who, being God of God, very God of very God, dwelling in the bosom of the Father with unspeakable blessedness from all eternity, at last, when the fullness of the time was come, came down from heaven, and became man, for us men and for our salvation.

For all thy mercies and favors, known to us and unknown, we give thee thanks. But most of all, we praise thee, the Father everlasting, for the gift of thine adorable, true, and only Son, our Saviour Jesus Christ, who by his appearing hath abolished death and brought life and immortality to light through the Gospel. We bless thee for his holy incarnation; for his life on earth; for his precious sufferings and death upon the cross; for his resurrection from the dead; and for his glorious ascension to thy right hand. We bless thee for the giving of the Holy Ghost; for the institution of the Church; for the means of grace; for the hope of everlasting life; and for the glory which shall be brought unto us at the coming, and in the kingdom, of thy dear Son.

Thee, mighty God, heavenly King, we magnify and praise. With patriarchs and prophets, apostles and martyrs; with the holy Church throughout all the world; with the heavenly Jerusalem, the joyful assembly and congregation of the first-born on high; with the innumerable company of angels round about thy throne, the heaven of heavens, and all the powers therein; we worship and adore thy glorious name, joining in the song of the Cherubim and Seraphim:

Here let the people join aloud in the Seraphic Hymn.

Holy, Holy, Holy, Lord God of Sabaoth; heaven and earth are full of the majesty of thy glory. Hosanna in the highest! Blessed is he that cometh in the name of the Lord. Hosanna in the highest!

Then the minister shall proceed:

The Lord Jesus, the same night in which he was betrayed [here he shall take some of the bread into his hands], took bread; and when he had given thanks, he brake it [here he shall break the bread], and said, Take, eat, this is my body which is broken for you; this do in remembrance of me.

After the same manner also [here he shall take the cup into his hands], he took the cup, when he had supped, saying, This cup is the New Testament in my blood; this do ye as often as ye drink it, in remembrance of me.

Let us pray.

Almighty God, our heavenly Father, send down, we beseech Thee, the powerful benediction of thy Holy Spirit upon these elements of bread and wine, that being set apart now from a common to a sacred and mystical use, they may exhibit and represent to us with true effect the Body and Blood of thy Son, Jesus Christ; so that in the use of them we may be made, through the power of the Holy Ghost, to partake really and truly of his blessed life, whereby only we can be saved from death, and raised to immortality at the last day. *Amen.*

And be pleased now, O most merciful Father, graciously to receive at our hands this memorial of the blessed sacrifice of thy Son; in union with which we here offer and present unto thee, O Lord, the reasonable sacrifice of our own persons; consecrating ourselves, on the altar of the gospel, in soul and body, property and life, to thy most blessed service and praise. Look upon us through the mediation of our great High Priest. Make us accepted in the Beloved; and let his name be as a pure and holy incense, through which all our worship may come up before thee, as the odor of a sweet smell, a sacrifice acceptable, well pleasing to God. *Amen.*

Remember in mercy, we beseech thee, thy Church militant throughout the whole earth. Let her ministers be clothed with righteousness, and her priests with salvation. Build up her desolations; restore her disorders; heal her divisions; and grant unto her prosperity, safety, unity and peace. *Amen.*

We commend unto thee especially this particular church and congregation, pastor, elders, deacons, and people, beseeching thee to accept their piety and faith, and to increase toward them thy heavenly grace, so that they may come behind in no gift, waiting for the coming of our Lord Jesus Christ. *Amen.*

We pray for all estates of men in Christian lands; for kings, princes, and governors, and for the people committed to their charge and care; especially for thy servant the President of the United States, and for all the rulers of this land and nation. Make us a righteous people, and give us power to serve thee in quietness and peace. *Amen.*

Vouchsafe unto us, we beseech thee, favorable weather, that the fruits of the earth may ripen and be gathered in for us in due season; and be pleased of thy great goodness to preserve us from war, pestilence, and famine. *Amen.*

Send forth thy light and thy truth unto the ends of the earth; cause the glorious gospel of thy grace to be proclaimed among all nations; and powerfully incline the hearts of men everywhere, that they may hear and obey the joyful sound. *Amen.*

Regard in tender compassion those among thy people, who are called to suffer heavy affliction, or sore temptation and trial of any kind: and be thou graciously nigh unto them with thy divine help, according to all their need. *Amen.*

Especially do we commend unto thee those departing this life. Let the arms of thy love be round about them in their last hour; defend them against the assaults of the devil; enable them joyfully to commit their spirits into thy hands; and so receive them to thy rest. *Amen.*

O God, the Father of our Lord Jesus Christ, of whom the whole family in heaven and earth is named; we rejoice before thee in the blessed communion of all thy saints, wherein thou givest us also to have part. We praise thee for the holy fellowship of patriarchs and prophets, apostles and martyrs, and the whole glorious company of the redeemed of all ages, who have died in the Lord, and now live with him for evermore. We give thanks unto thee for thy great grace and many gifts bestowed on those who have thus gone before us in the way of salvation, and by whom we are now compassed about, in our Christian course, as a cloud of witnesses looking down upon us from the heavenly world. Enable us to follow their faith, that we may enter at death into their joy; and so abide with them in rest and peace, till both they and we shall reach our common consummation of redemption and bliss in the glorious resurrection of the last day. *Amen.*

Here let the people join aloud in the Lord's Prayer.

Our Father who art in heaven, Hallowed be thy name. Thy kingdom come. Thy will be done in earth, as it is in heaven. Give us this day our daily bread. And forgive us our debts, as we forgive our debtors. And lead us not into temptation. But deliver us from evil. For thine is the kingdom, and the power, and the glory, for ever. Amen.

M. The peace of our Lord Jesus Christ be with you all.
C. Amen.

Here the Holy Communion shall take place. While a sacramental hymn is sung, the people shall present themselves in front of the altar, reverently and devoutly standing. The officiating minister shall first receive the Communion in both kinds himself, and administer the same to his assistants; and he shall then proceed with their help to administer it, first to the elders and deacons, and afterward to the people; distributing first the bread and then the cup.

Giving the bread, the minister shall say:

The bread which we break, is the communion of the body of Christ.

Giving the cup, the minister shall say:

The cup of blessing which we bless, is the communion of the blood of Christ.

After the people have communed in both kinds, the minister shall say:

May the Holy Communion of the body and blood of our Lord and Saviour Jesus Christ, keep and preserve you, each one, in body, soul, and spirit, unto everlasting life. *Amen.*

Depart in peace.

When all have communed, the minister shall say:

Let us pray.

Almighty and everlasting God, we give thee most hearty thanks for the great goodness thou has shown toward us at this time, in vouchsafing to feed us, through these holy mysteries, with the spiritual food of the most precious body and blood of thy Son our Saviour Jesus Christ; assuring us thereby, that we are very members incorporate in the mystical body of thy Son, and heirs through hope of thine everlasting kingdom, by the merits of his most blessed death and passion. And we most humbly beseech thee, O heavenly Father, so to assist us with thy grace, that we may continue in that holy fellowship, and do all such good works as thou hast prepared for us to walk in; through Jesus Christ our Lord, to whom, with thee and the Holy Ghost, be all honor and glory, world without end. *Amen.*

Then shall be said, or chanted, the Ambrosian Hymn (Te Deum laudamus), as follows:

M. We praise thee, O God:
C. We acknowledge thee to be the Lord.

M. All the earth doth worship thee, the Father everlasting.
C. To thee all angels cry aloud; the heavens and all the powers therein.

M. To thee cherubim and seraphim continually do cry:
C. Holy, Holy, Holy, Lord God of Sabaoth.

M. Heaven and earth are full of the majesty of thy glory.
C. The glorious company of the apostles praise thee.

M. The goodly fellowship of the prophets praise thee.
C. The noble army of martyrs praise thee.

M. The holy Church, throughout all the world, doth acknowledge thee,
C. The Father of an infinite majesty;

M. Thine adorable, true, and only Son;
C. Also, the Holy Ghost, the Comforter.

M. Thou art the King of glory, O Christ.
C. Thou art the everlasting Son of the Father.

M. When thou tookest upon thee to deliver man, thou didst humble thyself to be born of a Virgin.
C. When thou hadst overcome the sharpness of death, thou didst open the kingdom of heaven to all believers.

M. Thou sittest at the right hand of God, in the glory of the Father.

C. We believe that thou shalt come to be our Judge.

M. We therefore pray thee, help thy servants, whom thou hast re-deemed with thy precious blood.

C. Make them to be numbered with thy saints in glory everlasting.

M. O Lord, save thy people, and bless thy heritage.

C. Govern them, and lift them up forever.

M. Day by day we magnify thee;

C. And we worship thy name ever, world without end.

M. Vouchsafe, O Lord, to keep us this day without sin.

C. O Lord, have mercy upon us, have mercy upon us.

M. O Lord, let thy mercy be upon us, as our trust is in thee.

C. O Lord, in thee have I trusted; let me never be confounded.

After which the minister shall close the whole service with this Benediction.

The peace of God, which passeth all understanding, keep your hearts and minds in the knowledge and love of God, and of his Son Jesus Christ, our Lord: and the blessing of God Almighty, the Father, the Son, and the Holy Ghost, be amongst you, and remain with you always. *Amen.*

PART FOUR

✣

Heteronomous Authority and the

Autonomous Individual

JOHN WILLIAMSON NEVIN

Human Freedom

Editor's Introduction.

The words "autonomy," "heteronomy," and "theonomy" answer the question of the *nomos* or the law of life in three different ways: Autonomy asserts that man as the bearer of the universal reason is the source and measure of culture and religion — that he is his own law. Heteronomy asserts that man, being unable to act according to universal reason, must be subjected to a law, strange and superior to him. Theonomy asserts that the superior law is, at the same time, the innermost law of man himself, rooted in the divine ground which is man's own ground: the law of life transcends man, although it is, at the same time, his own.[1]

At the end of his first year at Marshall College, Nevin inherited the course in moral philosophy from Rauch, who had a manuscript on the subject almost ready for publication at the time of his death. Nevin, as his literary executor, handled the arrangements for the second edition of Rauch's *Psychology* in 1841. Apparently he did not feel that he could do the same for the manuscript on ethics, even though he probably built his own college course in ethics upon the Hegelian foundations of his predecessor. His own bent was primarily ethical, and it was this aspect of idealist philosophy that most interested him.

The essay that follows constitutes Nevin's best statement of the idealist philosophy as it was taught in the early days of Marshall College, to be set beside Rauch's *Psychology*. The basic concept of the inner reconciliation of moral freedom with objective law was worked out by Nevin in relation to the state and the family, as well as the Church, although he was most interested in the last. The essay was published early in 1848 in the *American Whig Review*. A briefeer statement, entitled "Faith, Freedom,

1. Paul Tillich, *The Protestant Era* (Chicago, 1948), 56, 57.

and Reverence," was delivered as a commencement address at the college, and published in *The Mercersburg Review*.[2]

All created life exists under two aspects and includes in itself what may be denominated a twofold form of being. In one view it is something individual and single, the particular revelation as such, by which, in any given case, it makes itself known in the actual world. In another view, it is a general, universal force, which lies back of all such revelation, and communicates to this its true significance and power. In this form it is an *Idea*, not an abstraction or notion simply, fabricated by the understanding to represent its own sense of a certain common character, belonging to a multitude of individual objects, but the inmost substantial nature of these objects themselves, which goes before them, in the order of existence, at least, if not in time, and finds its perpetual manifestation through their endlessly diversified forms. All life is at once Ideal and actual, and in this respect at once single and universal. It belongs to the very nature of the Idea (as a true subsistence and not a mere notion) to be without parts and without limits. It includes in itself the possibility, indeed, of distinction and self-limitation, but this possibility made real is nothing more nor less than the transition of the Idea over into the sphere of actual life. In itself it is boundless, universal, and always identical. It belongs to the very conception of the actual world, on the other hand, that it should exist by manifold distinction, and the resolution of the infinite and universal into the particular and finite. All life, we say then, is at one and the same time, as actual and Ideal, individual also, and general, something strictly single, and yet something absolutely universal.

These two forms of existence are opposite but not, of course, contradictory; their opposition involves, on the contrary, the most intimate and necessary union. The Ideal is not the actual, and the actual is not, as such, the Ideal; separately considered, each is the full negation of what is affirmed in the other, and still they cannot be held for one moment asunder. The Ideal can have no reality except in the form of the actual, and the actual can have no truth save as it is filled with the presence of the Ideal. Each subsists only by inseparable union with its opposite; each is indispensable to the other, as the complement of an existence that could otherwise have no force. The bond which unites them, accordingly, is not mechanical and outward merely. The life in which they meet is not

2. II(1850), 97–116.

to be regarded as, in any sense, two lives. The two forms of existence which it includes are at the same time the power of a single fact, in whose constitution they are perfectly joined together, in an inward way. The Ideal and the actual, the general and the particular, are both present in all life, not by juxtaposition or succession, but in such a way as to include each other at every point. The very same life is both general and particular at the same time — the Ideal in the actual, and the actual in the Ideal; and each is what it is always, only by having in itself the presence of the other, as that which it is not.

Take, for instance, the life of a particular plant or tree. Immediately considered, it is something single, answerable to the outward phenomenal form under which it is exhibited to the senses. But it is, at the same time, more also than this. It becomes a particular plant or tree, in fact, only as it is felt to be the revelation of a life more comprehensive than its own, a life that appears in all plants and trees, and yet is not to be regarded as springing from them, or as measured by them, in any respect. The general vegetable life is not simply the sum of the actual vegetation that is going forward in the world. It is before this in order of being, and can never be fully represented by its growth, for in its nature it has no bounds, while this last is always necessarily finite, made up of a definite number of individual existences. Still it is nothing apart from these existences, which serve to unfold its presence and power, and which, in doing so, and only in doing so, come also to be what they are in truth. The life of each particular tree is thus at once the universal vegetable life, in which all trees stand, and the single manifestation to which this life has come in that particular case. Abstract from it the invisible, Ideal, universal force or fact, which as mere particular tree it is not, but which belongs to it only in common with other trees, and you reduce its existence at once to a sheer nullity: an object absolutely *single* in the world could never be anything more than a spectral prodigy for the senses. So also, if it be attempted to sunder the particular from the general. Vegetable life can have no reality save as it shows itself through particular plants and trees. The claims of the particular here are just as valid and full as the claims of the general. We have no right to push either aside in order to make room for the other. The Ideal or general cannot subsist without the actual or particular, and it is equally impossible for this last to subsist without the first. They can subsist both, only in and by each other; and it is this mutual comprehension and inbeing of the two precisely, which gives life its proper realness and truth. The *real* is not the actual as such, nor the Ideal as such, but the actual and Ideal perfectly blended together, as the presence of the same fact.

The same order holds in the sphere of humanity. Every man comprehends in himself a life which is at once both single and general, the life of his own person, separately considered, and the life at the same time of the race to which he belongs. He is *a man;* the universal conception of humanity enters into him, as it enters also into all other men: while he is, besides, *this* or *that* man, as distinguished from all others by his particular position in the human world. Here again, too, as before, the relation between the general and the particular or single is not one of outward conjunction simply; as though the man were, in the first place, complete in and of himself, and were then brought to stand in certain connections with other men, previously complete in the same way. His completeness as an individual involves of itself his comprehension in a life more general than his own. The first can have no place apart from the second. The two forms of existence are not the same in themselves, but they are indissolubly joined together, as constituent elements of one and the same living fact in the person of every man.

All this belongs to our constitution, considered simply as a part of the general system of nature. But man is more than nature, though organically one with it as the basis of his being. His life roots itself in this sphere, only to ascend by means of it into one that is higher. It becomes complete at last in the form of self-conscious, self-active spirit. The general law of its existence, as regards the point here under consideration, remains the same — but with this vast difference, that what was mere blind necessity before, ruled by a force beyond itself, is now required to become the subject of free intelligence and will, in such way as to be its own law. It is as though the constitution of the world were made to wake within itself to a clear apprehension of its own nature, and had power at the same time to act forth its meaning by a purely spontaneous motion. Reason and will are concerned in the movement of the planet through its appointed orbit, in the growth of the plant, and in the activity of the animal; but in all these cases they are exerted from abroad, and not from within the objects themselves. The planet obeys a law which acts upon it irrespectively of all consent on its own part. So in the case of the plant: it grows by a life which is comprehended in itself, but in the midst of all it remains as dark as the stone that lies motionless by its side; its life is the power still of a foreign force, which it can neither apprehend nor control. The animal can feel, and is able also to move itself from place to place;

yet in all this, the darkness of nature continues unsurmounted as before. The intelligence which rules the animal is not its own, and it cannot be said to have any inward possession whatever of the contents of its own life. This consummation of the world's meaning is reached at last only in the mind of man, which becomes thus, for this very reason, the microcosm or mirror, that reflects back upon the whole inferior creation its true, intelligible image. Here life is no longer blind and unfree. The reason and will by which it is actuated are required to enter into it fully, and to become, by means of it, in such separate form, self-conscious and self-possessed. This is the idea of *personality*, as distinguished from the conception of a simply individual existence in the form of nature. Man finds his proper being at last only in such life of the spirit.

Personality, however, in this case, does not supersede the idea of individual natural existence. On the contrary, it requires this as its necessary ground and support. The natural is the perpetual basis still of the intellectual and moral. The general character of life, therefore, in the view of it which is before us at this time, is not overthrown by this exaltation, as has been already intimated, but is only advanced by it into higher and more significant force. It still continues to revolve as before, between the two opposite poles which we have found to enter into it from the start, and exhibits still to our contemplation the same dualistic aspect, resulting from the action of these forces, whose inseparable conjunction at the same time forms its only true and proper unity. It is still at once actual and Ideal, singular and universal; only now the union of these two forms of existence is brought to be more perfect and intimate than before, by the intense spiritual fusion to which all is subjected in the great fact of consciousness.

Consciousness is itself emphatically the apprehension of the particular and single, in the presence of the universal. The two forms of life flow together, in every act of thought or will. Personality is, by its very conception, the power of a strictly universal life, revealing itself through an individual existence as its necessary medium. The universal is not simply in the individual here blindly, as in the case of the lower world, but knows itself, also, and has possession of itself, in this form, so far, at least, as the man has come to be actually what he is required to be by his own constitution. The perfection of his nature is found just in this, that as an individual, inseparably linked in this respect to the world of nature, from whose bosom he springs, he shall yet recognize in himself the authority of reason, in its true universal character, and yield himself to it spontaneously as the proper form of his own being. Such clear recognition of the universal reason in himself, accompanied with such spontaneous assent to its authority, is that precisely, in the case of any human individual, which makes him to be at once rational and free. The person is necessarily individual; but in becoming personal, the individual life is itself made to transcend its own limits, and maintains its separate reality, only by merging itself completely in the universal life which it is called to represent.

Personality and moral freedom are, properly speaking, the same. By this last we are to understand simply the normal form of our general human life itself. As such, it is nothing more nor less than the full combination of its opposite poles, in a free way. In the sphere of nature this union is necessary and inevitable; in the human spirit, it can be accomplished only by intelligent, spontaneous action on the part of the spirit itself. The individual life in this form, with a full sense of its own individual nature, and with full power to cleave to this as a separate, independent interest, must yet, with clear consciousness and full choice, receive into itself the general life to which it of right belongs, so as to be filled with it and ruled by it at every point. Then we have a proper human existence.

Moral freedom, then, the only liberty that is truly entitled to the name, includes in itself two elements or factors, which need to be rightly understood, first in their separate character and then in their relation to each other, in order that this Idea itself may be rightly apprehended. It is the *single* will moving with self-conscious free activity in the orbit of the *general* will. The constituent powers by which it comes to exist are the sense of self on the one hand, and the sense of a moral universe on the other, the sense of independence, and the sense of authority or law. It is the perfect union of the single and the universal, the subjective and the objective, joined together as mutually necessary, though opposite, polar forces in the clear consciousness of the spirit.

Let us direct our attention now, for a moment, separately to each of these great constituents of freedom.

Freedom supposes, in the first place, entire *independence* on the part of its subject.

It can have no place, accordingly, as we have already seen, in the sphere of mere nature. God is free in upholding and carrying forward the world, in this form, according to its appointed laws, but the world itself is not free. Its activity is for itself altogether blind and necessary, accompanied with no self-apprehension, and including in itself no self-motion. It is actuated throughout by a foreign force, with no possible alternative but to obey, while yet its obedience carries in itself no light or love, no intelligence or will. Nature is held in slavish bondage to its own law, as a power impressed upon it perpetually from abroad, and in no sense the product of its separate life. The earth rolls round the sun, the sap mounts upward in the tree, the dog pursues its game, with like subordination to a force by which they are continually mastered, without the least power to master in return. Animal impulse and instinct are no better here than the plastic power that fashions the growth of the plant. There is individual existence in each case, included in the bosom of a general Ideal life, and comprising action powerfully turned in upon itself, but there is no independence: the subject of the action hangs always, with helpless necessity, on the action itself, and is borne passively along upon the vast objective stream of the world's life, without concurrence or resistance of its own.

It is only in the sphere of self-conscious spirit, then, that individual independence becomes possible. Hence it involves two things, the light of intelligence and the power of choice. Both of these, in their very nature, refer to an individual center, or *self*, from which their activity is made to radiate, and towards which, again, it is found continually to return. All knowledge begins and stands perpetually in the consciousness of self; and every act of the will may be denominated, at the same time, an act of self-apprehension.

It belongs to the conception of individual life universally that it should be in itself a center of the manifold activities by which it makes itself known. In the sphere of nature, this relation holds in the form only of a blind plastic law, or at least in the form of an equally blind instinct. In the sphere of consciousness, which is above nature, it is no longer blind, but clear. The subject is not simply an individual center, but knows and seeks itself under this character. In such form first, it attains to what we call subjective independence.

By means of intelligence, the individual self emerges out of the night of nature into the clear vision of its own existence, and is thus prepared to embrace itself as a separate living center. It is no longer an object merely as before, acted upon from abroad, but is constituted a *subject*, in the strict sense of this term, having possession of itself, and capable of self-action.

Mere intelligence, however, is not of itself independence. If a planet were endowed with the power of perceiving its own existence, without the least ability to modify it in the way of self-control, it is plain that it would be just as little independent as it is in its present state. Consciousness in absolute subjection to nature would be, indeed, a species of bondage that might be said to be even worse than that of nature itself. And so if the intelligence were ruled and actuated, not by nature but by some other intelligence in the like irresistible way, the result would be the same. No matter what the actuating force might be, if it were even the divine will itself which were thus introduced into the conscious life of the individual so as to carry this along with overwhelming necessity in its own direction, the subject thus wrought upon from abroad, without the power of self-impulse, could not be regarded as having the least independence. The case calls for something more than mere intelligence. To this must be joined also the power of choice.

The supposition, indeed, which has just been made, is in its own nature impossible. Reason and will necessarily involve each other, and the light of intelligence, therefore, can never be sundered in fact (but only hypothetically) from the motion of choice. Self-consciousness is itself always self-action.

Individual independence, we say, requires the power of choice — that the self-conscious subject shall not be moved simply from abroad, but have the capacity of moving itself, as though it were the original fountain of its own action. If the will be itself bound by a force which is foreign from its own nature, the man in whom it dwells cannot be free. It lies in the very conception of freedom that the subject of it should have power to choose his own action, and that this power should involve the possibility of his making a different choice from that which he is led to make in fact. He acts from himself, and for himself, and not in obedience merely to an extraneous power, whether in the sphere of nature or in the sphere of spirit. The action springs truly and fully out of his own conscious purpose and design, and is strictly the product of that separate living nature which he calls himself.

This is what Kant makes so much account of in his philosophy as the *autonomy* of the will. The idea is one of vast importance, notwithstanding the great abuse which has been made of it in his school. The will, in its very nature, must be autonomic in order that it may be free; that is, it must be a law to itself, in such sense that its activity shall be purely and strictly its own in opposition to the thought of everything like compulsion exerted upon it from abroad. It is a world within itself, no less magnificent than that with which it is surrounded in the external universe, and it may not be invaded by any form of power that is not comprehended from the beginning in its own constitution. All such power, proceeding from earth, or hell, or heaven, must be counted *heteronomic*, and contradictory to its nature. The will can endure no heteronomy. It must be autonomic, subjectively independent, the fountain of its own activity, wherever it is found in its true and proper exercise.

This then is the first grand constituent of Moral Freedom. The idea implies universally the presence of an individual will, which, *as such*, is perfectly unbound from all heteronomic extraneous restraints, and carries in itself the principle of its own action, in the way of law and impulse to itself. There can be no liberty where there is no subjective independence.

But such autonomic will is not of itself at once, as some appear to think, the *whole* conception of freedom. This requires another constituent factor, no less essential than the first, the presence, namely, of an objective universal *law*, by which the individual will is of right bound, and without obedience to which it can never be true to its own nature.

Self-consciousness is itself the power of a life that is general and universal as well as individual. All life we have already seen to be the union of these two forms of existence in fact; though in the sphere of nature, of course, the fact prevails only in an outward and blind way. With the light of intelligence, however, including in itself the force of self-apprehension and self-action, it must itself enter into the life of the subject under the same character. That is, the union of the general and individual must hold in the form of consciousness itself; so that the subject of this, in coming to know himself properly as an individual being, shall have at the same time the apprehension of a life more comprehensive than his own, and, indeed, truly universal, in the bosom of which his own is carried as the necessary condition of its existence. It is the complete sense of this, theoretically and practically felt, that gives us the fact of personality, which is just the consciousness of an individual life, in the form of reason and will, as the universal truth of the world's life. Reason cannot be something merely particular or private. It is universal in its very nature. It is so theoretically, and it is so, also, of course, practically. In entering the sphere of thought and will, then, as distinguished from that of mere nature, man comes into conscious union with a life which is more than his own, and which exists independently altogether of his particular knowledge or choice. He does not create it in any sense, but is simply received into it as a sea of existence already at hand, and altogether objective to himself as a separate single subject, while he knows it to be in truth, at the same time, the only proper form of his individual life itself subjectively considered.

If this were not the case, there could be no room, in his case, for the idea either of intelligence or freedom. A purely particular or single intelligence would be as blind as the stork, which knoweth, we are told, her appointed times in the heaven[Jer. 8:7]; and a purely particular or single will, in like manner, would be as little free as the wind, which is said to blow where it listeth, or as a wave of the sea driven of the same wind, and tossed hither and thither without object or rule. — Reason and will, to be truly subjective, must be apprehended always as truly objective, also, and universal. This necessity lies, as we have said, in the very idea of consciousness itself, and is the foundation of all personal life in the case of men.

But the idea now of such universal reason and will is itself the conception of law, in its deepest and most comprehensive sense. This is nothing more nor less than this boundless objective authority or necessity, in which the individual life of the human subject is required to enter freely that it may be complete.

The *law*, in this character, is of course an Idea, not an abstraction. It has in itself, accordingly, the two grand attributes of an Idea, universality and necessity.

Its universality is not simply this, that it represents collectively all individual wills, or objects of will. On the contrary, it excludes every sort of distinction and comparison. No individual will, as such, can enter into the constitution of the law. It is absolute, and one within itself, merely revealing its presence through the single wills into which it enters, without deriving from them at all its being and force.

So, again, its necessity is not simply this, that the world cannot be preserved in prosperity and order without it, or that the world itself may have been pleased to agree in establishing its authority as sacred. It is a necessity which is altogether unconditional, and which rests eternally and unchangeably in the nature of the law itself.

As thus universal and necessary, the being of the law is infinitely real. It is not simply the thought or conception of what is right, not a name merely or mental abstraction representing a certain order of life which men are required to observe; but it is the very forms of truth and right themselves, the absolutely independent power by which they exist in the world. As in the sphere of nature, the law is in no respect the product of the forces which are comprehended in nature itself, but forms rather the inmost life of its entire constitution, which could not consist at all if it were not held together by this bond; so here in the sphere of free intelligence also, it is by no other power that the order of life, as thus intelligent and free, can be upheld for a single hour. The world, in its moral no less than in its physical constitution, lives, moves and has its being only in the presence of the law, as a real existence in no sense dependent upon it for its character — not indeed as though it might be supposed to exist, with its own separate entity, in no connection with the actual world whatever. As the Ideal life of nature, it cannot be sundered from the actual manifestation in which this consists; and as the absolute truth and right of the moral universe, it cannot subsist except through the consciousness of the thinking and willing subjects of which this universe is composed. Abstracted from all subjective intelligence, its objective reality is reduced to a nullity. It is only in the form of reason and will, which have no being apart from self-consciousness, that the law can have any true subsistence whatever. It supposes an intelligible and intelligent universe. But still it is no creature of the universe, no mere image abstracted from its actual constitution. In the order of being, though not of time, it is older than the universe. Without reason and will there could be no law, and yet all reason and will stand in it from the very start, and can enter into no living subject whatever except from its presence, as their ulterior objective source and ground.

Concretely real in this way, and not simply an abstraction, the law has its seat primarily, as Hooker expresses it, in the bosom of God.[3] Not so, however, as if God might be supposed, in the exercise of any private arbitrary will of his own, to have devised and ordained it as a proper scheme after which to fashion the order of the universe. The universality of the law excludes, as we have already seen, the idea of all merely private or particular will, even though it were conceived to be in this form the will of God himself. God's will, however, is not private or particular but absolute — subjective, indeed, in such sense as is required by the nature of personality, but objective and universal at the same time; these two forms of existence, subjective and objective, being with him absolutely commensurate and identical. God is not the author of the law, as something standing out of himself and beyond himself; he does not *make* it, as a man might frame an instrument to serve some purpose which he has, under another form, in his own mind. Still less, of course, may the law be said in any sense to make *him*, as though it were a power before him in authority, determining the manner of his existence. It has its being only in God and from God, not, however, as something different from the divine

3. [ED.] Richard Hooker, *Laws of Ecclesiastical Polity*, Bk. I, III, [4].

mind itself. It is the necessary form of God's infinitely wise and holy will, as exercised in the creation and support of the actual universe, considered both as nature and spirit.

Thus resident primarily in the divine will, and identical with it throughout, the law, at the same time, in its objective character, passes over into the actual order of the world, and reveals itself here also as a power to be acknowledged and obeyed, under the most real and concrete form. In the sphere of nature the universal and singular are brought together, not directly and immediately, but through the medium of the particular, constituting what we denominate the species or kind, as distinguished from the genus. Thus the tree is not what it is by receiving into itself at once the universal vegetable life, but only as this life has previously undergone a distinction within itself, by which it may be recognized as vegetation under this or that specific form; it can become a tree only as it puts on at the same time the type of some particular tree, locust, for instance, or ash, or elm, so as to be known accordingly in this character and no other. And just so in the sphere of the moral world, where the law has to do with intelligence and will. As universal or Ideal, it is not carried over at once into the consciousness of each individual subject in an original and independent way; but the case requires necessarily that it should, in the first place, resolve itself into certain particular orders or forms of authority, through which intermediately its presence may afterwards thus actualize itself in full for the single will. As no single man is the human race, but only a part of it, having the truth of his being in the organic relations by which he is comprehended, through the family and state, in the whole, so the law, which is an objective rule and measure for the whole, and only for the parts as comprehended in this, and not as sundered from it, can never come near to any man in the way of an absolutely singular and exclusive revelation. It can reach him really, only by passing *through* the organic system, in which alone it takes cognizance at all of his existence. Under such view, it has an actual concrete being in the world itself, and is wrought objectively into the very constitution of its rational and moral life, as embodied in the form of human society and made to reveal itself continually in the process of human history.

Such, we say, is the conception in general of the law, which is the other grand factor or constituent of Moral Freedom; the first having exhibited itself to us before in the necessary independence or autonomy of the individual subject. It remains now to consider *how* these two great forces are joined together in its constitution.

Separately considered, they seem to oppose and overthrow each other. If the will be absolutely autonomic and independent in its subjective character, how can it be absolutely bound at the same time by a force that comes from beyond itself, the purely objective authority of law? And if it be thus bound, placed under necessity, comprehended in a power which is broader than itself and older than itself, how can it be said to be in any proper sense its own law, and the fountain of its own action?

It is clear that no merely mechanical union here can escape the power of this contradiction. If we suppose the single will to be, in the first place, something complete by itself, and then think of the law as existing in the same separate way, each including in itself the claims which belong to it, as they have now been described, the two conceptions must necessarily contradict each other, and cannot be brought in such form to any true reconciliation. If the subject feel himself in mere juxtaposition with the law, having it over against his consciousness as a form of existence different from his own, it will not be possible for him to assert his own independence without resenting and resisting the pretensions of the law at the same time, as a heteronomic, foreign force. Nor will it be possible for the law, in the same circumstances, to acknowledge or respect the independence of the human subject. It must necessarily assume the tone of command, arraying against him the majesty of its own everlasting nature, and with the weight of its terrible categoric imperative, *Thou shalt*, crushing his liberty completely to the earth. In such a relation there is no room for the idea of moral freedom. It is slavish in its very nature. The liberty which the subject may still pretend to assert for himself becomes necessarily licentiousness and sin, while on the other hand any obedience he may seem to yield to the law, as being thus forced and external, can have no reality or worth in the view of the law itself.

Such is the relation which holds in fact between human consciousness and the law in a state of sin. The two forms of existence are still incapable of being absolutely sundered, but they are bound together only in an outward, unfree way. The law cannot relax its right to rule the sinner's will, but it stands over him merely in the attitude of despotic commination. The sinner, too, can never emancipate himself entirely from the sense of the law, for that were to lose his hold upon himself at the same time; but he has it over against him only as an objective might, in whose favor he is required to renounce the separate self, which he has come to regard as his true and proper life. Hence continual rebellion only, and continual guilt.

The law, in such circumstances, has no power to bring light or freedom, strength or peace, into the soul. It is necessarily the ministration only of sin and death. Emphatically it works wrath.

In distinction from all such merely outward and mechanical conjunction of the two opposing forces, liberty and authority, from which can proceed at best only a powerless, unfree morality, the true idea of human freedom, we say now, requires their internal *organic* union as constituent elements of one and the same life. The opposition of the two forces, in this case, remains in its full strength; each is left in the possession of its separate independent character; neither is permitted to exclude or overwhelm the other, but the opposition is simply that which belongs to the contrary poles of the magnet, which fly asunder only that they may, at the same moment, be drawn together with the greater force, and whose union, as it is the result, is also the indispensable condition always of the separation out of which it grows. Such polar distinction enters, in fact, into the very idea of concrete existence. Where there is no distinction there can be no concretion, but only meaningless and powerless abstraction, or, at best, the ideal possibility of an existence which has not yet become real. Distinction, however, involves opposition, or the setting of one thing over against another. Only where this has taken place, then, is there any room for the union that all proper reality implies. But such union shows the two sides, thus sundered, to be at the same time necessary to each other. The opposition is polar only, and as such conservative and not destructional. All organized, concrete existence, physical or spiritual, will be found to carry in itself a polarity of this kind.

We may be assisted to a right apprehension of the point in hand by referring again to the constitution of life, as we have already found it to hold in the sphere of mere nature. The Ideal and the actual, a universal generic nature on the one hand and a particular single existence on the other, enter jointly into the constitution of every plant that springs from the bosom of the earth. These two forces, at the same time, are in their own character truly different and distinct. Their distinction takes the form of actual, direct opposition. What the one *is,* the other *is not.* Each is in itself the negation in full of the other. And yet they are here brought perfectly together, in the constitution of the same life, not by mechanical juxtaposition, but in the way of mutual interpenetration and interfusion, so that each is made to grow into the other, and by such concrescence only, comes to be at last what it is found to be in fact. The two sides of the plant's life still continue to be distinct, and their opposition to each other is by no means abolished in such sense as to be taken wholly out of the way; it still exists, but it exists as something comprehended in a higher action, which is at the same time the perfect union and reconciliation of the forces from which it springs. The opposition is polar. The union is organic.

Bring all this into the sphere of consciousness, so that the union in question shall be not blind and unavoidable but the movement of clear, spontaneous intelligence, acting from itself and for itself, and we have the conception of Moral Freedom. The existence here is not a mere object, wrought upon by an action strange to itself, but a subject which has come to be possessed of its activity as the very form of its own being. It is as though the planet, moving in its appointed orbit, were made to awake within itself to the clear knowledge of its own nature, with full power at the same time to pursue any course through the heavens that to itself might seem best, while it should still continue true notwithstanding, as before, to the path prescribed for it, no less *bound* by objective law but bound always only by its own consent. Should such a rational planet, in the exercise of its liberty, strike off from its orbit, affecting to play the part of some wandering comet, it must in the same moment become unfree — as much so, at least, as when carried forward in its true course by the force of mere blind natural law. Only the power of choice making it possible for it to become a comet, but yet spontaneously embracing the true planetary motion in fact, identified thus with the sense of law, could constitute it the subject of freedom. Neither as bound simply, nor as simply unbound, would the planet be free, but only as bound and unbound at the same time, and in the same continuous action — the two forms of existence joined together as the power of a single fact, in the sphere of consciousness, the law coming to its proper expression only in the independence of the subject, and the independence of the subject having no reality save under the form of obedience to the law.

What may thus be imagined in the case of a planet, to illustrate the conception in hand, is the very constitution of man in his normal state. He is formed for freedom, and becomes complete only in this character, by the possibility he carries in himself of such a living, conscious, free union, as has now been mentioned, of the great polar forces of the world's life. He has a will of his own, and he is at the same time under a law which is not himself; he is conscious of both, as making realities in his existence; and, to crown all, he is capable of so acknowledging both that they shall actually grow into each other as the same consciousness. The union of the two powers, in such case, is not mechanical but organic and real, as truly so as the flowing together of the Ideal and actual in the constitution of a plant or tree, only with the difference that what is blindly necessary there has become here the self-comprehending activity of the living nature itself. This is Freedom. In no other form can it exist for men at all. It is the action of the individual will, moving of its own accord and apart from all compulsion, in the orbit of the law, with clear sense of its authority, and clear private election in its favor, at the same time. This implies, of course, that the will is of the same nature with the law. They are thus related, in fact, as we have already seen. In obeying the law, the will obeys in reality its own true constitution, as much so as fire does, for instance, in exhibiting the properties which show it to *be* fire, and not water. So, in breaking away from the law, it necessarily becomes false to itself to the same extent. Thus all apparent contradiction is resolved in the idea of freedom as now described. Authority involves necessity, while liberty is the very opposite; and still both are here inseparably joined together, in such way, indeed, that neither can exist at all, in its true form, without the other. Freedom, in order that it may be free, *must* be bound. But in this case it is self-bound, not arbitrarily, however, to a rule of its own invention, which would be again to be unfree, but in obedience to the law, as the necessary form of its own existence. The will of the subject is ruled by a force that comes from beyond itself, and yet it is strictly autonomic at the same time; even as the rose blooms forth always its proper single life, though it is only as filled with the general law of vegetation that it has power to bloom at all. The law so enters the subject as to become within him a continually self-originated obligation, while his private will is so comprehended in the law as to find in it no foreign constraint whatever.

Such is the proper theory of human freedom, whether considered as religious or as simply political. It is formed by the union of liberty and authority, so joined together that neither is allowed to exclude or oppress the other; the two constituting thus the force of a single life. Where this inward organic conjunction of the elements now named is wanting, one of them either excluding the other altogether, or at best enduring its presence only in an outward way, the whole idea must be to the same extent necessarily overthrown. It matters not, in such case, which of the two factors may thus prevail at the cost of its opposite, the result will be the same. In the one direction, we shall have authority turned into despotism; in the other, liberty converted into licentiousness — both alike fatal to all true freedom. To be wholly bound, and to be wholly unbound, come here to the same thing in the end. Either state is to be deprecated as slavery.

The world has a continual tendency to fall over, either to one or the other of these extremes. Thus we have, on one side, authority coupled with blind obedience, and on the other a spirit of insurrection against all legitimate rule, making up to a great extent the history of human life. Our own age leans especially toward the extreme of exalting individual liberty at the expense of just authority. Time has been when the whole civilization of the world showed an opposite character. It was necessary, indeed, in the nature of the case, that the process of our modern culture, the fruit of Christianity, and the only culture that may be regarded as worthy of the name, should commence in this way. Its foundations were to be laid deep, in the first place, in the sense of law and a corresponding spirit of obedience to its authority. Long ages of discipline were required for this purpose, in the course of which it was hardly possible that wrong should not be done to the idea of freedom by an undue depression of its opposite element, the liberty of the individual subject. The discipline became, in fact, as we all know, tyrannical and oppressive just in this way, by refusing to recognize the rights of those who were subjected to it, as the time of their minority came to an end and made it proper that these rights should be brought into full and free exercise. Instead of making it their business to train their subjects for personal independence, the true design of all sound government, both Church and State pursued the policy only of repressing every aspiration in this direction, and sought to hold the world in perpetual vassalage to mere power on their own side, as though a parent, long accustomed to rule his children with absolute control, should at last insist on extending over their full adult life itself the same kind of rule, without any regard whatever to the wants and capabilities of their advanced state. The relation between authority and obedience became, in this manner, mechanical and altogether external. Free authority and obedience fell asunder, as though each belonged to a different sphere from the other. The authority claimed to be of divine force for itself, under a fixed outward form, while the merit of obedience was supposed to lie in its blind, uninquiring subjection to the will thus imposed upon it from abroad. In one word, the claims of the subjective were overwhelmed and well-nigh crushed by the towering pretensions of the objective. No wonder that this extreme should at length become insupportably onerous to the ripening consciousness of the Christian world. It opened the way gradually for a powerful reaction towards the opposite side. This gave birth finally, when the fullness of time had come, to the great fact of the Reformation, which may be regarded as a solemn *Decla-ration of Independence* on the part of the human mind against the tyranny by which it had been wronged for centuries, in the name of religion and law — a grand epoch, certainly, in the history of the world's life, whose consequences must continue to fill the earth to the end of time. These belong, of course, not simply to the Church in a separate view, but to every sphere, whether of thought or action, that is comprehended in our common human existence. Art, science, government, and social life all have been affected by the change. A new stadium is in progress for the universal life of the world, having for its object now the full assertion of what may be styled the subjective pole of freedom, in opposition to the long historical process that went before, in favor of its opposite side. Protestantism is the fountain thus of all modern liberty, religious and political alike. Its tendency has been, from the beginning, to break the chains of authority as previously established, and to engage the human mind to a bold vindication of its own rights in opposition to all blind obedience of whatever kind. Nor is it to be imagined at all that the new position which has been reached in this way can ever be surrendered again in favor of the order which prevailed before. The period of blind submission to the sense of the objective, whether in Church or State, when priest and king were held to be superior by divine right, to the divine constitution itself by which they were created, we may well trust, has forever passed away. But it does not follow at once from this that the past was all wrong, or that the present is all right. A just consideration of history would lead us rather to suppose that the new direction it has taken may itself be liable to abuse, in a way answerable to the wrong which existed before on the opposite side — which would not imply, certainly, that we must fall back again to the things we have happily left behind, but only that we should so far right our course as to steer clear of the rocks that threaten us from either side, and so press forward to the true and proper destiny of our race. That the principle of individual liberty has been, in fact, thus carried to an extreme, at least in some cases, in the progress of the Protestant era, is acknowledged on all sides; and it needs no very profound or extensive observation to see that our own age in particular is peculiarly exposed to danger just in this direction. It leans constitutionally towards an undue assertion of the prerogatives of the individual life, over against the idea of authority as something absolute and universal.

False liberty in this form does not consist, of course, in the open rejection of the law in itself considered. On the contrary, it usually affects to make great account of the law, but it is always only in a mechanical and outward way. The law is not viewed as a necessary constituent of freedom itself, but simply as an outward rule and measure of its supposed rights. The subject starts with his own independence as an interest full and complete in its separate character, and obeys the law accordingly in his way, not by entering it as a life beyond himself but by requiring it to come first into subjection to his own private will. He has no conception of freedom as the union of liberty and authority. It is for him, at last, the exercise only of separate personal independence on his own part. By the right of private judgment, he means to assert the right of thinking for himself, regardless of the thoughts of all other men; and so also in the case of private will. He does not deny, indeed, that truth and right are universal in their nature, and as such not to be created or controlled by his particular mind. But the authority which belongs to them in this view remains for him always more or less a mere abstraction. It does not come near to him under a concrete form in the actual constitution of the world with which he is surrounded. He is without reverence, accordingly, for the powers by which it is properly represented. He sees nothing divine in history. The Church is to him the mere aggregation of a certain amount of private thinking on the subject of religion. The State is taken to be the creature only of its own members, standing by their permission, and liable of right to be taken down by them, or changed into a new form, at their own good pleasure.

All this involves, of course, an immense error, though it is one which it must ever be difficult to bring home clearly to the consciousness of the popular mind. Liberty without law is licentiousness, whether in the sphere of thought or will; and law, to be real, must be the sense of a general concrete authority, actually comprehended in the constitution of the living world to which we belong. Where this may be wanting, it is not possible that there can be any true religious or political freedom. The exaltation of private independence, the rights of the individual, as they are called, at the cost of all proper objective authority, is just as fatal here as the exaltation of authority at the cost of individual rights. There is a vast amount of cant and falsehood abroad on this subject, which it is important we should understand, and against which we have need to stand continually upon our guard.

With any right conception of the nature of freedom as now explained, it will not be possible for us, on the other hand, to fall in with the views of those who would persuade us that the only remedy for the evils of a licentious individualism is to be found in casting ourselves once more blindly into the arms of mere outward authority. This were to fall backward to the period which preceded the Reformation, when we should seek rather to make our own period the means of advancing to one that may be superior to both. It is well to see and admit the difficulties of the present, but we are bound to remember also the difficulties of the past, that we may look for salvation only in the form of a brighter and more glorious future. It deserves to be continually borne in mind that mere authority is as little to be trusted for securing the right order of the world, as mere liberty. They are the opposite poles of freedom, and neither can be true to its constitution except as this is made to include both in a perfectly inward and free way. The evils incident to private judgment are not to be corrected by referring us to an infallible public judgment, ecclesiastical or political, that may do our thinking for us in every case, and then make it over to us in a merely outward way, without any activity on our own part. And just as little, of course, are the irregularities of private will to be reformed by handing us over to the rule of a foreign public will, as the measure of all right and wrong for our conscience. It is not in this way that Christianity, especially, proposes to make us free. The imagination of a mechanical system of notions and rules brought near to the mind from abroad, to be accepted by it in a blind way, on the ground of authority conceived to be divine, is wholly aside from the true character of the gospel. Christianity is indeed a law, but it is at the same time the "law of liberty," comprehending in itself the true normal mold of our general human life, into which it must be cast in every case in order that it may be complete, but into which it can be cast for this purpose only by its own consent and choice. In truth, no government can be rational and good in the case of men, that does not aim at making them able to govern themselves. The only proper use of government is to educate its subjects for freedom, if they have not yet come to be capable of its exercise; and if this be not proposed, the government becomes to the same extent tyrannical. He is an unfaithful parent who seeks to hold his children in perpetual dependence upon his own judgment, and in perpetual vassalage to his own will, instead of training them as quickly as possible to think and act for themselves. So neither the State nor the Church can have any right to bind the understanding and will of their subjects in slavish obedience to mere authority. The case demands a different relation between the two interests with which it is concerned. Though the authority should be never so benevolent and wise, and the subject of it never so well satisfied to be ruled by it in this way, the result would still be slavery and not freedom. No man can fulfill his true moral destiny by a simply blind and passive obedience to law. His obedience, to be complete, must be intelligent and spontaneous. In other words, the law must enter into him and become incorporated with his life. The remedy, then, for subjective license is not such an exhibition simply of outward authority as may supersede the necessity of private judgment altogether. Even an *infallible* authority in this form would not be desirable, for the divine will itself, if it were made merely to overwhelm the human as a foreign force, must lead to bondage only, and not to freedom.

The case requires, then, such an understanding of the true nature of freedom as may serve to secure its constitution on both sides. Mere theory, indeed, will not be sufficient, here or elsewhere, to preserve life in its right form, but it is at least a most important auxiliary to this object. It is much to know clearly, and still more, steadily to keep in mind, that liberty and law, the activity of private will and the restraining force of authority are alike indispensable to a right condition of human life, and they are required to enter into it always as polar forces, which organically complete each other, and that the exaltation of either interest at the cost of its opposite must prove alike fatal to true moral order. It is much to know that the idea of freedom can never be reached by simply opposing one of these powers to the other on either side, as though to insist upon authority were necessarily to wrong liberty, or as though to press the claims of this last required a rejection of the no less rightful pretensions of the first. That is at all times a very shallow philosophy, though it be unfortunately very common, which can see contradiction only in the polarity now mentioned, and is urged accordingly to affirm and deny with regard to it in such a way as to exclude the possibility of any reconciliation between the tendencies thus opposed. No authority can be moral that does not seek liberty as its end, and no liberty can be free that is not filled with the sense of authority as the proper contents of its own life.

That it may be difficult to bring this theory of freedom into practice is readily admitted, but this forms no proper argument against the truth and value of the theory itself. The difficulty lies in the nature of the subject to which it belongs. Still, however, there is no other way in which it is possible for the end to be secured that is here in view. Man must be at once independent and bound, self-governed and yet obedient to authority, in order that he may at all fulfill his own destiny, in distinction from the system of mere nature with which he is surrounded. For this he is to be educated and formed, under the influences which are comprehended in human society for the purpose. He comes not to moral freedom at once, but is required to rise to it by regular development out of the life of nature in which his existence starts, and in which it continues always to have its root. In our present circumstances, moreover, the process is greatly embarrassed and obstructed by a false law of sin, which is found too plainly seated in our constitution. It becomes accordingly a most complicated problem to bring our common human life, in this view, into its proper form — a problem whose solution in fact runs through the history of the world's entire social constitution, from the beginning of time to its end. The family, the State, and the Church are all comprehended alike in the service of this great design. They surround the human subject with the force of law from the cradle to the grave, and from the rudeness of savage life onwards through all stages of subsequent social refinement; but it is only that he may be educated for the full use finally of his own proper personal independence, in being set free from all bondage, whether objective or subjective, by the clear spontaneous union of his private will with the law to which it is necessarily bound.

It lies in the very conception of this vast educational process, including as it does not only all stages of the single life from infancy to old age, but all stages also of the general ethical life in the progress of nations, that the two great compound forces, by which the problem of freedom is in the course of being solved, should sustain to each other, in their legitimate action, a constantly fluctuating relation; the pressure of authority being necessarily greater, and the sense of independence less, in reverse proportion to the actual development of the true idea of freedom in the subject. Here, of course, a wide field is thrown open for the exercise of political and ethical science, in determining the claims of duty and right as related to each other in any given stadium of morality. On this, however, we are not called now to enter. It may be sufficient to conclude with the general rule, drawn from the whole subject, that no one can be true ethically to his own position, whether as a child or as a man, high or low, rich or poor, in power or out of power, who in the use of his liberty, whatever it may be, is not ruled at the same time by a sentiment of *reverence* for the idea of an objective authority extended over him in some form, in the actual social organization to which he belongs. To be without reverence for authority is to have always to the same extent the spirit of a slave. In no other element is it possible to think what is true, or to act what is right.

JOHN WILLIAMSON NEVIN

Theology within the Creed

Editor's introduction.

Nevin and Schaff were aware earlier than most American theologians of the challenge of "higher criticism" to the Protestant view of Scripture. Schaff had heard Baur at Tübingen, and both men were affected by Strauss' argument that the Gospels were the creation of the early Christian community and thus merely an element of uncertain ecclesiastical tradition.

Schaff reacted defensively, insisting like his mentor Hengstenberg on a high doctrine of inspiration [1] as a distinction of Scripture as against all later tradition. Nevin, by contrast, looked for help in much the same quarter as Grundtvig, the Danish theologian and embarrassed Biblicist who had made the "great discovery" of the Apostles' Creed as the normative declaration of the gospel, passed down the generations at baptism as the Church's living confession of faith. Quite independently, it would seem, Nevin made a similar discovery, and through the years the Creed played a distinctive role in his theology.

Nevin and Grundtvig alike distinguished the Creed from Scripture and from reflective doctrine. For Grundtvig it was the expression of living spirit in contrast to the dead letter. For Nevin the Creed was the direct spontaneous articulation of the realities of faith as felt in the consciousness of the community, "the sense of the New Creation in Christ Jesus." Christianity was to "stand in Christ, in the new world Christ creates," and say the Creed.[2] Such expression did not, as Schaff had held, rest upon Scripture. The Creed was older than Scripture, and independent of it.

1. See Theses 41 and 42, 129f., above.
2. "The Apostles' Creed," *The Mercersburg Review*, I (1849), 214.

The Grundtvigians attempted to buttress the authority of the Creed by tracing the text to the Apostles themselves, or even to the teaching of the risen Christ in the days before the Ascension — a speculation which exposed them to the mockery of Kierkegaard. Nevin was more critical and more profound. He derived the Creed rather from Peter's confession, "Thou art the Christ." As he saw it, confession of Jesus as Christ already implied the whole Trinity, which had been made explicit in the baptismal confession of the second century. The Creed had thus grown "organically" and was essentially the same in one article, in three, or in twelve, and indeed in the Nicene and Athanasian versions. The unity and consistency of the whole was not affected by some variation in the secondary articles. The internal organization of the Creed was dictated by the nature of the divine reality and was not subject to revision or improvement. From the birth of the Church to the end of history, the Creed would thus endure as the rule and frame of all sound theology.

The Reformers had honored the Creed in their confessions, catechisms, and liturgies, and had thought in this context. Such recognition, along with the recognition of real sacraments, was a mark of church consciousness in contrast to the sect mentality. To Nevin, in this connection, the prevailing neglect of the Creed in America appeared ominous.

The debate over the relative authority of Scripture and tradition was usually falsely stated, in Nevin's opinion. He never denied the crucial importance of Scripture. What he denied was the general assumption of his ultra-Protestant opponents that it was possible to approach the Scriptures without presuppositions. The real choice, as he saw it, lay between private and irresponsible interpretation of Scripture and interpretation in the context of the believing community, or, in other words, as guided by the Creed. Thus stated, it was another form of the reconciliation of the heteronomous authority and the autonomous individual, a resolution which, Nevin believed, must do justice to both terms. Conscience must never be constrained, but the tradition and authority of the Church must be reverenced.

The debate also involved divergent views of revelation, faith, and reason. Most of Nevin's opponents, including his old college classmate, Professor Proudfit of Rutgers, held a view of revelation as a body of "truth received on testimony" — propositions whose authority was external. Thus the authority of Scripture was demonstrated by various arguments based on such things as miracles or the fulfillment of prophecy, which were regarded as convincing to the natural reason. For Nevin this contention was a form of rationalism, equivalent to the ultramontane arguments for papalism.[3] For him the content of revelation was no body of propositions, but God, his "being, and presence, and glory." [4] A revelation demonstrated by rational arguments was not revelation. "Jesus Christ authenticates himself." [5] Faith was less an assent to propositions and arguments than it was a recognition, analogous to sense experience, of the divine reality. The motto on the cover of *The Mercersburg Review* came from Anselm: "*Neque enim quaero intelligere ut credam, sed credo ut intelligam* [For I do not seek to know that I may believe, but I believe that I may understand]."

The selection below is the conclusion of a three-part article, "The Apostles' Creed," from the first volume (1849) of *The Mercersburg Review*. Among the rebuttals were one in the Congregationalist *Puritan Recorder*, and another by Professor Proudfit of the Reformed Dutch Church in the *Princeton Review*. Nevin replied to both in *The Mercersburg Review*. He returned to the subject of the Creed repeatedly thereafter, notably in "Thoughts on the Church" [6] and in the "Answer to Professor Dorner." [7]

❖   ❖   ❖   ❖

1. The Creed does not spring from the Bible. This is plain from its history. Its main substance was in use before the New Testament was formed. Peter's confession, "Thou art the Christ, the Son of the living God," had no such origin. It was produced from the living sense of Christ's presence itself. And so, we may say, the whole Creed which lies involved in that confession is derived through faith out of the same living ground. It is, of course, in harmony with the Bible, for it has to do immediately with its central revelation, the mystery of the Word made flesh. It comes not, however, circuitously, in the way of reflection and study, through its pages. The early Church got it not from the Bible but from the fact of Christianity itself, which must be allowed to be in its own nature older even and deeper than its own record under this form. Strange that there should be any confusion in regard to what is in itself so palpable and clear. The Bible is not the *principle* of Christianity, nor yet the *rock* on which the Church is built. It never claims this character, and it can be no better than idolatry and superstition to worship it in any such

---

3. See below, 324f.   4. "The Apostles' Creed," *loc. cit.*
5. See above, 117.   6. *The Mercersburg Review*, X (1858).
7. *Ibid.*, XX (1868).

view — as much so as though the same worship were directed towards a crucifix or the Roman mass. The one only principle of Christianity, the true and proper function of its being, is the person of Christ; not any written account or notion of his person, but the actual living revelation of it, as a fact in the history of the world. The Church rests immediately on this foundation, and no other. The Bible is of force only as it proclaims this revelation. In such view it is of indispensable account for the preservation and advancement of the Christian life; it is the divinely constituted rule by which, through all ages, it must be measured and led. But still it is not this life itself; its relation to it is, after all, that of a condition, rather than that of a ground; and we are bound to see in Christianity always the presence of the Word under another form, as the true substratum at last of all its glorious power in the world. It is a fact, independently of the Bible and before it, which, as such, has a right to challenge our faith, whether we can show the Bible to be inspired or not. Indeed our ability to show the Bible inspired must ever turn on our ability to prove in the first place the reality of the revelation. So in all our systems of divinity we begin not with the inspiration of the sacred volume, as though this could be established in any wholly *ab extra* way, but with the truth of Christianity itself; feeling well assured that without this, it must be worse than idle to think of bringing the other question to any satisfactory issue. But what is this else than an acknowledgment that the Bible is not the principle of Christianity, but that this has its being in the world under another form, which is no less divine than the Scriptures themselves. Christianity is not only a written word, but a new creation in the form of life, starting from its founder Jesus Christ. In this last view, it *must* have, if it be what it claims to be, a real historical substance, which we are bound to respect as divine, no less than the Bible itself. There is not merely room thus, but an absolute necessity, for what may be styled a true Christian *tradition* in the Church, not as something against the Bible or foreign from it, but still not as a mere derivation either or efflux simply from its pages; a tradition which starts from the original substance of Christianity itself, as it underlies the Bible, and which in such form becomes the living stream into which continuously the sense of the Bible is poured, through the Holy Ghost, from age to age, onward to the end of the world. This divine tradition meets us under its clearest, most primitive, and most authoritative character, in the Apostles' Creed.

II. The idea of the Creed, as now given, throws light on the true character of the Church, as related to Christ in one direction and to the Bible in another. The Creed represents the primary substance of Christianity, as it has passed over from Christ in the form of life, into the general consciousness of his people. This general life is the Church. It is, of course, a divine fact in the world, and so of right an article of faith more immediately than the Bible itself. First the Church, and then the Bible. So in the Creed: "I believe in the holy catholic Church," instead of: "I believe in the Holy Inspired Bible"; not certainly to put any dishonor on this last, but to lay rather a solid foundation for its dignity and authority in the other article; for, after all, it is the Church, next to Christ, and not the Bible, save as comprehended in the Church, which according to St. Paul is "the pillar and ground of the truth" [1 Tim. 3:15]. Is this to throw Christ into the shade, as the opposers of the Church sometimes pretend? Just as little, we reply, as faith in the divine authority of the Bible tends to throw him into the shade. The Church *may* be so magnified as to wrong Christ, but it is just as possible, and at this time also just as common, to magnify the Bible in a like bad way, at Christ's expense; as where men, for instance, insist on sundering it from the objective fact of Christianity itself, the life of Christ in the Church, and force it to become instead the vehicle only of their own private judgment and proud self-will. Neither the Church, however, nor the Bible, can be held responsible for any such abuse. In their own nature, they do homage perpetually to Christ. The Church is but the living revelation of his presence and power, from age to age, in the world. The Bible is his written word. In this view, both are required to go together. Christianity is the proper union of both. Neither can fulfill its mission apart from the other. The Church, to be true to her vocation, must be ruled by the Bible; if any pretend to follow her voice without regard to this, they will be led astray. But the converse of this is no less certain. The Bible, to be a true word of Christ, must be ruled by the life of the Church; if any pretend to follow it without regard to this, they too will most assuredly miss the truth. Will it be said that this is a circle? Be it so. In such circle, precisely, is it the divine prerogative of faith at all times firmly and serenely to move.

III. Christianity, as such a divine fact in the consciousness of the Church, is historical. The idea of history is opposed both to dead tradition and to dead change. It moves; it lives; it grows. So the Creed originally came to pass. In its very conception, thus, it makes room for a continuous historical evolution of the Christian life on all sides. To take it as the end of all Christianity is to mistake its nature entirely. It is only the form in which it begins. Christianity must be far more than such beginning. Its mission is not merely to cover the earth with its outward presence, but to occupy and rule inwardly also the universal being of man. It must regenerate the thinking of the world and all its action; it carries in itself, accordingly, the possibility of becoming such a reconstruction or intensification of our universal life, from the start. The substance, then, which it exhibits primitively in the Creed, is by no means bound to that, either as a rigid shell or loose drapery, but widens itself continually, in the way of historical concrete growth, and unfolds its inward wealth in forms as manifold as the complex fact of humanity itself. So in particular it admits and requires a progressive theology; for why should not Christianity occupy our nature in the form of science as well as in the form of action or feeling? Theology implies doctrines. These come, for the understanding, by gradual process. Hence each single doctrine has its history, and theology is historical as a whole. The history in this case is not something outward only, but enters into the very substance of the Christian fact itself, so that in any right view of the case it is just as necessary for theology to be historical as it is for it to be biblical. History is one of the factors by which it is brought to pass and made to have in itself a real existence. True faith in the Creed, then, does not require us to renounce all interest in theology, and fall back on the primary Christian consciousness as the *ne plus ultra* of the new creation; on the contrary, it is just what we need to overthrow the idea of all such stability, and fit us for the right appreciation of theology as a continuously progressive science. To have faith in the Church is to have faith at the same time in history. The spirit of the Creed is not radical. It is the spirit of sect, ever violent and abrupt by its very constitution, that seeks to nullify the whole Christian process since the days of the Apostles. To a mind in sympathy with the Creed, that process is ever something sacred and divine, no less, we may say, than the primitive faith itself.

IV. With such historical character, all true theology at the same time grows forth from the Creed and so remains bound to it perpetually as its necessary radix or root. History is not progress in the way of outward local remove from one point to another, but progress that carries the sense with which it is freighted onward and upwards always into new forms. It resembles the growth of a tree or the gradual evolution of our individual human life. It is a river which carries itself forward with its own flow, ever changing and yet ever the same. The relation of the Creed, then, to the forms of sound Christian doctrine which have since appeared, is simply this, that they are to be regarded as lying silently involved in it from the beginning, though some time was needed to bring them to clear and distinct utterance. The great articles of Christian theology come from the Bible, but at the same time they are *mediated* or brought to pass for the mind of the Church only through the presence and power of the primitive Christian consciousness (expressed in the Creed), as something already at hand. It is no defect in the Creed that it contains not several most important and necessary articles of a sound theology as the Church now stands — the inspiration of the Scriptures, for instance, or the doctrine of justification by faith. On the other hand, however, such articles lose no credit or authority whatever by the fact of such omission. The only question is, do they flow from the substance of Christianity as given in the Creed, and do they hold in it and from it perpetually as their vital root? This, after all, is complete, under its own form, as an utterance of the primary *fact* of Christianity, and it only follows that other articles have their truth and importance, not in the same primary way, but all the more surely, for this very reason, in the way of derivation and outflow from what goes before. We reach thus this great practical conclusion, that the orthodoxy of every doctrine is fairly tested at last by its inward correspondence or want of correspondence with the Creed. It is not enough that it seems to be biblical from some other standpoint; its biblicity must be evident, as seen *through* the fundamental substance of Christianity embodied in this universal faith of the holy catholic Church. It is not enough that a doctrine be sound in form; if it refuse, notwithstanding, to coalesce inwardly with the spirit of the Creed, it convicts itself of substantial falsehood. Take in illustration the article of justification by faith, Luther's criterion of a standing or falling Church. It is not sufficient, surely, that it be accepted in a merely general and abstract way. Our sects, United Brethren, Albright Brethren, Winebrennerians, and a score of others to the same general tune, readily meet for the most part on this ground, one trying to outdo another in its zeal for this particular side of religion. And yet Luther would have denounced the whole of them as a worse plague than the locusts of Pharaoh. Do we ask, why? With Luther, the article had firm and fast root in the Creed, the historical substance of the old catholic Christian life; whereas, with these upstart sects, it is a mere abstraction or fancy, which makes no account of the old catholic faith whatever, and so proves itself to be the growth of some other soil, the product simply of the human brain. These sects have no sympathy with the Creed; they do not stand in it with their inward life; their theology starts not out of it at all, as its primitive ground. *Thus* held, the article of justification by faith ceases to be true, and is no longer safe but full of peril for all the interests of religion. So would all the Reformers say, with one voice.

v. Regard for the Creed, then, may be taken as a fair measure of sound Church character, as distinguished from the spirit of sect and schism. In its whole conception and life the Creed is catholic, inwardly bound to the true universal power of the Christian life as it stood in the beginning. Hence it will be found invariably that the sect spirit, whose essential nature it is to be abrupt, violent, unhistorical, and upstart, leads, if not openly, at least quietly, always to the abandonment of the venerable symbol altogether. Sect piety has no relish for the Creed; it cannot utter itself naturally in any such way; it makes no account, in truth, of Christianity in that form. The genius of Puritanism, as we have already seen, is also strikingly at variance with the same rule. The fact admits no doubt. It stares upon us in the almost universal neglect into which the Creed has fallen wherever Puritanism prevails. It will not do to say that this neglect is more apparent than real, and that the substance of the Creed is still in honor, though not its particular form. The difficulty is precisely that the form is such as will not easily allow another substance to be put into it than that which belongs to it in truth; on which account the use of it is felt to be uncongenial with the true life of Puritanism, as something which is, in fact, not inwardly harmonious with the life of the ancient Church. Hence such use in this case can never be easy, natural and free, but produces always some sense of awkward and stiff constraint. Puritanism must wrest the Creed into quite a different sense from its own original meaning to be able at all to acquiesce in its several articles. Left to itself, it would fall on a very different scheme of fundamental and necessary truth. It can see no reason why the Creed carries just its present form, or why so much should be left out of it that Puritanism is apt to think of first, in its own abstract way. The orthodoxy of New England, for instance, can hardly be said at all to grow forth organically from the primitive mind or consciousness of the Church as embodied in this symbol. Is not this strange and startling fact entitled to some consideration? We are firmly persuaded that it will be felt to be solemnly significant in proportion exactly as it is made the subject of earnest thought. An orthodoxy which owns no inward fellowship with the Creed, and which feels itself complete in a wholly different way without it, deserves to be regarded with distrust, and may well be asked to give a reason of the hope that is in it under such abstract and unhistorical form. We are free to confess that in our view any scheme of Christianity to which the voice of the Creed has become thus strange, labors under a most serious defect; and we need no other proof than the general fact here noticed, to show what is shown by so many proofs besides, that Puritanism, with all its great excellencies and merits, involves a material falling away from the faith of the sixteenth century as well as from that of the early Church.

vi. For the settlement of our existing theological and ecclesiastical difficulties, the first and most indispensable necessity is a true and hearty inward submission to the authority of the Creed, according to its original intention and design. Not that this is to be taken as of itself the sum and end of all theology; but all sound doctrine and true Church life must proceed forth from a common faith here, as their only sure ground, and it is vain to dream of their being prosperously advanced in any other way. It is mere loss of time, for instance, to argue the question of election, or that of infant baptism, with those who are not imbued in the first place with a true reverence for the Apostles' Creed. It is, in truth, of very little consequence in such case whether it be the affirmative or the negative of any such question that is maintained; as growing forth organically, not from the primary substance of the Christian faith at all, but from some other ground altogether, the opinion whether right or wrong in its notional and formal character, is sure to be in its inward material constitution, unchristian and wrong. So, as we have just seen, the doctrine of justification itself, in its right outward shape, may become, through such divorce from the life of the Creed, in the highest degree false and dangerous. Election, the Atonement, imputation, &c., can have no validity as Christian doctrines in an abstract view, but only as they can be developed from the concrete mystery here apprehended by faith. Theology in any other form is always necessarily rationalistic, an effort to build faith on intellection, whereas the true order is just the reverse. This, rightly understood and felt, would at once greatly narrow the field of theological controversy, as well as greatly facilitate the proper conclusion of its cardinal debates. How much, especially of our modern disputation, our *sect-fights*, we may say, generally, would be found by this rule to be little better than mere *skiomachy*, the battling of phantom shapes projected on the air. The first condition of all sound theology is active sympathy with historical Christianity, with the idea of the Church, with the catholic mystery of the Creed. So also as regards all Church questions; we do but run ourselves into endless talk if we propose to settle them from any other ground, or in any other frame of mind. For instance, the question of using or not using a settled liturgy in public worship: how much of the argument on both sides do we not find proceeding under a wholly different, and therefore wholly unsatisfactory form? The interest is vindicated or opposed on purely outward grounds instead of being referred, as it should be, first of all to the interior demands of Christianity itself, as embodied in the Creed. Or take the question of episcopacy. It has been much the fashion to place it all round, on such *ab extra* proofs and reasons, as though the point were to make out a simply external warrant for or against it, independently altogether of the contents of the Christian life itself. Thus Episcopalians often try to find it outwardly prescribed in the New Testament — a vain and hopeless task which only serves to countenance the equally vain and fruitless attempt, on the other side, to overthrow it in the same mechanical way. To make episcopacy the necessary hedge of Christianity, which we are to be sure of first on outside reasons, whether biblical or historical, in order that we may then be sure of the enclosed truth, is just again to subordinate faith rationalistically to the lower authority of the understanding; for how can such a purely outward and mechanical authority be a whit better at last, than any other form of thought and will which is not ruled by the very substance of the truth itself? Who may not see that if episcopacy be indeed the *first* thing towards a sound faith, it ought to come first also in the Creed, or at least to follow immediately the general article of the Holy Ghost? Whereas in truth, as we all know, it has no place in the Creed whatever. Are we then at once to infer from this, on the other hand, that episcopacy is false, or that no definite organization is required as the normal form of the Church? By no means. Only this is not the way in which the question can ever be settled. What we need for that, especially just now, is a general hearty return to the catholic life of the Creed, as the necessary point of departure for coming to a true solution of all our church questions. This we firmly believe is something that *can* take place extensively, long before we are able to see at all to the *end* of the perplexing difficulties with which we are now surrounded; and that *must* take place, indeed, before a single step can be successfully made towards their proper practical resolution. It is the idea of the Church, the mystery of Christianity as it is made sure to us by faith in the Apostles' Creed, something older certainly, and deeper in its own nature, than any mere outward hedge surrounding it, which we are bound first of all to embrace, which alone is sufficient to draw after it any right theory or practice, as regards all other church interests, and which therefore we have it in our power to begin with, as an *a priori* foundation for reaching in the end the results that the case requires. A convention of sects to negotiate a federal Church is much like a convention of the blind to settle the laws of light. We must be in the Creed, and so have faith in the Church, in order to find it, or settle its exact form and limits. This is the true method for bringing to an issue the sacramental question, the liturgical question, the question of festival days. An active revival of the consciousness expressed in the Creed would in due time restore all these great interests to their pristine authority. And we will just add, in the way of friendly hint to Episcopalians, that if their favorite system of church polity *could* be vindicated as necessary, in this way, to the conservation of the great catholic ideas that enter into the primitive faith, it would be, in our estimation, an argument of more weight and force in its favor than whole tomes of learning employed to establish its authority in an outward and abstract view.

III

JOHN WILLIAMSON NEVIN

Ultramontanism: Brownson's Quarterly Review

Editor's introduction.

There is a certain similarity in the careers of Nevin and Orestes Brownson, which may say something about the spiritual situation in the 1840's. The two men, both of "Puritan" nurture, each experienced a "churchly" conversion in middle life, and within the same year. Brownson became a Roman Catholic and the self-elected intellectual spokesman of that tradition in America. The gathered prelates of the Baltimore Council of 1849 seemed to concur with this assessment and gave him an unprecedented testimonial.

Brownson had followed with interest the developments at Mercersburg, and announced at the beginning of 1847 that he would discuss the movement in his *Review*. Schaff at once wrote urging him to wait until he had read *The Mystical Presence* and *What is Church History?* Later that year Nevin published what amounted to an indirect criticism of Brownson when he translated Gerlach's article on the "Infallibility of the Church" from the June *Evangelische Kirchenzeitung* for *The Weekly Messenger* (October 6, November 3, 1847). In this article Gerlach had defended "evangelical catholicity" against the ultramontanism of Goerres' *Historisch-politischen Blätter*, while maintaining common ground with Roman Catholicism against rationalist attack. The Mercersburg men wished to hold a comparable position in America, where Brownson was the most conspicuous and articulate ultramontane.

Something over a year later, Nevin challenged Brownson to produce his promised critique and took the offensive himself with "Brownson's Quarterly Review," which appeared in January 1850. Nevin had already described Brownson's advocacy of blind obedience as "immoral and irra-

318

tional." [1] He now declared that Brownson had simply rebounded from his earlier rationalistic autonomy to the opposite extreme of authoritarianism, without ever beginning to wrestle with the inner reconciliation of the two principles. Now that he had adopted a servile attitude to the hierarchy and asserted the personal infallibility of the pope, he was ready to "swallow a camel."

Nevin expressed admiration for Brownson's courage and vigor, but found his theology singularly unconvincing. He doubted whether Roman Catholicism, "rightly understood," involved so mechanical a view of infallibility as Brownson and the American episcopate supposed. He preferred to think that even in Roman Catholicism infallibility belonged to the ministry as a whole, of which the pope under certain circumstance might be the voice. Möhler's interpretation of Catholicism seemed far more persuasive and formidable than Brownson's ultramontanism. Nevin had to concede, however, that the first encyclical of Pius IX had made quite explicit claims of papal infallibility.

Brownson had also attacked the theory of historical development advocated by Newman and by Schaff. Such a view he found proper enough in a Protestant heretic like Schaff, but in Newman it amounted to a betrayal of Catholicism. The Roman Church, as Brownson pictured its history, had sprung into existence full grown and armed "as Minerva from the head of Jupiter." [2]

Nevin's essay ranged over a number of major issues: the relation of faith to reason, of the supernatural to the natural, of ecclesiastical authority to personal freedom. He argued strongly that Brownson's ultramontanism, like the rationalist supernaturalism on which he himself had been brought up at Princeton, was ultimately a form of rationalism. The whole apologetic tradition of "Christian evidences," he said, should be recast; "Christ authenticates himself."

Nevin broke off the dialogue after a second exchange, feeling already, apparently, the onset of the psychic enervation which was to disable him for a time. At any rate, the argument was already substantially complete.

The course of reasoning which . . . underlies Mr. Brownson's whole faith in Romanism,[3] and to which we are continually referred as the ulti-

1. "Reply to Berg," *The Weekly Messenger*, March 29, 1848.
2. *The Mercersburg Review*, II (1850), 47.
3. "We had already convinced ourselves of the insufficiency of naturalism, rationalism, and transcendentalism; we had also convinced ourselves of the necessity of divine

mate argument in his manifold debates with Protestantism, may be reduced briefly to the following statement: [4]

I. Christianity is a revelation made to men by God through his Son,
Jesus Christ, in other words, "the truth which Jesus Christ taught or revealed." As such it belongs, at least in part, to the *supernatural* order,
transcends nature, comes from beyond the limits of human knowledge. It
is something superadded to nature. "Grace, though having the same
origin, is above the order of creation, is not included in it, nor promised
by it. It is, so to speak, an excess of the divine fullness not exhausted in
creation, but reserved to be superadded to it according to the divine will
and pleasure." In this form it is indispensably necessary for our salvation,
but can be apprehended only by faith, whose vocation and prerogative it
is, as distinguished from science, thus to make us sure of what transcends
sense and reason. The object of faith here must be the very truth itself of
this supernatural revelation, and not something else in its stead. The problem of our salvation requires that the supernatural, as revealed by Christ
and transcending our knowledge, should be appropriated to our minds
notwithstanding in the way of faith or sure belief, so as to act upon us
with the reality which belongs to it in its own sphere.

II. "Faith, as distinguished from knowledge and science, rests on authority extrinsic both to the believer and to the matter believed." Knowledge is intuitive, finds its motives of assent in the subject or person knowing. Science is discursive, finds its motives of assent in the object or thing
known. "But in belief I must go out of myself, and also out of the object,
for my motives of assent." It rests on *testimony*. All turns then, of course,
on the authority or credibility of the witness, extrinsically considered.
The supernatural cannot be attested or made sure in this way by any
merely natural witness, but only by supernatural authority, that is, by
God himself. Nothing less than divine testimony can be a sufficient
ground for faith in what transcends nature. This, however, we may rationally trust in such case, if we have it, "because enough is clearly seen

---

revelation and of the fact that the Christian revelation was such a revelation. From this,
by a process of reasoning which may be seen in the first article of this number, we
arrived infallibly at the Catholic Church. The process is simple and easy. It requires
no metaphysical subtlety, no long train of metaphysical reasoning. All it needs is
good common sense, a reverent spirit, and a disposition to believe on sufficient evidence." April 1845, 262.

4. [ED.] The résumé that follows is based on a number of essays from *Brownson's
Quarterly Review*. The citations, admittedly somewhat casual, have been left as
Nevin gave them, save that they have been shifted from the text to the foot of the
page. A note promising a future discussion of two tracts of John Owen has been
omitted.

of God from the creation of the world, and understood by the things that are made, to establish on a scientific basis the fact that he can neither deceive nor be deceived; for we can *demonstrate scientifically*, from principles furnished by the light of natural reason, that God is infinitely wise and good, and no being infinitely wise and good can deceive or be deceived." But now to place our faith in contact truly with the authority of God, in the case of a divine revelation, the fact of the revelation must be authenticated to us by a competent witness, and also the true sense of it made certain in intelligible propositions; for if it be a question whether the revelation is really from God, or if it be taken in a wrong or doubtful sense, there can be no apprehension of God's testimony as it is in the case, and so no apprehension through this of the supernatural to which it bears witness. "Faith in the supernatural requires, then, in addition to the witness that vouches for the fact that God has made the revelation, an interpreter competent to declare the true meaning of the revelation." And as faith is required in all times and places, these necessary conditions of its exercise must be no less universal, at hand for all nations and through all ages, and of unmistakable authority for the poor and illiterate as well as for the high and learned. The witness and interpreter, moreover, must be *infallible*. Faith is a theological virtue, which consists in believing, without doubting, what God has revealed, on the veracity of God alone. "He who has for his faith only the testimony of a fallible witness, who may both deceive and be deceived, has always a reasonable ground for doubt, and therefore no solid ground for faith. Therefore, since with a fallible witness or fallible interpreter we can never be sure that we are not mistaken, it follows, if we are to have faith at all, we must have a witness and interpreter that cannot err, therefore infallible."

III. As God requires faith in his Word, in order to salvation, and this can have no place without the conditions now mentioned, we are bound to believe that these conditions *sine qua non* are by him provided for this end. Where then is the infallible witness and interpreter of God's Word, thus indispensable to the exercise of faith in what it reveals, to be sought and found? It is not *reason*, whether as intuitive or discursive. It is not the *Bible*, because this itself needs to be authenticated and interpreted by some infallible authority beyond itself. It is not *private illumination*, for that at best would give only a private faith, while what we are required to have is a public faith, such as can be sustained by public evidence, by arguments which are open to all and common to all. "No witness, then, remains to be introduced but the apostolic ministry, or *ecclesia docens*." Either this, or we have no witness.

IV. This conclusion is abundantly supported and made good also in the way of historical fact. "The ministry is the organ through which Jesus Christ *supernaturally* bears witness to his own revelation." It is infallible, not in virtue of what it is naturally, but by his supernatural presence. Such supernatural qualification or competency might seem to be a fact itself requiring again supernatural witness, but it is not so; the credibility of the witness may be "supernaturally established to natural reason by means of miracles." A miracle connects the natural and supernatural, "so that natural reason can pass from the one to the other. Natural reason can determine whether a fact be or be not a miracle; and if it be so, can conclude from it legitimately to the supernatural cause, and to the divine commission or authority of him by whom it is wrought. The miracle is God's own assurance to natural reason, that he speaks in and by the person who performs it; in which case we have the veracity of God for the truth of what the miracle-worker declares, and therefore infallible certainty; for God can neither deceive nor be deceived. So then the process of proof for the fact before us, namely the infallible authority of the *ecclesia docens*, is simple and easy." The miracles of Christ, historically certified or made sure for natural reason, are sufficient to accredit his divine commission, and authorize the conclusion that whatever he said or promised was infallible truth; for whether you say Jesus was himself truly God as well as truly man, or that he was only divinely commissioned, you have in either case the veracity of God as the ground of faith in what he said or promised. Suppose, then, the fact that Jesus Christ appointed a body of teachers, and promised to be always with them to make them infallible, and suppose also this fact made infallibly certain to natural reason, by proper historical evidence; have we not, in such case, infallible certainty that Jesus Christ does speak in and through this body, and that it is absolutely secure thus from error in all it believes and teaches? Here we have recourse to the New Testament, which as a simple historical document may be infallibly clear for private reason alone in *some* of its contents, though not in the whole. In Mt. 28:18, 19, 20; Mk. 16:15; Eph. 4:11, we have the well-known apostolical commission, which is declared to reach to the end of the world, and to have regard to all nations. In such view, it requires and implies a corporation or body always identical with itself. This is the *ecclesia docens*, which with such constitution must be considered corporately infallible, and whose voice all men consequently are bound to obey as the voice of God.

v. Where now is this corporate ministry to be found, at the present time? It cannot be in the Greek communion, still less in the Protestant. It is then the Roman Catholic ministry, because it can be found nowhere else, and because also its regular succession can be clearly identified here from the beginning. "Then we sum up by repeating that Jesus Christ has instituted and commissioned an infallible and indefectible body of teachers, and this body is the congregation of the Roman Catholic pastors in communion with their chief. The Catholic Church, then, is the witness to the fact of revelation. What its pastors declare to be the Word of God, is the Word of God; what they enjoin as the faith, is the faith without which it is impossible to please God, and without which we are condemned and the wrath of God abideth on us. What they teach is the truth, the whole truth, and nothing but the truth; for God himself has commissioned them, and will not suffer them to fall into error in what concerns the things they have been commissioned to teach." Out of this Church, of course, no act of faith can take place, for faith is a theological virtue, which can be elicited only in obedience to God's authority, propounding truth in a supernatural and also public way, which we have only in the body of pastors and teachers belonging to the Roman Catholic Church.[5]

The main force of this reasoning lies in this, that the view maintained is made to appear the only and necessary alternative to another view, starting from the same premises, which is found to be irrational and untenable. In both cases, Christianity is taken to be a revelation of supernatural truth, which men are to receive by faith, as something wholly out of themselves, that is brought near to them for their use in a purely outward way. As it has its source and seat beyond their proper nature altogether, so it cannot be allowed to find in this any rule or measure whatever for its apprehension. It must be taken as a matter of mere authority. The relation between the receptivity of faith on the one side, and the propounded truth on the other, the subject natural and the object supernatural, is held to be in no sense inward and living, but mechanical only and juxtapositional, the one remaining always on the outside of the other. How now is the necessary connection between the two to be mediated, so as to secure faith a real possession of the heteronomic supernatural? We take it only on God's testimony; God is true, and we may rationally trust his word, if we have it, in so great a case. Very good; agreed so far on all sides. Now comes, however, another question. How are we to be sure that God has

---

5. See the article particularly entitled, "The Church against No-Church," April 1845; also "The British Reformation," in the same volume; "Faith not Possible without the Church," January 1846; "The Two Brothers, or why are you a Protestant," July 1847; &c., &c.

spoken in the first place, and then in the next place that we have his very mind or sense in what he has spoken? It is not enough here to send us to the Bible; the question still returns, How do we know that the Bible is his Word, and how are we to ascertain the mind of the Spirit in what it teaches? Inspiration is itself something supernatural, of which faith needs to be infallibly assured in order that it may be infallibly sure of what it reveals. Here, however, a certain system of thought, which claims to be Protestantism, although it is not Protestantism in its true and genuine sense but a corruption of it rather on the side towards rationalism, is ready at once to respond: "We need no infallible witness to assure us of the revelation, other than the inspired Bible itself; the proofs of its divinity lie open to reason, and every man may there get the mind of God out of it for himself." But with the theory of revelation before noticed, by which it is taken to be wholly outward and transcendent, and which resolves faith into an assent to grounds which are extrinsic both to the object and the subject, and to be found only in an authority that lies between, it is plain that this short method of settling the matter must land us at last in something very like infidelity itself. It is in truth to subordinate the supernatural to the natural, and to make the private reason of every man the seal and certification of God's oracles, sounded forth from a world which has this same reason wholly on its outside. To say: "Man needs no revelation, but only the full development of his nature"; and to say: "He may by his nature assure himself infallibly that he has a revelation on the outside of him, and also make out what it means in the same outward view," are declarations that come to very much the same result in the end. In either case we have substantial rationalism, or a faith that has to do immediately and really not with the supernatural at all in its own kind, but only with the natural shoved in as a supposed intermediate witness in its name and stead. Faith becomes a conclusion of logic, and not the substantiation of things invisible, immediately and directly, as they are in their own nature. The case labors under a twofold difficulty. First, the merely individual judgment is made to be the measure of truth, without regard to the claims of mind in its general character — which is in contradiction to the idea of humanity itself, as it comes before us on all other sides. Private judgment, like private will, has no force of reason ever *as private*, but becomes rational only by ceasing to be private and showing itself to be truly general. Then again, if it *could* be regarded as sufficient and complete, it must still be held of no power to bridge over effectually, in a real way, the impassable gulf by which it is here taken to be sundered from the object of which faith needs to be infallibly certified and assured. The theory of the *Bible and Private Judgment*, then, under this abstract form, cannot possibly bear examination. It is not only false, but pernicious to the very life of faith. It runs at last into mere naturalism and rationalism. Over against it, the argument for the idea of the Church, the claims of Christianity in its universal or catholic and historical character, and the necessity of a truly divine certification or witness of supernatural truth for faith, is overwhelmingly conclusive. Without all this, Christianity has no power to save its proper divine credit. The alternative is, faith in this form or infidelity. Romanism thus far is fully in the right; and if it can cause it to appear that its own theory, as exhibited by Mr. Brownson, is the only way of escape from what is thus opposed, we must feel ourselves bound certainly, as we fear God and value his salvation, to throw ourselves into its arms.

At present, however, we do not see this theory to be such a necessary way of escape from the ruinous system it so justly condemns on the opposite side. On the contrary, it seems to us intrinsically defective in its own constitution, as being nothing less in truth than the reverse side of that same bad system itself; which as such is found, on close inspection, to labor under substantially the same difficulty and contradiction. Here, as there, the difficulty is again of a double sort. The general is made to exclude the individual, as there the reverse, in contradiction to the idea of humanity as we find it in the natural world. And then, as before, no real bridge is made to span the gulf that divides the visible from the invisible. Both views are alike in this, that they make faith to rest on a conclusion of mere natural reason, and will not allow the supernatural, as such, to come by means of it into any real union with the natural. We will try to make our meaning clear, as regards Romanism, by the following general observations, in the way of criticism on Mr. Brownson's argument in its defence.

1. The theory involves a general wrong against our human constitution, naturally considered, inasmuch as it will not allow its ordinary law of freedom to have force in the sphere of religion, which is that precisely in which it is required to make itself complete. The general law of our nature is that mind must fulfill its mission, not by following blindly a mere outward force of any sort, but by the activity of its own intelligence and will, both as general and individual. It must move in the light that springs from itself, and by the power it generates continually from within. This moral constitution includes complex relations, laws, organic

interdependence, action and reaction, as in the world of nature, on a vast and magnificent scale. Still, to the idea of it as a whole the conception of freedom appertains, in the form now stated, as a necessary universal distinction. The theory of Mr. Brownson, however, if we rightly understand it, requires us to assume that in the highest form of religion, that which is reached in Christianity, the human mind ceases to be directly active in the accomplishment of what is brought to pass in its favor, and is a passive recipient simply of foreign action brought to bear on it in an outward way. It does not help the matter that it is taken to be active with regard to Christianity in a different sphere; the difficulty is that no activity is allowed to it in the realization of Christianity itself as the highest fact of the world. Christianity claims to be the perfection of man's life; this, in its ordinary constitution, unfolds itself by its own self-movement in the way of thought and will; but just here all this is superseded by another law altogether; the supernatural comes in as the outward complement of the natural in such sort as to make the force of this last null and void in all that pertains to its higher sphere.

II. This wrong against human nature becomes most immediately plain in the violence which the individual mind is made to suffer, by the theory, in favor of what is taken to be general. The existence of truth is objective, and in such view of course universal and independent of all private thought or will; but as thus objective it must be at the same time subjective, must enter into particular thought and will, in order to be real. As object merely, without subject, it becomes a pure abstraction. Mere single mind can never be, in and by itself, the measure of either truth or right; it must be ruled, and so bound, by the objective or the authority of the general. On the other hand, however, the general as such, mere law or object, is no such measure either, in and by itself; to be so, it must take concrete form in the life of the world, which resolves itself at last into the thinking and willing of single minds. But now, in the case before us, Romanism sets aside the authority of this order, which is found to be of such universal force for the constitution of our nature in every other view. Christianity is taken to be of force for the world under a simply abstract form — an outwardly supernatural revelation, transcending the whole order of our common life, and not needing nor allowing the activity of man himself, as an intelligent and free subject, to be the medium in any way of its presence and power. Authority is made to be all, and freedom nothing. The authority, too, is cut off and sundered from the proper life of the subject, and in this way comes to no real union with his intelligence and will. It comes from abroad, stands over him in an outward way, and requires him to submit to it as a foreign force. Authority thus is not mediated at all by man's actual life, is in no sense living and concrete, but altogether mechanical, rigid, and fixed. It is from the start a given quantity, just so much, and nothing either more or less. It excludes private thought and will, according to Mr. Brownson. "The two authorities," that of private thought and that of the Church, "may indeed coexist," we are told, "but not in regard to the same matters; for one is the negation of the other." The right of private judgment is taken to be of force only where the authority of the Church ceases, as though each had its own territory separate from that of the other, without the possibility ever of any truly common jurisdiction. "To assume the authority of both private judgment and the Church on the same matters, is absurd. One authority necessarily excludes the other. If it is private judgment, then not the Church; if the Church, then not private judgment." The office of reason ends where authority begins. "We accept private judgment, as well as the Bishop (Hopkins), and give full scope to the individual reason, but only within its legitimate province. We reconcile reason and authority by ascertaining the province of reason, and confining it within its legitimate province. Questions of reason are to be decided by reason, but questions of faith are to be decided by authority; for all faith rests on authority, and would not be faith if it did not." [6] Authority may override private reason, and make it null. Its teachings and commands, in the case of the Church, "constitute the rule of truth and falsehood, right and wrong, good and evil. It is no matter what you prove she teaches and commands; for if it be clear that she teaches and commands it, we will maintain that it is true, right, and good, against all gainsayers, even to the dungeon, exile, or the stake, if need be." Articles of faith are first principles, or axioms in religion, over which "reason has no natural rights, never had any, never can have any; because they lie out of her province, and belong to the supernatural, where her authority does not extend." So again: "The articles of faith are not taken from the dominions of reason, but they are certain grants made gratuitously to her, extending, instead of abridging, her authority, and therefore serve instead of injuring her." [7]

This, and a great deal more to the same purpose, shows clearly enough the relation in which Mr. Brownson makes faith stand to reason, and so the view he takes of authority, or the claims of the general, as related to

6. See article on the "British Reformation," January 1845.
7. October 1845, 448-51.

the rights of the individual mind. He sees rightly enough that a purely unbound freedom, liberty without law, is the very conception of slavery itself; but does not stop to take into view the other side of the truth, this namely, that a purely bound authority, law without liberty, is slavery also. "Liberty to hold and teach," he tells us, "what the Sovereign Pontiff says we may, is all the liberty we ask"; for this is liberty to obey God's law, the only liberty he allows to any man. "Law is the basis of liberty, and where there is no sovereign authority there is no law. Liberty is not in being free of all law, but in being held only to the law. We believe the Church, and the pope as visible head of the Church, is the organ through which Almighty God promulgates the law. Consequently, in our own estimation at least, in submitting to the pope, we find, instead of losing our liberty." [8] Good. No law, no liberty. But still, the planet is not free in being true simply to the law that carries it round the sun, and the animal is not free that follows the law of its own instincts. Law here is not enough. It must be met by the spontaneity of a free subject, which with the power to go aside from its orbit, makes the law notwithstanding the very form of its own action, producing its authority purely and truly from within. Certainly, the theory before us is ready to say, the law must be obeyed freely, by the option and choice of the obeying subject; but this requires no autonomy of the subject in the constitution of the law, no voice in its legislation; all the case demands or allows is that on grounds extrinsic wholly to its constitution the subject be rationally persuaded that obedience is wise and right. Is this, however, more at last, we ask, than mere prudence, or a skillful calculation of profit and loss? Is the man free who obeys the law, *Thou shalt not kill*, to avoid the gallows? Is it liberty to say white is black or black white, though it should be said never so pleasantly and glibly, because we are required to do so by an authority which we feel it unsafe to resist? Am I free when I renounce my own intelligence and will, and accept in their place another measure of truth altogether *in no union whatever with my personal reason*, whether from the hand of an earthly prince to buy political distinction, or from the hand of a pope to buy a place in heaven? Freedom is more, a great deal, than any such outward consent to the authority of law. It is life *in* the law, union with it, the very form in which it comes to its revelation in the moral world. Place the law as an objective force on the outside wholly of the intelligence and will of those who are to be its subjects, and at once you convert it into an abstract nothing. This is the natural extreme of

8. January 1846, 101.

Romanism. Against it, the Reformation formed a legitimate and absolutely necessary reaction and protest. It is quite in the order of history that this protest should itself lead again to extreme results on the opposite side, making the subjective everything and the supernatural objective next to nothing. But the cure for this is not just the old error; and however much of force there may be in Mr. Brownson's polemics, as directed against Parkerism, socialism, and pseudo-Protestantism universally (a force which *we* have no wish certainly to deny or oppose), it does not follow by any means that Protestantism, as simply opening the way for such abuse, is to be considered unsound and false from the start; just as little as the abuses of popery show the Catholic truths to be false, from which they can be shown to have taken their rise. It is still as true now as it was at the beginning of the sixteenth century, that the *actualization* of truth in the world is something which can be accomplished only through the medium of intelligence and will on the part of the world itself, that liberty, in its genuine sense, is not simply the outward echo of authority, but the very element of its life, and the co-efficient of its power, in that which it brings to pass; that man is no passive machine merely in the business of his own salvation; that the free activity of the individual subject in the world of mind never can be paralyzed or overwhelmed by the sense of law, as a nature foreign and transcendent wholly to its own nature, without such bondage as involves in the end the overthrow of reason altogether.

The force of this position does not depend on the kind of authority that is to be obeyed. Whether it be divine or human is all the same thing, if it is taken to be something wholly on the outside of the subject, in no way congenerous with his natural constitution, a law beyond his own reason altogether and foreign from his life. It is not in such view that God exercises authority. His will is never arbitrary, and so never abstract. Where it touches men, it forms in truth the inmost and deepest reason always of their own being; and in such view, though it may not be fully comprehensible, and though it could never have been dreamed of without supernatural revelation, still it must be allowed, even to the mystery of the Blessed Trinity itself, to carry in itself such an organic agreement with the world's life as otherwise known, and such a felt suitableness to the demands of reason, as may serve to evidence its rationality at least afar off, and create thus a presumption in its favor from the start. It will not do to say that reason is absolutely passive in the reception of what is propounded by divine authority in such way, for instance, that it would be as easy to allow five persons in the Godhead as it is to allow three, or that a Hindu avatar might be believed as fully as the Christian Incarnation, on the strength simply of God's outward Word. It may be said, indeed, and with truth also, that to be sure of God's Word in the case is to be sure of the intrinsic rationality of what it is thus supposed to proclaim; but this just shows that we *cannot* be sure of his Word without some regard to the intrinsic reasonableness of what it propounds, and that this itself accordingly is ever to be taken as part of the evidence for the other fact. In other words, the authority of the revelation is not abstract and foreign wholly from the nature of the life for which it is made. Our difficulty here with Mr. Brownson, then, is not just that he arms the pope with divine authority, whereas he might seem to be only a common man; but that such authority, in the hands of the pope or anywhere else, should be taken to supersede and nullify so completely the true idea of human freedom. The theory rests on a wrong conception of what authority is in the world of mind, and so on a wrong conception of the true nature of the Church, as the divinely constituted organ and bearer of Christ's will among men (as we too take it to be) to the end of time.

III. For, as already intimated in some measure, the necessary result of such a separation of liberty and law, the rights of the subjective and the claims of the objective, is vast wrong in the end to the second of these interests as well as to the first. The true idea of authority, in the moral world, requires that it should come to its revelation, under a concrete form, through the medium of the general life and in the way of history. With the theory of Mr. Brownson, however, all this fails. The Church is taken to be the infallible witness of God's mind in the Christian revelation; but not in virtue of her living wholeness as the Body of him that filleth all in all, her life serving in such universal form as the natural medium for unfolding the full sense of its own contents; all this is precluded by the conception of an abstract ministry, or *ecclesia docens*, on which the gift of infallibility is conferred in a purely outward supernatural way. This gift is not mediated at all, in any way, by the life of the Church as a whole. *The ecclesia docens* is no organic product and outbirth of the new creation generally, which it is appointed to serve. Its prophetical, priestly, and kingly functions are not the activity of Christ's mystical body working itself forth collectively in such form, by appropriate organs created for the purpose. The ministry rather is independent of the Church; it has a life of its own; it is a separate organization, through which the higher powers of Christianity are carried forward, by a wholly distinct channel, for the use of the world from age to age. These higher powers too belong to it in a mechanical, magical way, and not according to the ordinary law of truth and power among men. It is objected to Mr. Newman, that he makes the general mind of the Church the medium of Christian knowledge. "This view, if followed out," we are told, "would suppress entirely the proper teaching authority of the Church, competent at any moment to declare infallibly what is the precise truth revealed; or at least would raise the *ecclesia credens* above the *ecclesia docens,* and reduce the office of the Church teaching to that of defining, from time to time, the dogmatic truth which the Church believing has gradually and slowly worked out from her implicit feelings. The secret supernatural assistance would then attach to the Church believing, and superintend the elaboration, rather than to the Church teaching; and if to the Church teaching at all, only so far as to enable it faithfully to collect and truly define what the Church believing elaborates." [9] There is no room with this view, of course, for the conception of anything like a progressive actualization of the life of the Church in the form of authority. As the infallibility which belongs to her is independent of her natural constitution, abstract and not concrete, so it lies also wholly on the outside of her proper human presence in the world. To be out of history is to be out of humanity. All this is encumbered with difficulty. We find no clear account of it in the New Testament. What is said there of the Church and its ministry leads of itself to no such conception. The two forms of existence are exhibited rather as one, the second proceeding organically from the first, the entire constitution holding, moreover, under the character of life, real human life, in unity with itself throughout. It is not easy, again, to withstand the universal analogy of the actual world in favor of the same view. Humanity, in all other cases, accomplishes its destiny by organic co-operation, carried forward in the form of history. Truth is brought to pass for it, through the medium of its own activity, the whole working towards its appointed end by the joint ministry of the parts, in such a way, however, as to be something more always than these separately taken. So it is in the sphere of science, so in the sphere of art, so in the sphere of politics and social life. In each case, we have association, organization, historical movement, intercommunity of powers and functions — in one direction activity to guide and rule, in another direction activity to obey and follow; but this distinction conditioned by the life of the corporation itself in its whole character, and so

9. July 1846, 354.

always more or less free and flowing, not fixed by arbitrary ordination from abroad. The same law is allowed to have place in the sphere of religion, too, beyond the precincts of Christianity. Even Judaism, we are told, was not exempt from its operation. But in the sphere of the Church, as it stands since Christ, we are required to take all differently. As a supernatural constitution, it must not conform to the order of nature. It must be neither organic, nor historical, nor human, in its higher life, but one long monotony, rather, of mere outward law and authority, superseding the natural order of the world, and contradicting it, age after age, to the end of time. The Roman system carries in itself thus a constant tendency to resolve the force of Christianity into magic, and to fall into the snare of the mere *opus operatum* in its bad sense. It must be confessed, at all events, that the theory, right or wrong, labors here under a difficulty which it is by no means easy for a truly thoughtful mind to surmount.

IV. This brings us to notice more particularly, in the next place, the general relation in which the supernatural is taken by this system to stand to the natural, and its corresponding view of divine revelation. The two worlds are held to be wholly disjoined and separate the one from the other, so that any connection which is formed between them is regarded as outward only and not in the way of common life. The truth with which faith has to do belongs to the "supernatural order," which transcends altogether, we are told, the order of nature, holds out of it, above it, and beyond it, and cannot come to any organic union with it, under its own form. The two worlds are sundered by an impassable gulf as regards inward constitution and being; only by the word of God, as an outward report, it is possible for faith, in the sphere of nature, to be infallibly assured of what lies beyond in a higher sphere.[10] This abstract conception of the supernatural, as something that refuses utterly to flow into one life

10. We have a strong assertion of such *transcendence* in the article, "Natural and Supernatural," Jan. 1847, 110, 111, in reply to the allegation of an opponent that man's capacity of knowing God, as far as it goes, can be only through kindred powers. "Why could not Newton's dog know Newton? Because he had not the kindred powers." Mr. Brownson accepts the case as in point, and turns it to his own use. The dog *did* know his master within the range of a dog's nature, but not in the order in which Newton transcended this; "no one can know naturally above the order of his nature," and so no one can know naturally the supernatural. But will the objector deny, asks Mr. B., "that Almighty God, if he had chosen, could, by a special act of his power, have so elevated the dog's powers as to have enabled him to know his master in the full sense in which one man may know another?" And so the mind of man may be supernaturalized, by the gift of faith, into a capacity for apprehending the super-

in any way with the natural, may be said to underlie the whole theory of Romanism, as we find it set forth by Mr. Brownson; and it is of so much the more force to lend it plausibility, as it is for substance very generally accepted as correct, only with a less broad application, by those who are most forward to oppose the pretensions of this system as vain and false. Much of our Protestant orthodoxy, it must be confessed, rests on precisely the same abstract supernaturalism, in the view it takes of the Bible as the medium of divine revelation, without seeing that from such premises we are shut up at last, without help or escape, to the Romanist conclusion; since if the matter of revelation be wholly without self-evidencing power for faith, and such that it can be received on the ground of outward divine authority or testimony only, it follows plainly that we need also an infallible outward witness in the Church, to assure us in like mechanical style where this authority is really and truly at hand. The reasonableness of faith turns not at all, according to this school, on any correspondence in which it stands directly with its own contents, but purely and exclusively on its relation to the extrinsic authority on which they are accepted as true. The principle that we must judge the speaker by the word, however sound within the sphere of nature, is taken to involve infidelity, or at least a strong leaning to it, when adopted in the sphere of religion; "for it cannot be adopted in the sphere of religion without first denying that in religion there is anything to be believed which transcends natural reason; therefore it cannot be adopted without denying supernatural revelation; and to deny supernatural revelation is what is meant by infidelity." [11]

It might seem enough to convict this theory of error, so far as the Bible is concerned, that this bears on the face of it throughout clear proof of a real union of the supernatural with the natural, in the persons of the sacred writers. The truth it reveals is conditioned in the form of its manifestation, always, by the mind and education of the men who give it utterance, and through them by the living human relations in the midst of which they stood. No two prophets think alike or speak alike. Their in-

---

natural; while all this implies no fitness in his nature previously for any such apprehension. But is not this now, we ask, to set the higher sphere wholly on the outside of the lower, and to make the translation from the second to the first a simple miracle? The dog, to ascend into the order of man's life, must be *essentially* changed, created over again altogether; and if the supernatural entering man's life be a like process, it must be virtually his demolition and the construction of a new being, by divine fiat, in his place.

11. October 1845, 510.

spiration, then, is no abstraction, no divine mechanism, but something that truly descends, with all its divinity, into the order of nature. And what shall we say of him in whom all prophecy and inspiration became at last complete? Was it his office simply to stand between the two worlds that met in his person, and report *mysteries* over from one to the other, for the use of faith, in a purely outward way? What is meant then by the declaration: The *Word* became *flesh*, and dwelt among us, and we beheld his glory, the glory as of the only-begotten of the Father, full of grace and truth [Jn. 1:14]? Surely if the gospel means anything, we have here at least the supernatural order linked in real organic union with the natural, and showing thus the capacity of this last, as well as its need, to receive into itself such higher life as its own proper complement and end. It will not do, in the face of such a fact as the Incarnation, to say that the realities with which faith has to do, in distinction from reason, are wholly without light or evidence for this last in their own nature, and as such to be taken on the mere authority of God ascertained in some other way, in such sense that a man might be supposed to be infallibly sure first that he has this authority to go upon, and so be prepared to accept any and every proposition as true, on the strength of it, with equal readiness and ease. What is revelation, if it be not the actual entrance of the supernatural in some way over into the sphere of the natural? That which remains wholly beyond the orb of man's life, naturally considered, and in no living contact with it at any point, cannot be said surely to be revealed at all for his apprehension and use. All revelation, as distinguished from magic, implies the self-exhibition of God, in a real way, through the medium of the world in its natural form. To a certain extent, we have such a revelation in the material universe. The outward creation is the symbol, mirror, shrine, and sacrament of God's presence and glory, as a supernatural fact, in the most actual way. The word of prophecy and inspiration is the gradual coming forth of eternal truth into time, in a like real way, through the medium of human thought and speech, a process which completes itself finally in the full domiciliation, we may say, of the Infinite Word itself in the life of the world by Jesus Christ. It is an utterly unevangelical conception of this fact, to think of Christ only as an outward teacher or reporter of secrets belonging to another order of existence wholly from that in which he appeared among men. Such a conception involves in fact the old Gnostic imagination, by which the supernatural side of his existence was never allowed to come to any really inward and organic union with its natural or simply human side, in consequence of which this last became always a phantom, and the first at the same time an extra-mundane abstraction. In Christ, most literally and truly, the supernatural order came to a living and perpetual marriage with the order of nature, which it could not have done if the constitution of the one had not been of like sort with that of the other (man made in the image truly of God), so as to admit and require such union as the last and only perfect expression of the world's life. It lies, then, in the nature of the case, that Christ can be no abstraction, no solitary portent, in the midst of the world. If his Incarnation involved a real entrance into its life at all (and not simply an avatar, whether for an hour or for ten thousand years), it must stand in living inward relation, and this fundamental, too, and central, with its entire organization and history under every other view. The lines of truth must fall in upon it as their necessary center, from all sides, out to the farthest periphery of nature. It must be found to carry in it the inmost and deepest sense of the universal sphere to which it belongs. It is a fact, therefore, which must come harbingered and heralded by voices from the deep, and long shadows thrown before, signs, prophecies, and types, from every quarter; all made clear at last, indeed, only by the event itself; whilst with equal necessity the powers of history may be expected to throw themselves subsequently, always more and more, into its train, the world before and the world behind joining thus in one and the same loud acclamation: "Hosannah to the Son of David! Blessed is he that cometh in the name of the Lord" [Mt. 21:9]! But now, if this be the relation of the supernatural in Christ himself to the sphere of nature, it is not easy, certainly, to acquiesce in any theory of the Church by which this is taken to be the medium of divine revelation in a wholly different style. An abstract Church is as much at war with the true mystery of Christianity as an abstract Christ. The Church, according to Mr. Brownson, is the infallible witness of God's word, not in the way of any really human mediation in the case, but in a wholly outward and unearthly way, by a special fiat of grace investing it with such infallibility, as a fixed mechanical fact, in no union whatever with the laws of our life under its ordinary form.[12] This we find it by no means easy to admit. The view works back

12. Mr. Brownson sees the Church always as an order extrinsical to the life of nature, or to humanity in its own proper form. Human institutions, he admits, allow a mixture of good and bad; but the Church, he will have it, is no *human* institution. "If Christian, she is divine—for Christ is God; and then she is not a human institution, unless God and man are identical;" and so she must be taken as only and wholly true, right, and good. (July 1849, 310.) But Christianity in the individual believer is divine too; does it then make *him* to be also free from all error and sin? Even

unfavorably on the whole idea of revelation, and especially wrongs, in the end, the character of Jesus Christ. We are very far from believing that the divinity of a revelation turns on its having no common life with humanity; on the contrary, it seems to us to become complete in proportion, precisely, as the supernatural, by means of it, is brought to enter most fully and truly into the conditions of the natural.

v. The theory carries with it, finally, as it seems to us, a wrong conception of the true nature and power of faith, involving in the end the very consequence it seeks professedly to shun, namely the subordination of faith to reason or its resolution into mere logic. It goes on the assumption that the supernatural, with which faith has to do, is so sundered from the natural as to admit no direct approach or apprehension from that side; that truth in such form is inevident for the mind wholly in its own nature, and without force of reason intrinsically to engage its assent; that the mind is moved to such assent in its case accordingly, not by any motives either in itself or in the object set before it, but by something extrinsic to both, the weight of an intermediate authority which is felt to be fully valid as a ground of certainty, without regard to the nature of what is thus taken on trust one way or another. "In belief," says Mr. Brownson, "I must go out of myself, and also out of the object, for my motives of assent." Subjective and objective come to no union or contact whatever. The gulf between them is sprung only by means of outward *testimony*. The case requires indeed divine testimony; but still it is this always as something *between* the subject and object, in a purely separate and external way. As such, the testimony itself needs of course to be authenticated before it can be rested upon as sure and certain, and this authentication must be again infallible. Such a witness of God's veracity we have in the Church, whose voice accordingly is to be taken as the true sense always of his word. The divine authority of the Church, it is supposed, may be established for natural reason in its own sphere, although this of itself is not enough to produce faith. For that we need what is termed the *donum fidei*, a supernatural benefit conferred by the ministry of the Church itself through the holy sacrament of baptism.

We object to the way in which faith is here opposed to reason. Its

---

an apostle, it seems, might do wrong. And is the Church in fact so good, as to be literally *sinless* as well as infallible? Her divine side, of course, is both one and the other; but she has also her human side, her divinity shines through humanity; she is not only the heavenly leaven of Christ's life in the world, but the true and proper life of the world itself also *in the progress of being leavened*. The progress here is not at once the end.

opposition is properly to sense, and to nature as known through sense; to reason, only so far as this is taken for the understanding in its relation to such knowledge. Faith is the capacity of perceiving the invisible and supernatural, the substantiation of things hoped for, the certification of things not seen (Heb. 11:1); which, as such, does not hold on the outside of reason, any more than this can be said of sense, but opens to view rather a higher form of what may be called its own proper life, in which it is required to become complete, and without which it must always remain comparatively helpless, blind, and dark. It requires of a truth, in our present circumstances, a supernatural influence to call faith into exercise; no force of logic, and no simply natural motives, can bring it to pass; there must be for the purpose a new life by the Spirit of Christ. But still all this forms at last but the proper education, or drawing out, of the true sense of man's life as it stood before. Faith does not serve simply to furnish new *data* for thought in an outward way, but includes in itself also, potentially at least, the force of reason and knowledge in regard to its own objects. It stands in rational correspondence with its contents, and involves such an apprehension of them as makes the mind to be in some measure actually in their sphere. Faith touches its object as truly as sense. This requires indeed the medium of God's veracity; we can perceive the supernatural only as we feel and know that God exists; faith thus sees all things in God. But the veracity of God here is no abstraction; it reaches us in and by the things it verifies and affirms. So in the world of nature. Mr. Brownson will not allow the revelation of God in nature to be for faith at all; we have it, he says, by mere reason; "regarded solely as the author, upholder, and governor of nature, he is natural, and hence the knowledge of him as such is always termed *natural theology*." In this character, "he is naturally cognoscible, according to what St. Paul tells us, Romans 1:20." [13] But surely mere logic can never conclude from the world of sense to the world of spirit, from the finite to the infinite. To perceive God in nature requires far more than any syllogism. We see him there only when he authenticates himself to us by his works, as the immediate felt symbol of his presence, and then our perception is faith. So St. Paul, Hebrews 11:3: "*Through faith* we understand that the worlds were framed by the Word of God, so that things which are seen were not made of things which do appear." Through the world of sense, faith looks continually, not the logical understanding, to the vast and glorious Reality that lies beyond, and of which it is only the outward

13. April 1845, 146.

type or shadow. Nature in this view is a divine word (as in the Nineteenth Psalm), always showing forth the supernatural, having its seal or witness, too, in the veracity of God, that is, in his being, as a fact underlying the phenomenal creation; while, however, at the same time, this fact makes itself immediately certain, not from beyond, but in and by the very document which it thus seals and certifies for faith. And why should it be different in the case of revelation, under its higher view? God speaks in the Bible, and he must himself authenticate his own voice. This implies, however, no merely outward certification, apart from the Word itself. He reveals himself for faith, in and by the Word, as the very medium of his own presence. This becomes most clear in the person of Jesus Christ, the Word Incarnate, by whom all previous revelation is made at last complete. How is *he* authenticated for faith? By divine testimony. In what form? Miracles, according to Mr. Brownson. "From the miracle the reason concludes legitimately to the supernatural cause, and to the divine commission or authority of him by whom it is wrought." Jesus Christ performed miracles, and stands accredited by them as a divine teacher. But could a miracle legitimate the pretensions of the Mormon prophet, Joseph Smith? Certainly not. The miracle itself needs to be authenticated, by the living person and word of him whose commission it is appointed to seal. This is plain from Deuteronomy 13: 1-3, which is of itself sufficient to show that reason is concerned, in faith, not simply with the seal of God's word outwardly considered, but with the intrinsic reasonableness also of the Word itself. A miracle in favor of a lie proves nothing. Is the Word itself then enough, without the miracle? By no means. Only they are not to be sundered one from the other. They are wedded together as body and soul. The body authenticates the presence of the soul; but it is only as the soul, at the same time, authenticates the life of the body. Christ's miracles then are indeed a divine attestation of his character and mission; but their true force for this end holds at last in their relation to his person. *That* underlies all truth in the world besides; and how then could it be proved or made sure by any other form of truth, taken as something separate from itself? Christ thus authenticates himself, and all else that is true. Not abstractly again, however, but concretely, in and by the living relations of his presence in the world. The supernatural in his life, including his miracles, forms but the natural and proper expression of what his life was in its own power. The force of all falls back finally on his person itself; and it is with this, accordingly, that faith has to do primarily, in accepting his divine mission. The voice of God for it, attesting the revelation, comes not from abroad, but in and through the revelation itself. Thou art the Christ, it says with Peter, and to whom else shall we go? Thou hast the words of eternal life [Jn. 6:68, 69]. "He that believeth on the Son of God," says St. John, "hath the witness in himself; he that believeth not God" — in and by this revelation — "hath made him a liar" (1 Jn. 5:10). Not to own and obey Christ, is the greatest possible wrong to truth which any man can commit. It is such a blow at God's veracity as can be aimed at it in no other way; for the Truth of truth itself is Christ, the alpha and omega of life, the same yesterday, today, and forever. Faith here is not indifferent to the word and work of Christ, but still it sees these in the light of his person, and does not so much conclude to this as from it, in the view it takes of their significance. It is not by establishing his miraculous conception, or the fact of his Resurrection, in an abstract separate view, that we prove him to be the Son of God; but we must feel him in the first place to be the Son of God, with Peter, before we can truly believe, on any evidence, either the first of these facts or the last. *He* is in the last proof of both. So in the Creed. Christ authenticates himself for faith not by mere outward warrant and seal of any sort, but by direct communication, in some way, with the rational nature of men, as being himself indeed the life of reason and the only true light of the world. Faith here, as in all other cases, is led by motives of assent in its object, and not simply by motives drawn from some other quarter; or, in other words, the authority of God moving it is not on the outside of the object, but comes to view in and by the object bearing its proper seals, these last having no conclusive force save in union and connection with the first.

Mr. Brownson himself is forced to allow something like this in the end, though as it seems to us not without contradiction to his own general theory. Reason may conclude in its own sphere, he says, from the natural to the supernatural by the miracle, but not so as to generate faith; this comes in another way as a free donation from God. It is not given to us in the fact that we are human beings, but supernaturally, so as to lift us from the order of nature to the order of grace. Supernaturalized in this way, "the creditive subject is placed on the plane of the supernatural credible object, and they are thus *correlatively* creditive and credible; and if no obstacle intervene, the act of faith is not only elicitable, but elicited, *without other motive than is contained in the subject and object,* as is the case with every act of faith, whether human or divine." Faith then is not blind and regardless of its object. "The *donum fidei* is not a general *vis creditiva,* but simply *vis creditiva* in relation to its special correlative, the supernatural credible object." What it believes is the authority of God, but this authority in identification always with the object it commends to faith; just as light, in the natural world, bears witness to the objects of sense, shows them as they are for the eye, by making them at the same time the medium of its own revelation. Such is the view given of the subject in the article [14] which, however, as we have just said, seems not to agree fully with what is said, when we are told [15] "that faith or belief, as distinguished from knowledge and science, rests on authority extrinsic both to the believer and the matter believed." If this be meant simply to exclude the notion that reason is the mother of faith, the so-called Vulgar Rationalism, it is all very well. But in the hands of Mr. Brownson, it is made to mean much more. It sets faith out of the sphere of reason altogether, and reduces it to the character of a mere blind assent to outward authority, contrary to what we find him saying again of the *donum fidei*, as an actual bringing of the subject into inward correlation with the object believed. Where the authority for faith is thus taken to be extrinsic to the supernatural object, as with the system generally, we are thrown at last on the very rationalism, which it is sought in this way to avoid. So our common abstract supernaturalism, on the Protestant side, is in the habit of concluding *logically*, from miracles and other evidence in the sphere of nature, to the supernatural authority of the Bible, and then pretends to make this, in such outward view, a complete succedaneum subsequently for all reason besides — as though reason and revelation were only contiguous spheres, the one ending where the other begins; not considering that the whole authority of the Bible itself thus can be no better at last than the strength of the logic on which as an arch it is made in this way fundamentally to rest. To make the Church, however, a succedaneum for reason, in like outward style, comes precisely to the same thing. Allow the *donum fidei*, as an elevation of the mind to the plane of the supernatural, and the case is changed; but then also it is no longer easy to see why faith should be bound so mechanically to the voice of the Church, as an authority extrinsical to the truth itself. The Church we hold, too, to be the medium of the Christian revelation, the organ by which Christ makes himself known in the world, and which is to be reverenced on this account, through all ages, as his body, the fullness of him that filleth all in all [Eph. 1:23]. But it is all this, not in a mechanical quasi-magical way, as a witness set forward to propound the truth in outward style only, a supernatural automaton with the pope at Rome for its

14. "Liberalism and Catholicity," July 1846.   15. April 1845.

mouthpiece. The Church is the Body of Christ only as it serves to reveal Christ under a truly living and historical form in the history of the world; in which view all the power it has to propound Christ as an object of faith is found in the fact of its being itself an object of faith through Christ and from him, the form in which his life completes itself among men. Faith starts then in Christ. *Because* we believe in him, we believe also the holy catholic Church, and not in the reverse order. The Church is still necessary as an indefectible witness to the truth; but her indefectibility is a moral fact, not a physical necessity, made good through the activity of the general Christian life itself, the life of Christ in his people, working out its own problem in a truly human way. Why should not the supernatural in this form be quite as accessible for the *donum fidei*, as when exhibited or propounded in a purely outward and abstract style? Nature, we know, is not grace. This pertains to a higher order. But why may not the higher order reveal itself through the very life and constitution of the lower, supernaturalizing it for its own ends, as well as in an abrupt outside way, in such sort as to be for faith still all the authority that is needed, to place it in the infallible possession of Christ's Word?

PART FIVE

❖

The Ministry

THE ORDINATION OF MINISTERS [1]

Editor's introduction.

The Mercersburg theologians had from the beginning a higher view of the office of the ministry than most American Protestants, although the issue was little debated at first. In this, too, they endeavored to recover at once the Catholic and the Reformation heritage. The ministry as a continuing organ was of divine institution and commission in the Church. It did not derive its rights and powers from the people by delegation from the priesthood of all believers. They came rather in unbroken succession from the Lord's commission to the Apostles.

Schaff asserted in *The Principle of Protestantism* that the Reformers received their ordination regularly from the Catholic Church. Nevin admitted that there might have been some unavoidable defect in the outward genealogy of the Protestant ministry, but contended that the true line of succession "lay in the life of the Church as a whole." [2] Neither seemed to take seriously Calvin's charge that the Catholic succession, having abandoned the teaching of the Apostles, had already lost its efficacy before the Reformation. Neither raised the question as to whether the intention of Roman Catholic and Protestant ordination was the same. But they were strict on genealogical succession. In 1849, for example, a preacher of the Albright Association was received into the Mercersburg classis of the German Reformed Church only after having received ordination by that Church, on the ground that his previous ordination was invalid. No such question, apparently, would have been raised about Roman Catholic ordination.

The Mercersburg conception is exhibited in the following excerpts

1. *Order of Worship for the Reformed Church* (Philadelphia, 1866), 215–20.
2. "The Classis of Mercersburg," *The Mercersburg Review*, I (1849), 385. This idea was apparently rejected five years later, to judge from the sermon "The Christian Ministry," which follows.

from the ordination service. They consist of the exhortation to the candidate and two of the questions to which he is required to give affirmative answer. Dorner objected that this service made ordination into a "third sacrament"; but Calvin had not taken offense at a like suggestion, nor did Nevin.

❖   ❖   ❖   ❖

Dearly Beloved Brother: It is now our part, solemnly and for the last time, before proceeding to lay upon you irrevocably the burden and responsibility of the holy ministry, to remind you how great is the dignity of the office, and how weighty and momentous also are the duties which it involves.

The office is of divine origin, and of truly supernatural character and force; flowing directly from the Lord Jesus Christ himself, as the fruit of his Resurrection and triumphant Ascension into heaven, and being designed by him to carry forward the purposes of his grace upon the earth, in the salvation of men by the Church, to the end of time.

All power, we hear him saying after he had risen from the dead, is given unto me in heaven and in earth; Go ye, therefore, and teach all nations, baptizing them in the name of the Father, and of the Son, and of the Holy Ghost; teaching them to observe all things whatsoever I have commanded you: and lo, I am with you alway, even unto the end of the world.

To this answers in full what is written also by St. Paul: Wherefore he saith, When he ascended up on high, he led captivity captive, and gave gifts unto men. Now that he ascended, what is it but that he also descended first into the lower parts of the earth? He that descended is the same also that ascended up far above all heavens, that he might fill all things. And he gave some, apostles; and some, prophets; and some, evangelists; and some, pastors and teachers; for the perfecting of the saints, for the work of the ministry, for the edifying of the body of Christ; till we all come in the unity of the faith, and of the Son of God, unto a perfect man, unto the measure of the stature of the fullness of Christ.

Consider well, dear brother in Christ, how much all this means, as declaring and setting forth the true nature and significance of the holy office. The first ministers were the Apostles, who were called and commissioned immediately by Jesus Christ himself. They in turn ordained and set apart other suitable men, as pastors and teachers over the churches which they had gathered and established in different places; and these again, in the same way appointed and sent forth others to carry onward and forward still the true succession of this office; which, being regularly transmitted in this way from age to age in the Christian Church, has come down finally to our time. The solemnity of ordination, through which this transmission flows, is not merely an impressive ceremony, by which the right of such as are called of God to the ministry is owned and confessed by the Church; but it is to be considered rather as their actual investiture with the very power of the office itself, the sacramental seal of their heavenly commission, and a symbolical assurance from on high, that their consecration to the service of Christ is accepted, and that the Holy Ghost will most certainly be with them in the faithful discharge of their official duties.

These duties are of the same order with the high origin of the office, and its glorious design. The ministers of Christ are set in the world to be at once the representatives of his authority, and the ambassadors of his grace. As my Father hath sent me, he says, even so send I you. He that heareth you, heareth me; and he that despiseth you, despiseth me; and he that despiseth me, despiseth him that sent me. Let a man so account of us, says St. Paul, as of the ministers of Christ and stewards of the mysteries of God. Again: We are ambassadors for Christ, as though God did beseech you by us. To them it belongs to baptize, to preach the word, to administer the holy Sacrament of the Lord's Supper. They are appointed to wait upon and serve the Church, which is the spouse of Jesus Christ, his body mystical; to offer before him the prayers and supplications of his people; to feed, to instruct, to watch over and guide the sheep and lambs of his flock, whom he hath purchased with his own blood. They are charged also with the government of the Church, and with the proper use of its discipline, in the way both of censure and absolution, according to that awfully mysterious and solemn word: I will give unto thee the keys of the kingdom of heaven; and whatsoever thou shalt bind on earth, shall be bound in heaven; and whatsoever thou shalt loose on earth, shall be loosed in heaven.

Such being the character of the office to which you are now called, beloved brother in the Lord, and such the high and arduous nature of its duties, it is easy to see with what seriousness and godly fear, with what solemn forethought, with what holy caution, you should approach unto it, as you are now doing, in the present transaction; and with how great

care and study also you ought to apply yourself, that you may appear
hereafter to have been worthy of being put into the Christian ministry,
by being found faithful to its mighty trust. Know, at the same time, that
for this you are by no means sufficient of yourself. All proper sufficiency
here is from God alone; to whom therefore you should pray earnestly,
through the mediation of our only Saviour Jesus Christ, for the heavenly
assistance of the Holy Ghost; that giving yourself wholly to this office,
with daily meditation, and study of the Scriptures, you may be able to
make full proof of your ministry, being nourished up in the words of
faith and good doctrine, and showing yourself a pattern to others in
piety and godly living. In doing this, thou shalt both save thyself, and
them that hear thee. And when the Chief Shepherd shall appear, you shall
receive a crown of glory that fadeth not away.

And now, that this congregation of Christ may also understand your
views and will in these things, and that you may yourself also the more
feel the binding force of what you thus publicly profess and promise, we
call upon you to make answer plainly to these following questions, which
we now propose to you in the name of God and of his Church.

[The candidate is questioned with regard to the Scriptures, the Creed, and the
Heidelberg Catechism. Then the questions continue:]

Are you truly persuaded in your heart, that you are called of God to
the office of the holy ministry, and do you desire and expect to receive,
through the laying on of our hands, the gift and grace of the Holy Ghost,
which shall enable you to fulfill this heavenly commission and trust?

Ans. Such is my persuasion, and such my desire and hope.

Do you acknowledge the rightful authority of this Church, from
which you are now to receive ordination, as being a true part in the succession of the Church Catholic; and do you promise to exercise your ministry in the same with faithful diligence, showing all proper regard for its
laws and ordinances, and all suitable obedience to its lawful government
in the Lord?

Ans. So I confess, and so I promise.

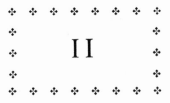

II

JOHN WILLIAMSON NEVIN

The Christian Ministry

Editor's introduction.

If high-churchism may be maintained apart from the papacy, we do not see why it should not be maintained apart from the episcopacy. . . . On the supernatural power of the Church, the efficacy of the sacraments and the authority of her priesthood, Dr. Nevin expresses his views as strongly as the Catholics are in the habit of doing.[1]

The sermon reprinted here was preached at the installation of Nevin's successor as professor of theology, Bernard C. Wolff, in Zion's Church, Chambersburg, at the end of November 1854. Wolff was a Baltimore pastor whose interests were more practical than speculative, but whose personal ties put him usually in the Mercersburg camp. He was to be succeeded a decade later by Henry Harbaugh, an even more decided adherent of the movement. The installation of Wolff had dramatic significance since Nevin's participation was an apparent demonstration that he had decided not to go over to Rome.

The sermon is enigmatic in that it gives no hint of the practical conclusions to be drawn from its definition of a valid ministry. Is there still such a ministry in existence? Or is this the Ideal ministry still struggling for actuality among us?

Less ambiguous is the emphasis on the governmental role of the minister, bolstered by a strong analogy between ecclesiastical and political power.

❖ ❖ ❖ ❖

Ephesians 4:8–16. Wherefore he saith, When he ascended up on high, he led captivity captive, and gave gifts unto men. (Now that he as-

1. Joseph Berg, "Dr. Krummacher and Mercersburg," *Protestant Quarterly Review*, July 1847.

cended, what is it but that he also descended first into the lower parts of the earth? He that descended is the same also that ascended up far above all heavens, that he might fill all things.) And he gave some, apostles; and some, prophets; and some, evangelists; and some, pastors and teachers: For the perfecting of the saints, for the work of the ministry, for the edifying of the body of Christ: Till we all come in the unity of the faith, and the knowledge of the Son of God, unto a perfect man, unto the measure of the stature of the fullness of Christ: That we henceforth be no more children, tossed to and fro, and carried about with every wind of doctrine, by the sleight of men, and cunning craftiness, whereby they lie in wait to deceive; But speaking the truth in love, may grow up into him in all things, which is the head, even Christ: From whom the whole body fitly joined together, and compacted by that which every joint supplieth, according to the effectual working in the measure of every part, maketh increase of the body unto the edifying of itself in love.

We propose to consider from this passage, without farther introduction, the origin, nature, and design of the Christian ministry.

1. In the first place, its *origin*. This is here referred by St. Paul explicitly to what may be denominated the *Ascension Gift* of our Lord Jesus Christ. When he ascended up on high, we are told, leading captivity captive, far above all heavens, that he might fill all things, he gave gifts unto men; and he gave some apostles, and some prophets, and some evangelists, and some pastors and teachers. The ministry was the result and fruit of his glorification at the right hand of God, when he became "head over all things to the Church, which is his body, the fullness of him that filleth all in all" (Eph. 1:22,23.) All lay in the Gift of the Holy Ghost, as his presence began to reveal itself in the world on the day of Pentecost.

This Gift forms in a certain sense the end or completion of the gospel. In it the "Mystery of Godliness," the economy of redemption, came first to its full perfection as the power of God, not in purpose merely but in actual reality, for the salvation of the world. What was begun when the Word became flesh in the Virgin's womb, was brought here to its proper consummation. The Incarnation of Christ and the Mission of the Holy Ghost stand related to each other, not simply as cause and effect, but as commencement and conclusion of one and the same grand fact. The first was in order to the last, and looked forward to it continually as its own necessary issue and scope. Short of this, the design of Christ's coming into the world could not be reached. He took upon him our nature, that he might die for our sins and rise again for our justification, that is, that having by his death exhausted the curse which lay upon the world through the fall, and having broken thus the power of death and hell, he might be constituted by his resurrection and glorification the head of a new creation, the principle and fountain of a new order of life among men, in the bosom of which it should be possible for the believing and obedient, through all time, to be saved from their iniquities and made meet for the inheritance of the saints in light. All this took place by the mission of the Holy Ghost, for which it was necessary that room should in this way be first made by the whole previous manifestation and work of the Redeemer.

The New Testament is full of this thought, so that it is truly wonderful there should ever be any doubt in regard to it, with those who pretend to take the Scriptures as their guide. The gospel goes throughout upon the assumption that the power which Christ carried in himself for the salvation of the world could not make itself felt with free, full, constant action among men, till it had gone through a certain course of qualification previously in his own person. The Spirit dwelt in him, we know, without measure; but so long as he continued in our present mortal state, it was necessarily confined to his own individual life. Between it and the surrounding world of humanity, comprehended as this was in the order of mere nature, rose as a high wall of separation, the law of sin and death which reign throughout this constitution, making it impossible for the law of spiritual life in Christ Jesus to reach it under its own form. Death and sin must first be conquered on their own territory by the Son of God himself; which, however, implied, of course, that he should with real victory transcend, at the same time, their domain, and so take possession of the world under the form of a new, higher existence, no longer natural but supernatural, from the plain of which it might be possible for him to extend to men generally the power of his redemption in a corresponding real and truly supernatural way. The order of nature could never be the platform of any such work, and therefore it must be left behind for the sake of the work itself, and room must be found for the mystery of righteousness in another system altogether, in the order of grace, as this was to be constituted and made permanent in the world by the resurrection of Jesus Christ from the dead.

This great idea underlies all our Saviour's instructions, as it may be said also to be the actuating sense of his own entire life. "Except a corn of wheat fall into the ground and *die*," we hear him saying (Jn. 12:24), "it abideth alone; but if it die, it bringeth forth much fruit." This refers to himself; but then he adds immediately, as the standing law and general conception of the Christian salvation: "He that loveth his life shall lose it; and he that hateth his life *in this world,* shall keep it unto life eternal." So after his resurrection (Lk. 24:25, 26): "O fools, and slow of heart to believe all that the prophets have spoken! *Ought* not Christ to have suffered these things; and to *enter into his glory?*" Everywhere we may see that, in the mind of our Saviour, the whole purpose and force of his life were felt to be conditioned by his dying, and so entering upon a new mode of existence, in which he should no longer be subject to the limitations of his mortal state, but have his humanity itself exalted above nature, and clothed with dominion over it for the benefit of his Church. His removal from the world of sense in this way was to be no loss to his disciples, but on the contrary great gain. He would be put to death in the flesh, as St. Paul expresses it, only that he might be quickened *in the Spirit.* His presence with his people, under this form, would be not less real than it had been before, but in some sense, we might say, even more real, as being at the same time far more unrestrained, and intimately near, and powerfully efficacious for the ends of the gospel, than it was ever possible for it to be previously to his glorification. For it is by the Spirit that he enters into living communication with the members of his mystical body; and the Spirit or Holy Ghost, we are told (Jn. 7:39), could not be given, or *was* not, as the original text has it—that is, was not as the actual revelation of the Saviour's higher presence in the world—till Jesus was glorified. "I will not leave you orphans," he says (Jn. 14:18,19), "I will come to you. Yet a little while, and the world seeth me no more; but ye see me: because I live, ye shall live also." So again (Jn. 16:7), *"It is expedient for you* that I go away; for if I go not away, the Comforter will not come unto you, but if I depart, I will send him unto you." The presence in the flesh must be withdrawn, to make room for a higher, better, and far more glorious presence in the Spirit.

The great burden, indeed, of our Saviour's valedictory discourse may be said to turn upon this thought; and after his resurrection, accordingly, all is made to depend with him on what was to be now brought to pass by his formal ascension into heaven. "Behold, I send the promise of my Father upon you," it was said (Lk. 24:49; Acts 1:5); "but tarry ye in the city of Jerusalem, until ye be endued with power from on high. For John truly baptized with water; but ye shall be baptized with the Holy Ghost not many days hence." The mission of the Spirit is made thus to be the great object of his whole previous life. It formed the travail of his soul, from the commencement of his sufferings to their close. For this he wrestled with the powers of hell. This was emphatically the purchase of his death, the boon of salvation which he came into the world to obtain for our fallen race. He became the author and finisher of our faith (Heb. 12:2) by enduring the cross, with all its shame, and so being set down at the right hand of the throne of God; ascending up far above all heavens, that he might fill all things; leading captivity captive, and taking possession of the world as its supernatural king and head, that he might bestow gifts upon men. And all these gifts were comprehended primarily in the Holy Ghost, as the form under which it was now made possible for the power of his glorified life to reveal itself with free effect in the world. The Holy Ghost, in this view, is not one among other gifts for which the world is indebted to Christ, but the sum and absolute unity at once of the whole, the Gift of gifts, that without which there could be no room to conceive of any other, and through which only all others have their significance and force. It is that which men need as the very complement of their life, that they may be redeemed from the power of the fall, and raised to a participation of the divine nature (2 Pet. 1:4), having escaped the corruption that is in the world through lust. For "except a man be born of water and of the Spirit, he cannot enter into the kingdom of God" [Jn. 3:5]; and only what is thus born of God, as distinguished from all that is the birth of mere flesh (1 Jn. 5:4), can ever have power to overcome the world. So wide and vast is the grace procured for men by the death and resurrection of the Son of God, and bestowed upon them after his ascension through the gift of the Holy Ghost.

This Gift now forms the origin and ground of the Christian Church; which by its very nature, therefore, is a supernatural constitution, a truly real and abiding fact in the world, and yet, at the same time, a fact not of the world in its natural view, but flowing from the resurrection of Christ and belonging to that new order of things which has been brought to pass by his glorification at the right hand of God; a fact not dependent, accordingly, on the laws and conditions that reign in "this present evil world" [Gal. 1:4] and not at the mercy of its changes in any way — "against which the gates of hell shall not prevail" [Mt. 16:18, adapted], and that is destined to outlast and conquer in the end all other institutions, interests, and powers of the earth. As a supernatural presence among men in any such constant and really historical way as the Gift and Promise of Christ seem necessarily to imply, the Spirit must have his own supernatural sphere, in distinction from the order of nature, within which to carry forward his operations as the power of a new creation over against the vanity and misery of the old. This constitution or order of grace is what our faith is taught to receive in the article of the holy catholic Church; that great mystery which is denominated Christ's Body, and within which is comprised, according to the Creed, the whole supernatural process of man's salvation, from baptism for the remission of sins, onward to the resurrection of the flesh and the life everlasting. It is not of the first creation, like the art and science and political institutions of mankind in every other view. It holds directly from Christ in his capacity of glorified superiority to the universal order of nature. He is "head *over all things* to the Church" [Eph. 1:22]. It is in virtue of his having conquered, and ascended up on high, leading captivity captive, far above all heavens — "far above all principality, and power, and might, and dominion, and every name that is named, not only in this world, but also in that which is to come" (Eph. 1:21) — that he has by his Spirit created for himself this glorious constitution, and continues to reign over it through all ages as "the beginning and first-born from the dead" (Col. 1:18). So when he commissioned his Apostles for their great work, all was made to depend on what had thus been accomplished in his own person. "All power," he said "is given unto me in heaven and in earth: Go ye *therefore*" — because it is so and I am able, as the conqueror of sin and death and hell, having all power in my hands, to become the author, the principle and ground of a new creation, against which the gates of hell shall not prevail; because it is so, go ye therefore — "and teach all nations, baptizing them in the name of the Father, and of the Son, and of the Holy Ghost; teaching them to observe all things whatsoever I have commanded you: And, lo, I am with you always, even unto the end of the world" (Mt. 28:18–20).

And here we are brought directly to the point which we have now before us for particular consideration, namely, the origin of the Christian ministry. It is, by the terms of this commission, identified with the institution of the Church itself. The two things are not just the same. The Church is a much wider conception than the ministry. But still they are so joined together that the one cannot be severed from the other. The idea of the Church is made to involve the idea of the ministry. The first is in truth constituted by the commission that creates the second; for it has its whole existence conditioned by an act of faith in the reality of this commission, and this tested again by an act of real outward homage to its authority, the sacrament of baptism being interposed as the sign and seal of every true entrance into the system of grace thus mysteriously consigned to its charge. "He that *believeth* and is *baptized*," it is said (Mk. 16:16), "shall be saved; but he that believeth not shall be damned."

The appointment of the ministry in the form now mentioned took place just before our Saviour's ascension; but it was not until the day of Pentecost that the appointment was fairly armed with its own proper supernatural force, as an institution springing from the glorious sovereignty with which Christ was invested when he took his seat at the right hand of God as head over all things to the Church. The Apostles were directed to wait at Jerusalem, accordingly, till they should be endued with power from on high. Then, when the right time was fully come, the Spirit descended in symbols of wind and flame. The great promise of the gospel was fulfilled. The ministry received its baptism of fire. The Church came to its solemn inauguration, all as an order of things proceeding really and truly from the Saviour's glorification. "Being by the right hand of God exalted," the people were told at the time (Acts 2:33), "and having received of the Father the promise of the Holy Ghost, he hath shed forth this which ye now see and hear."

II. We are to consider, in the next place, the *nature* of the Christian ministry, the peculiar quality and constitution of the office, as related to its origin in one direction and to its general purpose or design in another.

And what we need first and chiefly to fix in our minds, here, is its *supernatural* character. This lies in what we have now seen to be the source from which it springs. It refers itself at once to the ascended and glorified Christ. When he went up, leading captivity captive, far above all heavens, and was constituted head over all things at God's right hand, then it was, and in this capacity and posture, that he gave gifts unto men, and foremost among these the institution of the ministry, endued with power from on high for its own heavenly ends.

Let us endeavor to apprehend well the full force of this thought. We may speak of a divine agency in the order of nature. "The heavens declare the glory of God, and the firmament sheweth his handiwork" [Ps. 19:1]. And still more room is there to refer the life of man, in its higher forms, to his ordination and care. "The inspiration of the Almighty giveth him wisdom" [Job 32:8, adapted]. In this way we are prompted to ascribe remarkable providences to his hand, and are accustomed to talk of nations and men as having been raised up by him for the accomplishment of particular ends. There may be a vocation thus, and along with it a corresponding commission, for purposes embraced in the economy of our present life, which are as truly referable to the divine will as this economy itself is in all its parts. Cyrus had his mission from God; so had Alexander the Great; and so also our own more illustrious Washington. Great statesmen, great artists, and great scholars may be regarded as men sent of God for their own special work. We ascribe to them at times an actual inspiration from on high, a sort of truly divine afflatus, answerable to the idea of such a mission. And so the Bible itself teaches us to look upon the domestic constitution and upon civil government, as existing by the authority and will of heaven. Parents have a divine right to the respect and obedience of their children; and magistrates, according to St. Paul, are to be obeyed for conscience' sake. "The powers that be," he tells us (Rom. 13:1,2), "are ordained of God: Whosoever therefore resisteth the power, resisteth the ordinance of God; and they that resist shall receive to themselves damnation." Thus it is, we may see, that the order of nature admits not only the idea but the actual reality also of heaven-appointed functions and functionaries, in its own sphere, on all sides.

But is the Christian ministry now a divine institution only in the same general view? Such seems to be the opinion of many. They attach much the same force to the commission claimed by Calvin or John Wesley that they are ready to allow also to that of Oliver Cromwell. Both the authority of the office, and the vocation to it, are supposed to be lodged in some way in the moral constitution of the world under its ordinary form, and to be divine only in virtue of those general relations to God, which this must be allowed on all hands to carry in its bosom. But this is in truth to mistake and deny the supernatural character of the ministry altogether, and to turn it into an institution of mere nature, the very thing which our faith is required to contradict. The peculiarity of the office is that it does not originate in any way out of the order of this world naturally, but proceeds directly and altogether from a new and higher order of things brought to pass by the Spirit of Christ in consequence of his resurrection and ascension. It belongs to that constitution which we call the Church, which starts from him who is the resurrection and the life, and who has passed into the heavens as its glorified head; which is by its very conception, therefore, a supernatural fact; and whose whole existence in the world, accordingly — its actual relations, capabilities, and powers — is a mystery that can be apprehended only by faith. To conceive properly of the divine character of the sacred office, we must make full earnest with the relation it bears to the glorification of Christ, as the cause and source of an order of things higher than nature in the world, which was not and could not be in it before. It holds from him immediately as head over all things to the Church.

And as regards this point, it is plain that no account is to be made of the distinction that is justly enough drawn between the ordinary and extraordinary forms of the office. "He gave some, apostles," it is said, "and some, prophets, and some, evangelists, and some, pastors and teachers"; various classes and orders, some special and for a time only, others for the ordinary use of the Church through all ages; but so far as their origin is concerned, all of precisely the same character and nature; since all alike are referred to the same Ascension gift. The source of the apostleship is the source also of the common pastoral episcopate. As the Church is a supernatural constitution and so an object rightly of faith, in its ordinary history, no less than in the midst of Pentecostal miracles, so does the ministry also derive its force really and truly from Christ, in his capacity of head over all things to the Church, whether exercised by inspired or by uninspired men. This deserves to be well considered and laid to heart. Either the office in its ordinary form is a mere sham, an idle mockery without reality or power, or else it must be allowed to represent and embody in itself actually the force of a supernatural commission.

It becomes easy, in this view, to determine its relation to the world as it exists in the order of nature. The office is no product, in any sense, of the life of humanity in this form. It holds, as we have seen, from another economy or system, founded in a power which has actually surmounted the order of nature, and reigns above it in its own higher sphere. On this ground it is that we declare the Church to be higher and greater than the State. Patriotism after all is not the first virtue of man, if we are to understand by it devotion to the will of the State regarded as an absolute end. To make this will the absolute measure of truth and duty, to find in it the last idea of right and wrong, to denounce the conception of a real jurisdiction on the part of the Church that shall be taken as owing no subordination whatever to the jurisdiction of the State (in the style of some who carry on the war blindly with the Church of Rome), is in fact to betray Christ into the hands of Caesar, and to treat the whole mystery of his ascension and glorification as a cunningly devised fable. Governments have no right to place themselves at the head of the Church, or over it, in its own sphere, converting it into a department of state, as in Prussia, or making the civil power the source and fountain of ecclesiastical authority, as since the days of Henry the Eighth and Cranmer in England. What can be more monstrous than the conception of such a pretended headship of the Church, resting as it does at this moment in the person of Queen Victoria, because she happens to be the political sovereign of the British nation! But if it be monstrous for any civil power to usurp this sort of lordship over God's heritage, affecting to play the part of sovereign in the sphere of powers that belong not to this world, can it be at all less monstrous to think of making these powers dependent on the constitution of the simply natural world in any other view? The people have just as little right here as parliaments and kings to shape the Church to their own ends, or to take the creation of its ministry into their own hands. The fond notion which some have of a republican or democratic order in Christianity, by which the popular vote, or the will of any mass or majority of men, shall be regarded as sufficient to originate or bring to an end the sacred office wherever it may be thought proper, and even to create, if need seem, a new *Church*, as they dare to prostitute that glorious name, for its service and use — is just as far removed from the proper truth of the gospel as any other that could well be applied to the subject. It is completely at war with the Creed. It makes no account of the strictly supernatural character of Christ's kingdom, as a real polity not of this world, and yet from its own higher sphere entering into it and taking hold upon its history in the most real way. It drags the whole mystery down continually to the level of the simply natural understanding, and forces it thus to lose itself at last altogether in the world of mere flesh and sense.

The relation of the ministry to the world on the outside of the Church, however, as now described, does not determine at once its relation to the mass or body of men who belong to the Church itself; and there is room here, accordingly, for the democratic notion just dismissed to return upon us again under another and much more plausible form. The office may be viewed as something which proceeds from Christ, not indeed through the constitution of nature, as is the case with that of the civil magistrate, but yet through the constitution of grace itself as this is comprehended in the general Christian community. We are thus confronted with the question concerning the order which the ministry and the Church hold to each other, in the system of Christianity. Both spring from the same source, and date from the same time. Still there is room to distinguish between them, as regards inward priority and dependence, and to ask whether the Church is to be regarded as going before the ministry, or the ministry before the Church. To this question, however, an answer has been in fact already returned, in speaking of the commission originally given to the Apostles. The terms of that commission are such as of themselves plainly to show that the Church was to be considered as starting in the Apostles, and extending itself out from them in the way of implicit submission to their embassy and proclamation. They were to stand between Christ and the world, to be his witnesses, his legates, the representatives of his authority, the mediators of his grace among men. They were to preach in his name, not merely a doctrine for the nations to hear, but a constitution to which they were required to surrender themselves, in order that they might be saved. The new organization was to be formed, and held together, by those who were thus authorized and empowered to carry into effect officially its conditions and terms. Hence the Church is said to be builded upon Peter, as the central representative of the college of the Apostles (Mt. 16:18) and in another place, again (Eph. 2:20), "upon the foundation of the apostles and prophets, Jesus Christ himself being the chief corner stone." So in the passage we have taken for our text, the ministry both in its extraordinary and ordinary character is exhibited as the great agency which Christ is pleased to employ for the edification of his Mystical Body. There is no room then for the theory by which the Church at large, or any particular part of it, is taken to be the depository, in the first instance, of all the grace and force which belong to the ministerial office, just as in a political organization the body of the people may be supposed to contain in themselves primarily the powers with which they choose to invest their own officers and magistrates. The order of dependence here is not ascending but descending. The law of derivation is downwards and not upwards, from the few to the many, and not from the many to the few. The basis of Christianity, as it meets us in the New Testament, is not the popular mind and popular will as such in any form or shape. It starts from Christ. It reaches the world through the mediation of his ministers. Their mission is from him only. "As my Father hath sent me," he says (Jn. 20:21), "even so send I you." They are overseers set over the house of God by the Holy Ghost. By whatever names they may be distinguished, apostles, prophets, presbyters, rulers, or pastors, their office is in its essential constitution episcopal. They are shepherds under him who is the Chief Shepherd, clothed by delegation with his authority, and appointed to have charge of the flock in his name (1 Pet. 5:2–4), with a power so real in its own sphere, and so absolutely irresponsible, at the same time, in any democratic or republican sense, that they are warned before Christ not to use it as lords over God's heritage. However well, then, the famous watch-word may sound for the popular ear: "A Church without a bishop, and a State without a king," it must be held to be, so far at least as the first part of it is concerned, absolutely treasonable to the true conception of Christianity. The question is not of the episcopal office in some special given form, but of the office in its broad New Testament sense, as involving the idea of a real pastoral jurisdiction over the Church, representing in it immediately the authority of Jesus Christ, and deriving its force from the sovereignty of heaven and earth to which he has been advanced by his resurrection from the dead.

To say that there may be a Church without a bishop, in such view a purely republican assembly of Christians in simply lay capacity, able to generate and produce from itself a full, valid ministration of the mystery of grace contained in the gospel, without the intervention in any way of the ministry constituted and commissioned for the purpose by the ascended Saviour himself; to say, in other words, that the Church is before the ministry in the order of existence, and in no way dependent upon it, but complete without it (the very thing the maxim *does* mean to say, if it has any meaning whatever), is a heresy which at once strikes at the root of all faith in the supernatural constitution of the Church, and turns both the apostolical commission and the gift of Pentecost into a solemn farce.

Both from its origin, as already considered, and from its design, which yet remains to be considered, it may be inferred with necessary consequence that the office in question must be a single institution, in harmony with itself in all its parts. The commission given to the Apostles implied that they were to act in concert. It was not an authority which each one of them was left to himself to exercise in his own way and for his own pleasure. It belonged to them only in their collective capacity. They were bound by it to the real and fixed constitution of grace with which it was concerned, in the capacity of a college or corporation. And so as the ministry assumed other forms, whether ordinary or extraordinary, it remained necessarily subject still to the power of the same law. Just as among the Jews the priesthood was one, though the priests were many and of different orders, so in the Christian Church, however the ministers might be multiplied and the forms of their office varied, the office itself could be of force only as it retained always the character of a single body bound together, and in union with itself. As there can be, by the very conception of Christianity, but one faith, one baptism, and one Church, so can there be also but one ministry, and this unity must be taken to extend to all times and ages, as well as to all lands.

And thus we have, in the next place, the idea of apostolical succession; and along with that the conception also of ordination, as the veritable channel through which is transmitted mystically, from age to age, the supernatural authority in which this succession consists. It is easy, of course, to deride everything of this sort, and to make sport with the notion of a tactual communication, as it is sneeringly styled, of heavenly powers, and of grace that is supposed to trickle from consecrated fingers in the imposition of hands, but it comes certainly with a very bad grace from those who pretend to make a merit of their respect for the Bible. The Old Testament is full of this way of ordering spiritual things, and in the New Testament also exemplifications of it occur on all sides. The derision in question only serves to reveal and expose the unbelieving habit of mind from which it proceeds. What is in truth the subject of skeptical scorn in the case, is the existence in the world of any such supernatural constitution, any such mystery of faith, as the Church claims to be in virtue of her derivation from him who has "ascended up far above all heavens, that he might fill all things." The mockery regards the whole reality of the order of grace, as an abiding economy among men, different from the order of nature and above it. Let this first conception be admitted, with some felt sense of its being a fact, and not merely a speculation or notion; and then it will be easy comparatively to allow also all other points belonging in any way to the same grand article of faith. Sacramental grace will follow as a matter of course. And so will the idea of the ministry as an institution proceeding from Christ's commission, and armed with power by his Spirit, and having all its force accordingly in the unity and perpetuity of its first appointment. This involves succession; and the succession, to be valid, must be kept up in some way within the bosom of the institution itself. For, as we have seen, this holds not from the natural life of the world, nor even from the higher life of the Church collectively taken, but directly and wholly from the commission and ordination of Christ; and so can be maintained with its original character from age to age, only as it may have power to transmit the actual virtue of this first supernatural appointment from one generation still onward to another.

It remains to notice, finally, under our present head, the force and power of the office. It is not properly of this world; for the sphere of existence to which it belongs is that higher economy of the Spirit which has been introduced by the triumph of Christ over the whole constitution of nature. The virtue which it carries in itself for its own ends, therefore, is not to be measured by any merely natural or worldly standard. The preaching of the cross is foolishness to the Greek and a stumbling block to the Jew, we are told, and yet the wisdom and power of God for salvation to them that believe. "The weapons of our warfare," St. Paul says (2 Cor. 10:4), "are not carnal, but mighty through God to the pulling down of strongholds." The power of the ministry stands not in the wisdom, or eloquence, or art and policy of men in any form. It is a quality derived from the kingdom of Christ, and answerable to its heavenly constitution. In its own form and sphere, however, it has to do with relations that are most real, and takes hold of interests which are lasting and solemn as eternity itself. It involves the stewardship of the mysteries of God (1 Cor. 4:1), the administration of the keys of the kingdom of heaven (Mt. 16:19; 18:18; Jn. 20:23), the negotiation of the terms of eternal life (Mk. 16:16; 2 Cor. 2:15, 16; 5:18-20). All this supernatural force, in the case of those by whom it is thus exercised, is, of course, official and not personal. It belongs to the institution of the ministry, and not to the men privately considered who may be charged at any given time with the sacred trust. Their personal character may come in to enforce or to prejudice its claims to respect; but the claims themselves are independent of this, and rest upon other ground altogether. They go with the office; and the whole case supposes that so long as it may be held to its legitimate form this will be found true and equal to the purposes of its original institution. Even a simply human organization, where the mind and action of the individual functionary are necessarily ruled by the spirit of the body as a whole, is found to have a wonderful power of self-consistency and self-conservation in this way; as we may see, for instance, in the case of our civil courts, where the decisions of a judge, circumscribed and controlled by the fixed relations of his office in the general system of which it is a part, are something very different from his merely personal will, and carry with them rightly and safely an authority to which, out of such position, he could lay no good claim whatever. And why should it be thought strange, then, if the same law of organized corporate life, raised from the sphere of nature to the sphere of grace, and having to do with the "powers of the world to come" [Heb. 6:5], be represented as carrying with it in the Church, by virtue of Christ's Spirit, not only a general moral security, but an absolutely infallible guaranty, for the truth and trustworthiness of its results? What less than this can the commission mean, that clothes the ministry with Christ's own authority, and requires the nations to bow to it under penalty of damnation? Whatever may be said of single ministers in their private character, or in particular acts of their office, the institution as a whole, and taken in its corporate unity, must be held to be equal in full to the terms of this appointment. It cannot prove false and recreant to its supernatural trust. "On this rock," Christ says, "I build my Church" [Mt. 16:18]; "He that heareth you, heareth me; and he that despiseth you, despiseth me" [Lk. 10:16]; "Lo, I am with you always, even to the end of the world" [Mt. 28:20].

III. We come now, in the third place, to the *design* of the Christian ministry.

The whole office is, as St. Paul expresses it, "for the perfecting of the saints, for the work of the ministry, for the edifying of the body of Christ: till we all come in the unity of the faith, and of the knowledge of the Son of God, unto a perfect man, unto the measure of the stature of the fullness of Christ. That we henceforth be no more children, tossed to and fro, and carried about with every wind of doctrine, by the sleight of men, and cunning craftiness, whereby they lie in wait to deceive; but speaking the truth in love, may grow up into him in all things, which is the head, even Christ: from whom the whole body fitly joined together, and compacted by that which every joint supplieth, according to the effectual working in the measure of every part, maketh increase of the body unto itself in love."

Here we have the great thought, which may be said to form the keynote of this whole Epistle to the Ephesians, Christ "head over all things to the Church, which is his body, the fullness of him that filleth all in all" [1:22,23]. The Church is no congregation merely of persons professing Christianity, brought together in an outward way, the result in such view of private and separate piety supposed to be brought to pass under such form on the outside of its communion. It is a living constitution which starts from Christ himself, in virtue of his resurrection from the dead, forms the home of the Spirit in the world, and includes in itself powers altogether above nature for the accomplishment of its own heavenly ends; within the bosom of which only is comprehended all the grace that men need for their salvation, as truly as deliverance from the Flood was to be found only within the Ark in the days of Noah. Here is the forgiveness of sins, the illumination of the Holy Ghost, the manna of heaven, the communion of saints, the victory of faith, the resurrection of the dead, and the life everlasting. And these benefits are conditioned by the vitality of the whole system or constitution to which they belong. Thus the Church is viewed as being to Christ in the world of grace, what the body is to the head in the natural world. It is the form in which he reveals his presence among men through the Spirit, and the organ by which he carries into effect the purposes of his grace. His people in this view are members of himself, and at the same time "members one of another," by their common relationship to the Church. "For as the body is one," the Apostle writes (1 Cor. 12:12,13; cf. Rom. 12:5), "and hath many members, and all the members of that one body, being many, are one body; so also is Christ. For by one Spirit are we all baptized into one body, whether we be Jews or Gentiles, whether we be bond or free; and have been all made to drink into one Spirit." It is as comprehended in the general organization of the Church that its members grow up more and more into him who is the Head, and this process of growth on their part is, at the same time, the edification of the Church as a whole.

The mystery of the general Christian life goes forward thus by the activity of its several parts, working unitedly together for a common end, in obedience to the law of its own supernatural constitution. The whole is an organic process. The growth of the Church is carried forward by the growth of its members, while at the same time the plastic power from which this last comes resides only in the Church itself. There it flows from Christ, through the Spirit, fashioning and building up the new nature according to its own divine type. Its operation is primarily by the faith and knowledge of the Son of God, that living apprehension of the truth as it is in Christ, which faith only has power to produce, when brought into communication with the realities of the gospel in their own sphere. Such knowledge is, as far as it goes, an actual entrance into the truth itself, and so a real participation in the life of him who is the absolute light of the world. What serves thus to redeem the understanding from darkness, brings into the will also the law of charity or love, which becomes then a perpetual fountain of grace, and the source of all Christian sanctification. Such wealth of salvation, according to the Apostle, is comprehended in the knowledge of Jesus Christ as it is made possible to men in the Church! His prayer for Christians was accordingly that God might give unto them the Spirit of wisdom and revelation in this form, the eyes of their understanding being enlightened, to know the hope of his calling, and the riches of the glory of his inheritance in the saints, and the exceeding greatness of his power towards them who believe (Eph. 1:17–19). His soul struggles seemingly with the greatness of the theme, and no language is found strong enough in its service. "For this cause," he says (Eph. 3:14–19), "I bow my knees unto the Father of our Lord Jesus

Christ, of whom the whole family in heaven and earth is named, that he would grant you, according to the riches of his glory, to be strengthened with might by his Spirit in the inner man; that Christ may dwell in your hearts by faith; that ye, being rooted and grounded in love, may be able to comprehend with all saints, what is the breadth, and length, and depth, and height; and to know the love of Christ, which passeth knowledge, that ye might be filled with all the fullness of God."

So in our text, the edification of the body of Christ is represented as going forward by the perfecting of the saints in this very process of faith and knowledge; whose scope is "the measure of the stature of the fullness of Christ"; and through which, "speaking the truth in love," or rather as the original word means, *being one with the truth* in love, it is their privilege to "grow up into him in all things," which is the head from whom the power of growth and spiritual completion is conveyed to the whole Church.

And here it is precisely, we say, that the Christian ministry has its grand purpose and use. It is the agency through whose intervention in the Church, Christ is pleased by his Spirit to provide for the building up of his people in the faith and hope of the gospel unto everlasting life. The representation of the Apostle implies that the faith and knowledge of the Son of God, by which the saints are carried forward towards their proper perfection, are conditioned by this arrangement as its necessary medium. And how much again this involves may be understood by considering what results are supposed to be reached after and gained by its means. The case has to do with the mysteries of the kingdom of God, with the treasures of wisdom which are hid in Jesus Christ, with the deep things of the Spirit which surpass all natural thought and comprehension. It has to do with a knowledge that begins altogether in faith, and supposes, therefore, an actual order of supernatural life and truth answerable to such faith, brought home to the soul in the form of revelation, and challenging its implicit submission. The obedience of faith, as it is called, is made to be in this way, over against all speculation and opinion, the ground of the whole Christian salvation. Men are required to surrender themselves to the economy of the gospel, in order that they may be formed by it to its own purposes and ends; and it is assumed that in doing so they will come really and truly under the action of the truth as it is in Christ, so as to be no longer children, tossed to and fro, and carried about with every wind of doctrine, by the sleight of men, and cunning craftiness, whereby they lie in wait to deceive, but having their very being in the element of truth and charity, may grow up in all things into him who is the Head, even Christ. When we are told, then, that the ministry is the agency by which all this is brought to pass, we are not only enabled to form some right conception of its design, but from this come to see again what must necessarily be its constitution, agreeably to what we have already found to be true of the same, in looking at it from the side simply of its supernatural origin. The nature of the office is determined and explained by the object it is formed to serve no less than by the source from which it springs; and from this view, full as much as from the other, may be easily found to require all the qualifications which we have before shown it to possess. In no other form could it mediate safely between Christ and his Church, and promote the perfecting of the saints, "till we all come in the unity of the faith and of the knowledge of the Son of God," as distinguished from the winds and waves of all merely human doctrine, "unto a perfect man, unto the measure of the stature of the fullness of Christ."

In conclusion, it becomes us to consider seriously, from the whole subject, what are the general tests and conditions of a true ministry, and to ponder well the misery and danger of a false one, both for those who exercise it and for those who trust themselves to its care.

The ministry under its true form supposes, as we have seen, a divine commission, a strictly supernatural appointment and source. And as there has been in fact but one such commission, that which was given by Christ when he passed into the heavens as head over all things to the Church, it must be able, all the world over and through all time, to refer itself to this as the actual charter of its authority, in clear exclusion of every other title pretending to take its place.

From this it follows necessarily, in the next place, that the ministry under its true form, wherever it exists, must be comprehended in the unity of the office as a whole, and so also at the same time in the unity of that one true Church which we all own and acknowledge, as an object of faith, in the Apostles' Creed. One Lord, one faith, one baptism. All starts from Christ; all subsists by his Spirit; all rests on the same foundation of the apostles and prophets. The very thought of a loose and divided ministry, in such a constitution, destroys itself, by overthrowing the conception on which alone the whole authority of the office must rest. To see and feel the reality of the commission from which it flows, is at once to see and feel also that it must be in union and harmony with itself through all its parts, that it must have the character of a single organization, and that the whole force of it must fall to the ground whenever it is pretended to sever it from such connection, and to exercise its functions in an independent and isolated way. In any government, the powers by which it exists and carries on its affairs must form one single constitution. However they may be distributed, they must remain still bound together as one orb, whose parts all meet in the unity of a common center. Laws, titles, offices, functions, all have force only by virtue of their comprehension in the order which originates and sustains the whole. To think of powers being validly exercised, or rights validly claimed, in the name of the government without regard to this order, would be a monstrous contradiction. And can it be any less monstrous to suppose the possibility of any similar disruption of authority and office in the kingdom of Christ, and under the great seal which imparts to the Christian ministry its supernatural warrant and force? "Is Christ divided?" [1 Cor. 1:13] May the same seal be attached here to different ministries, in no connection with one another, held by no common law, and moving in no common sphere? Is the connection something which a man may carry away with him wherever he pleases, to use in his private capacity as to himself shall seem right and good? The imagination is preposterously absurd. The force of the commission holds only in the office considered as a whole. To rend it from this unity is to reduce it to nothing.

And so from this we have, by necessary consequence again, the third condition of a true ministry, namely submission to a living rule or order in which this unity of office may be actually exhibited in a real way, as a fact coming down from the time of the Apostles. To act officially in any polity, the single functionary must not only join himself with its general organization, but in doing so must bow also to the authority which already belongs to it as an actually existing constitution in its own sphere. How much more is it meet and fit that this should be the case also, where the administration regards the supernatural constitution of the Church, and the mysteries of the kingdom of God! Christianity, in its very nature, involves the idea of authority under a form not dependent on human thought or will; so that here above all, the conception of office must be taken to imply, at the same time, submission to the actual polity or order from which it springs, regarded as a living permanent constitution. And if this polity be represented by the unity of the ministry, as we have seen it to be, there must be a line of historical continuance by which both together shall be found falling back to the great commission in which the Church originally took its start. The unity of the ministry in this way is not the consent merely of any number of men, whether many or few,

who may agree to take the office upon them and exercise it in the same
way. It exists always as a historical fact already at hand, and dating from
the day of Pentecost, to the authority of which, in such view, accordingly, all must bow who are brought from time to time to have part truly
in its commission.

Such seem to be necessarily, from the nature of the subject, the great
tests of the Christian ministry in its legitimate and true form. Where
these are wanting we may have the show and sham, but not, it is to be
feared, the reality of the sacred office. It is hardly necessary to say, however, how widely different from all this is the reigning popular view of
the subject, especially in our own country at the present time. Few appear
to make serious account either of the supernatural commission of the ministry, or of its necessary unity, or of its dependence upon an actual succession in this form, handed down from the time of the Apostles. Indeed
nothing is more common than to hear ministers themselves, those at least
who call themselves such, openly deriding every requirement of this
nature, as a sort of exploded superstition, fit only for Catholics and Old
Testament Jews. Any evangelical sect, they take it, has power to originate the office for its own use; or at all events may be satisfied if it has
been able to carry off with it some small fragment or particle of an older
succession, in breaking away violently from some other Church; as Micah
felt that all was right when he obtained a wandering Levite for his priest
(Judg. 17:7-13), or as the children of Dan considered it an object afterwards to steal away the same unprincipled priest, and to make him the
source of a new, separate priesthood for their own false worship (Judg.
18:18-31). The flaw of schism, in such a case, is not felt to be of any
consequence, for the persons in question have no sense whatever of the
necessary oneness or corporate solidarity of the sacred office. They laugh
at the idea of its legitimacy and force being conditioned, in their own
case or in the case of others, by any such relation. They are bound by no
such consciousness. Their commission is felt to be a sort of private property, which holds good to themselves directly and separately, from the
great head of the Church. Enough, it may be, that it is acknowledged by
a single congregation, or at most that it is comprehended in the organized
ministry of some particular sect. They care for no wider comprehension.
And with such unbelieving indifference to the idea of the Church as a
present whole, how should they be expected to have any such faith in its
historical character, as to feel the least real concern about the derivation
of their title through its living succession in past ages? The only authority

they think it necessary to bow to, in such view, is the constitution and tradition again of their own sect. What though this be only of yesterday, and its creed confessedly a mere opinion or "persuasion"? They are willing to trust themselves blindly to its guidance, and then make a merit of what they call their Christian liberty and independence by throwing off all respect for Church authority under every broader and older view.

Need we say that such a habit of thought always involves, in its last analysis, an entire want of faith in the supernatural constitution of the Church, and in the divine order of the ministry as we have had it under consideration at this time? We have a right to say of it, indeed, that it is absolutely at war with the mystery of Christianity from first to last. It substitutes for it another gospel.

By comprehending what the ministry involves in its true form, we are prepared to understand how great must be the calamity of a false ministry for all who are concerned with it in any way. It is by its very nature an imposture and usurpation, where it is most dreadful to think of any such outrageous wrong. By pretending to be the truth, at the same time, under such false character, it contradicts and opposes the truth itself in its own proper form. It belongs in this way necessarily to the realm of Antichrist. For this precisely is the true conception of the power we call Antichrist, that it exalts itself against Christ by wickedly thrusting itself into his place, and seeking to pass itself off under his name. The grand criterion of the spirit, according to St. John (1 Jn. 4:3), is just this, that it "confesseth not that Jesus Christ is come in the flesh," is not willing to know and own the actuality of a new and higher order of life in him as the Word made flesh for us men and our salvation, but pertinaciously insists on resolving the whole "mystery of godliness" (1 Tim. 3:16), either directly or indirectly, into the form of a mere abstract spiritualism belonging to nature in its own sphere. Thus a spurious Christ, existing only in the thought and fancy of men, and having no power to effect a real union, and so a real reconciliation between the natural and supernatural worlds, is set up in mockery and rivalry of the true Christ, and made to challenge the faith of the world under the usurpation of his glorious name. And what else is it but the same spirit at work when the true supernatural constitution of the Church, proceeding as this does from the mystery of the Incarnation "justified in the Spirit" — the Son of Man received up into glory — is ignored, or virtually denied, and made to be practically of no account, by the substitution for it of another conception altogether, reducing it in fact to a simply rationalistic and natural form! Or when, in full conformity with this, the supernatural origin of the ministry is sublimated into a sort of Gnostic idealism merely, its commission converted into a religious myth, the idea of its necessary unity and apostolical succession derided as a silly dream of the Middle Ages, and an institution of a wholly different form and nature, excluding these characteristics in their true sense altogether, is brought forward and exhibited as fully equal to all the purposes and ends of the sacred office? Could any presumption more certainly refer itself, by St. John's criterion, to the domain of Antichrist? Whatever any such false ministry may affect or pretend, it is a ministry, in truth, not of faith but of unbelief, not of righteousness but of sin. It practically proclaims God a liar (1 Jn. 5:10), by "not believing the record that he has given of his Son," not owning the mystery of the gospel in its own form, but daring to put it into another form agreeably to its own taste. Christ, having risen from the dead, establishes his Church as a constitution above nature, and in virtue of the power that belongs to him as the fountain and head of this new creation, solemnly commissions the ministry in his own form, clothing it in a real way with powers answerable to the economy to which it belongs, and promising to surround it with the guaranty of his own presence in the Spirit through all time; bids it go teach all nations, baptizing them into his name; makes salvation to depend on believing and obeying the order which he has been pleased thus, in his sovereign goodness, to appoint. And now, in the face of all this, the false ministry of which we are speaking stands forward, and preaches to men that salvation depends on no such special constitution whatever, and that if they will but trust themselves to *its* guidance all may be expected to come out right in the end. Is not this, we ask again, the very spirit of Antichrist? And what shall we say of those who commit themselves to the care of such an episcopate, in the prosecution of eternal life? The very thought is dismal in the extreme, and the case, if Christianity be more than a dream, one of the most deplorable that can well be presented to the contemplation of a believing mind.

Of such vast significance is the question concerning a true ministry and the true Church. It has to do not merely with the accidental form of Christianity, but with its inmost constitution and life. All are bound, as they value their salvation, to look well to the nature of the commission and charter under which they propose to secure this all important object. Indifference with regard to the matter is itself a just occasion for apprehension and alarm; for it implies at once serious infidelity towards the whole subject — infidelity at the very point, too, where Christ makes all to depend on faith, when he says: "He that *believeth*, and is baptized, shall be saved, but he that believeth not shall be damned" [Mk. 16:16]. As every minister is bound to be well assured that he is a minister not merely of this or that sect, but of the true Church Catholic, and has part thus in that one great commission from which hangs the unity of the whole office; so also are all other persons under obligation to satisfy themselves, on good and sufficient grounds, that they are in the bosom of the Church in its true form, and under the guidance and care of a legitimate and true ministry.

Selected Bibliography

I. PRIMARY SOURCES

1. PHILIP SCHAFF

Die Sünde wider den Heiligen Geist (Halle, 1841).
Das Princip des Protestantismus (Chambersburg, 1845).
The Principle of Protestantism, translated with introduction and appendix, "Catholic Unity," by John W. Nevin (Chambersburg, 1845).
What Is Church History? translated by J. W. Nevin (Philadelphia, 1846).
Geschichte der Apostolischen Kirche, nebst einer allgemeinen Einleitung in die Kirchengeschichte (Mercersburg and Philadelphia, 1851).
History of the Apostolic Church, with a General Introduction to Church History, translated by E. D. Yeomans (New York, 1853).
Amerika (Berlin, 1854).
America, translated by E. D. Yeomans (New York, 1855).
Germany: Its Universities, Theology, Religion (Philadelphia, 1857).
History of the Christian Church from the Birth of Christ to Gregory the Great, 1–600 A.D., Vol. I (New York, 1858).
Der Heidelberger Katechismus, edited by Philip Schaff (Philadelphia and Bremen, 1863).
Gedenkbuch der Dreihundertjährigen Jubelfeier der Heidelberger Katechismus in der Deutsch Reformirten Kirche der Vereinigten Staaten, edited by Philip Schaff (Chambersburg and Philadelphia, 1863).
Der Buergerkrieg und das Christliche Leben in Nord Amerika (Berlin, 1865).

2. JOHN WILLIAMSON NEVIN

The Anxious Bench (Chambersburg, 2nd ed. 1844).
The Mystical Presence (Philadelphia, 1846).
History and Genius of the Heidelberg Catechism (Chambersburg, 1847).
The Church (Chambersburg, 1847).
Antichrist, or the Spirit of Sect and Schism (New York, 1848).
Heidelberg Catechism in German, Latin and English, Tercentenary Edition, introduction by J. W. Nevin (New York, 1863).
W. H. ERB, ed. *Dr. Nevin's Theology, Based on Manuscript Class-room Lectures* (Reading, 1913).

3. OTHER WRITERS

GERHART, E. *Institutes of the Christian Religion* (2 v., New York, 1891–94).
HARBAUGH, H. *Christological Theology* (Philadelphia, 1865).
RAUCH, F. A. *Psychology, or a View of the Human Soul, including Anthropology*, 2nd edition with a notice by J. W. Nevin (New York, 1841).

4. Liturgy

A Liturgy, or, Order of Christian Worship (Philadelphia, 1857).
Nevin, J. W. *The Liturgical Question* (Philadelphia, 1862).
Order of Worship for the Reformed Church (Philadelphia, 1866).
Bomberger, J. H. A. *The Revised Liturgy: A History and Criticism of the Ritualistic Movement in the German Reformed Church* (Philadelphia, 1867).
Nevin, J. W. *A Vindication of the Revised Liturgy* (Philadelphia, 1867).
Bomberger, J. H. A. *Reformed, not Ritualistic* (Philadelphia, 1867).
Dorner, I. A. *Der Liturgische Kampf in der Deutsch-Reformirten Kirche von Nord-Amerika* (Philadelphia, 1868).
Proceedings of the Convention of Ministers and Laymen Belonging to the German Reformed Church Held at Myerstown, Pa., September 24th and 25th, 1867 (Lancaster, 1867).
The Liturgical Conflict and the Peace Movement of the Reformed Church in the United States as Exhibited by the Official Records of the General Synod (Dayton, 1896).
Higbee, E. E. "The Pericopes," seven articles as indexed in *The Mercersburg Review*, 1911.

5. Modern Editions

A modern paperback edition of the major texts of the Mercersburg theology is now being published in six volumes by the United Church Press as the Lancaster Seminary Series in Mercersburg Theology, edited by Bard Thompson and George H. Bricker. The contents as announced are:

1. P. Schaff. *The Principle of Protestantism* (Philadelphia and Boston, 1964).
2. J. W. Nevin. *Early Writings.*
3. P. Schaff. *Historical Writings.*
4. J. W. Nevin. *The Mystical Presence and other Writings on the Lord's Supper* (Philadelphia and Boston, 1966).
5. *Miscellany of the Mercersburg Review.*
6. *Writings Illustrative of the Mercersburg Liturgy.*

There have been other recent reprints:

J. W. Nevin. *My Own Life: The earlier years* (Lancaster, 1964).
J. W. Nevin. *The Mystical Presence*, with an introduction by R. E. Wentz (Hamden, 1963).
Philip Schaff. *America*, edited with an introduction by Perry Miller (Cambridge, 1961).

6. Periodicals

That about half of the selections in this volume are taken from *The Mercersburg Review* is a fair indication of its importance in the bibliography of the movement. The first four volumes (1849–52), edited by Nevin, are especially rich in significant items. An index to articles published from 1849 to 1911 is found in the *Reformed Church Review*, XV (1911).

Other periodicals which should be mentioned include *Der Deutsche Kirchenfreund* for the period of Schaff's editorship, through 1853; *The Weekly Mes-*

senger, The Christian Intelligencer, published in New York for the Reformed Dutch Church, and the *Lutheran Observer,* published in Baltimore. A typescript index to *The Weekly Messenger,* compiled by Guy B. Bready, is at the library of the Historical Society of the Evangelical and Reformed Church, Franklin and Marshall College. The *Reformed Church Review* for July 1913 contains a list of articles and reviews about the Mercersburg theology, compiled by C. H. Ranck and entitled "As Others See Us in the Magazines, 1840–1860."

7. MANUSCRIPTS

There is a substantial amount of unpublished correspondence, lecture notes, and other manuscript material of the leaders of the Mercersburg movement. The library of the Historical Society of the Evangelical and Reformed Church, located at Franklin and Marshall College, is the most important collection. Correspondence mentioned in the text is to be found here unless otherwise noted. Other materials are deposited at the Theological Seminary in Lancaster and at Eden Theological Seminary in St. Louis. The Schaff-Mann correspondence is at Mt. Airy Lutheran Seminary in Germantown, and Nevin's exchanges with Brownson and McMaster are at the University of Notre Dame, South Bend, Indiana.

II. SECONDARY WORKS

1. AMERICAN

APPEL, T. *Life and Works of John W. Nevin* (Philadelphia, 1889).

APPEL, T. *Recollections of College Life at Marshall College* (Reading, 1886).

BINKLEY, L. J. *The Mercersburg Theology* (Lancaster, 1953).

John H. A. Bomberger Centenary Volume (Philadelphia, 1917).

DUBBS, J. H. *History of Franklin and Marshall College* (Lancaster, 1910).

DUBBS, J. H. *The Reformed Church in Pennsylvania* (Lancaster, 1902).

FERM, V. *The Crisis in American Lutheran Theology* (New York and London, 1927).

GOOD, J. J. *History of the Reformed Church in the United States in the Nineteenth Century* (New York, 1911).

HAGEMAN, H. *Pulpit and Table* (Richmond, 1962).

HARBAUGH, LINN. *Life of the Reverend Henry Harbaugh, D.D.* (Philadelphia, 1900).

KIEFFER, E. C. *Henry Harbaugh, Pennsylvania Dutchman* (Norristown, 1945).

KLEIN, H. M. J. *Century of Education at Mercersburg, 1836–1936* (Lancaster, 1936).

KLEIN, H. M. J. *History of the Eastern Synod of the Reformed Church in the United States* (Lancaster, 1943).

NICHOLS, J. H. *Romanticism in American Theology: Nevin and Schaff at Mercersburg* (Chicago, 1961).

RANCK, H. H. *Life of the Reverend Benjamin Bausman* (Philadelphia, 1912).

RICHARDS, G. V. *History of the Theological Seminary of the Reformed Church in the United States, 1825–1934, Evangelical and Reformed Church, 1934–1952* (Lancaster, 1952).

RUSSELL, G. B. *Four Score and More* (Philadelphia, 1908).

SCHAEFFER, C. B. *A Repairer of the Breach* [B. C. Wolff] (Lancaster, 1949).
SCHAFF, DAVID S. *Life of Philip Schaff* (New York, 1897).
SPAETH, P. F. A. T. *Memorial of William Julius Mann* (Philadelphia, 1893).
THOMPSON, BARD, et al. *Essays in the Heidelberg Catechism* (Philadelphia and Boston, 1963).
WENTZ, A. R. *A Basic History of Lutheranism in America* (Philadelphia, 1955).
WHITMER, A. C. and RICHARDS, G. W. *Addresses on the Life and Theology of Henry Harbaugh and Emanuel Vogel Gerhart* (Philadelphia, 1918).
ZIEGLER, H. J. B. *Frederick Augustus Rauch — American Hegelian* (Lancaster, 1943).

There are also a number of unpublished theses on Mercersburg topics.

2. EUROPEAN

BARTH, K. *Die protestantische Theologie im 19 Jahrhundert* (Zollikon-Zurich, 1947).
BRILIOTH, Y. *The Anglican Revival* (London, 1925).
BRILIOTH, Y. *Three Lectures on Evangelicalism and the Oxford Movement* (London, 1934).
BOLSHAKOFF, S. *The Doctrine of the Unity of the Church in the Works of Khomyakov and Moehler* (London, 1946).
CHADWICK, OWEN. *From Bossuet to Newman: The Idea of Doctrinal Development* (Cambridge, 1957).
EBRARD, J. H. A. *Das Dogma vom heiligen Abendmahl und seine Geschichte* (2 v., Frankfurt a. M. 1845-46).
ELERT, W. *Der Kampf um das Christentum seit Schleiermacher und Hegel* (München, 1921).
FAGERBERG, H. *Bekenntnis, Kirche und Amt in der deutschen konfessionellen Theologie des 19 Jahrhunderts* (Uppsala, 1952).
HERMELINK, H. *Geschichte der evangelischen Kirche in Württemberg* (Stuttgart, 1949).
HEPPE, H. L. J. *Die confessionelle Entwicklung der altprotestantischen Kirche Deutschlands* (Marburg, 1854).
HIRSCH, E. *Geschichte der neuern evangelischen Theologie*, Vol. V (Gütersloh, 1954).
JEDELE, E. *Die Kirchenpolitischen Anschauungen des Ernst Ludwig von Gerlach* (Ansbach, 1910).
SCHLEIERMACHER, D. F. E. *The Christian Faith*, translated from the 2nd German edition of 1832 by H. R. Mackintosh and J. S. Stewart (Edinburgh, 1948).
SCHNABEL, F. *Deutsche Geschichte im neunzehnten Jahrhundert. IV: Die religiösen Kräfte* (Freiburg im Br., 1937).
SCHOEPS, H. J. *Das andere Preussen* (Stuttgart, 1952).
SEEBERG, R. *Die Kirche Deutschlands im neunzehnten Jahrhundert* (Leipzig, 2nd ed. 1904).
SHAW, P. E. *The Catholic Apostolic Church* (New York, 1946).
VERMEIL, E. *Jean-Adam Möhler et l'école catholique de Tubingue (1815-1840)* (Paris, 1913).

Index